12

ICT & COMPUTER STUDIES

PNG UPPER SECONDARY

Greg Baker
Tom Bowen

OXFORD

Oxford University Press is a department of the University of Oxford. It furthers the University's objective of excellence in research, scholarship, and education by publishing worldwide. Oxford is a registered trademark of Oxford University Press in the UK and in certain other countries.

Published in Australia by
Oxford University Press
Level 8, 737 Bourke Street, Docklands, Victoria 3008, Australia

First published 2015
Reprinted 2019, 2023, 2024, 2025

ISBN 978 0 19 557816 4

Illustrated by diacriTech, Chennai, India
Typeset by diacriTech, Chennai, India
Printed in Hong Kong by Sheck Wah Tong Printing Press Ltd.

Contents

Introduction

This book has been published to provide the information required by students in order to successfully complete both the Upper Secondary syllabus in Information Communication Technologies (ICT) and the Computer Studies syllabus at Grade 12 in Papua New Guinea. A detailed syllabus coverage chart showing how this book covers both courses is set out on p. vi. Please refer to that chart for guidance.

For students of Information Communication Technologies, Units 12.1 to 12.5 in this book follow the same order as Units 12.1 to 12.5 in the Grade 11 Information Communication Technologies Syllabus:

Unit 12.1 Information and Communication Systems

Unit 12.2 Database 2

Unit 12.3 Internet 2

Unit 12.4 Multimedia

Unit 12.5 Computers and Employment

Within each Unit the Topics follow the main subheadings and bullet points in the Syllabus. For students of Computing Studies, some Units of the Grade 12 syllabus were covered in the *Save Buk ICT & Computer Studies Grade 11* book, while the remaining Units of the Grade 12 syllabus are covered in this book:

Unit 12.1 Information and Communication Systems

Unit 12.2 Multimedia (covered in Unit 12.4 in this book)

Unit 12.3 Spreadsheets (covered in Unit 11.4 in the *Save Buk ICT & Computer Studies Grade 11* book)

Unit 12.4 Databases (covered in Unit 11.5 in the *Save Buk ICT & Computer Studies Grade 11* book)

Unit 12.5 Computers and Employment

Please use the syllabus coverage chart on p. vi as a guide.

The influence of information technology has gained tremendous momentum in Papua New Guinea in the last decade. It will be of increasing importance in driving the economy and the social and political environment of our country. The two syllabus documents are designed to support our growing needs and this book is designed to provide the necessary structure and content in a concise and compact format.

If you have any suggestions about how this book might be improved in future editions, please make contact with Oxford University Press:

Fax: 00 61 3 9934 9100

Customer Service Email: exportsales.au@oup.com

We wish you every success in your studies.

The authors

Syllabus coverage chart

The chart below shows how each Unit and Topic relates to the ICT syllabus and the Computer Studies syllabus.

Unit 12.1 Information and Communication Systems	**ICT Syllabus Grade 12**	**Computer Studies Syllabus Grade 12**
Topic 1: Information systems	**12.1** *p.33*	**12.1** *p.30*
Topic 2: Networking	**12.1** *p.33*	**12.1** *p.31*
Topic 3: Communication systems	**12.1** *p.34*	**12.1** *p.32*
Unit 12.2 Database 2	**ICT Syllabus Grade 12**	**Computer Studies Syllabus Grade 12**
Topic 1: Introduction to Microsoft Access		
Topic 2: Exploring advanced table features	**12.2** *p.36*	
Topic 3: Using relationships	**12.2** *p.37*	
Topic 4: Creating advanced queries	**12.2** *p.37*	
Topic 5: Forms	**12.2** *p.37*	
Topic 6: Integrating main form and subforms	**12.2** *p.37*	
Topic 7: Working with report sections	**12.2** *p.37*	
Unit 12.3 Internet 2	**ICT Syllabus Grade 12**	**Computer Studies Syllabus Grade 12**
Topic 1: Creating a new web page	**12.3** *p.38*	
Topic 2: Working with images and multimedia effects	**12.3** *p.39*	
Topic 3: Creating hyperlinks	**12.3** *p.39*	
Topic 4: Working with special effects	**12.3** *p.39*	
Unit 12.4 Multimedia	**ICT Syllabus Grade 12**	**Computer Studies Syllabus Grade 12**
Topic 1: Introduction	**12.4** *p.40*	**12.2** *p.33*
Topic 2: Creating interactive presentations	**12.4** *p.40*	**12.2** *p.33*
Topic 3: Delivering and controlling a presentation	**12.4** *p.41*	**12.2** *p.34*
Topic 4: Integrating multimedia with other applications	**12.4** *p.41*	**12.2** *p.34*
Unit 12.5 Computers and Employment	**ICT Syllabus Grade 12**	**Computer Studies Syllabus Grade 12**
Topic 1: Career options in ICT	**12.5** *p.42*	**12.5** *p.42*
Topic 2: Job search on the Internet and in other media	**12.5** *p.42*	**12.5** *p.42*
Topic 3: Formatting resumes or CVs	**12.5** *p.42*	**12.5** *p.42*
Topic 4: Formatting job application letters	**12.5** *p.42*	**12.5** *p.42*

Acknowledgments

There are many people to be thanked for their help and assistance in enabling the publication of this series to happen. First, we acknowledge the cooperation and generosity of Mark Sayes at ESA Publications in New Zealand, who responded with interest and support when the proposal to adapt his Study Guide series was put to him.

We would also like to acknowledge many other individuals who have been happy to advise and assist in different ways: Joy Sahumlal, Greg Kapanombo, Anne Sangi, Safak Deliismail.

Copyright acknowledgments

The author and the publisher wish to thank the following copyright holders for reproduction of their material.

Alamy/John Crowe, 44/David J Green Technology, 46; Courtesy of Cisco Systems, Inc. Unauthorized use not permitted, 22, 26; Getty Images/Andreas Rentz, 164; IstockPhoto/ Alec051, 47/SKashkin, 43 (bottom)/PickStock, 45 (bottom); Reproduced courtesy of The National, 30; Reproduced courtesy of The Post-Courier, 19; Reproduced courtesy of The Post PNG, 39; Shutterstock/a_v_d, 45 (top)/Bloom Design, 235/ bochimsang12, 43 (top)/ Celal Erdogdu, 13/Jon Le-Bon, 238 (top)/Denis Rozhinovsky, 23/sbko, 238 (bottom)/ Vasily Smirnov, 15.

Every effort has been made to trace the original source of copyright material contained in this book. The publisher will be pleased to hear from copyright holders to rectify any errors or omissions.

Unit 12.1 Information and Communication Systems
Topic 1: Information systems

Information systems use people and processes to change data into information. In this unit students learn about the role computers play in an information system and how data is communicated across networks. These systems support people who are working together by enabling them to exchange and share data and information.

Unit 12.1 Information and Communication Systems is a year-long unit that is taught as the theory component of the course. Topic 1 focuses on information systems, specifically:

- What an information system is.
- Characteristics of an information system.
- Types and purposes of information systems.
- Designing and planning an information system.
- Issues related to information systems.

What is a system?

A system is a set of related components that work together to fulfil a purpose. In daily life there are many different systems that impact on our lives – water cycle, digestive systems, knowledge databases, transaction systems, accounting systems, expert systems, etc. Nations have different political systems.

A system has structure and a number of components that are related.

What is an information system?

An **information system** is an integrated set of components for collecting, storing, processing, and communicating information. An information system involves people and information technology. People use information technology to solve problems and to communicate. Thus, the way people interact with the technology is part of the information system.

An information system involves:

- People.
- Hardware.
- Software.
- Data.
- Processes.

Most information systems now use computer systems to process, store and modify data and to provide solutions to problems.

Many organisations rely on information systems to manage their operations in an effective and efficient manner.

In particular, an information system must have:

- A purpose – a reason to exist (eg managing sales in a store, managing students and recording results in a school).

- A structure – the various components of the system need to be related in a meaningful way.
- Interdependence – systems rely on inputs from other systems (eg a school may rely on funding from a government's economic system).

Data becomes information

When data becomes organised and has meaning, it is **information**. It enables decision making if it meets the needs of the recipients of that information.

Where, what and why?

Almost every day we interact with information systems. These systems include:

- People.
- Information processing equipment.
- Procedures that are designed to make the information system effective.

Nearly all the transactions we make daily are recorded on an information system somewhere. Many of these are linked to our personal files; some of them are for use only within a particular organisation. Some of these information systems may be linked to each other, while others will be separate and independent.

Some typical examples of recording transactions on an information system are:

- Making a purchase at a supermarket.
- Making a telephone call.
- Borrowing a book from a library.
- Booking a concert ticket.
- Booking an airline ticket.

In using some of these systems, you will have provided your name or some other identification. Other information systems may not require any identification.

Unit 12.1 Activity 1A: Identifying information systems

1. List ten different information systems you have interacted with during the last week. In each case, identify whether or not your name or some other identification was included as part of that system.

2. Many supermarkets and other stores have an electronic funds transfer point of sale (EFTPOS) system in place.

   a. What does an EFTPOS system allow you to do?

   b. What security provisions are in place to ensure that the transaction is secure?

Planning an information system

Planning is needed so that:

- The goals of the system are clearly identified.
- The information needed by users can be obtained from the system.
- The correct items of data are captured.

- The business rules of the organisation are defined and modelled.
- The costs of the system are worked out and controlled.
- Resources including computers, network infrastructure and peripheral devices are made available.
- The system can be integrated with existing resources and information systems.

Goals for an information system

The goals for an information system will cover information needs, technical needs, costs and staffing. These goals will also reflect and be consistent with the goals of the organisation.

The information system might be developed as a multi-user system for internal use only, as a single-user system for a small business or home business, or it might provide business opportunities on the Internet using the World Wide Web.

Goals can be high-level system goals, such as:

- To provide up-to-date information for management.
- To provide accurate information about employees (eg names, addresses, salary).
- To provide for the efficient use of resources.
- To minimise the costs of storing and retrieving information.
- To accurately track the use of resources.

Goals can be lower-level and specific, such as:

- To provide accurate information about stock levels in a store operating a point-of-sale system.
- To provide accurate, up-to-date account balances following every transaction in a financial institution.
- To provide the current address and contact telephone number of every employee of an organisation.

Case study: An information system for a school

Each school has an information system to meet its needs. While some of the system is paper-based, much of the information will be stored and accessed on an electronic computer system.

Goals

The goals of an information system for a school include the provision of:

- Up-to-date and accurate data regarding:
  - Students.
  - Staff.
- Complete and accurate data about a student's progress at the school including:
  - Attendance.
  - Classes in which the student is enrolled.
  - Academic assessments.
  - Sporting and co-curricular records.
- Access to records for authorised staff.
- Different levels of access to data depending upon needs of the people involved.

Structure

The structure of the information system will provide data about the various entities that have been identified with the school. These will include, among others:

- Students.
- Teachers.
- Classes.
- Assessments.

Some of the assumptions include:

- Each student interacts with many teachers.
- Each teacher interacts with many students.
- Each student is enrolled in many classes.
- Each student has many assessments for each class in which he or she is enrolled.

The local library as an information system

Many schools and local district libraries use a computer-based library automation system. These systems have replaced card catalogues and manual borrowing systems.

The goals of these automated systems include:

- Accurate catalogues.
- Up-to-date catalogues.
- Efficient borrowing procedures.
- Effective tracking of borrowed items.
- Better-quality information for borrowers.
- Easier ways of searching for information.

Types of organisations

Organisations can be broadly divided into the following categories:

- Government and public service organisations.
- Privately-owned commercial businesses.
- Partnerships.
- Publicly-owned commercial businesses in which shares may be traded on a stock exchange.
- Non-profit, non-government associations such as charities and clubs which people join as members.

The reasons for the existence of these organisations and the functions they perform vary considerably. These differences are reflected in the information systems that they develop and operate.

Stakeholders

A stakeholder is a person who has a particular interest in a business or organisation and who will typically have an interest in the success of the organisation. The types of stakeholders will vary with different types of organisations.

The designers of an information system need to consider the stakeholders in that system and ensure that their needs are met. They must also ensure that the stakeholders have the opportunity to express their wishes when a system is being designed and implemented.

Stakeholders in a club

The stakeholders in a club or organisation are those people who have an interest in the activities of the club. Those interests will differ according to the role taken in the club.

Members of a club committee, for example, will need different information to the members of the club. Within the committee, the information needs will also differ. The treasurer will require detailed financial information that is not needed by other committee members.

Many clubs are incorporated bodies under law and must provide information to the relevant government department at both a national and regional level.

Stakeholders in a rugby club could include:

- Members – active, social, playing, non-playing.
- Committee.
- Selection panel.
- Medical support staff.
- Supporters.
- Sponsors.
- The club's bank.
- The local community.
- The regional government.

Unit 12.1 Activity 1B: Stakeholders in a club

1. Consider a sporting team that you support or with which you are involved, and identify the stakeholders in that club or team.

2. Imagine that the club needs to raise money to build a new clubroom.

  a. Who are the stakeholders in the planning process of the clubroom?

  b. What types of information would each of the stakeholders need to help make a fundraising process for that clubroom a success?

Stakeholders in a privately-owned business

The key stakeholders in a privately-owned business are the owners and any other investors in the business.

A privately-owned, incorporated business has a number of legal requirements that must be fulfilled on an annual basis, including the completion of an annual report and a profit and loss statement.

The owners and investors in a business are seeking a suitable return on their investment. Governments receive income from such businesses in the form of taxes and other regulatory fees that must be paid.

Stakeholders in a publicly-owned business

Operating a business requires management of information for use both inside the company and by people, organisations and government outside the company.

Some information is required by law, while other information is needed for organising and running the business and to provide the information needed for analysis to meet its short-term and long-term goals.

The stakeholders in a public company include shareholders, governments, management, employees and business partners.

Shareholders

Shares in a publicly listed company are traded on the stock market. Each shareholder has made a financial investment in the business. The shareholders require information so that they can decide whether or not the business is:

- Providing an adequate return on the investment in terms of dividends paid.
- Providing satisfactory capital growth (ie the share price is increasing in value over time).
- Being managed in a sound and responsible manner.
- Communicating its policies and performance in an open and frank manner.

Governments

Governments receive money from businesses through the taxation system. Taxes such as company tax and payroll tax provide funds to governments.

Governments also use businesses to collect tax from consumers using valued added tax (VAT) or goods and services tax (GST). Governments thus have a financial interest in business performance.

Government business policies can affect the financial viability of businesses and the employment of people.

Management

Management is entrusted with ensuring that the business is profitable and remains viable. Staff members need information that will help them achieve this.

The remuneration of some senior management is based upon the performance of the company. They therefore have a direct personal interest in that performance.

Management needs information to make decisions about whether the business is being effectively managed and whether the resources under management's control should be increased or decreased. It also needs to decide whether the business is meeting the future needs of the marketplace and make decisions that will ensure the viability of the business.

Employees

The employees of a company have an interest in the wellbeing of the company because it provides their livelihood through the payment of wages and salaries. Some companies also include an employee share scheme that allows for some sharing of profits.

Business partners

Business partners need the same information about the viability of their business as management does to help them make decisions about how it is run.

Business partners operating in a franchiser–franchisee relationship usually have excellent information resources. These forms of business arrangement tend to have higher than normal success rates. This can often be because of the detailed information that is made available to the operator of the franchise.

Unit 12.1 Activity 1C: Stakeholders in a company

1. What types of information do companies release?
2. How do companies make information available?
3. Why is an annual general meeting of a company important?

Systems development and implementation

Information systems development and implementation describes the process of identifying and defining a problem, specifying a solution, testing the solution, putting the solution into action and then evaluating and modifying the solution.

This is a dynamic process. In a large system, a team of people will work to analyse and solve the problems. The team will work with key stakeholders throughout the process. Often the stakeholders will have difficulty in defining the problems to be solved and in setting out their expectations of the preferred solution. A systems analyst is a key member of the team.

Systems analysts

A **systems analyst** is a person who can work with stakeholders to develop the system requirements and the desired outcomes. The analyst must be able to interpret user needs and translate them into formal system requirements that can be used by designers and programmers. The analyst must ensure these needs are consistent with the goals of the organisation.

The analyst must also ensure that technical concerns, such as design specifications for input and output procedures, are met.

Systems life cycle

The **systems life cycle** is a step-by-step process for the development of an information system. These steps are:

- Preliminary investigation.
- Analysis.
- Design.
- Development.
- Implementation.
- Evaluation.

Although these steps are shown as sequential, some of them may be happening at the same time. The process is dynamic; needs and specifications will change during the process.

Preliminary investigation

A number of issues need to be addressed before a system can be designed and implemented. These include:

- Why is the information system needed?
- What is expected from the system?
- What problems are going to be resolved?
- What opportunities will be provided?

Note the distinction between a problem and a solution: 'I need an online system' is a solution; 'I need immediate access to customer data' is a problem to be solved. The true nature of a problem needs to be identified – the symptoms of a problem and the problem itself may be easily confused.

The scope of the system needs to be defined early in the investigation. The features that the system *must have* need to be distinguished from those that it would be *nice to have* but are not really needed.

Of critical importance is the establishment of key objectives: without defining and knowing them, they cannot easily be satisfied. If the objectives keep changing, a system will never be able to meet its expectations.

The preliminary investigation should result in:

- A definition of the scope of the project and its objectives.
- A summary of the constraints on the project.
- A recommended approach to the project.
- A recommendation as to the feasibility of the project.

The feasibility recommendation must include:

- Financial feasibility – what funding is required?
- Organisational feasibility – whether or not the organisation has the capacity to create and manage the system and whether there is active management support.
- Technological feasibility – ensuring that the technology exists to meet the needs.

Analysis

To create an information system, those involved must have a clear understanding of the current system. During the analysis stage, key tasks are:

- Data gathering.
- Data analysis.
- System requirements analysis.

The analysis should provide a clear and detailed specification of the information system. The analysis must include the information and data flows within the organisation. From whom does data flow and for what purpose? For example, from management to employee it could be:

- Procedures.
- Personnel practices.
- Pay details.

A number of design and analysis tools are used in this process. A data flow diagram is a graphic tool that models how data is used by an organisation and how it is changed and acted upon. A data flow diagram is a picture of an information system from the point of view of the data. Data flow diagrams are useful in identifying the processes involved in the collection, processing and storing of data.

If the information system involves a database, the analysis should determine the entities involved in the system and how they relate to each other.

Design

The analysis and system requirements are used to design the information system. In the first instance, the requirements are reviewed and a preliminary design is done to work out an overall plan.

Preliminary design

The preliminary design should resolve a range of questions, including:

- What is the nature of the system's online presence?
- Is the system only for internal use or will customers and clients have access to it?
- How will the data be integrated?
- What processing of the data will be carried out?
- Is new hardware required?
- What are the networking requirements?
- Will the system be designed and developed in-house or are external consultants required?
- What data models will be used?
- What software tools will be used to develop the application?
- What user interface will the software support?

Prototypes of parts of the system are often built at this stage of the development. A prototype is a working model of the system. These prototypes are tested with users and reviewed for suitability and usefulness.

Detailed design

The detailed design specifications consider every part of the system in detail. These include:

- Design of the forms that will capture the data.
- Design of the user interface.
- Detailed design of the data structures and the database.
- Detailed design of the standard reports to be generated.
- Designated access requirements for the users.
- Network integration design.
- Security processes.
- Selection of processing languages to be used.
- The development of a test plan.

This is not a comprehensive list; there will be other factors to consider.

Development

A system is developed from a detailed design. Programmers work with the analyst and a project manager to ensure that the needs are met and the specifications are adhered to.

Technical issues will require classification during this time and minor changes may need to be made to the specifications. During the development process, key users are taken through the procedures and they provide feedback to the developers.

Tools used by the developers include system flowcharts, structure charts, entity relationship diagrams and detailed data dictionaries.

A range of test data is used to ensure that processing is carried out correctly. The types of tests used include the following:

- Users ensure that entry layouts and reports work as required.
- Test data, for which the correct answers are known, is run through the system to ensure it is operating correctly.
- Data is used that will test the validation procedures. In particular, data that is known to be incorrect and out of range is tried to ensure the validation works.
- Response and processing times are measured to ensure that they will meet the required standards.

Developers look particularly for errors of logic and errors in calculations. An acceptance test should be done at the completion of the process. The users agree to a specified range of tests to be carried out and agreement is reached when these operate correctly.

Implementation

Once the system is tested and accepted, it is time for it to be implemented. The following need to be done at this time:

- User training to ensure the system is understood.
- Operating procedures established and documented.
- Help desk procedures established.
- Files converted and fully tested.

In some cases, an old system and a new system will run in parallel (at the same time) to ensure that all is well with the new system.

Evaluation and review – an iterative process

System specifications often change during the development process as business requirements may change. Sometimes system constraints force changes. All information systems are constantly under review and will be changed and improved.

Information systems need to be adaptable to cater for changes in business needs and a changed environment. Businesses need to respond quickly to changes in technology and methodology. The dramatic growth of the World Wide Web and the widespread use of social media are examples of the need for system adaptability.

Characteristics of an information system

As noted above, an information system involves:

- People.
- Hardware.
- Software.
- Data.
- Processes.

People interact with information systems using a variety of devices. Most information systems involve the storage of data on **computers**.

People have differing needs and interests with regard to an information system.

News organisations

Many news organisations provide news online for people to access. Users often access the stories with a device that has access to the Internet (eg a computer, a smartphone or a tablet). The software on the device displays the data in the manner that is specified by the designers.

Many people contribute data to the information system. In the case of an online news service, reporters write stories and load them into the information system. Photographers provide photographs. Editors and sub-editors check, arrange and manage the content.

The news organisations develop processes to ensure that the information is up to date and accurate.

The Post-Courier *provides an online news service*

Library systems

A library system is another type of information system. Registered users can log into the library system and carry out a number of functions including:

- Searching the catalogue.
- Renewing loans.
- Reserving items.
- Suggesting a purchase.
- Getting help.

Again, the system involves people (users and librarians), hardware (used to store and access the data), software and processes.

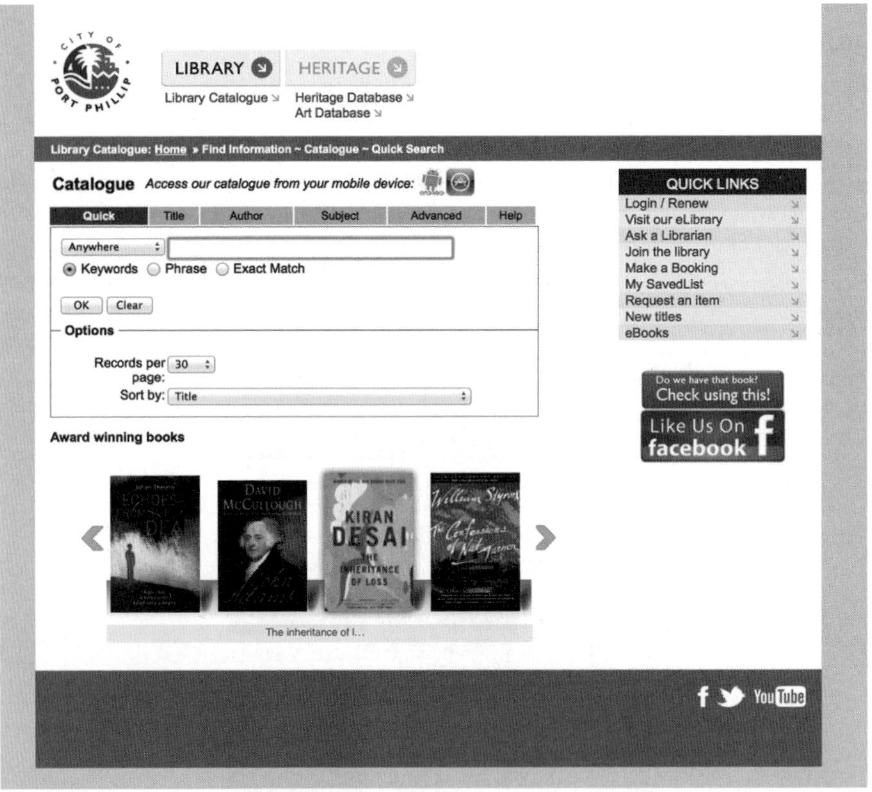

Using a library system

Types and purposes of information systems

Organisations use information systems to provide information to clients and employees in an effective, efficient and timely manner.

A bank uses its information system to manage its clients' financial matters and to provide those clients with information about their finances.

A library uses its information system to catalogue its many items and to manage the borrowing of them by its clients.

Information systems are used to educate and inform people. Many organisations use information systems to keep in contact with clients and to inform them about their products and services.

Information systems use information technology hardware and software to operate in a reliable and effective manner.

Databases

Databases are key elements in all information systems.

Data is made up of recorded facts, figures, images and sounds about people, objects, events or other items. Data is collected and stored in a database.

A database is made up of data that is arranged so that it can be searched, organised and selected. Each item of data is related to each other item in some way.

A database has a predefined structure that allows the designer to provide consistency and reliability of data.

More information about databases, and Microsoft Access in particular, is provided in Unit 12.2.

Communications

People interact with information systems in a number of ways. They do this using a variety of communication methods.

For example, bank customers can interact with the bank's information system using an automatic teller machine (ATM). Typically, the customer inserts a card, enters a PIN and then carries out a transaction.

Transaction processing

A transaction is an interaction between an individual and an organisation that results in an outcome. For example, buying a pair of shoes in a store is a transaction between a customer and the store that has as its outcome the customer receiving the pair of shoes and the store receiving payment for the shoes.

Transaction processing is a type of computer processing in which the computer responds immediately to requests from a user or a customer. Each of these actions is regarded as a transaction. Banks use automatic teller machines (ATMs) to carry out transaction processing when a customer withdraws funds from the bank.

An automatic teller machine

Another example of a transaction is booking a room online in a hotel:

- The customer checks whether or not a room is available on a particular date.
- The customer checks the price and the conditions of use.
- The customer makes a booking.
- The booking is secured by a deposit or a credit card receipt.
- The hotel's information system is updated.
- The customer receives an email and a receipt confirming the booking.

The whole process is one transaction. For busy organisations there will be many transactions in a day.

Decision support systems

A decision support system (DSS) analyses business data to provide information that helps users make decisions. It typically uses data that is collected in the normal process of business operation and then presents it to the user.

For example, a decision support system might provide comparisons of sales figures from one week to the next and lead to projected sales figures for future weeks.

Automation in manufacturing

Manufacturing lines often operate 24 hours a day, seven days a week. Many manufacturing tasks are repetitive and boring and can be dangerous. These tasks are well suited to automation.

Manufacturing production can be particularly suited to computer-aided processes. Some processes such as car assembly make considerable use of robots on automated production lines. Robots are programmed and can perform sophisticated movements at high speed with very low error tolerance levels. Some robots in warehouses move by having sensors that detect wires embedded in the floor; a processor manages the path the robot will take.

Sensors can measure sound, contact, heat, light and proximity, among other things. **Microprocessors** then interpret the data for manufacturing processes. For example, a sensor may determine if an empty packet is in place to accept the measure of a product prior to being sealed.

Control processes manage the steps in the manufacturing process and how sensors pass this information to the processors. A processor could be:

- A computer.
- A programmable logic device.
- A microprocessor embedded in a product such as a microwave oven. Motor vehicles have a large number of microprocessors to control aspects of the vehicle's operation, such as fuel injection, speed and security.

Automation can save on labour costs and it also conserves energy and materials. Automated processes can be accurate and precise and reduce the errors that are made.

An automated production line

Managing information in an organisation

The purpose of an organisation and the products and/or services it provides dictate the information needs of the organisation. Organisations such as a:

- School
- Airline
- Clothing manufacturer
- Retail store
- Mining company

all have different needs and use information in different ways.

All organisations need to create, maintain and keep records including:

- Employee records.
- Payroll.
- Invoicing for sales services.
- Financial information for balance sheets.

For employees of an organisation, those records could include:

- Personal details such as full name, address and contact details.
- Remuneration and taxation details.
- Sickness and leave entitlements.

A payroll system to manage the employees' entitlements would need to manage information including:

- Pay rate, hours worked and frequency of payment.
- Special allowances and overtime rates if applicable.
- Method of payment, such as cash or deposit to bank account (and those details).
- Taxation rates applicable and their application to the gross pay.
- Employee benefits such as sick leave, annual leave and allowances.

These, and other, information systems must be managed within an organisation. Who actually manages those systems is dependent on the organisation, its personnel and its size. For example, payroll and accounting systems may be managed within an accounts department. However, large organisations will have dedicated information technology professionals to manage the many diverse systems required by the organisations. Some organisations will outsource some of these functions to an external provider.

Data security and protection in the network

Backup and restore

All information systems need to be backed up and must have the ability to restore the system from the backup.

A **backup** is a copy of an original file that is kept on a storage medium. Backups are kept so that they can be used if anything happens to the original file or files.

Organisations keep backups to ensure that a system can be restored in case of failure.

Types of backups

The types of backups are:

- Full backup – every file is copied to an appropriate storage medium. This can take a long time and other activity on the computer should be stopped to ensure the task is completed.
- System backup – only the system files are copied so that the operating system can be recreated but user data is not backed up.
- Incremental backup – only those files that have changed since the last backup will be done. Specialist software is used to do this task.
- Selective backup – the user selects particular files to be backed up.

Making backups

Most organisations will have formal procedures for backing up their systems. They will typically use specialist software to carry out the backups.

They will use a combination of:

- Regular full backups, perhaps weekly.
- Incremental backups, perhaps daily.

They may replicate data across the organisation's network. Tape systems may be used for data storage. RAID systems will be used to help ensure the integrity of the data.

Many organisations will:

- Store backup tapes off site, or
- Replicate backup data across the network to different physical locations.

Some organisations will use backups in the cloud (ie by using the Internet). The backup procedure needs to account for:

What	What data and or system files will be backed up?
When	At what time will it be backed up and how long will it take?
Who	Who makes sure that the backup occurs and takes responsibility for the backup?
How	How will the backup be saved and how will it then be physically stored safely?

Testing of backup strategy

It is necessary to check that a backup strategy is working to plan. A test environment could be set up and checks put in place to ensure that the backup is correct and can be restored to equipment.

Restoring an information system

The backup strategy must be able to restore the information system in an agreed time.

Firewalls

Personal computers use software **firewalls**. A firewall is a system that protects a personal computer from unauthorised access. The figure below shows the control panel for the Windows firewall.

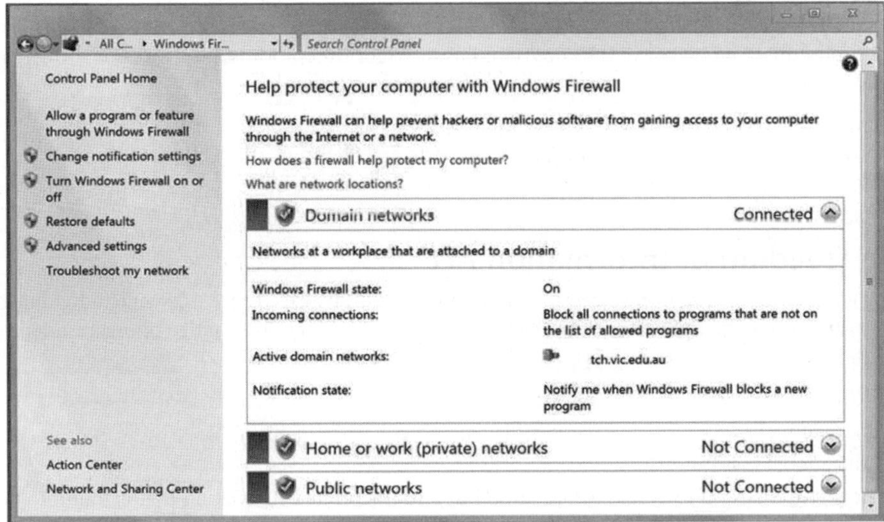

Windows firewall control panel for personal computers

Unit 12.1 Activity 1D: Firewalls

Examine the Windows firewall control panel on a computer.

1. What information does the control panel give regarding the current settings on the computer?
2. What settings can be adjusted in this panel?

Replication

Some database management packages provide database mirroring that can be used in conjunction with replication. Database mirroring involves two copies of a single database that typically reside on different computers. At any given time, only one copy of the database is currently available to clients.

Designing and planning an information system

Careful and thorough planning of an information system is of vital importance in the successful development and implementation of such a system. Only with careful planning can an organisation identify the information necessary for its continued successful operation.

Careful planning is also important because of the costs involved. A well-planned system can allow for growth and the integration of different elements. Poor planning that does not allow for growth and different needs within an organisation can prove to be costly in the long term. The integration of different systems, if not carefully planned, can cost an organisation a lot of money.

Issues related to information systems

Acknowledgement of data sources (copyright)

Copyright refers to the rights of the author or creator of creative works including text, graphics, music and films. The owner of the copyright has the right to reproduce the works or show the works in public.

Other people need permission to reproduce, display or use material that has a copyright. However, people do have a limited right to use parts of a copyrighted work providing the source of that work is acknowledged.

The Freedom of Information Act

Many governments have introduced Freedom of Information Acts. These Acts give individuals and organisations the right to request documents held about them by a range of organisations including:

- Governments.
- Local councils.
- Educational institutions.

The Acts give the right to access information but also to correct information that is found to be incorrect.

The scope of such Acts varies according to the legislation in each dominion.

Privacy principles

Many governments have also introduced laws with regard to the privacy of information.

In Australia, the Privacy Act sets out Information Privacy Principles and Privacy Regulations which organisations must follow.

The Privacy Principles include guidelines regarding:

- The manner and purpose of collection of information.
- The storage and security of personal information.
- Access and amendment of information.
- The use of information.

Principles such as these have significant implications for organisations and their creation and use of information systems.

Accuracy and reliability of data sources

Organisations are obliged to ensure that the data they hold about people is accurate and reliable.

Data integrity and accuracy is of paramount importance in ensuring the accuracy and usefulness of information. Managing both the accuracy and the reliability of data is a significant task for organisations.

To ensure that accuracy, an organisation must have:

- Standardised rules for the collection of data.
- Validation processes for data input.
- Procedures for regularly checking the accuracy of data.
- Procedures to ensure that data is not duplicated.

Most organisations will endeavour to ensure that there is a single source of data that can always be relied upon.

New trends in the organisation, processing, storage and retrieval of data

Data warehousing

Data warehousing refers to the retention of transaction data over a long period of time. The objective of data warehousing is to provide management with historical data that can be used to support the decision-making process.

Data warehousing is also used by organisations so that:

- The data warehousing technology ensures that transaction processing response times remain acceptable to users.
- It simplifies the process of reporting historical data.

However, data warehousing can:

- Increase costs to organisations for both hardware and software.
- Complicate business processes.

Data mining

Data mining is the extraction of hidden predictive information from large databases. The information can be used to analyse and predict customer behaviour. In particular, many online stores use data mining rules to make suggestions to customers about products based on the behaviour of other customers.

For example, the online store Amazon suggests other products that the customer might be interested in after a selection has been made.

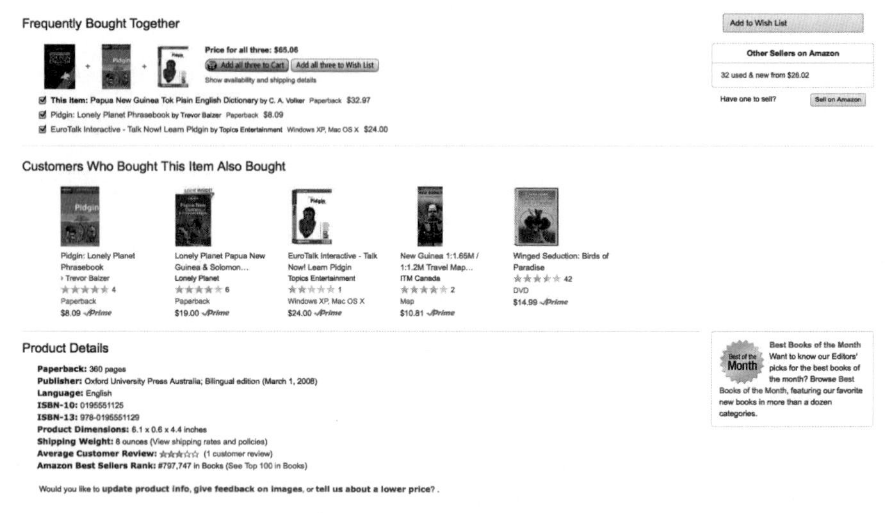

Suggestions from the Amazon online store

Unit 12.1 Information and Communication Systems

Topic 2: Networking

Topic 2 focuses on networking. It covers:
- Definition of a network.
- Characteristics and functions of network devices.
- Specification of local area network (LAN).
- Network software.
- Application software.
- Basic LAN setup.

What is a network?

A computer **network** consists of two or more computers linked together to enable the use of shared resources such as printers, storage, software and the exchange of files. The devices on the network can be linked by cable, telephone lines, or a range of wireless devices.

Computer networks use devices such as **hubs, switches** and routers to connect the various computers together and to transmit the signals.

A computer network allows users to:

- Work on a file that is on another computer.
- Print a document on a printer connected to a network.
- Send a message to another user on the network.

A computer network can span the whole world or be confined to a single room.

A network is made up of:

- Nodes – points that allow the input or output of data (such as printers, scanners, other computers and disk storage devices).
- Connections or links between the nodes.
- Computer and network software to allow and manage the connections.

Network node

A **node** is a connection point on a network that allows the input or output of data. It can be any device that is connected to the network, such as a:

- Computer.
- Printer.
- Hard disk.
- Scanner.
- Another peripheral device.

Network hardware

Server

A **server** is a software and hardware package that provides access to particular services. A server may be a dedicated computer that provides a specific service or a single computer that provides a range of services.

Providing access to resources and files for many users requires management and control. For example, rules are usually put in place for different users to access different files on a network. Users need to know that their files are safe and protected from unauthorised or unwanted access.

Servers that are often used on a network are:

- **File servers** – these store files for sharing access, storage and backup. They usually have differing levels of permission depending on the owner of the file and the type of file.
- Print servers – these manage files for printing and send them to the appropriate printer.
- Mail servers – these manage the receipt, delivery and storage of mail.
- Web server – this manages web pages and delivers content to legitimate users.

Many organisations with networks use 'client-server' as the basis for their local area network. A number of servers can be run on the same computer hardware, acting as 'virtual' servers.

What is a network switch?

A **switch** is used to connect devices on a network. A switch controls the connection of the devices so that they can communicate with each other efficiently and effectively. A switch processes and sends data from one device to another on a network.

Switches are used to create networks.

An unmanaged switch is one that works out of the box – it does not need to be configured by a user or technician. It does not need to be configured when it is connected to a network. However, unmanaged switches have less capacity than a managed switch. An unmanaged switch is useful in a small network such as one used at home.

A managed network switch is configured by the user and is required for larger and more complex networks. The switch is set up and monitored by a network engineer. A managed switch provides greater network control and capacity than an unmanaged switch.

Switches are generally a major financial investment in corporate and government networks. Their capacities, features and **functions** vary greatly. For example, the number of ethernet ports that connect to a switch varies greatly. Some of the switches support redundant power supplies to enhance their reliability.

Cisco and Hewlett-Packard are two well-known companies that develop and market network switches.

A Cisco Catalyst 3650 Series switch

What is a network hub?

A **network hub** is a device that allows multiple ethernet devices to be connected together. A signal can come into a hub and be distributed to a number of devices on the network.

A hub does not manage the traffic on a network; it typically broadcasts its signal to all the ports on the hub.

What is a router?

A **router** is a hardware device that is used to connect networks. A router links computers to the Internet so users can share the connection. A router chooses the best path for information to travel so it is received quickly.

Home networks will often have a router built into a network **modem** that will allow a number of users to connect to the Internet. A router can transmit data using different media including coaxial cable, CAT 5 cable, fibre optical cable and wireless.

A router

Client server

The best example of client and server is a web server and a client computer with a **web browser**. An **HTTP (hypertext transfer protocol)** request from the browser over the network to the web server is met when the server sends the HTML page and associated files to the client computer. The browser can read the HTML instructions and content and render the contents.

Most networks have proxy servers that sit between the client (person who requests server access) and the server on the World Wide Web. When the client requests access, the request goes to the proxy server, which then determines whether access can be granted according to its filters.

These usually sit inside the firewall and frequently accessed content may reside there. The practical effect is that the user does not distinguish if the content was delivered from the actual or the proxy server.

Intranets (a local network set using internet protocols) operate using a server within the organisation. With appropriate security (such as user names and passwords with secure tunnelling) such as a VPN (virtual private network) the intranet can be accessed from the Internet, with a client server relationship.

Peer-to-peer network

A **peer-to-peer network** is where all computers on a network can share files and resources with each other. Networks such as these are mostly used in homes or in small organisations.

The extent to which the files on a computer can be shared depends on setting appropriate permissions for access.

There can be delays in file sharing as requests are made and files are sent from a computer. Peer-to-peer could be suitable for a small home network and for file sharing over the Internet.

Internet peer-to-peer file sharing enables files to be transferred with suitable software. There are security issues with this practice as malware can be easily accessed and open a computer to hackers and viruses.

System software

Information systems within organisations could be employed on a variety of computer hardware using a variety of operating systems.

Operating system software is created by companies to operate using particular computer chips. Most software companies do not make the computer hardware the software will operate on, although some companies such as Apple sell their hardware and operating system as an integrated package. Microsoft offers 'Surface' tablets that include an integrated package.

Most systems administrators will endeavour to implement a Standard Operating Environment (SOE) that will specify the particular operating system that is to be used throughout the organisation.

Compatibility needs to be maintained between the operating system and:

- Computer hardware.
- Peripheral devices.
- Application software.
- Utility software.

When software upgrades occur, compatibility needs to be reassessed and tested to ensure that, if the upgrade is made, compatibility is maintained and the information system is not interrupted. Organisations often do not engage an upgrade process until compatibility issues are fully examined.

Specification of local area network (LAN)

Network topology refers to the layout of a network. It represents how the various nodes of a network are connected to each other and how they communicate with each other.

Design topology of LAN (star, bus, ring)

Star topology

In a star topology, all the network nodes are connected to a central computer called the **hub**. All the nodes on the computer communicate by passing through the hub that controls the network traffic.

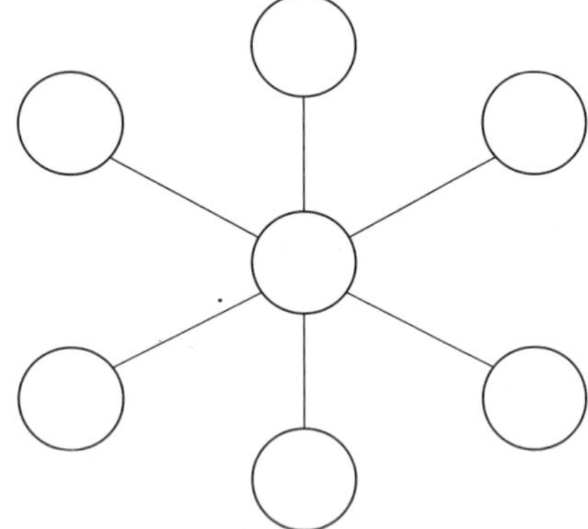

Star topology

Bus topology

Bus networks (not to be confused with the system bus of a computer) use a common backbone to connect all devices. A single cable, the backbone, functions as a shared communication medium that devices attach or tap into with an interface connector. A device wanting to communicate with another device on the network sends a broadcast message onto the wire that all other devices see, but only the intended recipient actually accepts and processes the message.

Ethernet bus topologies are relatively easy to install and do not require much cabling compared to the alternatives. 10Base-2 ('ThinNet') and 10Base-5 ('ThickNet') both were popular ethernet cabling options many years ago for bus topologies. However, bus networks work best with a limited number of devices. If more than a few dozen computers are added to a network bus, performance problems will likely result. In addition, if the backbone cable fails, the entire network effectively becomes unusable.

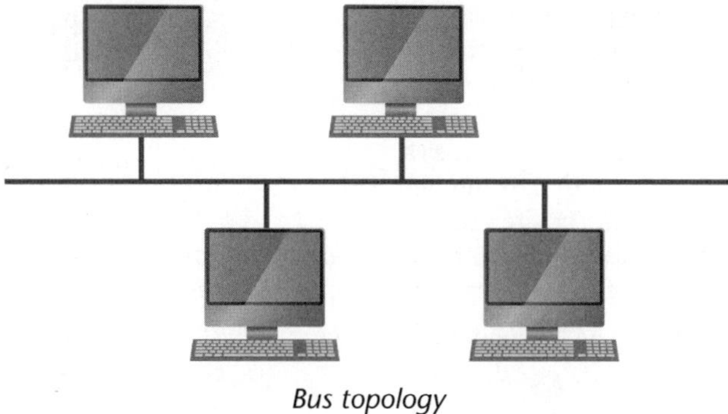

Bus topology

Ring topology

In a ring network, every device has exactly two neighbours for communication purposes. All messages travel through a ring in the same direction (either clockwise or anticlockwise). A failure in any cable or device breaks the loop and can take down the entire network.

To implement a ring network, one typically uses FDDI, SONET, or Token Ring technology. Ring topologies are found in some office buildings or school campuses.

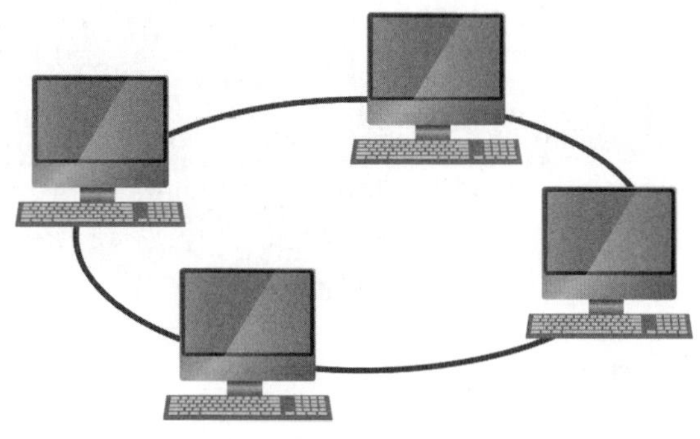

Ring topology

Network software

Network operating systems

A **network operating system**, often abbreviated to NOS, is specialised software that is designed to enhance an operating system by adding networking features. Examples of such software are Microsoft Windows Server, Novell Netware and LANtastic from Artisoft.

Firewall

A **firewall** is a system that protects a computer system or network from unauthorised access. On a network, a firewall is made up of:

- Hardware.
- Software.

Large companies such as Cisco and Norton typically provide firewalls for networks in organisations. Every message that enters or leaves a network must pass through the firewall. The firewall blocks those messages that do not meet the security requirements. Firewall products often include logging and reporting of perceived attacks.

Cisco security devices that are used for a firewall on a corporate network

The following illustration shows how a firewall works.

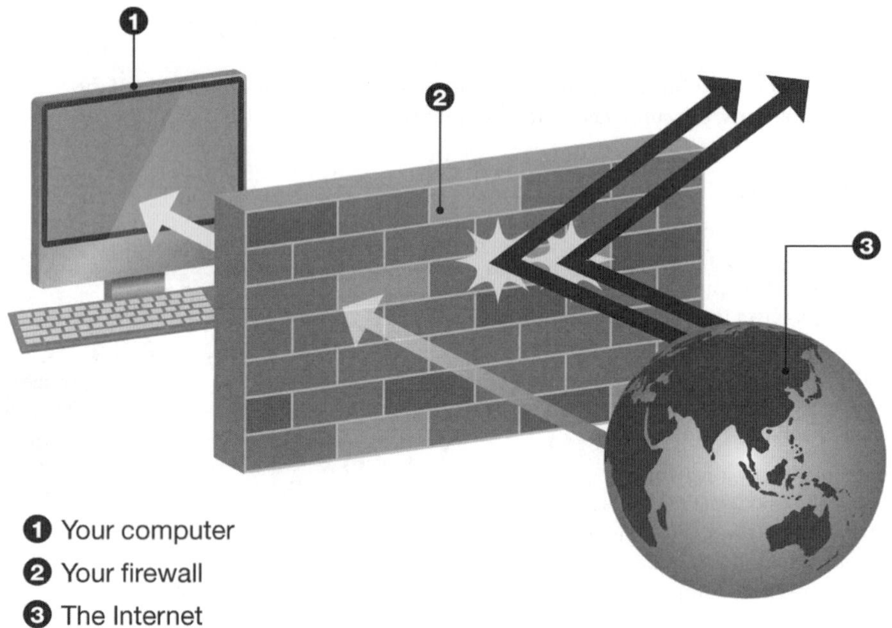

How a firewall works

Personal firewall

Windows includes a personal firewall that is set up to block requests to connect to a computer. This firewall is an application that is accessed via the Control Panel.

Device and utility drivers

A **device driver** is a small piece of software that tells the operating system and other software how to communicate with a piece of hardware. For example, each printer comes with a driver that is installed on the computer. The printer driver communicates with the operating system to ensure that information on the screen is printed correctly on the paper in the printer.

A printer driver

A **utility driver** is a program that performs a specific task in the management of computer functions (eg password management, file protection). The utility driver is the software that enables these tasks to be carried out.

System software – operating system

Each computer has an **operating system**. For example, operating systems designed by Microsoft include Windows XP and Windows 7. This software makes the computer usable – it provides a link between the hardware and the person using the computer. When the computer is turned on, the operating system starts up the computer.

Operating programs are generally purchased with the computer.

Some computers are able to use more than one operating system, although only one operating system can run at any one time. The operating system consists of a large range of smaller programs, each of which will have a specific job to carry out.

Operating systems are being continually modified and upgraded. For example, Microsoft offers service packs that include updates and security improvements.

Application software

Application software is a **program** or a group of programs designed to be operated by end users. These include word processing, spreadsheets and database applications.

General-purpose software

General-purpose software is used by a range of users. Most people in an organisation will use packages such as Microsoft Office. The actual modules used vary according to the needs of the users.

Word processing

Word processing software is used to produce, modify, save and print documents.

For many years, businesses and organisations used typewriters to create documents. The development of the electronic typewriter provided the first editing facilities, although these were very limited.

The first word processing applications were really only text formatting programs. Special codes needed to be entered for each formatting command and it was difficult to insert graphics.

The introduction of the **graphical user interface** and **'what you see is what you get' (WYSIWYG)** editing transformed the word processor into a popular and useful application. The ability to see on the screen exactly what a document would look like was a huge advantage. Early word processing programs included MacWrite (on the Apple Macintosh), WordPerfect and Microsoft Word.

Microsoft Word is now the most widely used word processing package and it can also be used to produce documents for the Internet. It is generally purchased as part of the Microsoft Office package.

Both Microsoft and Google now offer word processing packages online. There is also a range of other free online word processors available.

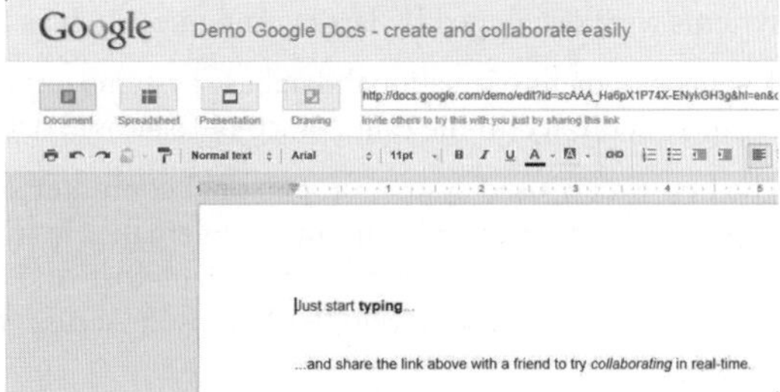

Google Docs provides an online word processor.

Spreadsheets

A **spreadsheet** is made up of a two-dimensional grid of cells arranged in rows and columns. Each **cell** is defined by its row number and its column number. A cell can contain text, numbers or a **formula** that displays the results of a calculation.

The spreadsheet had its origin in paper-based accounting applications. The paper spreadsheets were used for displaying and calculating financial information.

The ability of electronic spreadsheets to immediately re-calculate results once the data was altered made them compelling to use.

The first implementation of a spreadsheet on a personal computer was VisiCalc, which was released in 1979 for the Apple II computer. This was one of the first applications on a personal computer that was successful in business. VisiCalc was then developed for a range of other personal computers.

The first important spreadsheet application for IBM-based computers was Lotus 1-2-3. This became the leading spreadsheet application for DOS-based computers.

Microsoft first developed Excel in the 1980s and it was later moved across to a DOS-based application. Excel eventually became part of Microsoft's Office suite of programs and it has become the dominant spreadsheet application.

A number of vendors including Microsoft and Google now provide spreadsheet applications online and store the files in the 'cloud'. These applications are available via the Internet.

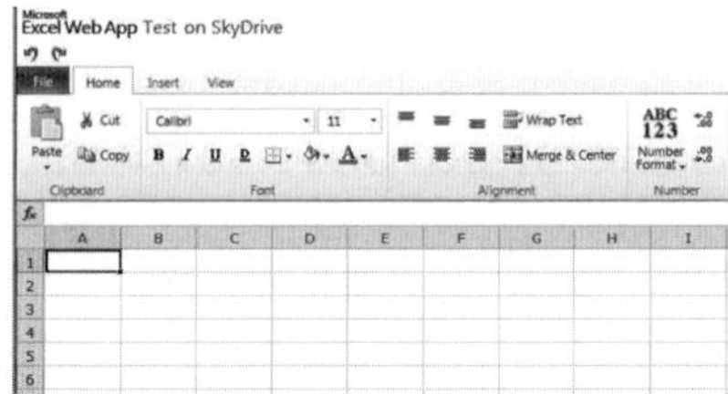

Part of an Excel spreadsheet on the Internet

Databases

A **database** is a collection of information that is organised to allow efficient retrieval and reporting of data.

Databases were originally collections of printed information arranged in an agreed format. Examples included:

- Telephone directory.
- Address book.
- Dictionary.

In the 1960s database management systems were developed for use on computers. The first systems were developed by large companies such as IBM and Oracle.

The development of relational database systems in the 1970s, based on the work of Edgar F Codd, led to the dominance of relational database management systems.

The first widely used system on personal computer systems was Dbase II, which became very popular on IBM personal computers. Filemaker was another popular database management system, first developed for the Apple Macintosh and later extended to Windows-based computer systems. Microsoft also developed Microsoft Access, which is included in some Microsoft Office packages.

Database management packages are of great importance to large organisations. Specialist positions including database administrators (DBA) and systems analysts are need to support the design and implementation of database systems.

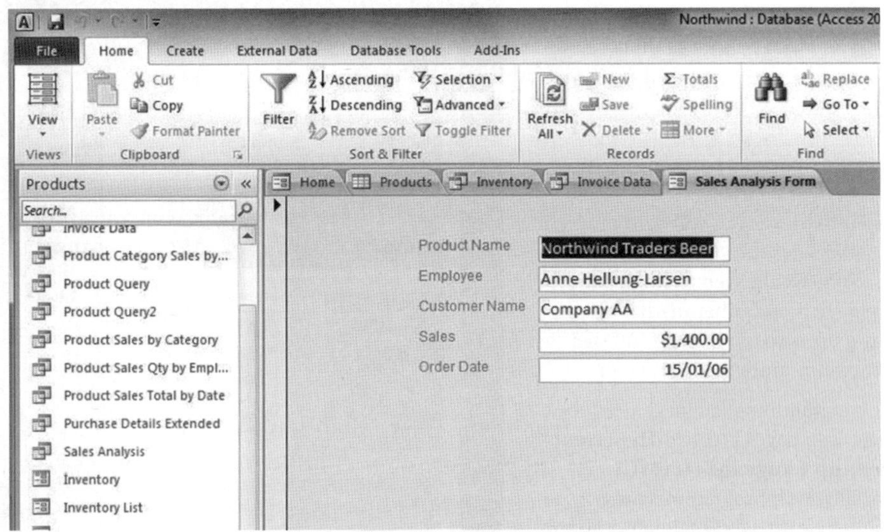

Part of a Microsoft Access database

Desktop publishing

Desktop publishing refers to the use of page layout software on a personal computer to produce documents. Page layout software is a tool for designers who create newsletters and magazines to create the documents online. Page layout programs make it easy to integrate text and graphics on the one page. These programs make it easy to manipulate multi-page layouts and to create different layouts.

The focus of word processing programs is on the creation and modification of text. Microsoft Word has incorporated some of the features of a desktop publishing package but does not offer the same flexibility in terms of laying out pages and moving elements around.

Desktop publishing suddenly became popular in the mid-1980s with the invention of the Apple LaserWriter – the first general purpose laser printer – and the software PageMaker from a company called Aldus. PageMaker was able to use the 'what you see is what you get' (WYSIWYG) layout of the Apple Macintosh computer to design and lay out pages on the screen.

Another important factor was the development of PostScript. This is a programming language invented by Aldus that is a page description language. This optimised pages for printing text and graphics. Publishers were able to lay out documents and proof them accurately using PageMaker and a LaserWriter before sending them to a professional printer for a final production. Apple's LaserWriter was the first PostScript printer.

PageMaker quickly became the de facto standard for page layout programs. Other competitors followed and QuarkXPress became widely used in the industry. Aldus was taken over and PageMaker was replaced by InDesign by Adobe. Microsoft's page layout software is Publisher.

Web browsing

A **web browser** is a software program that translates the coding in files on the World Wide Web to render and display text and other media. This allows users to browse the Internet using point-and-click navigation.

The programming language used to create web pages is called **Hypertext Mark-up Language (HTML)**. Specialist web programmers use HTML to create and maintain websites. The source code of a website can be viewed: in Microsoft Internet Explorer, this is done by right-clicking within a web page and choosing **View Source**.

Part of the homepage for The National, *http://www.thenational.com.pg/*

```
http://www.thenational.com.pg/ - Original Source
File Edit Format
<!DOCTYPE html PUBLIC "-//W3C//DTD XHTML 1.0 Strict//EN" "http://www.w3.org/TR/xhtml1/DTD/xhtml1-strict.dtd">
<html xmlns="http://www.w3.org/1999/xhtml" lang="en" xml:lang="en">

<head>
<meta http-equiv="Content-Type" content="text/html; charset=utf-8" />
  <title>The National | PNG's Top Selling Newspaper</title>
  <meta http-equiv="X-UA-Compatible" content="IE=EmulateIE7" />
  <meta http-equiv="Content-Type" content="text/html; charset=utf-8" />
<link rel="shortcut icon" href="/misc/favicon.ico" type="image/x-icon" />

  <link type="text/css" rel="stylesheet" media="all" href="/sites/default/files/css/40d088fce04ed8e4d7220e499d06ff79.css" />
  <script type="text/javascript" src="/sites/default/files/js/243eb62e7881192df3fa5d63742005f5.js"></script>
<script type="text/javascript">
<!--//--><![CDATA[//><!--
jQuery.extend(Drupal.settings, { "basePath": "/" });
//--><!]]>
</script>
  <!--[if IE 6]><link rel="stylesheet" href="/sites/all/themes/news/style.ie6.css" type="text/css" /><![endif]-->
  <!--[if IE 7]><link rel="stylesheet" href="/sites/all/themes/news/style.ie7.css" type="text/css" media="screen" /><!
[endif]-->
  <script type="text/javascript"> </script>
</head>
```

Part of the HTML code for the homepage of The National

The first web browser to be available to the public was called Mosaic and it was released in 1993. Following that, Netscape became the most popular browser. Then a new, open source browser named Mozilla became popular and this later evolved into Firefox. Microsoft challenged the browser market with Internet Explorer and this gained a significant share of the market.

Web pages are designed to be browser independent; that is, they should display the same no matter which browser is being used. However, browsers do not always display pages in the same manner and developers need to take care to ensure that their software is useable by a large number of sites.

2011	Internet Explorer	Firefox	Chrome	Safari	Opera
November	21.2%	38.1%	33.4%	4.2%	2.4%
October	21.7%	38.7%	32.3%	4.2%	2.4%
September	22.9%	39.7%	30.5%	4.0%	2.2%
August	22.4%	40.6%	30.3%	3.8%	2.3%
July	22.0%	42.0%	29.4%	3.6%	2.4%
June	23.2%	42.2%	27.9%	3.7%	2.4%

Browser usage as reported at http://www.w3schools.com/browsers/browsers_stats.asp

Specialised software

MYOB

Mind Your Own Business (MYOB) started more than twenty years ago and was a single package to handle double-entry accounting for small to medium businesses. MYOB was one of the accounting packages that helped transform the industry.

All businesses require bookkeeping which is the recording of the financial records of the business. These records include purchases, sales, receipts and income. Using MYOB, small business operators were able to record their transactions online rather than requiring handwritten entries in a ledger. At the end of a particular financial period, businesses must balance their books (ie produce a profit and loss statement and a balance sheet as well as other financial reports). Products such as MYOB:

- Reduced the time needed to produce these reports.
- Made it much easier to produce these reports.

MYOB has now expanded its product range to include payroll software, marketing software and a range of other software for specialised businesses such as hospitality.

Accpac

Accpac is an example of Enterprise Resource Planning (ERP) software. It provides a range of modules that are integrated and are designed to manage a business effectively. The modules include accounting but also include customer relationship management, human resource management, payroll and project management.

Accpac has been developed by a UK-based company, The Sage Group, that operates internationally. It is one of the leading vendors worldwide in the ERP market and is a large supplier to small businesses.

Customers can purchase Accpac modules and operate them within their business, and there is an online offering that can be purchased with a monthly fee.

Pronto

Pronto is a company that provides Enterprise Resource Planning (ERP) software. Pronto operates throughout the Asia–Pacific region, North America, Europe and the Middle East. It also operates in Port Moresby.

Pronto started as Prometheus Software in Australia in the mid-1970s. It was sold to Sausage Software in 1999 and then emerged as Pronto Software in 2002 following a management buyout.

It consists of a number of modules that can be customised for different industry groups. The modules include financial management, distribution, sales and marketing, and facilities management.

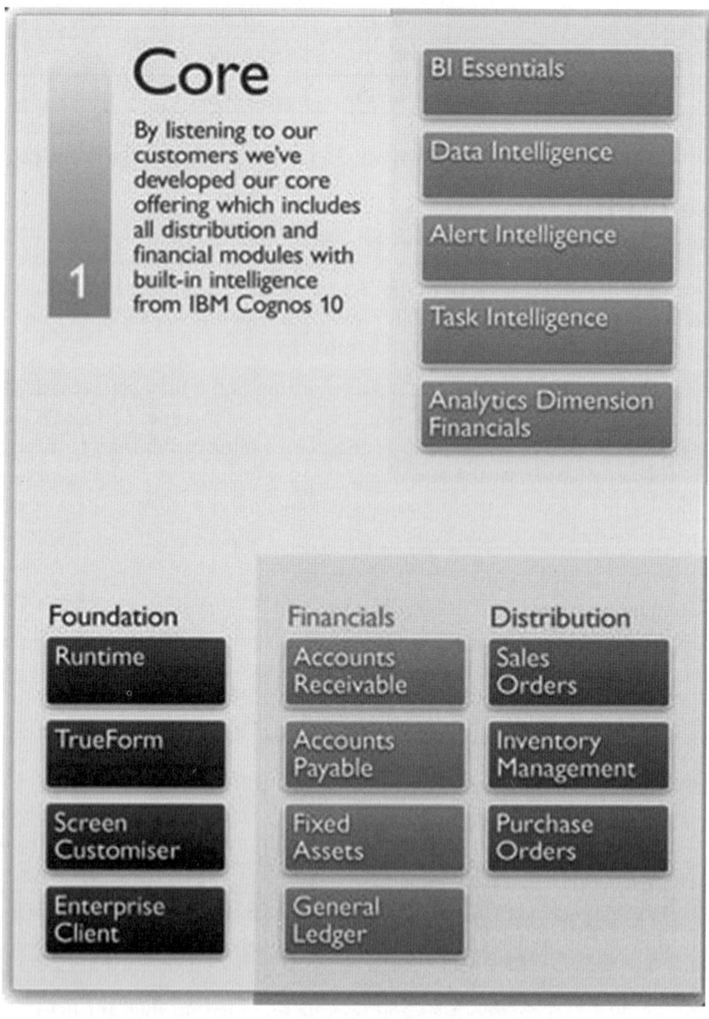

Part of the Pronto software modules

QuickBooks Pro

QuickBooks Pro is an accounting package for small businesses. It was developed by Intuit Inc, an American company that is based in Silicon Valley, California.

QuickBooks provides modules that:

- Organise finances for a business, including sales and expenses.
- Track sales and allow the creation of invoices.

QuickBooks can be purchased as a package or as a subscription to an online service.

Intuit produces a range of software products for small businesses, including point of sale software and payroll services.

AutoCAD

AutoCAD is a computer-aided design program that helps people design buildings and other structures. It was first released for personal computers in 1982 by AutoDesk Inc. It was the first software that could be used on a personal computer to replace expensive, powerful computer workstations.

AutoCAD has become the de facto standard for computer-aided design and it has expanded the range of different applications over time. It can now be used for three-dimensional design and there are specific enhancements for electrical, civil engineering and architectural applications.

AutoCAD is a relatively expensive program for personal computers. Some of the AutoCAD applications have security devices to ensure that they cannot be copied or distributed to other users.

Adobe Illustrator

Adobe Illustrator is a widely-used vector graphics editor. It allows users to create complex, high-precision graphic images.

Vector graphics is the creation of digital images using a sequence of commands or mathematical statements that place lines and shapes in a given two-dimensional or three-dimensional space. In vector graphics, the file created by a graphic artist is saved as a sequence of vector statements.

In contrast, a bitmapped graphics editor such as Photoshop saves and then displays the characteristics of each pixel on the screen. Bitmapped images are often used to edit and display digital photographs.

Adobe Illustrator came onto the market early in 1987 as one of the products that took advantage of the PostScript file format developed for the Apple Macintosh. It became an important part of the first desktop publishing systems, allowing graphic artists to produce illustrations for computer-generated publications.

After some years, a version of Illustrator was developed for Windows computers, but it took some time before the Windows version had the same capabilities as the Macintosh version.

Illustrator is now part of Adobe's Creative Suite Design range of products that also includes Photoshop, InDesign and Acrobat as well as other packages used in design for both the Web and the printed format.

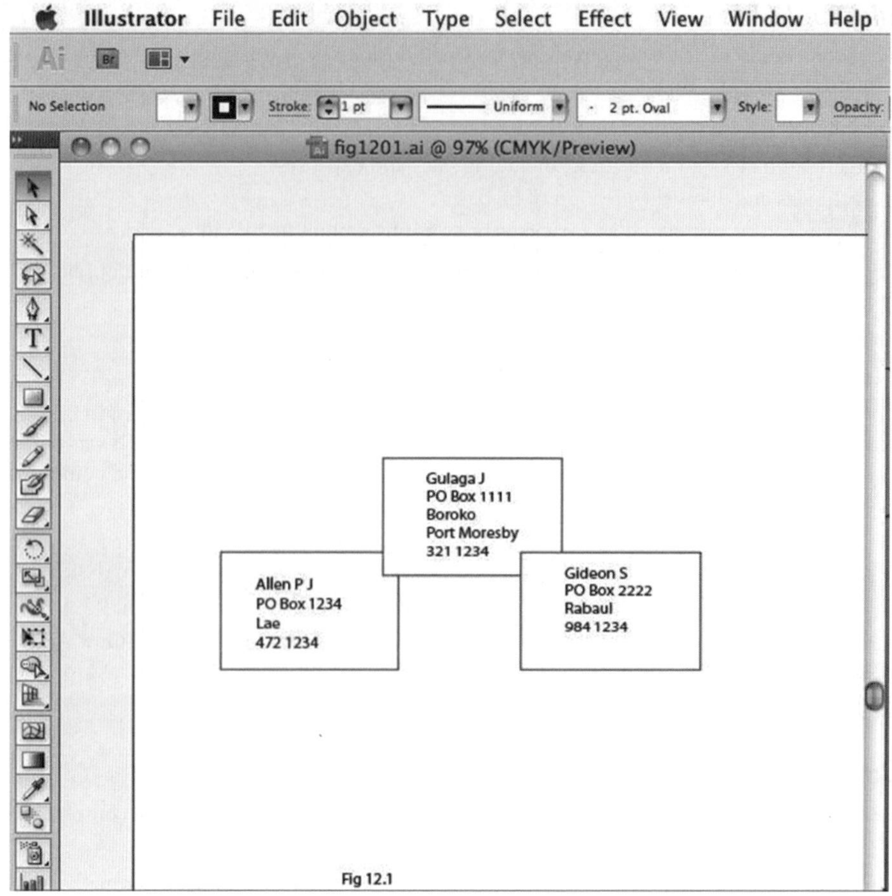

Part of an Adobe Illustrator window with a simple diagram

Basic LAN setup

Cable connections and connecting equipment

Setting up a single computer, **monitor**, peripherals and the Internet with connecting cables and power cords requires some skill and care to make sure it is successful.

Cable connections to computers, servers and peripheral devices are a common cause of system failure, simply because they are not connected correctly or securely. Connections need to have the correct cable, and be secure. Some cables require screws, some have sockets and others have pins. Even when connected, cables can be dislodged easily, particularly if equipment or cables are moved, either intentionally or accidentally. It is possible that connectors can fail and also the cables can be faulty.

In a situation where a computer has been functioning normally and is suddenly no longer working, it is useful to work backwards in time and reconstruct a timeline to see where things have been altered. For example, if the monitor is not working, check that the power cord is attached correctly both at the rear of the monitor and at the power switch. Check also that the monitor itself is turned on.

Protocols

Protocols are rules and procedures that are developed over time by manufacturers and international standards organisations. These become the basis for standard industry practice. Protocols for a network manage how the hardware and software will interact to exchange information.

In particular, protocols for network communication will determine:

- How a device can be identified on a network.
- How a device shows that it is ready to receive communication.
- How a device will start transmission.
- How a transmission will proceed regarding signal levels, speed, codes and data compression.
- How errors will be detected and then corrected.

Using ipconfig.exe

Ipconfig.exe is a program that is included as part of the system software with Microsoft Windows. It is a command line tool that is used to control the network connections of a computer.

The ipconfig command displays the network configuration values. This command is mostly used when there is an issue connecting to the Internet. The three main commands are:

- All.
- Release.
- Renew.

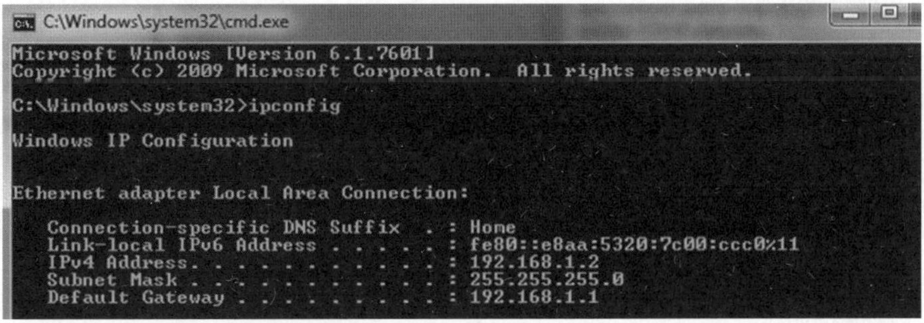

```
C:\Windows\system32\cmd.exe
Microsoft Windows [Version 6.1.7601]
Copyright (c) 2009 Microsoft Corporation.  All rights reserved.

C:\Windows\system32>ipconfig

Windows IP Configuration


Ethernet adapter Local Area Connection:

   Connection-specific DNS Suffix  . : Home
   Link-local IPv6 Address . . . . . : fe80::e8aa:5320:7c00:ccc0%11
   IPv4 Address. . . . . . . . . . . : 192.168.1.2
   Subnet Mask . . . . . . . . . . . : 255.255.255.0
   Default Gateway . . . . . . . . . : 192.168.1.1
```

The ipconfig command shows networking information

PING utility

The PING utility is a tool used by a system administrator to see if a computer's network connections are working.

This is another command line interface utility. The command sends a packet of data through the network to a particular IP address and waits for a return packet.

This utility can also be used to help resolve issues with regard to duplicate names or IP addresses on a network.

```
C:\Windows\system32\cmd.exe
Microsoft Windows [Version 6.1.7601]
Copyright (c) 2009 Microsoft Corporation.  All rights reserved.

C:\Windows\system32>ping

Usage: ping [-t] [-a] [-n count] [-l size] [-f] [-i TTL] [-v TOS]
            [-r count] [-s count] [[-j host-list] | [-k host-list]]
            [-w timeout] [-R] [-S srcaddr] [-4] [-6] target_name

Options:
    -t             Ping the specified host until stopped.
                   To see statistics and continue - type Control-Break;
                   To stop - type Control-C.
    -a             Resolve addresses to hostnames.
    -n count       Number of echo requests to send.
    -l size        Send buffer size.
    -f             Set Don't Fragment flag in packet (IPv4-only).
    -i TTL         Time To Live.
    -v TOS         Type Of Service (IPv4-only. This setting has been deprecated
                   and has no effect on the type of service field in the IP Head
er).
    -r count       Record route for count hops (IPv4-only).
```

The PING command

Windows networking options

Access rights to a network for a user primarily depend on authorisation. This is done with a user name and password. These are created and maintained by the systems administrator.

A particular user's level of access to files and **folders** on the network can be set according to the user's needs. There is a variety of operating system software. The figures below are from versions of Windows.

This image is typical of the dialog boxes used. It shows some of the folder options that are applied by a network administrator to users of a network.

These permissions determine if a user can, for example:

- Create a folder.
- Delete folders.

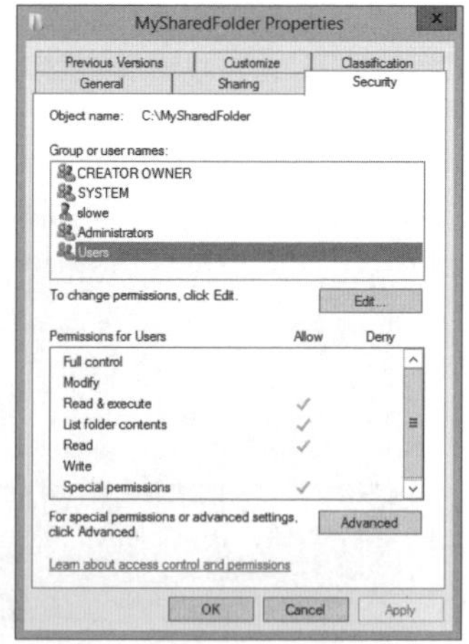

Permissions for a user

- Read files in a folder.
- Write files to a folder.

The figure below is an example of folder options in Windows that will determine the appearance with regard to the look and feel of files and folders. It also specifies what the user 'sees' as he or she navigates through folders on the network. For example, the 'Drive' letter of the volume will be shown as that option is ticked.

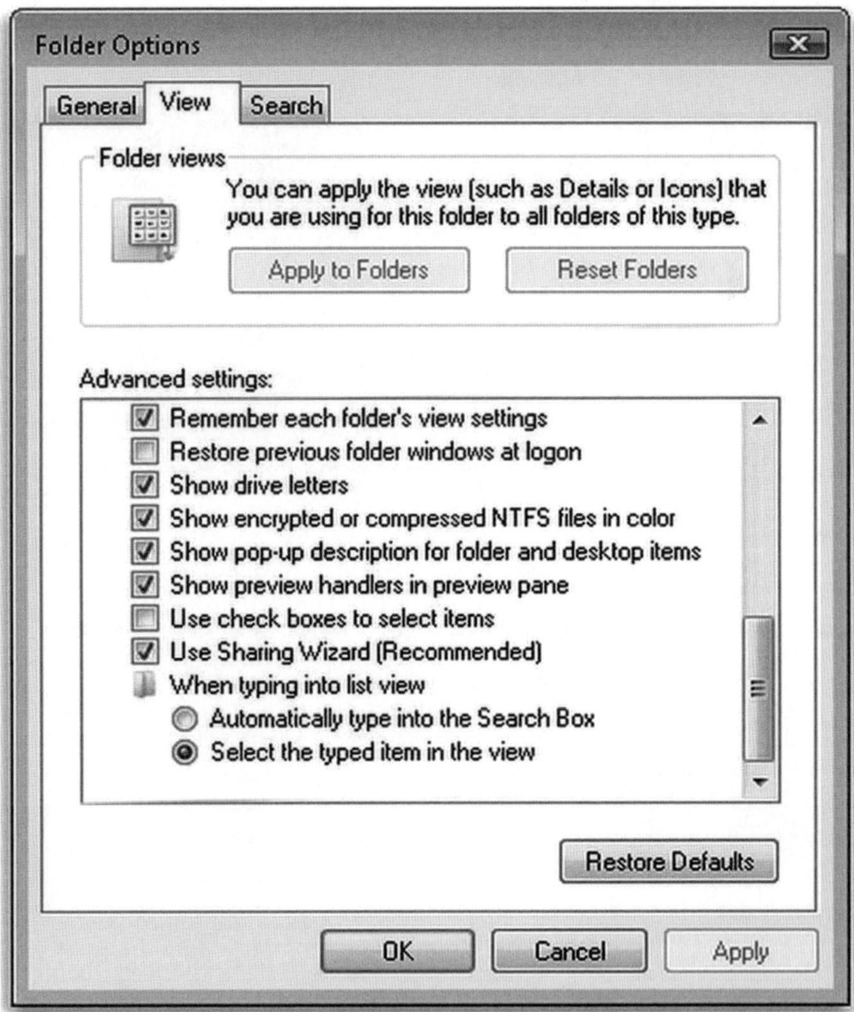

Look and feel of folders in network settings

Connecting a computer to a network

The network and sharing control panel for Windows shows the settings for connecting a workstation to a network, shared folders, peripherals and the Internet.

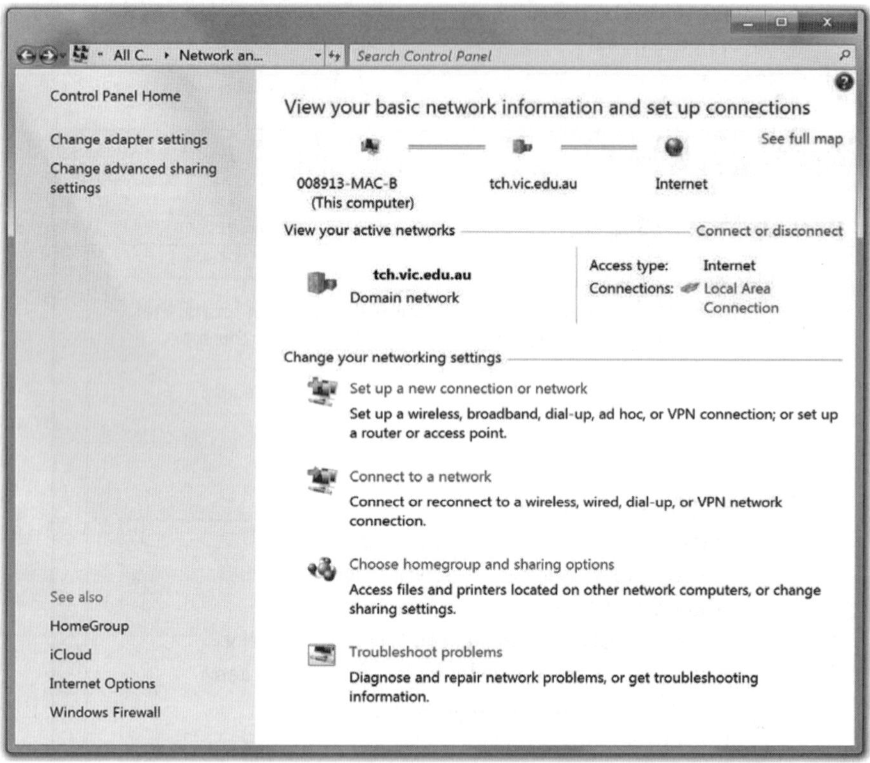

Windows options for adding a workstation to a network

A user can determine how files and folders on their computer can be shared with others in a similar manner to those on a network.

Unit 12.1 Information and Communication Systems

Topic 3: Communication systems

Topic 3 focuses on the various communication systems used in computing. It explores the following areas:

- What a communication system is.
- Examples of communication systems.
- Essentials of communications.
- Methods of communication (media).
- Hardware and software associated with communications via the Internet.

What is a communication system?

A **communication system** consists of the various processes that enable information to be passed between people. The systems vary in complexity and in the range of hardware devices that are used to enable the communications to take place.

Examples of communication systems

Some examples of communication systems are:

- **Mail network.** The mail network in most countries provides a means of sending and receiving letters and parcels. For many years, the mail network was the most important method of communication between people and organisations. For example, PostPNG Ltd provides a mail service throughout Papua New Guinea and forwards mail to other countries.
- **Telephone network.** For many years, the standard telephone network in many countries was the Public Switched Telephone Network (PSTN). This network was connected by copper wires that were connected

to a local telephone exchange. In some countries, mobile telephone networks are replacing the PSTN devices.

- **Email network.** Many people and organisations now regard an email network as a basic communication method.

Electronic mail (email)

Electronic mail, or email, allows people to exchange messages and documents using a computer network. With Internet access, email is a quick and efficient method of communication.

Email is one of the services that have driven the dramatic growth of the Internet. As such, it is one of the core services of the Internet and one that is used worldwide.

People in many organisations routinely exchange email addresses as contact points in much the same way as telephone numbers.

Why do people use email?

People use email because:

- Messages can be created and delivered quickly.
- It is geographically independent – messages may be sent anywhere in the world on the network.
- It is quick and easy to reply to a message.
- It is time-independent – messages can be sent at any time and read at the discretion of the user.
- It is platform-independent – messages can be viewed on any computer regardless of operating systems.
- Messages can be easily stored and retrieved.

An electronic mail system is made up of:

- People with email addresses.
- A computer network.
- Software.

What is an email address?

An email address is made up of:

- A person's email identity.
- The symbol @.
- The address of the mail server provider.

For example, an email address is in the form: myname@netmail.png.

Transmitting and receiving in communication systems

A communication system requires:

- A person to start a communication.
- A method of contacting another person or organisation. This could be:
  - An address.
  - A telephone number.
  - An email address.
- A method of forwarding a communication. This could be:
  - A written letter.
  - A telephone call.
  - An email.
- A method of delivery and receipt of the communication. This could be:
  - A postal employee and a mailbox.
  - A telephone.
  - An email inbox.

Current issues related to communication systems

There is no perfect communication system and all systems have issues relating to performance. Some examples of issues relating to these communications systems are:

- Mail network:
  - Mail can be addressed incorrectly and thus lost.
  - Incorrectly addressed mail cannot be returned to a sender unless the sender's address is included.
  - Mail can take an excessive amount of time to be delivered.
  - Mail is sometimes lost by the postal service.
- Telephone network:
  - Telephone numbers often change.
  - Many calls are missed because the receiver of the call is not home.
  - The PSTN service relies on a wired network that can be damaged.
- Email network:
  - This relies on the availability of the Internet.
  - The sender of an email message does not necessarily know that the message has been received.
  - Email networks are subject to **spam** and there are many junk emails.
  - Emails are not always delivered and the sender may not be aware of this.

Essentials of communications

Hardware required

Modem

Modem is short for modulator-demodulator. A modem is a device that converts digital signals from a computer into frequencies that can travel over a medium such as a telephone line. The receiving modem converts the signal back into a digital signal.

The first modem to become popular was the 300 baud modem. It could transmit at the rate of 300 characters per second. This would transmit each **bit** (a 1 or 0) as a certain frequency and the receiving modem would respond with its own dedicated frequencies.

These were the first dial-up modems and they operated across the public switched telephone network (PSTN) that ran on copper wire.

With the evolution of the Internet, higher data speeds were required and dial-up modems eventually increased in speed to 56 Kb per sec.

The dial-up modem also had the significant disadvantage that it required the use of a dedicated telephone line.

Transmission Control Protocol/Internet Protocol (TCP/IP)

TCP/IP is the basic set of communication protocols for the Internet. These protocols have been developed by the industry in general and not just a single company. The addressing scheme allows devices to have a unique address regardless of the size of the network. It uses a **client/server** protocol for communication and can also be used for networks within organisations.

Thus organisations can use the same skills to manage both Internet access and their local area networks. A local area network that is developed and maintained using Internet technology is called an **intranet**.

Synchronous and asynchronous transmission

Synchronous and asynchronous transmission both refer to the electronic transmission of data. Synchronous transmission sends data between devices in a continuous form. Asynchronous transmission sends data in spurts and waits on a response before continuing the transmission.

These types of transmissions are often used between Internet Service Providers and consumers using modems.

Parity

A parity bit, or check bit, is a bit added to the end of a string of **binary** code. This is used in transmitting data, particularly across networks.

It is a very simple form of error detection and can be used in communications between devices to reduce errors.

Methods of connection (media)

Cables

UTP cable

UTP cable is unshielded twisted pair cable. Two unshielded wires are twisted around each other. This type of cable is often used in local area networks and in telephone connections because it is cheap. However, it does not have high bandwidth. UTP cables have been used for wired telephone networks in many countries. These networks are gradually being replaced throughout the world.

Category 5 (Cat 5) cable is an industry-standard cable for both network and telephone wiring. It is made up of four pairs of twisted copper pairs. It is terminated in an RJ45 jack. This cable supports data speeds of up to 100 Mb per second and it usable for distances up to 100 metres. It is often called ethernet cable. This cable is widely used for computer networks and is also used to connect devices on small home networks.

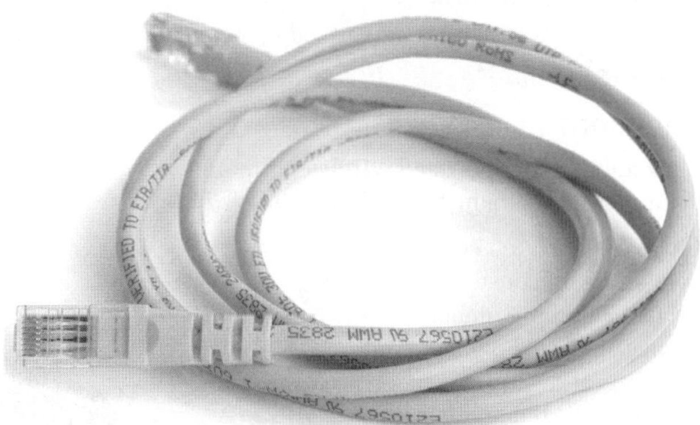

A UTP cable

Cat 5E cable is an enhanced version of Cat 5 cable that supports data speeds of up to 1000 Mb per second and cable runs of up to 100 metres.

Cat 6 cable is the sixth generation of twisted pair cable used in ethernet networks. Like Cat 5 cable, it is made up of four pairs of twisted copper pairs. It supports Gigabit ethernet (ie 1 Gb per second), and higher communication speeds than Cat 5E.

Fibre optic cable

Fibre optic cable

Optical fibre uses glass threads to transmit data. Fibre optic cable consists of a number of glass threads. Each of the glass threads transmits data using light waves.

Fibre optic cables:

- Have very high bandwidth and can thus transmit large amounts of data.
- Are far less susceptible to interference than copper cables.
- Are thinner and lighter than copper wires.
- Can carry data long distances – up to 100 km.

However, they are:

- Expensive to install.
- More fragile than wire.
- More expensive than wire.

Wireless

Bluetooth

Bluetooth is a low-powered **wireless** communication technology that is used to connect computers and other devices. This technology works well over only very short distances.

It was designed to allow the networking of consumer devices including mobile phones, personal digital assistants and wireless headsets. For example, Bluetooth is often used in motor vehicles to allow hands-free use of a mobile phone while the user is in the vehicle.

Bluetooth can be used with some printers. Such a printer includes a Bluetooth adaptor that can enable wireless printing from a mobile phone or other compatible device.

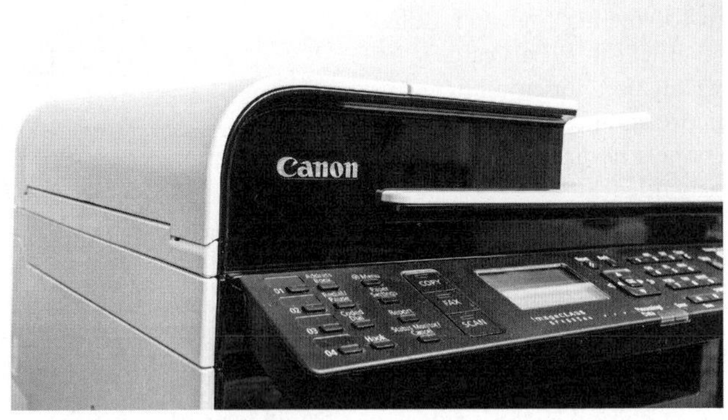

Bluetooth printer. This printer can use Bluetooth to print wirelessly from a mobile phone

Infrared

Infrared technology can be used to connect computing devices. Infrared is electromagnetic radiation that uses charged particles (both magnetically charged and electrically charged) to communicate.

Microwave

Microwave technology uses radio waves that have small wavelengths to provide point to point communications. The communication is done using antennas that point to each other and that transmit microwaves to each other.

Microwave communication has the capacity to transmit large amounts of data. However, it is limited to point-to-point communication and it cannot pass around hills and mountains.

Microwave communication is used in satellite communications.

A satellite dish

Satellite

A satellite can be used to provide Internet access. Geostationary satellites that can offer high data speeds are used. A geostationary satellite orbits the Earth at the same period as the period of rotation of the Earth; that is, approximately every 24 hours.

A user needs a dish antenna and the system requires line of sight between the satellite and the antenna. The dish is set to face in the same direction at all times to ensure the signals can be received and transmitted.

A satellite modem is connected to the dish and uses either ethernet or coaxial cable to access the network in the home or business.

A typical mobile phone tower

3G network

A 3G network is the third-generation mobile phone technology. This is a set of standards that is widely used in mobile telephone applications.

The 3G network uses a packet-based, wireless communication service. Devices on such a network are always 'on'; that is, the connection remains active as long as the telephone, or other device, is within range of the service. The service is transmitted by mobile telephone towers.

The 3G network can be used to provide a range of services to smartphones and other devices such as tablet computers. These services include telephone, instant messaging and Internet access.

In countries that do not have a wired telephone service, 3G networks are used to provide ubiquitous telephone access.

4G network

A 4G network is the fourth-generation mobile phone technology. This is a set of standards that is replacing those used in 3G networks. It provides higher data transfer rates and is used by smartphones, laptops and tablet computers that have USB wireless modems, and other mobile devices.

Manufacturers are producing devices that can use the 4G networks and telecommunication companies are installing these networks throughout the world.

Access to the Internet and a network

Access to the Internet and network resources requires:

- A computer or handheld device such as a smartphone.
- A means of communication, such as a telephone line, cable, wireless.
- A service provider to enable access to the Internet.
- Software on the computer or the handheld device.
- A means of access to the network, such as a modem or a network card.
- Funds to pay the cost of access and charges for time and downloading data.

Telephone and dial-up connection

A **modem** is a device that transmits digital data over a telephone line. This makes it possible for the telephone line to be used for access to the Internet and email.

The public switched telephone network (PSTN) is the network that was set up in many countries to provide telephone access. It consisted of unshielded twisted pair (UTP) cable that ran between the telephone access point and a telephone exchange. This fixed line system transmitted an analogue signal.

A dial-up modem is connected to a fixed telephone line and to a computer that has had the appropriate software installed. The modem acts to convert the analogue signal to a digital signal for use on the computer and then back to an analogue signal.

To access the Internet:

- The software dials a phone number to connect to the **Internet Service Provider (ISP)** through the modem.
- The modem connects and provides Internet access.
- The ISP has a bank of modems that allow the connection to take place.

This mode of access prevents use of the telephone line for voice calls when connected to the Internet.

For many years, this was the standard mode of access to the Internet in homes and some businesses. The disadvantages of this form of access are:

- Speed of access – it is now relatively slow.
- It requires shared access to a telephone line.
- Limited bandwidth.

The advantages of this form of access are:

- It made use of existing infrastructure.
- It may be the only method of connection in remote areas.

A dial-up modem

Broadband connection

Broadband connections provide a much higher bandwidth than a telephone connection. There are two types of broadband connections available in major cities:

- Cable.
- ADSL.

Cable connection

A cable connection uses a coaxial cable. This type of connection was developed in the USA and is widely used for both Internet access and television (in particular, pay television). This requires a cable connection into the house and a cable modem connected to the computer. Network access can then be provided within a home organisation using a wired or wireless connection.

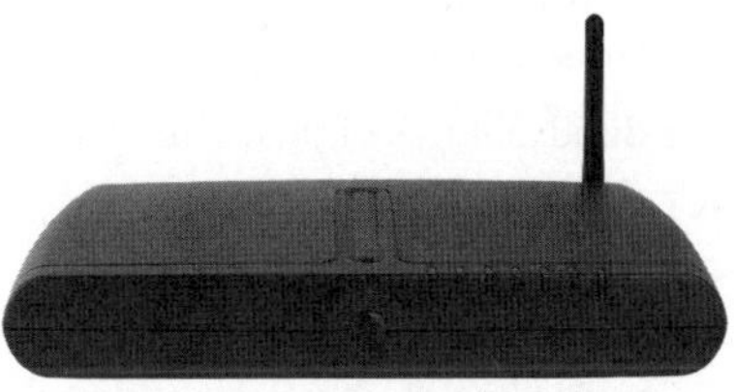

A cable modem

Cable provides a much higher connection speed than a dial-up modem.

A cable modem usually allows connections to a number of computers. The cable modem is used to connect to the ISP and then to a computer in a home or business.

A cable connection requires a coaxial cable to be installed in the location. This requires either a telecommunication company or a pay television company to run the cable in the area.

The disadvantages of this form of access are:

- Cost – it can be relatively expensive to use.
- It requires a significant wired infrastructure, usually provided by telecom companies or pay television companies.
- It is a shared service – if there is significant demand for television programs it may slow the service.

The advantages of this form of access are:

- It is high speed.
- It is very reliable.

ADSL (asymmetric digital subscriber line)

ADSL provides data to the user at a rate of between 256 KB per second and 1.5 MB per second and the user can transmit data at up to 256 KB per second.

ADSL is transmitted into the home using the existing PSTN telephone network. It allows dual usage of the telephone line for both phone calls and data transmission.

As with a cable modem, the ADSL modem can be used to allow a number of devices to connect to the Internet. ADSL modems usually allow both a physical connection (ie via a cable), and a wireless connection.

The disadvantages of this form of access are:

- Cost – it can be relatively expensive to use.
- It requires access to a PSTN network.

The advantages of this form of access are:

- It is high speed.
- It is very reliable
- It can be used by a small organisation or in a home to establish a network.

Satellite connection

A **satellite connection** is useful in areas where there is not fixed cabling and 3G and 4G networks are unavailable.

The disadvantages of this form of access are:

- Cost – it can be relatively expensive to set up and to operate.
- Latency – there can be some time delay for the signal to be received.
- Line of sight – there is a need to ensure that foliage and other obstacles are kept clear to ensure line of sight is always available.

The advantages of this form of access are:

- This is useful in remote areas, provided line of sight is available.
- It provides high bandwidth.

Hardware and software associated with communications via the Internet

Videoconferencing

Making a one-to-one video call is available using clients such as Microsoft Skype on a personal computer that has a camera and an Internet connection. Video is displayed in a window on the computer screen.

Videoconferencing is more sophisticated: it could require multiple locations and a number of people being involved. The video may be projected using projectors onto large screens in rooms specially designed for the conference.

Video communication over networks is an area of considerable potential but the pathway so far has met some difficulties in implementation. Some of these factors are:

- Network security and threats from **hackers**.
- People issues, including self-consciousness and the need to focus on the camera.
- The synchronisation of video and audio for the transmission.
- Time delay over networks that affects interaction. This is often referred to as 'latency'.
- Bandwidth – high-speed data interchange is needed for effective use.

Rather than videoconferencing achieving widespread adoption, it has uses in niche areas such as:

- Communicating with people in remote locations with good Internet access.
- Medical conferencing.
- Business meetings between offices in different countries.

Unit 12.1 Activity 3A: A library system

Consider the process of borrowing a publication from a library and answer the following questions:

1. Does the library record the transaction?
2. Is the borrower given a record of the transaction? If so, what does the transaction record?
3. Does the library inform borrowers of the process to renew a loan?
4. How does the library deal with books that are overdue?
5. Are computers used in the information system of the library?

Unit 12.1 Activity 3B: An airline system

The Air Niugini homepage enables bookings to be made online (see www.airniugini.com.pg).

1. List the information needed for a passenger to enter before they make a booking enquiry.
2. Three radio buttons are shown for Price (dates flexible), Price and Schedule. How does the information displayed differ according to the selection?
3. Which button would you select in these situations?
   a. You must travel next Wednesday for an important meeting.
   b. You wish to travel in a particular week, and would fly according to the best price you can obtain.
   c. You want to know the options for travel on a particular day.
4. What happens when you select the 'Multi City' option?
5. How can you get the airline's flight schedules? In what format are they available?
6. What is an e-ticket and how is it obtained?

Unit 12.1 Activity 3C: An airline check-in system

Air Niugini to Implement New Airport Check-in and Boarding Pass System

Air Niugini Chief Executive Officer, Mr Wasantha Kumarasiri wishes to inform our valued customers that as part of Air Niugini's continuing efforts to improving customer services, the airline from Tuesday 08th May will implement the new Airport Check-in and Boarding Pass System starting at the Port Moresby Domestic Airport then gradually across all Domestic Airports in the country.

Called MACS, the new Airport Control System is hosted by Mercator, a leading provider of technology solutions for the aviation industry. MACS is currently being used by Emirates Airline, who is amongst a number of other major carriers who use the system to manage their passenger operations.

MACS is the first phase of Mercator's Jupiter suite of Passenger Services Solutions being implemented for Air Niugini and will be followed by Mercator Airport Reservations System (MARS), the advanced Internet Booking and staff travel solutions. Upon completion, the airline's sales, airport, loyalty and revenue accounting systems will be fully integrated enhancing passenger experience, better internal controls and efficiency.

Our Loyalty Program customers will benefit once both the Airport and Sales Systems are implemented – with up to date profile and points details and redemptions available at Sales Offices.

1. Who is the vendor of the new Check-in and Boarding Pass System?
2. Why do airlines use systems created by specialist providers rather than developing their own? In your answer, discuss the advantages and disadvantages of this approach.
3. Who are the major vendors of airline reservation systems?
4. What are the main features of an airline reservation system? In your answer, discuss:
   a. Airline inventory (available flights, seats and seat classes)
   b. Availability (available flights, paired to cities with seats and classes)
   c. Passenger Name Record (PNR) – name and contact details, other passenger details, special requests and issued tickets.
   d. Fare data – used to construct the price of a ticket, the booking conditions, tax and other charges.
   e. Electronic ticketing

Unit 12.1 Activity 3D: Banking

1. What banks in PNG offer online banking for customers?
2. Outline the process a customer needs to go through to be able to bank online. In your answer include the role the following may play:
   a. The personal details the bank may require.
   b. The verification process for the personal details.
   c. The suitability of the username and password used to access the account
   d. The type of 'security' questions that are used so that the bank can verify identity at a later stage.
3. What precautions should you take regarding your online access to a bank in order to protect your account?

Unit 12.1 Activity 3E: A computer network

Select a computer network that is readily accessible to you – it could be in a school or business, for example. Investigate the network and answer the following questions.

1. How many desktop computers are linked to the network?
2. How many peripheral devices are linked to the network?
3. What is the network operating system?
4. Can wireless devices access the network?
5. How are devices authenticated when they access the network?

Unit 12.1 Activity 3F: An invoice receipt

Consider this invoice:

Magnetic Oil Company
Service Station
Hubert Murray Highway
Port Moresby

Terminal ID:	002782001
Stan	331152
Card No.	xxxx 7820
Expiry Date:	10/17

Purchase: 70 litres @ K3.51 = K245.7
K245.7

Signature

19/01/2014 Approved: 07:07

1. Outline the steps that occurred prior to this document being produced.
2. Describe the key elements of the document.
3. Is there any vital information missing?
4. How could you design the document template to improve its presentation to make it easier to understand?

Unit 12.1 Activity 3G: A supermarket or small business

Select a business that has a computer terminal at the point of sale that records transactions and prints receipts at time of sale.

1. Examine the print-out provided for the sale. Is the following information recorded on the receipt?
   a. Date of transaction
   b. Name of business

   c. Address of business
   d. Phone number of business
   e. Quantity of each item purchased
   f. Price of each item purchased
   g. Total kina for each item
   h. Total GST for the transaction
   i. Total kina for all items
   j. Name of customer
   k. Time of transaction
   l. Number of items in the transaction
2. Is there any additional information on the receipt? What information would be automatically generated by the information system and be printed at the time the receipt is generated?
3. What information input occurs at the time of the transaction? How is this data entered into the information system?
4. What formatting has been applied to the receipt and what information in particular stands out because of the layout?
5. Find an example of a receipt from at least one other comparable business. What are the differences and similarities on the receipt?

Unit 12.1 Activity 3H: A school

Consider the information a school collects about its students and the reports that it provides.

1. What information is collected about each student? Why?
2. Schools issue reports about the academic progress of students at regular intervals. At what intervals are reports issued? Describe the nature of the report.
   a. How does it identify the school?
   b. How does it identify the student?
   c. How does it identify the subjects and teachers?
   d. What information does it contain about other activities and co-curricular student involvement?
   e. What is the format of the grades and comments?

Unit 12.1 Activity 3I: Transaction processing

Banks offer a range of technologies that allow users to interact with the accounts. These technologies include:

- **a.** Online access with a web browser using the internet
- **b.** Telephone banking
- **c.** ATM – automatic teller machine
- **d.** Electronic funds transfer at point of sale (EFTPOS)
- **e.** Over the counter face-to-face at a bank branch

1. What are the advantages and disadvantages of each from the point of view of the bank and the customer?

2. What type of transactions is a customer able to perform using an ATM?

Unit 12.1 Activity 3J: Ipconfig.exe and ping

Find out the configuration values on the computer you are using. Choose **All Programs** > **Accessories** > **Run** and enter 'cmd'. This will display the command line.

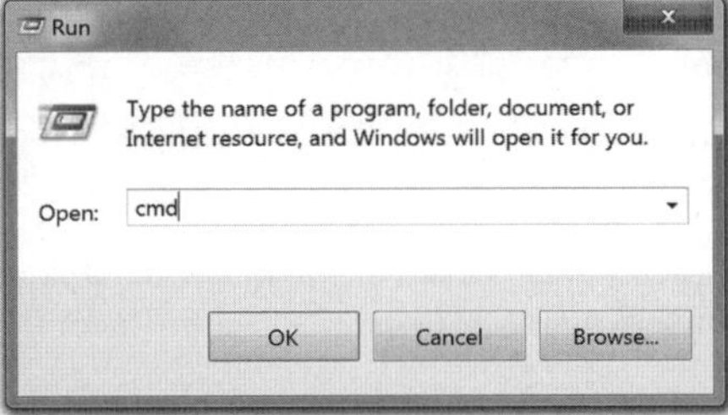

1. At the cursor, enter 'ipconfig' to display the network information. What is the IPv4 address?

2. At the cursor, enter 'ping'. What is displayed?

Unit 12.1 Activity 3K: Using the internet

1. In your local area, what are the options available for connecting to the Internet? In your answer, distinguish between access for:

- **a.** Educational institutions.
- **b.** Small business.
- **c.** Homes.

2. Are there significant differences between the providers and plans they offer for internet access?

Unit 12.1 Activity 3L: Data mining

This is an extract from a Google page about data mining.

> At Google, much of our work on our primary products like search, social, and ads relies on large-scale data mining. Data mining applications arise in several specific projects including speech processing, machine translation, and visual processing. Machine learning at Google raises deep scientific and engineering challenges. The statistics of the data we observe shifts very rapidly, the features of interest change, and the volume of data often precludes the use of standard single-machine training algorithms.

1. Why would Google be conducting research about data mining?
2. Would 'data mining' have implications for how search results are returned in response to a search query?

Unit 12.1 Activity 3M: Networks

A school is developing a computer network for the first time. It has internet access available for computers and other devices connected to the network. The systems analyst presents three different options:

- **a.** A wired network only.
- **b.** A combination wired network and wireless network.
- **c.** A wireless network only.

Give a brief explanation of each of these main factors that need to be considered in making a decision about the type of network to be installed. Factors that may need to be considered include:

- **a.** Cost of the installation
- **b.** Security considerations
- **c.** Speed of access
- **d.** The area covered by the network and the nature of the site.

Unit 12.1 Activity 3N: Software

1. The following are examples of tasks commonly performed using a computer. For each task, indicate the software type you would use. For some tasks there could be more than one software type that could be used.

	Task	Software used
1	Write a letter	
2	Create a budget for your next holiday	

	Task	Software used
3	Organise your personal finances for the coming year	
4	Connect to the world wide web	
5	View a page on the world wide web	
6	Send a message to another person	
7	Create an image to use on a newsletter	
8	Manipulate an image taken with a digital camera	
9	Design a new layout for a garden	
10	Organise your daily events for the next three months	
11	Play a music CD from your computer CD drive	
12	Create a system to organise your CD collection	
13	De-compress a file downloaded from the internet	
14	View a video file from a CD	
15	View a 'PDF' file	
16	Compose a web page	
17	Record a sound as a digital file	
18	Make a presentation to accompany a talk	
19	Communicate with a computer by speaking	
20	Create a sophisticated newsletter with three columns	

2. For a piece of software you like using, fill in the table below outlining the key features of the software.

	Feature	Software example
1	Easy to use	
2	Menu commands are suitably organised	
3	Help system is well organised and is easy to use	
4	Manuals (printed or online) are easy to use	
5	Software works well with other software types	

Unit 12.1 Activity 3O: Evaluation and review

ICT projects are prone to failure. Many organisations now have ICT Governance procedures in place.

1. What is the meaning of the word 'governance'?
2. What is meant by this statement: 'IT departments are not an end to themselves; they exist to enable an organisation to meet its goals.'
3. Research 'ICT disasters' on the internet. What are some examples? Are there any common reasons for failures?

Unit 12.1 Activity 3P: Privacy principles

Visit the Niu Ford homepage and find its privacy policy (see www.fordpng.com/privacy-policy.html).

1. What information does the company collect and how will it be used?
2. Are there any situations where the company may give information to others without your consent?
3. What are 'cookies'? What control can the user have over 'cookies' using settings in the browser?

Unit 12.1 Activity 3Q: Firewall

This is a diagram of a network with access to the WWW. Unfortunately the firewall has not yet been put in place. Where is the best position for it and why?

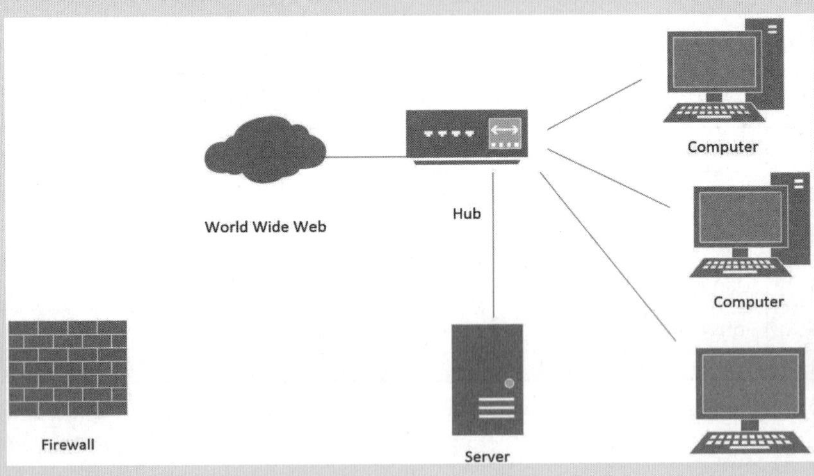

Unit 12.1 Activity 3R: Servers on a network

What role do these servers play on a computer network – web server, print server, mail server, file server?

Unit 12.1 Activity 3S: Peripheral devices on a network

The following peripheral devices may be connected to a network – printer, copier, scanner, multi-function device, fax, digital camera.

1. What functions do they perform in information processing?
2. How can each one of these be physically connected to a network?
3. What software may be required for the device to operate effectively?

Unit 12.1 Activity 3T: Communication systems

Letter, email and telephone are three main methods of communication used by individuals and organisations. Complete the following table comparing the methods.

Method	Examples of use	Advantages	Disadvantages	Potential for issues and failure
A letter		Established mail network		
An email		Cheaper than normal mail.	Has the email been received and read?	
A telephone call		Immediate	Missed calls	

Unit 12.1 Activity 3U: Creating a good working environment

Creating a working environment that demonstrates good working practices reduces the incidence of errors and accidents. Adline Pty Ltd is a shipping and transport agency with ten employees. There are twelve computers that are networked. Three people work in the main office. Florence and Samuel are full-time employees; Tabitha works three half-days per week. Florence mainly operates the accounting software; Samuel operates the switchboard and does general office duties; Tabitha provides technical support including hardware installation and software support.

Describe how each of these practices could be improved.

	Practice	Comment
1	Florence is the only person who knows how to back up the accounting software. This is regarded as not being a problem as she is full time.	
2	Florence currently backs up the accounting software once per week.	
3	Florence backs up the accounting program as well as the data files on a 100 Mb removable disk.	
4	Florence locks the 100mb backup disk in the office safe.	
5	Samuel enters meeting times in the calendar which is accessed by the employees. Samuel makes a backup of the meeting files at irregular intervals.	
6	Samuel on one occasion worked from a backup copy stored on the hard disk which did not have the current week's entries.	
7	Samuel is a novice computer user and reads computer magazines and manuals at work to find out how to use a computer.	
8	Samuel logs all deliveries to the office in a database created by Tabitha. The database is still work in progress and Tabitha will complete it when she has time. Sometimes Samuel will enter into the database information about the same delivery twice.	
9	Samuel creates letters to send to clients. He does not usually save the file until after it has been printed. Sometimes the computer freezes as it is being printed.	
10	Tabitha has recently installed new browser software on the computers in reception after working late one evening. Both Florence and Samuel are mystified about the changes when they turn on their computers the next morning.	
11	At the end of the day, Florence turns her computer monitor off and leaves the central processing unit running. Sometimes the cleaner requires the same power point and disconnects the computer.	
12	Samuel sometimes works at home on work documents. When he returns to the office, he continues working on the documents on the USB device only.	
13	Florence also creates letters for clients. She simply adds a new letter to a single document which contains all the letters for a particular month for all clients. She says it easy to copy and paste the address details from one letter to the next.	
14	For important office memos, Samuel does not keep an electronic copy of the memo, but rather prints the memo and stores it in the filing cabinet.	

	Practice	Comment
15	Tabitha purchased a single copy of a new database management program. She installed a copy on two computers at work and also her home computer so she could learn the package for work purposes.	
16	Samuel has been given a program downloaded from the internet by his best friend. He wants to try the software on the work computer.	

Unit 12.2 Database 2

Topic 1: Introduction to Microsoft Access

In Unit 12.2 students learn to appreciate that computer database systems have a capacity to store, retrieve and manipulate data better than non-computer systems. Students develop skills in modifying existing databases and designing new databases for specific purposes (ICT syllabus p. 36).

The database program described in Unit 12.2 is Microsoft Access. Topic 1 provides a general introduction to the use of Microsoft Access.

Data is made up of recorded facts, figures, images and sounds about people, objects, events or other items. Data is collected and stored in a database.

A **database** is made up of data that is arranged so that it can be searched, organised and selected. Each item of data is related to each other item in some way.

Information systems manage their daily operations and decision making using data stored in databases. Transactions conducted online require access to information stored in databases to enable ordering, payment and delivery of goods. These also provide access to services such as buying an airline ticket.

The **systems life cycle** referred to in Unit 12.1 is a way of illustrating the process for information systems to be created and maintained. An information system is always a 'work in progress' in the sense that the needs and demands of systems change over time. In fact, those needs can change very quickly at times.

The stages of the systems life cycle are:

- Preliminary investigation.
- Analysis.
- Design.
- Development.
- Implementation.
- Evaluation.

Microsoft Access

Microsoft Access is a relational database developed and supported by Microsoft. It is widely used by small organisations and businesses. This Unit focuses primarily on the analysis, design and development stages as it relates to an information system developed with Microsoft Access.

Approach to using Access

Microsoft Access is a sophisticated piece of software that can create a simple database but can also be used for a complex information system. It takes time to be able to understand the menus, ribbons and the other features of the software.

There can be different ways to build an information system and achieve the same result. The examples in this Unit may be only one of a number of ways of achieving the same result.

Microsoft Access templates

Microsoft Access has a variety of templates and working examples that can illustrate information systems and their design.

A **template** is a sample database that can provide an excellent starting point for many widely used types of information systems.

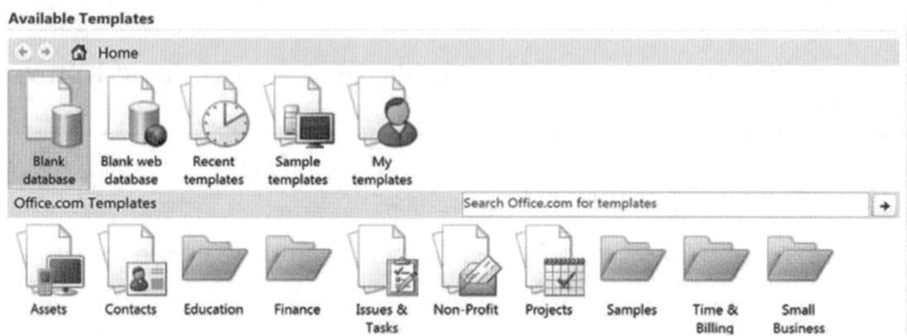

Template types available in Microsoft Access

These templates can be examined to see how they are set up and how they manage the information they contain. A template can be used to form the basis of an information system and can be modified by the developer to suit particular needs.

A sample from a template

Shown below is a screen from a sample database solution. It shows a form for entering information about a student. The form's appearance has been designed so that the items of data will be entered for a student in a logical order.

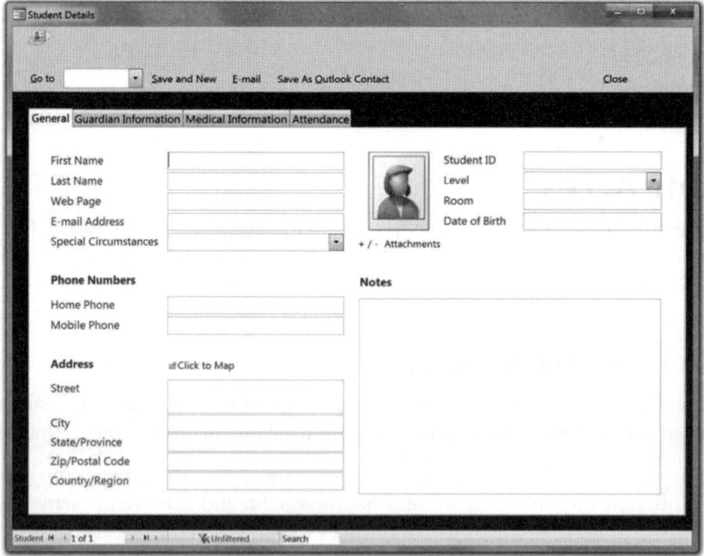

Example of a data entry form in a Microsoft Access template

The user interface for a database

The term **user interface** refers to the way in which the user interacts with the information system. The elements that make up the user interface include the menu bar, buttons, field layouts and descriptions, scroll bars and links.

The student entry form in the figure above is indicative of an information system created in Access that has a modified user interface. The ways in which the interface can be modified include:

- Using forms with buttons, links and tabs for navigation.
- Placing images and icons on the interface.
- Customising menus.
- Using different security levels with passwords to manage the level of access for different users.

An information system that is essentially a database may not appear to be a database to the user. In fact, an information system should have an intuitive user interface so the various screens do not appear like a database authoring environment. An intuitive interface means that when a user sees the interface, he or she is able to interact with it without having to refer to a manual or other documentation.

The design of a database usually starts with a pen and paper analysis of the information problem to be solved. There is no unique solution to an information problem using a database.

Many decisions need to be made during the design process. These decisions range from basic issues, such as what to name 'fields', to more complex issues involving queries and the process of producing reports.

The analysis of the data and decisions about tables to be used and their relationships form the basic building blocks of the database.

A student sport selection information system

A simple sport selection information system is able to demonstrate many of the key aspects of Microsoft Access.

The system is designed as a sport selection information system for a secondary school. It is designed to keep track of students and the sports that they have selected. The system shown in this Unit is simplified, and not all parts of a real-life system are shown.

Entity

A **database** is made up of a collection of files about somebody or something, referred to as an entity. An entity is a person or an object about which data needs to be recorded.

A person who is a student at a school is an entity. Depending on the problem being solved, that student could exist as part of a number of other entities, such as:

- A student in a particular class.
- A student in a particular sporting team.
- A student in a particular year level.

All the students at a particular school form an entity.

Entity relationship diagram (ERD)

An entity relationship diagram shows the data elements and how they relate to each other. It is a useful tool in the analysis of the system and helps in defining the tables and their relationships.

Entity relationship diagram symbols

Each entity has a number of attributes. An attribute is a component of the entity for which data needs to be collected. For example, attributes for a person would include **First Name** and **Family Name**. Note that the attributes for each entity do not represent all the attributes that would be created for the information system and are indicative only.

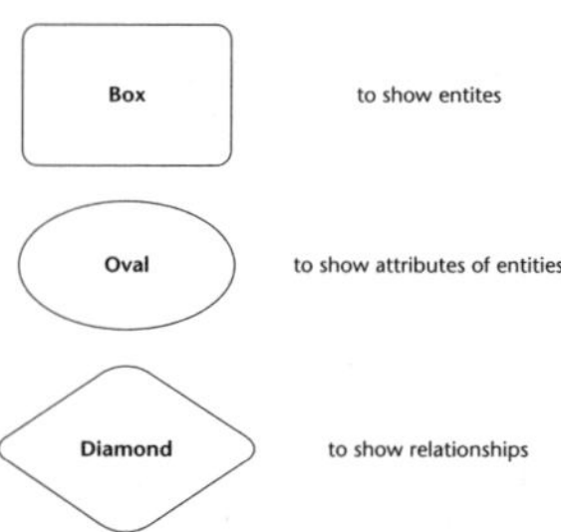

The symbols used and their meanings in an entity relationship diagram (ERD)

Entity relationship diagram (ERD) for a sports information system

Each entity that is used in a database has a name. Many databases consist of only one entity. These databases are often called 'flat file databases'.

A **relational database** is one that is composed of a collection of tables. The tables are related to each other by key fields.

The process of **normalisation** is used to analyse data and to identify the tables that are to be used in a relational database. Normalisation is a set of rules that is applied to the data to eliminate redundant data and duplicated fields. The process leads to the definition of the tables that will be used in the structure of the database.

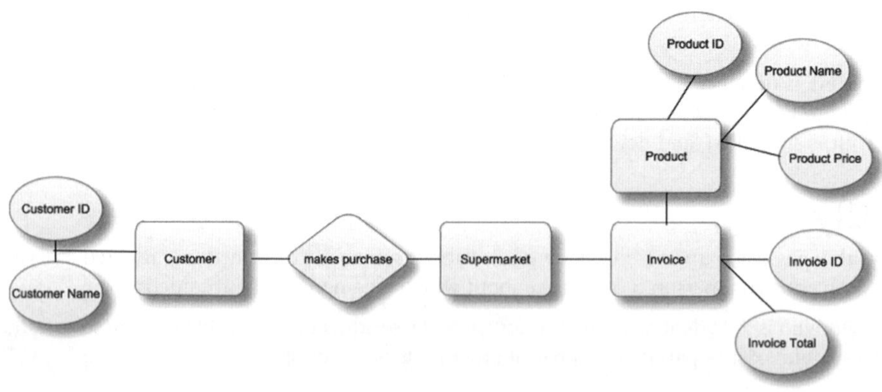

An ERD for a sports information system

Tables for the sports information system

For the sports information system, there are three key tables to hold the data. These are:

Object (Table)	Data	Role
Student table	StudentID, Name, Year Level, Date of Birth.	Student details need to be kept up to date as they can change over time.
Sport table	SportID, SportSeason and SportName. Essentially a lookup table of values.	Sports may be added to or deleted from the sports offered; the name of the sport may change.
Sports List table	StudentID, SportID. The sports list table is a table that stores the unique StudentID and the unique SportID so that reports and lists can be created.	Provide reports and lists of students and sports.

Three tables are required for a sports information system

An input, processing and output (IPO) chart

An IPO (input, processing and output) chart identifies:

- Input – data required to solve the problem.
- Processing – tasks and manipulation of data.
- Output – what the information system produces (screen and paper reports).

There is a storage component that ensures that the data that is input and manipulated can be retrieved at any time.

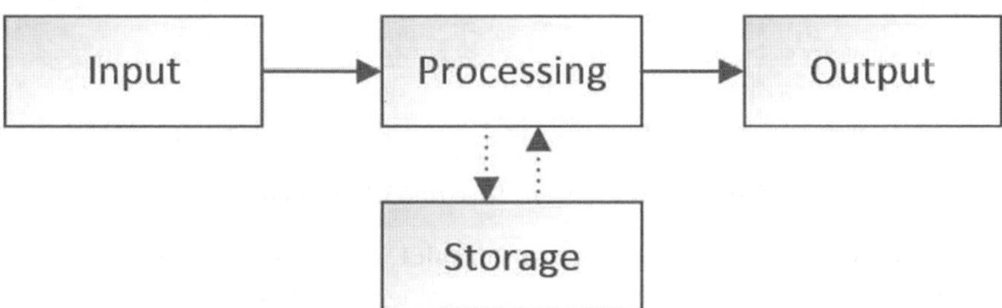

Information processing output (IPO) chart (storage component appended)

Storage is the ancillary stage where data is stored for use at another time.

Input	Processing	Output
Students' names, date of birth. Student sport selection is recorded. List of sports available.	Student selection is matched to the sport selected.	Lists of sports and students who have selected them. (Reports)

Main IPO tasks

Creating a table in Microsoft Access

Access has many features that are consistent with other Microsoft Office Applications. The ribbon is predominant, showing the options available. The **File** menu deals with general file handling, while the other menus invoke the respective ribbons that relate to their functions.

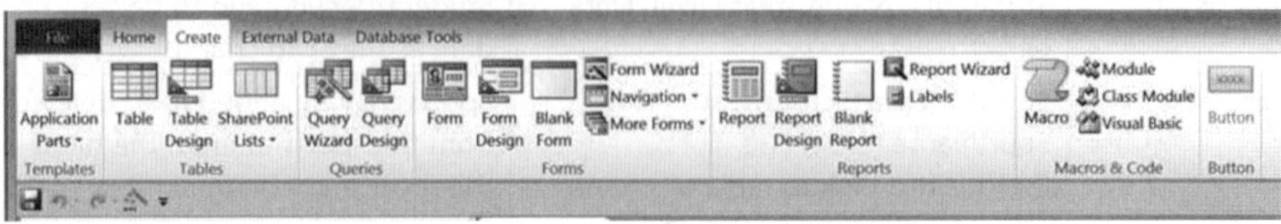

The Create menu ribbon in Microsoft Access

The figure above shows the options for the **Create** menu. This shows the key elements that are to be used in an information system.

The central elements of a database are the tables that store the data. Where there is more than one table, relationships are created so that data in one table is accessed from another table.

To begin creating information system with Microsoft Access, select **Blank database** using the **File** menu.

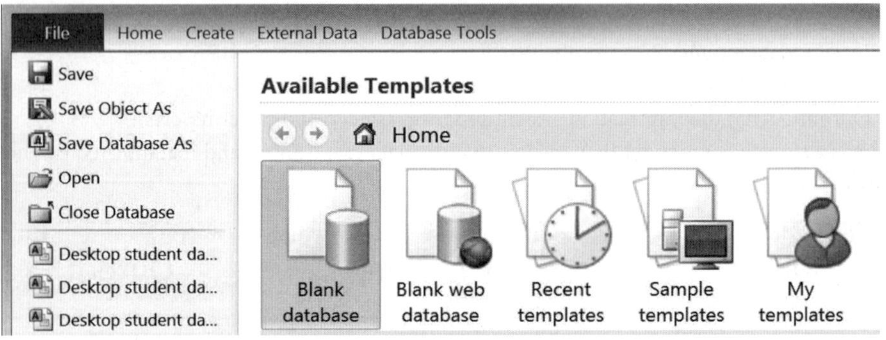

File menu with Open, Save and Close options

This creates a new table that has the default name **Table1**, with an ID field and a new field ready to be created.

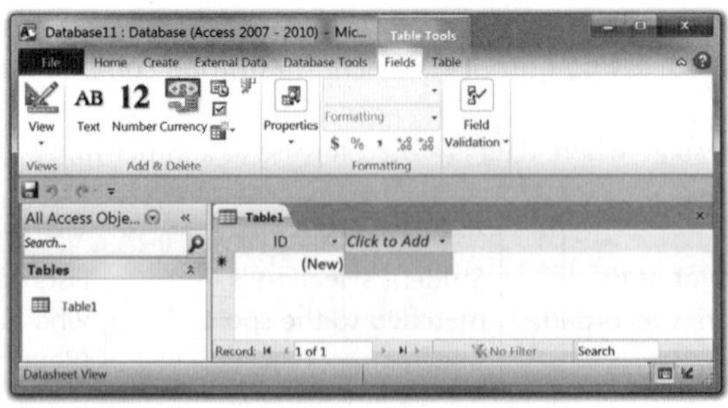

Creating a new table

Unit 12.2 Database 2

Topic 2: Exploring advanced table features

Topic 2 deals with exploring advanced table features with a focus on setting table fields properties, specifically:

- Controlling field size.
- Customising text format.
- Customising number and currency format.
- Customising date and time format.
- Controlling input pattern using input mask.
- Changing the display of field name using caption.
- Specifying a default value.
- Prompting error using validation rule.
- Customising an error message.
- Making a field compulsory.
- How to index a field.
- Creating lookup value for a field.
- Updating values in a lookup list.

A new table in Microsoft Access has the default name of **Table1**, with an **ID** field and subsequent fields **Field1**, **Field2** and so on.

The ID field is the primary key for that table. Each table has only one primary key. It is unique and can be used to identify any record. It is also indexed, which enables a search to be done quickly and efficiently.

A primary key in one table can be used as a foreign key in another table when relationships are created.

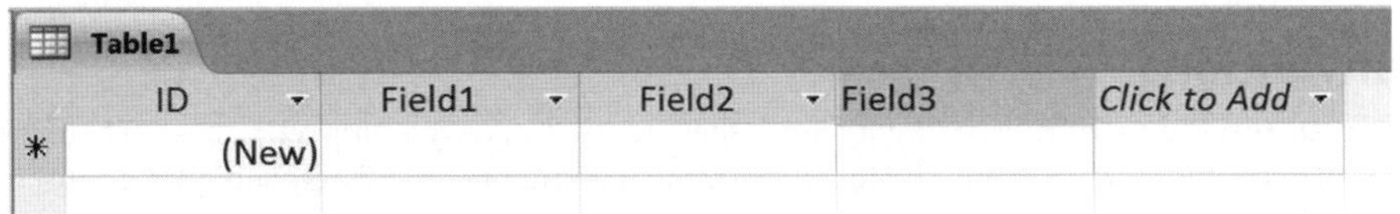

The default field names in Access

The table and fields need to have names that relate to the entity on which the table is based. In particular, each of these elements requires a name to assist in identification.

The **Help** file for Microsoft Access provides rules relating to naming, as shown in the figure below.

Guidelines for naming fields, controls, and objects

Names of fields, controls, and objects in Microsoft Access:

- Can be up to 64 characters long.
- Can include any combination of letters, numbers, spaces, and special characters except a period (.), an exclamation point (!), an accent grave (`), and brackets ([ ]).
- Can't begin with leading spaces.
- Can't include control characters (ASCII values 0 through 31).
- Can't include a double quotation mark (") in table, view, or stored procedure names in a Microsoft Access project.

Applies to:
Access 2010, Access 2007, Access 2003

Extract from the Microsoft Access Help file with guidelines for naming

Although you can include spaces in field, control and object names, most examples in the Microsoft Access documentation show field and control names without spaces. It is better to avoid using spaces in names because they can produce conflicts in some circumstances.

Some words are 'reserved' by Microsoft Access. For example, an attempt to name a field as 'Date' would bring up the error message shown below.

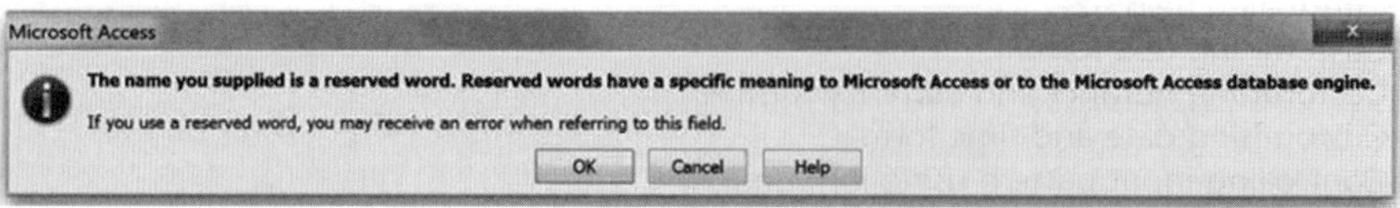

An error message identifying a naming conflict

Just as a table is required to have a name, so are the other elements associated with the tables and the database, including:

- Fields.
- Forms.
- Queries.
- Reports.
- Macros. (A macro is a tool that allows you to automate tasks and add functionality to reports, forms and controls.)

Naming of fields, controls and objects

The name of a field or object should be related to its content and provide guidance to its contents. Similarly, the name of a control should give guidance as to the function of that control.

Conventions

A **convention** is a set of rules and guidelines that are used in developing a database. There is a range of conventions that should be followed in the naming process. Essentially they are used to:

- Enable consistency.
- Make it easier for others to understand how the information system has been set up.
- Enable the name to provide guidance to its content or functionality.
- Keep to a minimum the typing of field names when referencing the field in other aspects of the database.

'Camel case' naming is where a compound word has each component word begin with a capital letter: for example, 'Student Identification' is often abbreviated to 'StudentID'. 'ID' is itself an abbreviation for 'Identification number'.

Underscore, rather than using the space character, is also another common convention for word separation: for example, 'Student_ID'

There is a wide variety of conventions that can be applied to naming. Essentially, it is the consistency of practice within the information system that is most important. For example, it would be normal to have either the camel case or the underscore convention apply in a system, but not a mixture of the two.

Variations on field naming

The following table shows fields that are used in many different databases with some alternative names they may be given. These use the conventions of underscore and camel case.

Field	Alternative field names	Field name (underscore)	Field name (camel case)
A person's first name	First Name Given Name	First_name Given_name	FirstName GivenName
A person's second name	Last Name Family Name	Last_name Family_name	LastName FamilyName
A person's date of birth	Date of Birth DOB	Date_of_birth DOB	DateOfBirth DOB

Variations in field names and examples of conventions

A **data structure table** referred to in this chapter is used in the design phase of a database and it reflects the decisions made regarding what the various fields will be named. Using such a table makes it easier to create the fields in Access and across the tables in the information system.

Setting table field properties

When a field in a table is defined, a data type must be assigned to that field. The default field type in Access is the **Text** data type. All the data that is stored in a particular field must be of the same data type.

There is a range of data types that can be assigned to a field when it is defined. These data types include:

- **Text** that consists of characters (eg A to Z, 0 to 9, punctuation and symbol characters).
- **Numbers** (0 to 9) that consist of different number types such as whole numbers or currency.
- **Calculated** that rely on the results of a calculation between other fields.
- **Logical** that consist of Yes/No options.
- **Web** addresses that are stored as hyperlinks.

When adding a field in a table, a drop-down list of field types appears in the window as shown in the figure below.

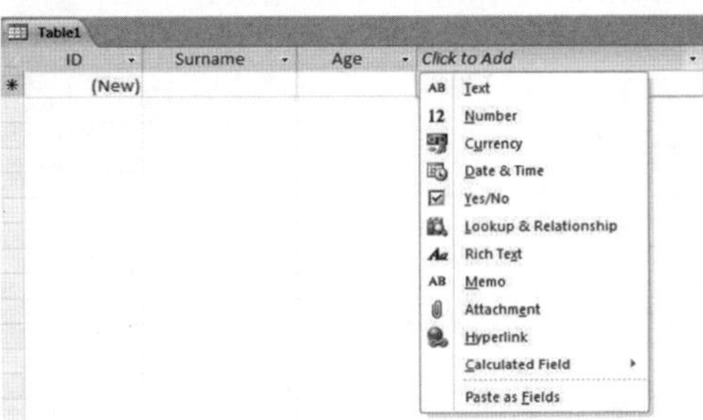

Selecting a field type

The figure below shows the key parts of the datasheet view for the table **Students**. It shows the fields, field names, data type, and navigation for the window.

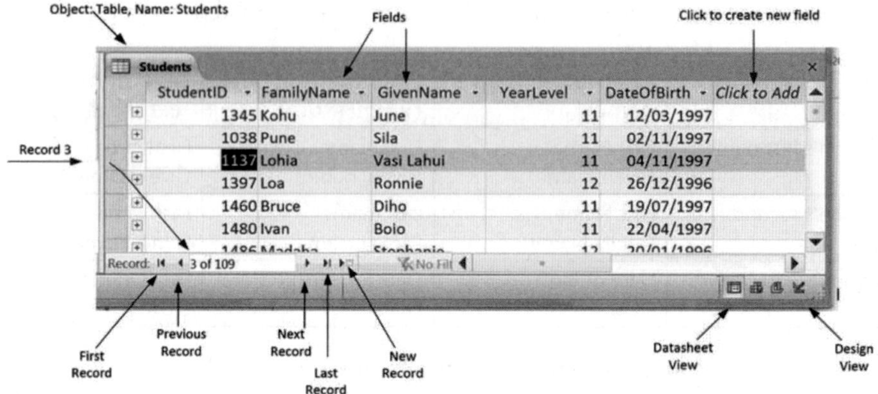

Datasheet view for a 'Students' table

The datasheet table view is very similar to a spreadsheet with cells, rows and columns.

The **Design View** for the table is shown below. Note the description details. The properties show the **format** for the 'DateOfBirth' field, being 'dd/mm/yyyy', and that an **input mask** has been created to assist the user in entering data in the appropriate format. An input mask provides a set format for data entry in a field by using characters and symbols.

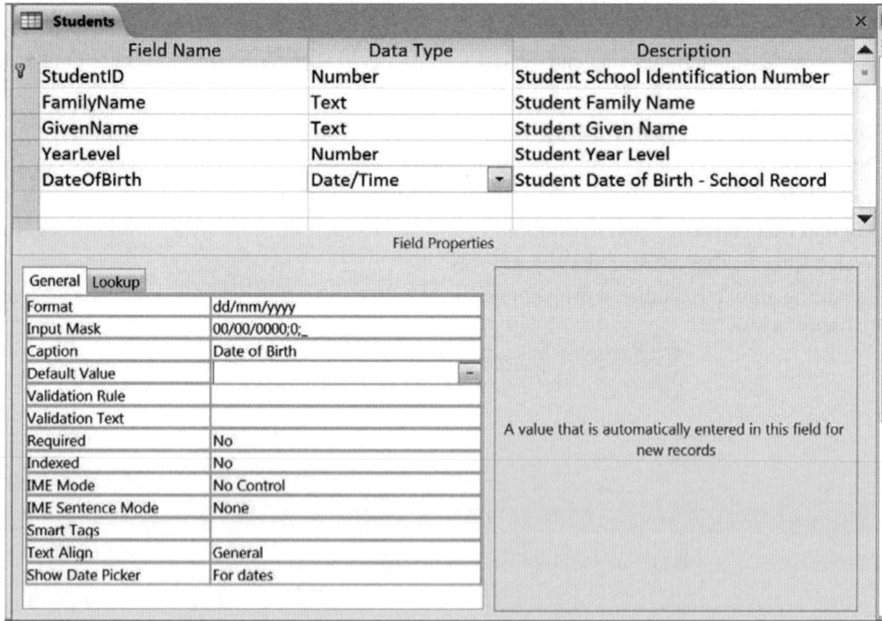

Design View for 'Students' table

The details provide a reference for the developer and others who may need to modify and develop the information system at a later date.

Data structure table

A **data structure table** is usually prepared in the design process prior to developing the system. It enables care and thought to be given to the construction of the database and it enables faster development using the software.

Field	Data type	Field size	Caption	Description
StudentID	Number	4	Student No.	Student Unique Identification Number
FamilyName	Text	30	Family Name	Student Family Name
GivenName	Text	30	Given Name	Student Given Name
YearLevel	Text	2	Year	Student Year Level
DateOfBirth	Date/Time	8	Date of Birth	Student Date of Birth
SportID	Text	3	Sport No.	Sport Unique Identification Number
SportName	Text	30	Name	Sport Name
SportSeason	Text	10	Season	Sport Season

Data structure table for 'Students' table showing field size

Field type selection is determined by what the database intends to do with the data contained in the field. For example, a phone number normally consists of only numbers. However, because the data is not used in calculations (such as addition, subtraction, multiplication), a text field would be used rather than a number field.

Controlling field size

The field size is determined when the field is defined. A text field has a default value of 255 characters.

The field size can be modified in the **Field Size** entry box on the **Fields** tab of the **Table Tools** menu.

Types of number fields

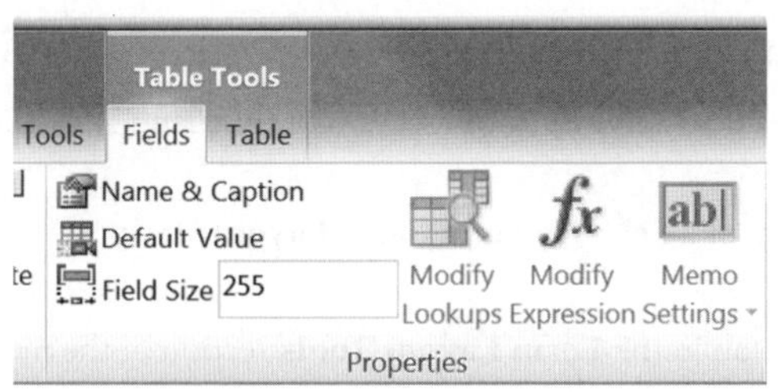

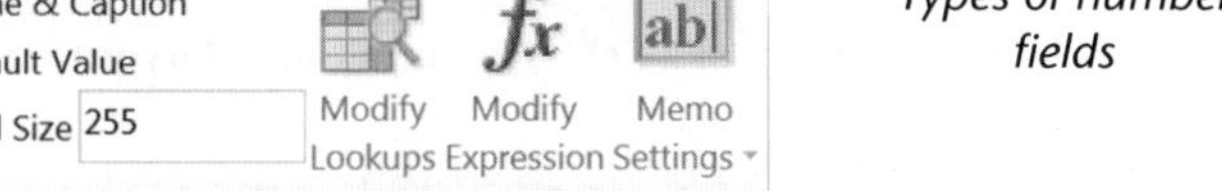

Text field with default field size prior to modification

Similarly, a number field can have its type selected from a range of possibilities.

Abbreviation of field names

It is normal to abbreviate field names. Access itself, for example, uses 'ID' for 'identification number'. Usually the ID is given as the suffix of the table name. Keeping names short helps readability and saves time entering field names.

Primary key field with name and data type, 'AutoNumber'

For the 'primary key', Access shows a key symbol. **Design** > **Primary Key** accesses the properties for the primary key. In the figure above, a number is entered automatically on the creation of a new record. This is entered as a serial number.

Primary key symbol

Significance of a primary key

A primary key is used as a unique identifier. There is only one record in each table that has the value of a primary key. A primary key could be numeric or alpha-numeric. Most information systems will automatically generate a primary key that has no direct relationship to any other item of data in the record. For example, a student ID in a school system could be a number. Invoices in a sales system could be prefixed with 'Inv' to indicate an Invoice, such as 'Inv58390'. In the USA, citizens and permanent residents are issued a 9-digit unique Social Security Number that serves as a primary key for many different databases.

Unit 12.2 Activity 2A: Unique identifiers

1. Would it be a good idea to use the 'Family Name' as a unique identifier in a school information system? Why/why not?
2. How is a student uniquely identified in a school information system?

Customising text format

The **Format** tab on the **Form Layout Tools** section of the menu allows control of the text format.

To change the text format of a field in a Form in the **Layout** view:

- Select the field.
- Choose the **Format** tab in the **Form Layout Tools** section of the menu.
- Choose the:
  - Font.
  - Size.
  - Formatting characteristics.

This is done on the **Font** section of the menu bar.

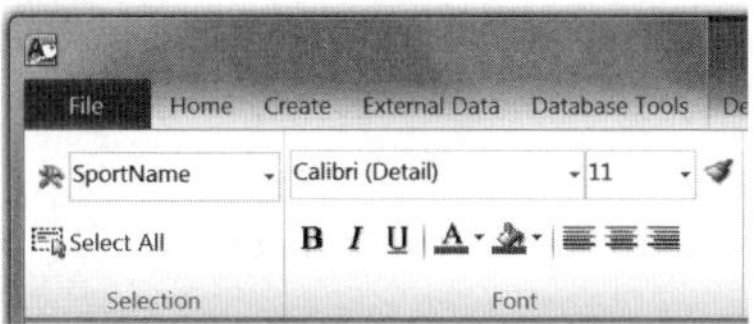

The Font section of the menu bar is used to customise text format

Another method of customising the text format is to use **Themes** section of the menu. The **Themes** section gives a consistent set of fonts, sizes and colours that can be used throughout an application.

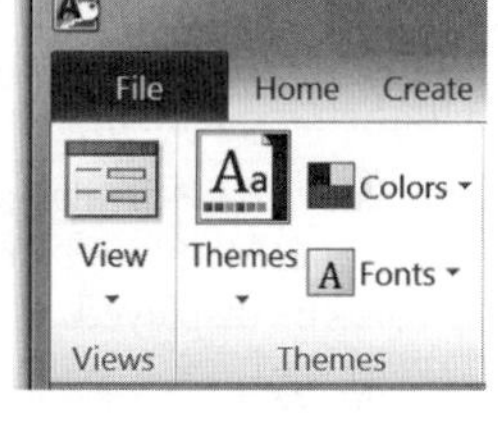

The Themes section of the menu bar can be used to format text

Customising number and currency formats

There is a range of options for formatting number and currency fields. It is also possible to create custom formats. A **custom format** is where the creator of the database creates his or her own particular format from a number.

Where a field is a number, the format can be selected in the Property Sheet.

Format | Data | Event | Other | All

Format		
Decimal Places	General Number	3456.789
Visible	Currency	$3,456.79
Show Date Picker	Euro	€3,456.79
Width	Fixed	3456.79
Height	Standard	3,456.79
Top	Percent	123.00%
Left	Scientific	3.46E+03

Property Sheet showing drop-down list with options for formatting numbers

Number

The default is **General Number** and the number will be displayed exactly as it is entered. For example, if the number entered is 3456.789 it will be displayed as 3456.789.

Currency

The default **Currency** format will display the '$' or currency symbol as selected in the 'Control Panel' setting, with the comma separator for '000s' and 'period' separator for the decimal point with two places.

$34,000.50 is an example of a number using the **Currency** format.

Customising date and time format

Dates and times can be used in Access in two main ways:

- As data in fields.
- As placeholders on forms and reports for information produced by an information system to show when a report has been produced.

A date field type is a number field. It starts with the number 1 referring to the date 31 Dec. 1899 and the number 2 referring to 1 Jan. 1900, then continues with the number 3 for 2 Jan. 1900 and then sequentially onwards.

The date can be displayed in a number of formats including Long Date, Medium Date and Short Date, and a custom format can also be displayed.

A **Long Date** is in the form 'Monday, 25 May, 2015' whereas the **Short Date** format is '25/05/15'.

Different formats for date fields

A placeholder is an area in a form or other layout that allows the developer to add content to that form whenever data is added or posted. A date field might be used in a placeholder to automatically record the date on which data is added or modified.

Unit 12.2 Activity 2B: Date formats

1. What are the differences in the format for dates shown in the figure above? Provide an example of how each would appear.
2. What is the default date and time format in Access?

Date (mdy or dmy)

Dates are critical information for an information system. The dd/mm/yyyy format is used in many countries. An example of this format is 23/12/2015.

In the USA, the format that is most often used is mm/dd/yyyy. An example is 12/23/2015.

A variety of options exist for displaying a date. It is best to choose a format that is unambiguous and to make sure that this format is used consistently throughout the application.

Date pickers

Using a **date picker** is a method of choosing a date. This enables the correct input of data. The day number, month name and year are shown during the selection.

Date picker can be used to select data for a date field

Unit 12.2 Activity 2C: Different date formats

1. How many different ways can the date 10/2/15 be expressed?
2. What date format do you prefer? Give reasons for your answer.

Times (12-hour or 24-hour clock)

Both 12-hour and 24-hour clocks are used to represent times. The 12-hour clock uses a.m. and p.m. notation to indicate morning or afternoon/evening.

A 24-hour clock counts from 00:00 to 23:59. The 24-hour clock is very common in Europe and is often used by airline information systems. The 24-hour clock is unambiguous as a time cannot be confused as a.m. or p.m. as with a 12-hour clock.

The figure below shows an airline booking with the use of a 24-hour clock.

Flight	Departure	Arrival	Stops	Equipment	Class
OUTBOUND **Port Moresby** (POM) to **Singapore** (SIN) | Sat, 26-Apr-14					
PX392	Jacksons International Airport (POM) **14:25** | Sat, 26-Apr-14	Changi International Airport (SIN) **18:45** | Sat, 26-Apr-14	0 Stop(s)	Boeing 767-300	Economy

Example of times shown using 24-hour clock

Unit 12.2 Activity 2D: 12-hour and 24-hour clocks

1. The flying time from Port Moresby to Singapore is approximately 6 hours and 40 minutes. If an aircraft departs Port Moresby at 10:00 am
   a. What time will it be in Port Moresby when the plane lands in Singapore?
   b. What is the time zone difference between Port Moresby and Singapore?
   c. What time will it be in Singapore?
2. Can you identify information systems that use an example of each clock format?
3. Why is a 24-hour clock commonly used by airlines? What are the advantages of using this format?

Control input pattern using input mask

Dates, times and data with a set sequence of numbers (such as phone numbers) are well suited to **input masks** to limit the input options.

Where a pattern is required for correct data entry, the input mask can give visual clues to assist in entry. For example:

- Phone numbers, particularly where country and area codes are required.
- Credit card numbers, particularly as the number of digits is lengthy. Validation of credit card type also often depends on the first four digits of the number.

The input mask can contain a variety of 'separators' to improve readability:

- 0, a digit (0–9).
- 9, a digit (0–9) is optional.
- L, a letter (A to Z).
- -, a separator character.

For example, the following input mask could be used for phone numbers where the main number consists of seven digits:

(000) 000-0000 Example: (675) 342-1234

The first three digits are the country code. For PNG, the country code is 675.

The input mask limits data entry to the number of digits; no additional characters or digits are accepted.

Creating the input mask

In **Design** mode, clicking on **Input Mask** invokes the wizard. By selecting **Short Date** the 'default' mask is shown.

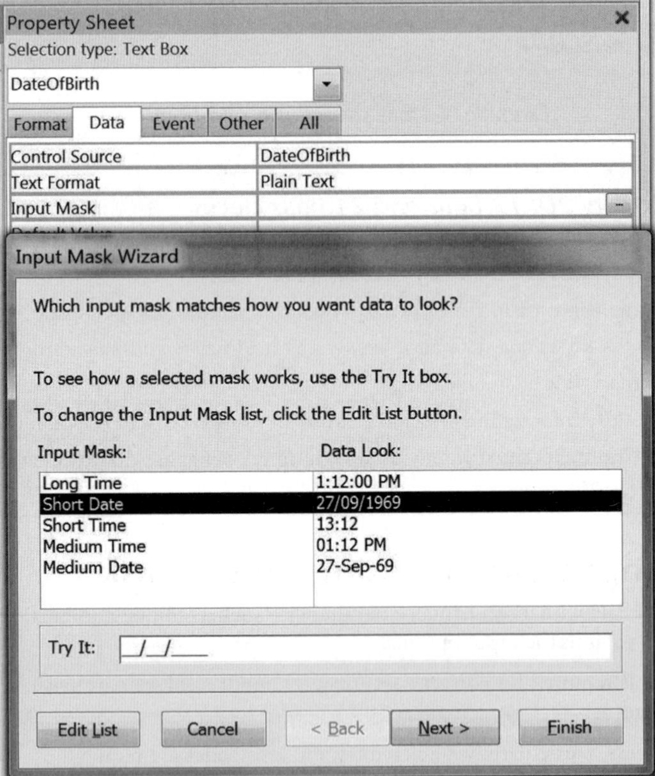

Input Mask Wizard dialog box with options and 'Try It:' window

The mask and placeholder character can be altered if desired.

Input Mask Wizard with 'Mask' and 'Placeholder' option

When clicking on the field on the form the mask is displayed ready for input.

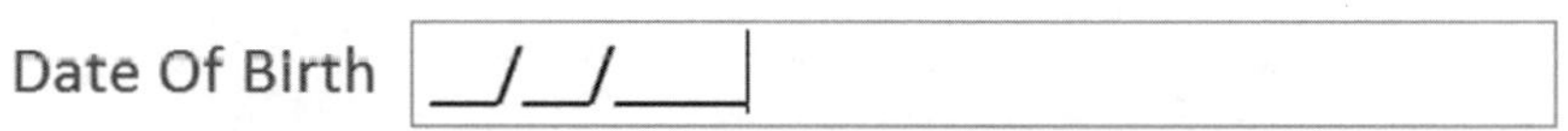

An input mask for a date of birth

Shown below is a date accepted by the mask as it conforms to the dates allowed.

Date Of Birth 12/12/1111

A date of birth is entered using an input mask

Depending on the information system, a range check may need to be used to limit dates to those that are reasonable and acceptable for the particular application.

Unit 12.2 Activity 2E: Input mask

1. What could be an issue with the date 12/12/1111 being entered into a system?
2. Are there systems where the date might be allowed?
3. Create an input mask with the example above. What happens as you enter a date in the field with the input mask?

Changing the display of a field name using a caption

The display of a field name in a form can be changed by using a different caption. To do this:

- Open the form in **Layout** view.
- Double-click on the field name.
- Enter the replacement caption.

Student Number	1819
Family Name	Tava
Given Name	Meleani

Modify the caption by entering different text

Specifying a default value

A default value for a field can be defined in the **Field Properties** window. The figure below shows the field 'RecordDate', a Date/Time field type. RecordDate is a field to display the date the record in the information system is created.

It has a default value that is entered automatically. The date is retrieved from the system clock of the computer.

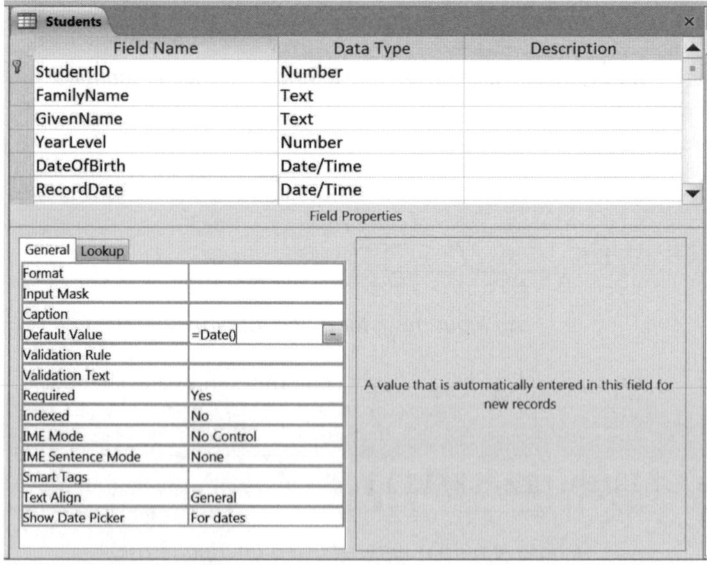

A default value for RecordDate is automatically entered

Prompting error using validation rule

Validation is checking that data is correct at time of entry.

Manual validation

Manual validation means that a person reads the data to check that it makes sense and is correct.

Some data, such as people's names, is difficult to validate other than by proofreading. There is such a wide variety of spelling and combinations that reference to an original document is usually required so the spelling can be verified.

For example, some schools will require a copy of a birth certificate to verify the name and date of birth of a student.

Unit 12.2 Activity 2F: Variation in spelling

1. What examples do you know of where there is variation of people's names?
2. Can you identify similar-sounding names where the spelling is different?

Spell check and AutoCorrect

A spell checker does have a role to play in the spelling of names. It can add words to the dictionary and this can save time with future checks.

Home > Spelling brings up the dialog box to check spelling.

Using a spelling check

Choosing **Options** in the dialog box shown in the figure above enables selection of other options for AutoCorrect.

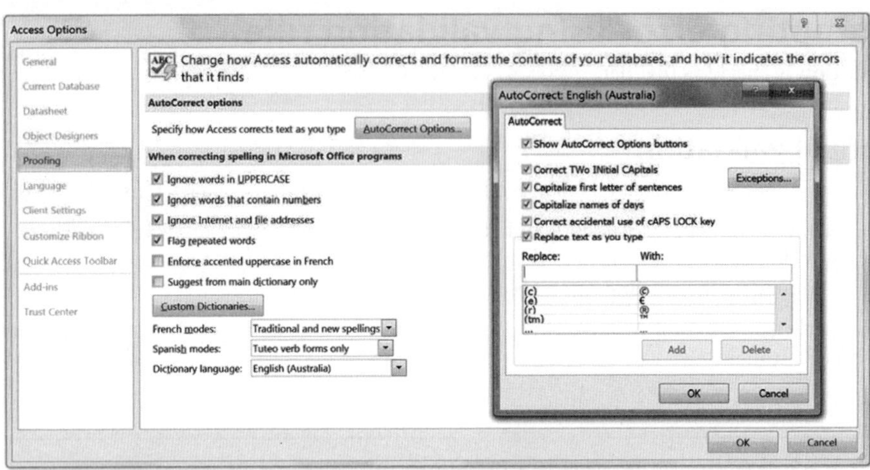

Options to customise AutoCorrect

Keyboarding errors are particularly suited to being corrected with AutoCorrect.

Automatic validation

Microsoft Access does automatic validation on fields such as:

- Date/Time.
- Yes/No.
- Number/Currency.

Data that does not conform to the rule will not be accepted by Access.

The figure below shows an attempt to enter data in a 'Date' field. Access will not enable the user to proceed until it is deleted or correct data is entered.

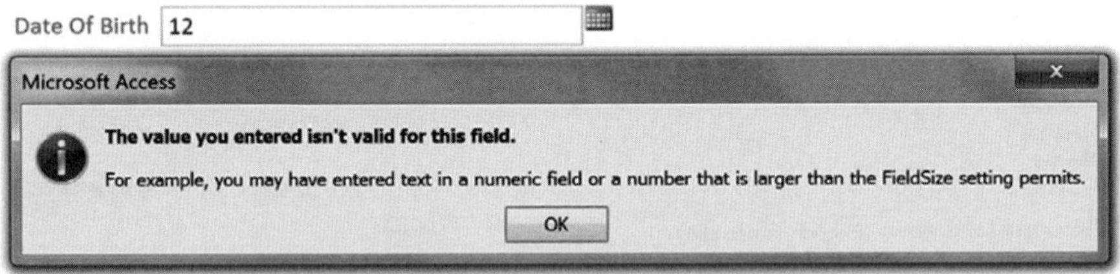

Default error message provided by Access

The default validation message provided does not provide specific feedback about the reason the data is invalid and will not be accepted.

Information systems endeavour to have data entered that is correct at time of entry. Often a simple keyboarding error can result in incorrect data being entered.

Access enables validation in two main places:

- Field.
- Table.

Electronic validation

Microsoft Access enables validation to be set for fields and records using rules that can be customised according to the desired check. These apply to the data *before* it is committed to the database.

The validation check will usually only allow data to be entered if it satisfies the check or, if it does not meet the check, the user can sometimes override the check for that specific item of data.

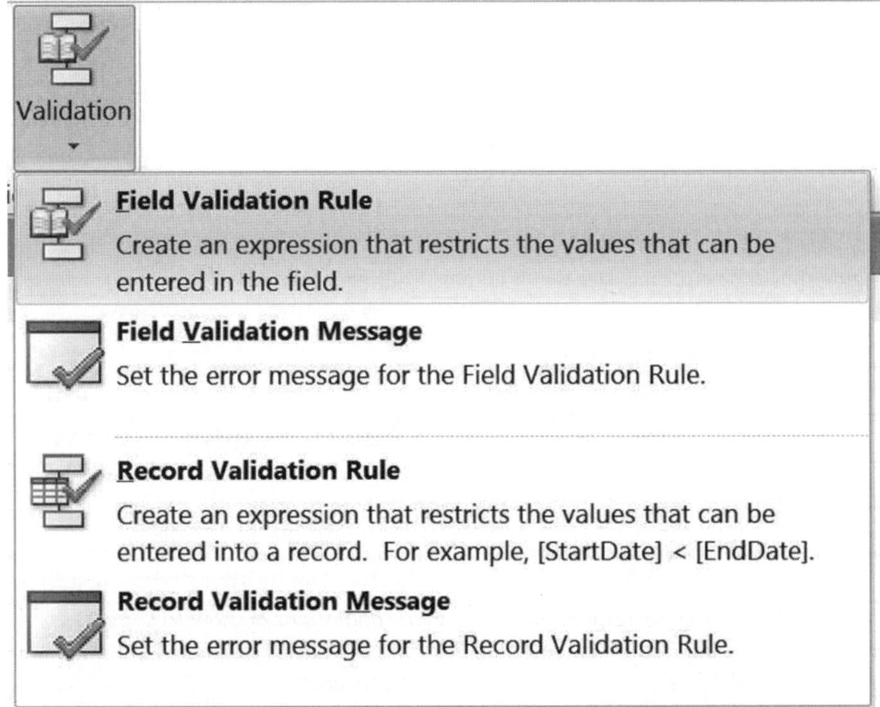

Options for setting validation rules and messages

The main types of validation include:

- Data type.
- Range check.
- Field not empty, required value.
- Input masks.

Data type

The field type definition can limit the type of data accepted by the field. For example, a text field can contain alpha-numeric characters, which are essentially the characters shown on a keyboard.

A number field will accept numbers 0–9. Access will automatically validate a number field. For example, a letter has been entered in the number field shown below.

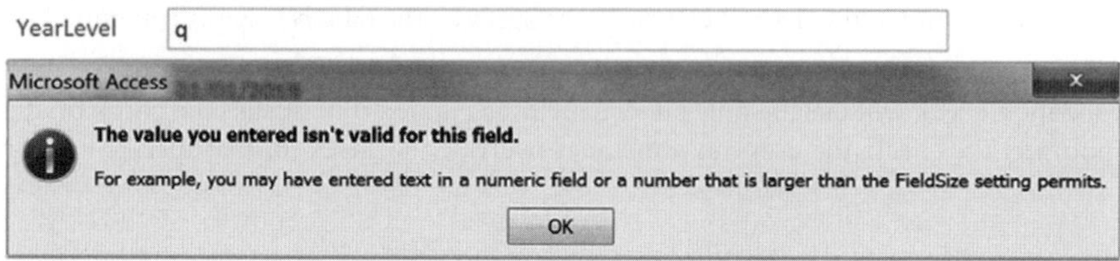

Automatic validation on a number field

Range check

A **range check** can see if values meet a particular test or set of tests.

Date fields are checked automatically by Access to the extent that the day and month must be valid. For example, the date 30/2/2014 would not be accepted as there are not 30 days in February.

The figure shows the error message that is automatically generated.

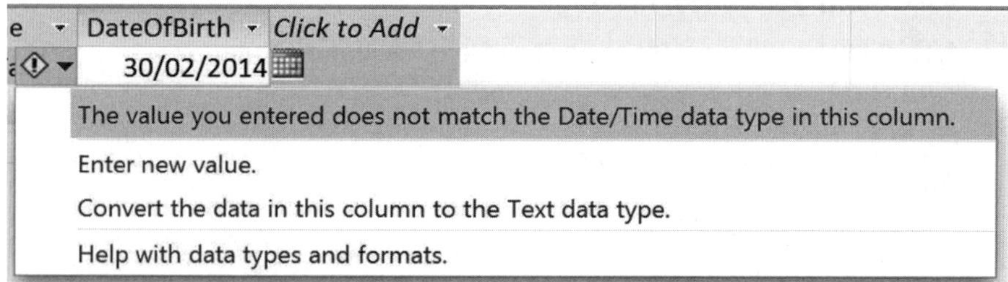

Default error message for date field with suggestions on how to correct

For a date field such as DateOfBirth, the rule **">=#1/01/1996#"** would exclude a person born before that date.

Validation rules have certain syntax that must be followed. For example, to restrict dates for a date field to those in the year 2015 the rule would be **">=#01/0/2015# AND <#01/01/2016#"**.

Lists

A list of values can be created that will form the data options for a field. The following figure shows the property sheet for a popup menu called a 'Combo Box' that will hold values for the field 'Year Level'.

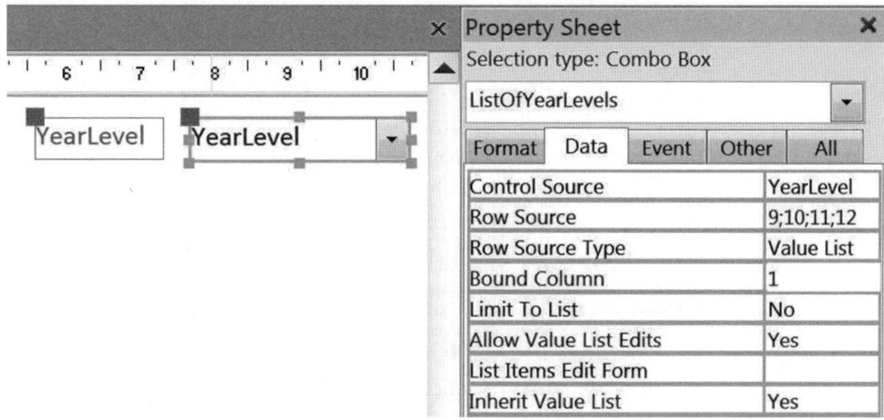

Combo box with range of values

The values accepted are shown in 'Row Source', that is, the values 9 through to 12 to represent those year levels. Note that the values can be edited in this case on the form as **Allow Value List Edits** is set to 'Yes'.

The figure below shows how the values available for selection would appear on a form.

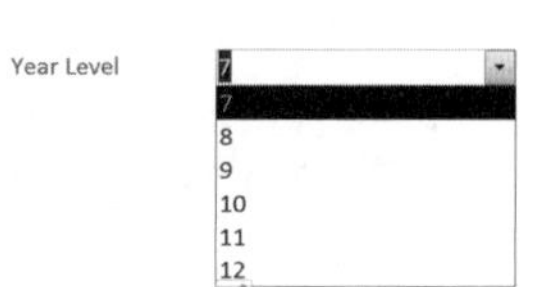

Selecting a value from a list

Field not empty

When entering student information, the system requires the student's family name to be entered.

The default error message generated by Access, although specific, may not be easy for all users to understand. The figure below shows the default message if the field does not have an entry and the user tries to leave the form.

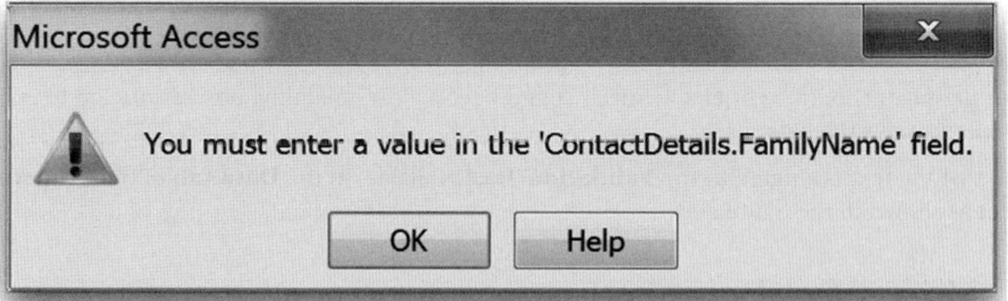

Default error message with table and field name

The error message would be useful for the developer, as it indicates the table and field that require the value.

With a validation rule, the message can be customised to be brief and simple and to include an instruction for the user.

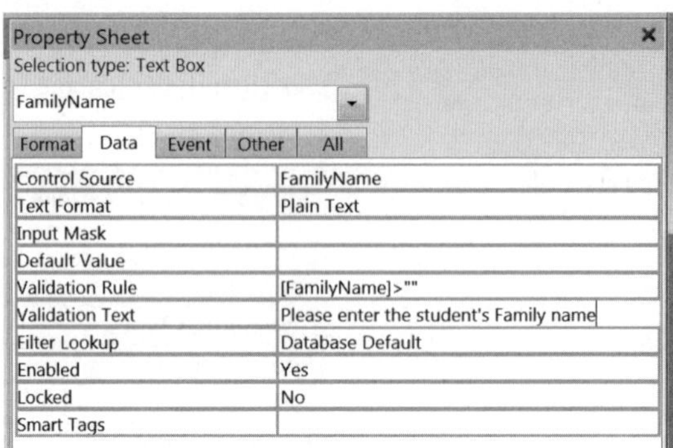

Using the Property Sheet to enter text from a custom validation rule

Shown is the alert with the customised message that prompts the user to the action required to resolve the problem.

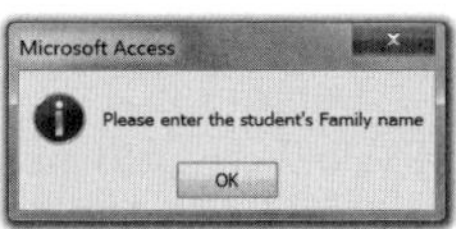

Example of a custom validation message

Customising an error message

If a user enters incorrect data, a validation message can be created to inform the user.

Dialog box to enter text for a custom message

Error messages should be brief and succinct and have a clear, unambiguous instruction to enable the user to enter the data.

Note that the text is entered in the **Validation Text** available on the **Data tab** of the **Property Sheet** as shown in the figure above.

Making a field compulsory

A field can be made compulsory using the **Fields** tab and the **Table Tools** tab. In the **Field Validation** section of the tab, click in the **Required** box to make it compulsory.

For some data items it is essential that a value be entered, for example, date of birth for a student at a school.

While developing and testing a database, making a field compulsory can be a nuisance as it restricts movement around the system if a value is required to be entered each time. However, after testing is completed and prior to implementation, the compulsory field validation should be activated.

How to index a field

An **index** is a data structure that speeds up the search for records that contain certain types of data. An index in a database is rather like an index in a book.

When a new table is created, Access automatically creates an index for the primary key field in the table. The primary key is used to uniquely identify a record.

To create an index on a particular field:

- Open the table in which the field is defined.
- Select the field name.
- Go to the **Field Validation** section of the **Fields** tab in the **Table Tools** tab.
- Click on the **Indexed** box in the **Field Validation** section.

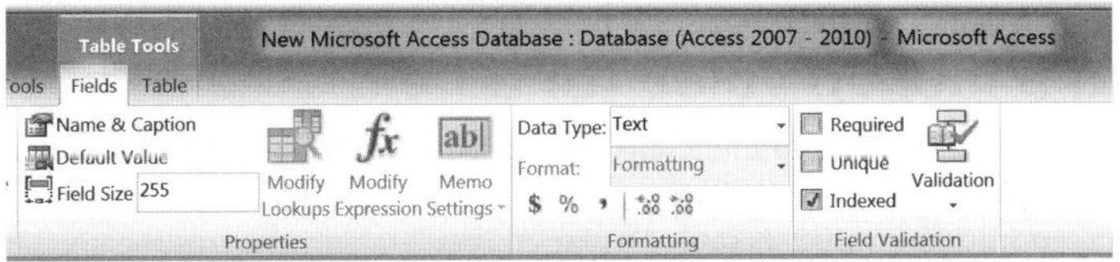

Field index option checked in Fields ribbon

When a new record is added to an information system, it is added at the end of the current set. However, it may be that the information system requires the records to be in a different order.

Indexing makes it quicker to sort and search a database; otherwise the sort or search has to traverse all records during the process.

For example, students in a school would often be sorted in A to Z order by family name. The figure below shows the field '**FamilyName**', which is indexed and allows for duplicates. Note that there may be more than one person with the same family name.

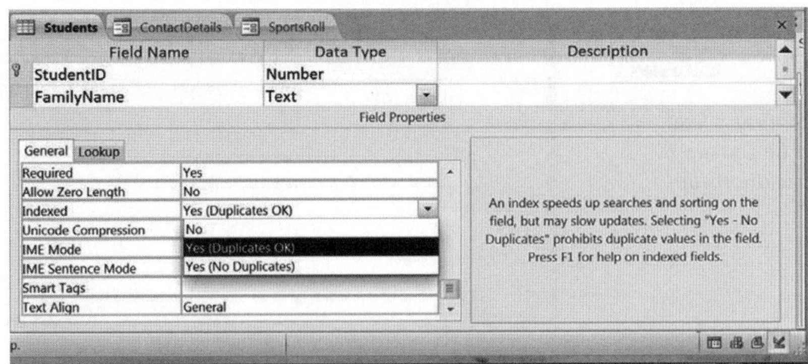

Selection to allow or disallow duplicate values in a field

The menu item **Design > Indexes** shows the indexes applying to this table. Microsoft Access automatically creates an index on primary key fields.

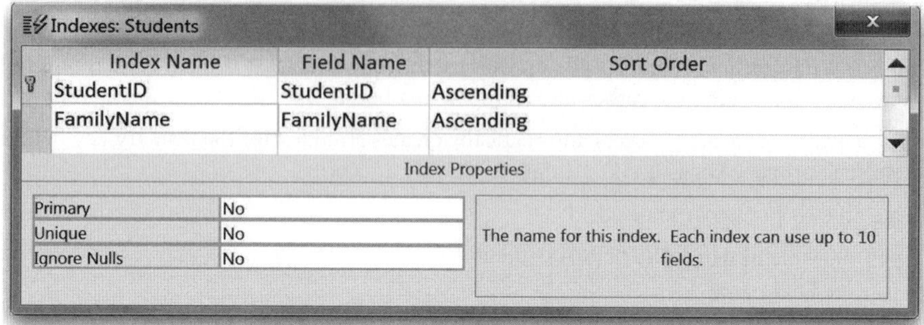

Index with a Sort Order selection

Creating a lookup value for a field

A lookup value is stored in its own table and therefore limits the values that can be entered. For example, the towns and provinces of Papua New Guinea could be stored in a table, enabling selection of the appropriate value. It saves keying in the data and ensures the spelling is correct and that the correct province for each town is entered if required.

A lookup field displays a list of values from which the user can choose. This can be set up so that only those values can be entered into the database. This prevents duplication of data and eliminates possible errors.

A lookup field can be created at the time the field is defined. To do this:

- Add a new field and select **Lookup & Relationship**.

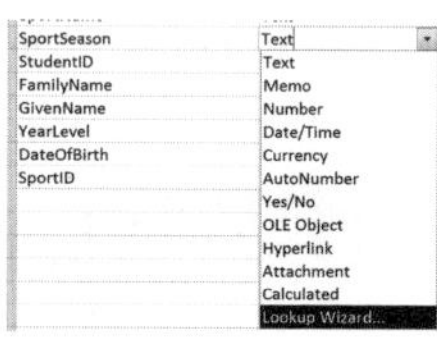

Setting a field to be Lookup & Relationship

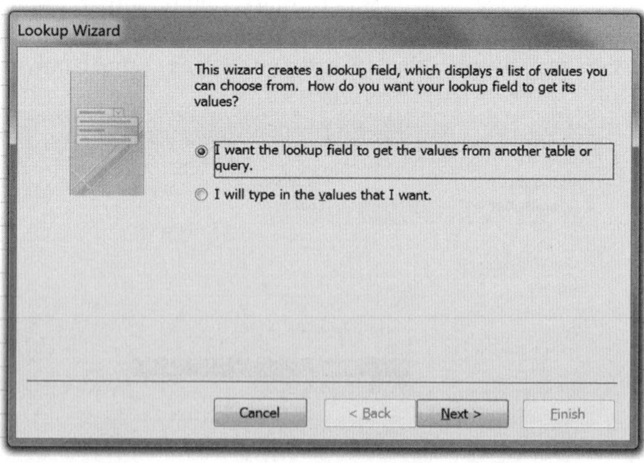

Lookup Wizard can obtain values from another table

The figure below shows the tables that are available; in this case 'Sports' is selected.

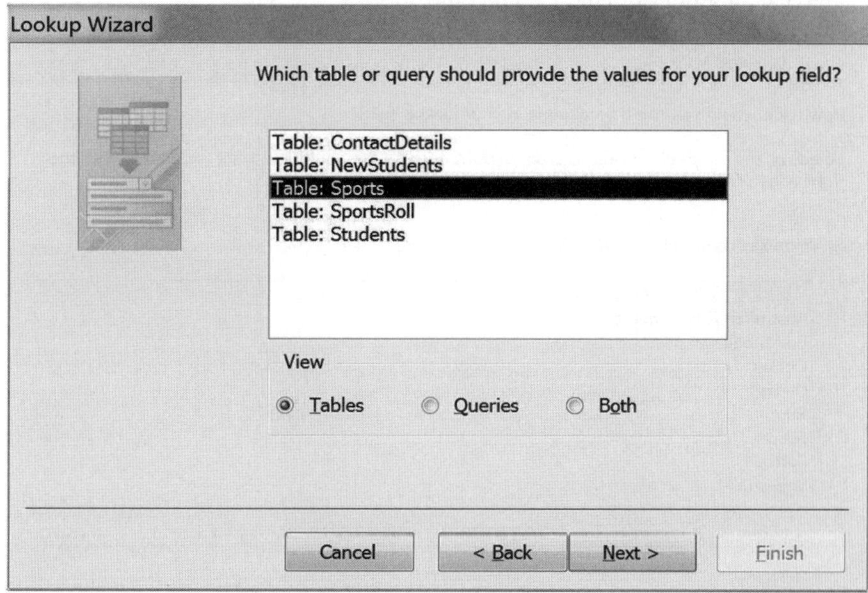

Selection of Sports Table

The figure below shows that the SportName field is selected.

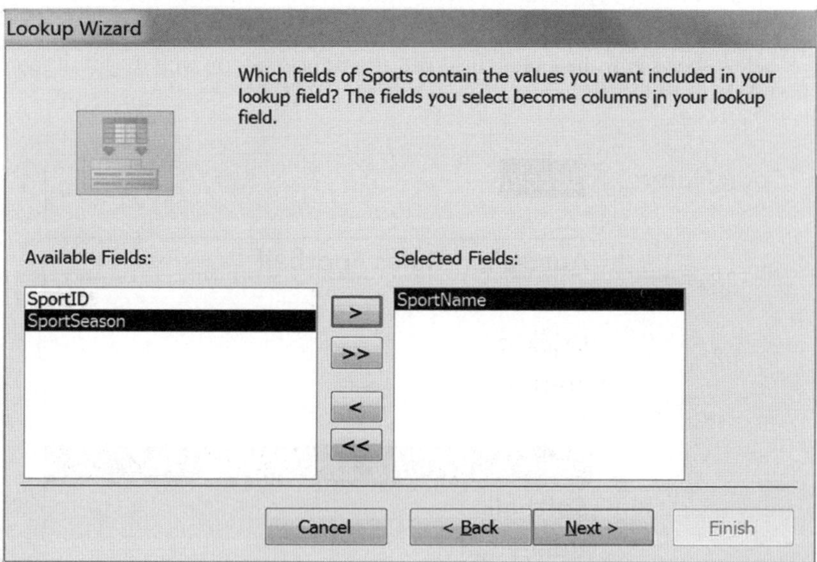

Selection of the SportName field

The sort order of items for the field (not shown) is selected. The figure below shows the step of setting the column width (with the sort order that was selected, A–Z).

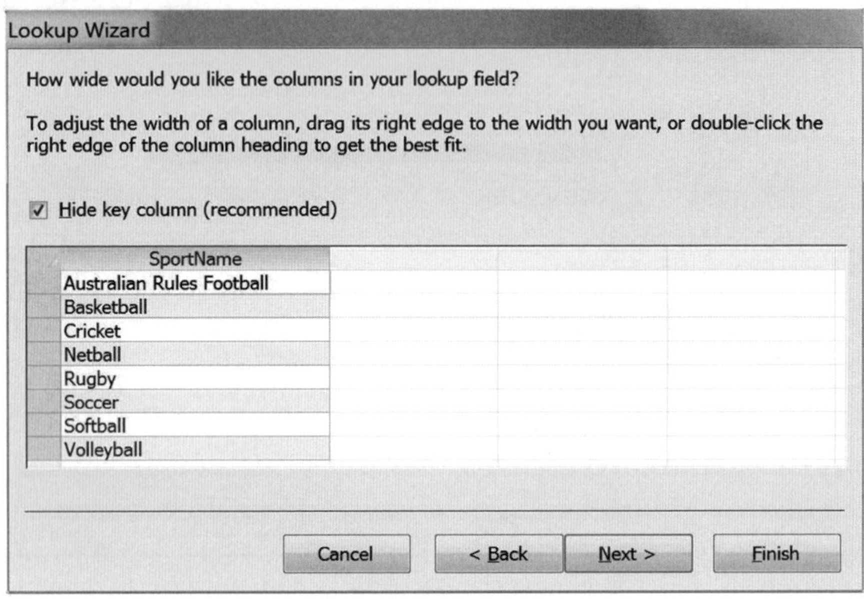

Setting the column width to display a lookup field

The next step sets the name of the lookup field which should be the same as the field in the other table.

The figure below shows how the lookup field will appear on the form with the list of sports offered for selection.

SportNames in alphabetical order with 'Soccer' the active selection

Updating values in a lookup list

The values available for the list are updated in the original table. These could be a product list or a list of stores, for example. As there are changes in those values, the updated values are available in the lookup list.

Unit 12.2 Activity 2G: Creating a sports information system

Create the sports information system that has been used as an example in the Topic. There are three tables required.

1. Create the tables with the following minimum fields, as shown in the table below.
2. For the student table, create fields that you think would be used for a student information system.

Student		Sports		SportRolls
StudentID				*StudentID*
FamilyName				*FamilyName*
GivenName				*GivenName*
YearLevel				*YearLevel*
DateOfBirth				*DateOfBirth*
		SportID		*SportID*
		SportName		*SportName*
		SportSeason		*SportSeason*

Fields for a sports information system

Updating values in a lookup list

Unit 12.2 Database 2
Topic 3: Using relationships

Topic 3 focuses on using the different types of relationships in a database:
- One-to-one relationships.
- One-to-many relationships.
- Solving many-to-many relationship problems.

Relationships enable data to be shared between tables. Most information systems consist of a number of tables; the primary keys in each table are the basis of the relationship.

The menu item: **File > Database Tools > Relationships** displays the ribbon shown below.

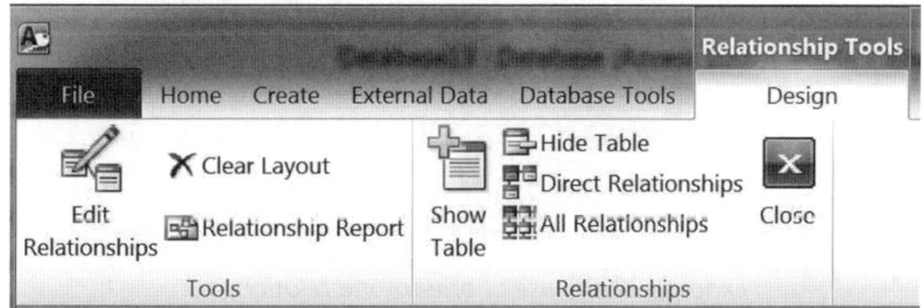

The Relationships Tools ribbon

Primary key

A table should have a field that is used to uniquely represent that record in the table. This can also be referred to as an 'ID' or 'unique identifier'. This field will not contain any duplicate data (ie each value is unique).

Microsoft Access adds the primary key column by default, using auto numbering. Only one record in this table will have this value.

The primary key field must:

- Always have a value.
- Be unique, so that only one record in the table has that value.
- Never change.

The primary key is usually independent of any data in the same record.

A primary key can be a number or a combination of numbers and characters.

Creating one-to-one relationships

A one-to one-relationship means that there is only one record in each table that has the same primary key value.

The following figure shows an example where the security password is stored in another table.

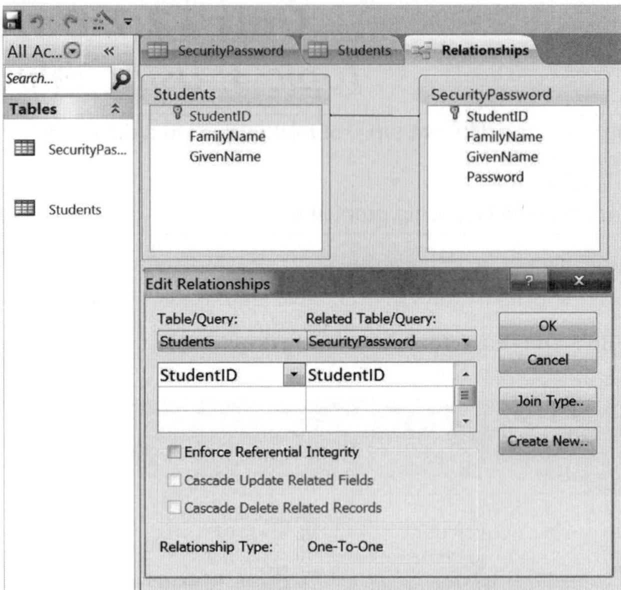

Example of the use of one-to-one relationship

Apart from a flat file situation, the one-to-one relationship is not usual. It could, however, occur because:

- The physical size of the table is very large.
- Sorting times can be less with a smaller file size.
- There is a security feature, such as storing a password or other sensitive data in another table.

A one-to-many relationship

Most databases are built using **one-to-many relationships**. A one-to-many relationship usually occurs when each record in Table A has many linked records in Table B, but each record in Table B has only one corresponding record in Table A.

In the sports information system example there are three tables. The SportsRolls table is linked to the table of *Sports* and the table of *Students* using:

- SportID.
- StudentID.

Note that the primary key symbol is only shown on the side of the relationship where the primary key resides.

The primary key is referenced in other tables with the same name; however, it is called the 'foreign' key in those instances.

The figure below shows the relationships between the tables. They are 'one-to-many'; that is, each Sport appears many times in the Sports Roll. Similarly, each Student appears many times in the Sports Roll (ie a student can participate in more than one sport).

The fields that the relationship is dependent upon are shown by clicking on the join. That is, each student is identified in the Sports Roll based on field *StudentID* and each sport name is identified by the field *SportID*.

The figure shows the relationship diagram for the three tables. The fields are linked by clicking on the primary key and dragging to the field of the same name (without the key symbol) in the other table. Shown in the dialog box is the nature of the relationship with the *Students* and *SportsRolls* tables.

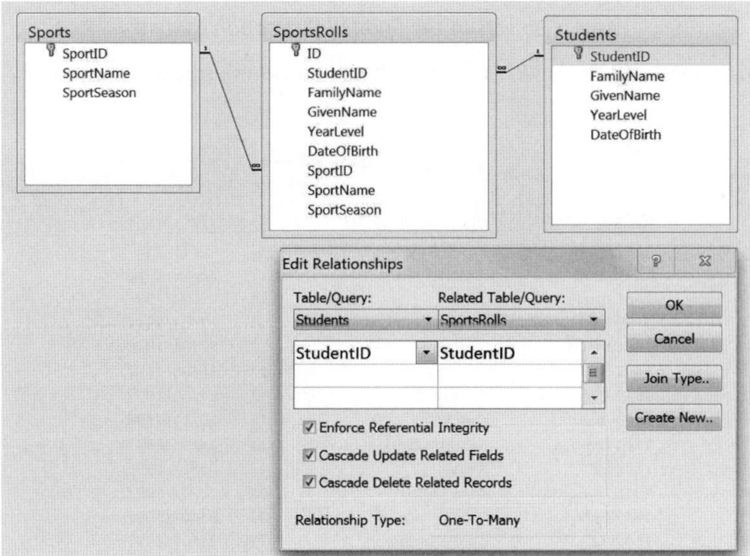

Creating the relationships between the tables

A **join** is the way in which data from multiple tables is displayed at the same time. It is usually based on a query. The nature of the 'join type' can be selected as shown in the figure below.

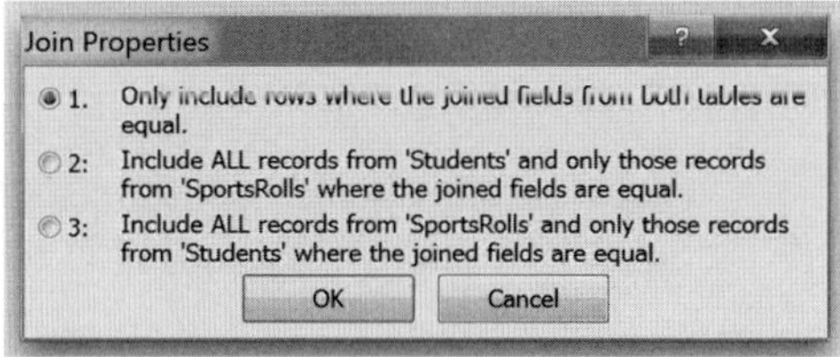

Join type options with radio button selection

The three figures below show the three tables created for the sport system (*Sports*, *Students* and *SportsRoll*).

The first figure shows the *Sports* table, with the eight sports offered; the primary key is the 'SportsID'.

SportID	SportName	SportSeason	Click to Add
1	Australian Rules Football	Winter	
2	Basketball	Winter	
3	Cricket	Summer	
4	Netball	Winter	
5	Rugby	Winter	
6	Soccer	Winter	
7	Softball	Summer	
8	Volleyball	Summer	
(New)			

Access objects in the Sports Information System

The second figure shows the *Student* table with basic student information; the primary key is the 'StudentID'.

StudentID	FamilyName	GivenName	YearLevel	DateOfBirth	Click to Add
1038	Pune	Sila	11	02/11/1997	
1137	Lohia	Vasi Lahui	11	04/11/1997	
1397	Loa	Ronnie	12	26/12/1996	
1460	Bruce	Diho	11	19/07/1997	
1480	Ivan	Boio	11	22/04/1997	
1486	Madaha	Stephanie	12	20/01/1996	
1497	Rei Simoi	John Lega	11	18/08/1997	
1523	Vagi	Tonga	11	24/09/1997	
1763	Avou	Kenny	12	10/11/1996	
1771	Maitisa	Ranuinu Dairi	11	13/01/1997	
1840	Eli	Andy	12	04/12/1996	
1910	Tamarua	Kone lamo	11	28/07/1997	
1947	Gabutu	Sula	11	01/07/1997	
2142	Rei	Daulin Daure	11	20/03/1997	
2196	Gabutu	Sula	11	01/07/1997	
2198	Igo	John	11	08/10/1997	

Datasheet view of the Student table

The third figure shows the *SportsRoll* table with student and sport information. The 'SelectionID' is the primary key; it indicates each separate selection made.

SelectionID	Stude	FamilyName	GivenName	YearL	DateOfBirth	Spo	SportName	SportSe	Click to Add
1	9723	Tava	Meleani	12	20/03/1996	6	Soccer	Winter	
2	7073	Pune	Sila	11	02/11/1997	1	Australian Rules Football	Winter	
3	4777	Benstead	Hebou Isiani	11	09/10/1997	2	Basketball	Winter	
4	3305	Torepa	Valo	11	04/05/1997	8	Volleyball	Summer	
5	3683	Igo	Patrick	12	29/01/1996	5	Rugby	Winter	
6	6060	Gabutu	Sula	11	01/07/1997	4	Netball	Winter	
7	1472	Lohia Sisia	Joe	11	19/08/1997	1	Australian Rules Football	Winter	
8	3349	Dikana	Arau	11	21/11/1997	3	Cricket	Summer	
9	8080	Pune	Sila	11	02/11/1997	2	Basketball	Winter	
10	3663	Benstead	Hebou Isiani	11	09/10/1997	3	Cricket	Summer	
11	1059	Torepa	Valo	11	04/05/1997	4	Netball	Winter	
12	9081	Ruby	Francis	12	05/06/1996	3	Cricket	Summer	
13	1679	Gabutu	Sula	11	01/07/1997	6	Soccer	Winter	
14	3836	Luke	Hila	12	04/01/1996	4	Netball	Winter	
15	7184	Teina	Igo	11	18/06/1997	3	Cricket	Summer	

SportsRoll table with student sport selection

Unit 12.2 Activity 3A: SelectionID

1. In the figure above, look at the SelectionID. Number 10 shows the selection for which student?
2. What sport has he or she selected?

Solving many-to-many relationship problems

A **many-to-many relationship** is one where each record in a table has many entries in another table and vice versa. An example of a many-to-many relationship is a school with students studying a number of subjects and who are also in a number of classes. A student studies a number of subjects and thus is in many classes. Each class also has many students.

In this case, an intermediate table is used to link the *Students* table to the *Subjects* table.

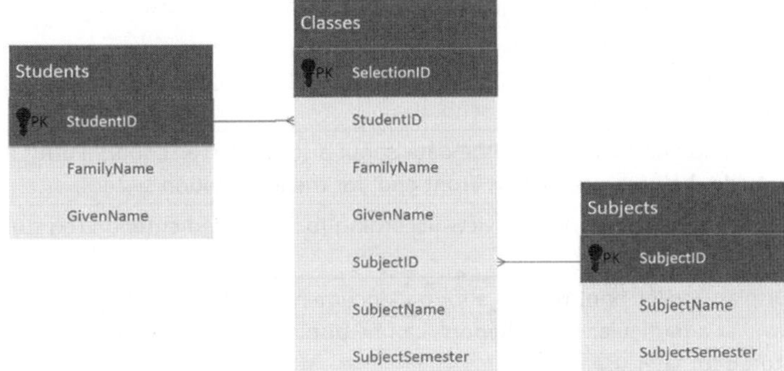

Example of a many-to-many relationship

Unit 12.2 Activity 3B: Solving many-to-many relationship problems

The allocation of students in a school to subject classes with teachers is an important aspect of the administration of a school. For example, it would be common to have tables for the following:

- Teachers.
- Students.
- Academic subjects.

1. How many tables would you use for the information system?
2. What data would form the basis for the tables?
3. What names would you give to these fields?
4. What data types would be used for these fields?
5. What ID fields would you use for the tables so the necessary relationships could be created?

Objects in Microsoft Access

Creating tables and their relationships enables an information system to be dynamic, thereby enhancing the ability to change data into information.

The figure below shows the navigation pane for Access with the key Access objects. Each has an important role in creating an information system.

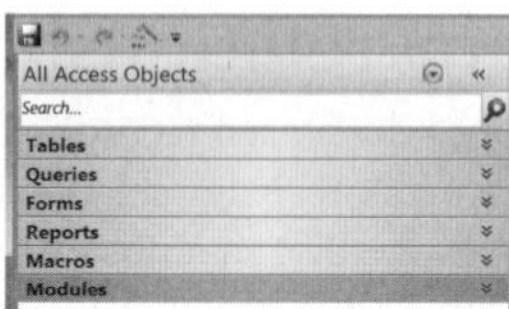

Microsoft Access objects

The basic roles and purpose of the objects are shown in the table below.

Objects	*Use in Access*
Table	Store data (eg students in a school).
Forms	Enter and edit data (eg change data about a student in a school). Forms are used to provide the user interface or 'front end' for the information system.
Query	Retrieve a subset of data to view according to a specified criterion (eg students in a school year level).
Reports	Display and/or print data as a formal document (eg A to Z listing of students in a year level at a particular date). Reports can be displayed on screen but may be printed or stored for later use.
Macros	Automate tasks; this saves a series of steps that can be replayed on running the macro.

Purpose of objects in a database

Naming objects

Although not used in the example in this Topic, some systems prefix the Access object with three letters to indicate the nature of the object.

Object	*Prefix*	*Examples*
Tables	tbl	tblStudents, tblSports, tblSportsList
Forms	frm	frmStudent, frmSport
Reports	rpt	rptSportsRoll
Queries	qry	qrySport
Macros	mcr	mcrPrintReport

Objects in a database

A **query** enables a view of data that meets specified criteria (eg all the sales made in a particular month, or sales to a particular customer). Macros enable automatic generation of information according to set criteria.

Using 'wizards' to build components of an information system

A **wizard** is essentially a series of steps used to create an element of the information system. The steps provide options and selections to create the element. Wizards are useful for beginners as a learning experience and also if a solution needs to be created quickly.

However, many experienced developers of information systems using Microsoft Access would examine carefully what they wish to do and manually build their system without the use of a wizard. A wizard does not necessarily solve a problem in the best or most appropriate manner.

In this Topic, many of the wizards available in Access are used to illustrate the creation of an information system. For example, Wizards can be used in the creation of a:

- Form.
- Button.
- Query.
- Import of records.
- Mask.
- Report.

Once a wizard has been used to create an element, it is still possible to manually adjust the properties.

Unit 12.2 Database 2

Topic 4: Creating advanced queries

Topic 4 explores the methods of creating advanced queries, with an emphasis on running queries:

- How to run make table queries to create new tables.
- How to run append queries to add records.
- How to run delete queries to remove records.

A **query** on a database is a search according to certain criteria so that a subset of information can be displayed. A subset of records is referred to as a 'recordset' by Access. The query itself is called a 'select query'.

Action queries are those that may perform an action on the subset when they have been displayed. This is discussed later in the Topic.

The sports information table could be queried, for example, to show a list of:

- All students who have selected basketball, or
- Year 11 students who have selected basketball, or
- Students who have not selected basketball.

Query in table view

A table can be used to sort and find data with information or a subset of information displayed in the table view. A right click on the cell enables simple sorts (Sort A to Z, Sort Z to A) and the use of filters to see a subset of the table records.

It is useful to examine a table and apply a variety of queries to fine tune the type of query you will create.

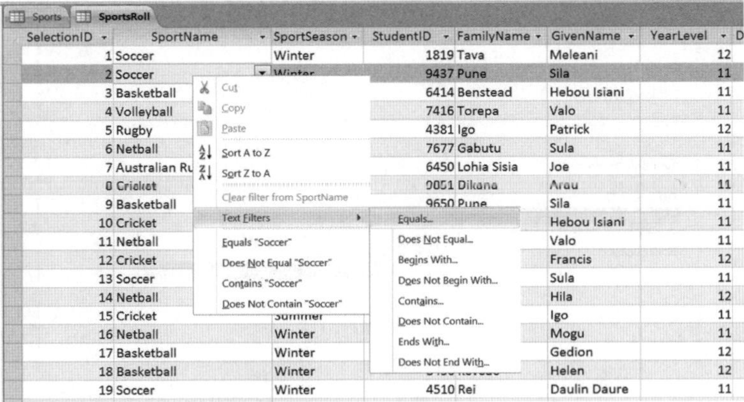

Using the datasheet for a simple query

Queries

Queries can be created, saved and used when required to produce real-time information (this means that over time the data changes).

The **Query Wizard** walks through the steps that enable a subset of records to be retrieved from a table or tables.

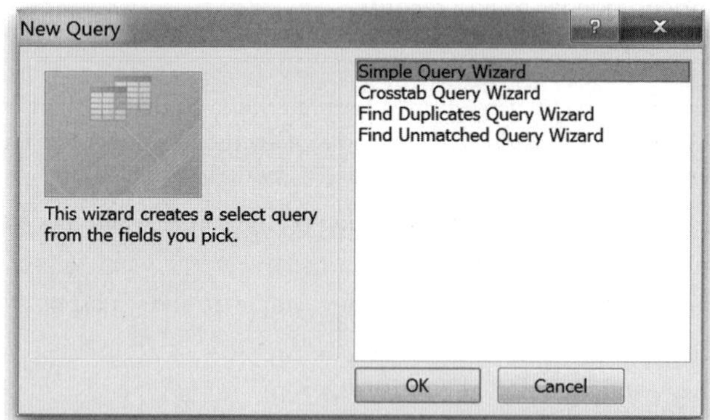

Activation of a New Query using the Simple Query Wizard

From the appropriate tables, the fields can be selected.

If the tables are related, then fields from the related tables can be selected. This query is selecting the students who have selected a particular sport. It is, in fact, the roll for a particular sport.

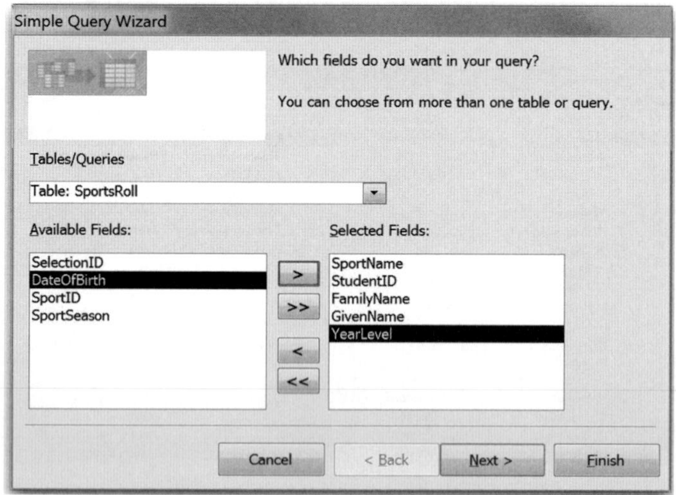

Selection of tables from the drop-down list and fields from tables

The option shows a 'detail' or 'summary' query.

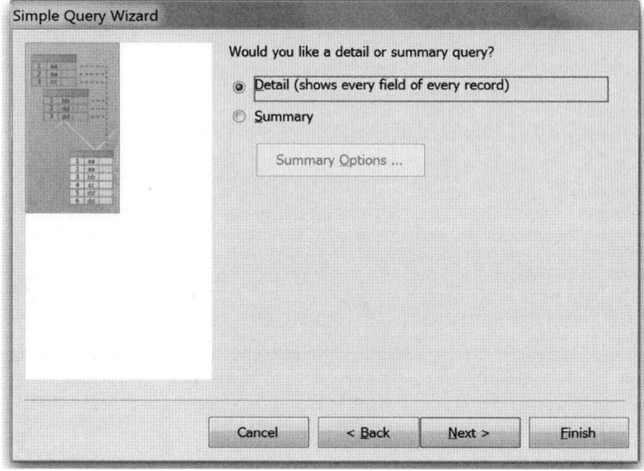

Detailed selection that displays each field of every record

The query is given a name for future use; this will appear in the left-hand navigation pane.

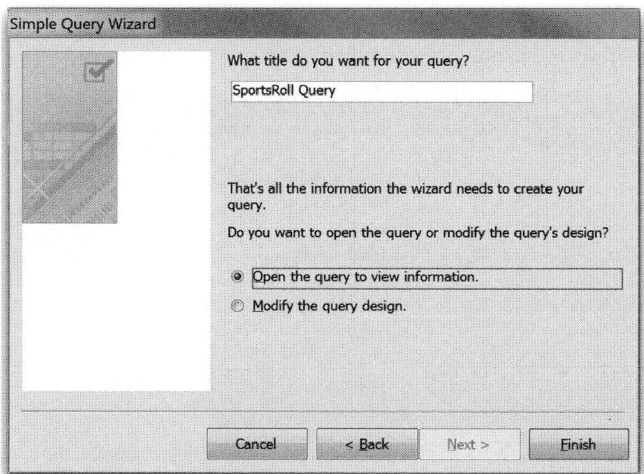

Naming a query

The **Design View** shows the fields:

- From the table that relate to the query.
- That form the basis for the query.
- With the sort order being applied to particular fields.
- With any criteria applying.

The criterion shown is that the 'SportName' should include 'Soccer'.

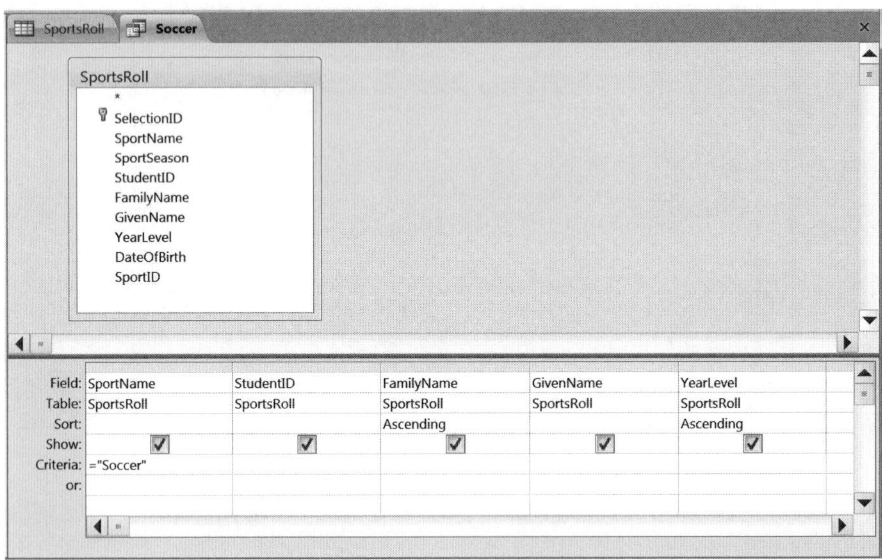

Query for 'Soccer' with fields to be displayed and 'sort' order for two fields

The figure below shows the listing provided by the query.

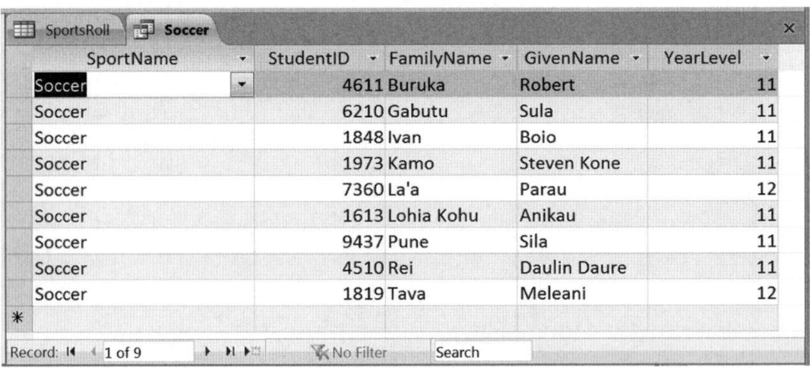

SportName	StudentID	FamilyName	GivenName	YearLevel
Soccer	4611	Buruka	Robert	11
Soccer	6210	Gabutu	Sula	11
Soccer	1848	Ivan	Boio	11
Soccer	1973	Kamo	Steven Kone	11
Soccer	7360	La'a	Parau	12
Soccer	1613	Lohia Kohu	Anikau	11
Soccer	9437	Pune	Sila	11
Soccer	4510	Rei	Daulin Daure	11
Soccer	1819	Tava	Meleani	12

Record: 1 of 9 No Filter Search

Result of a simple query

From 108 possible selections, there are nine students who have selected Soccer.

The Soccer query shows students grouped by 'YearLevel' and sorted in ascending (A to Z) order; that is, alphabetical order by family name.

Action queries

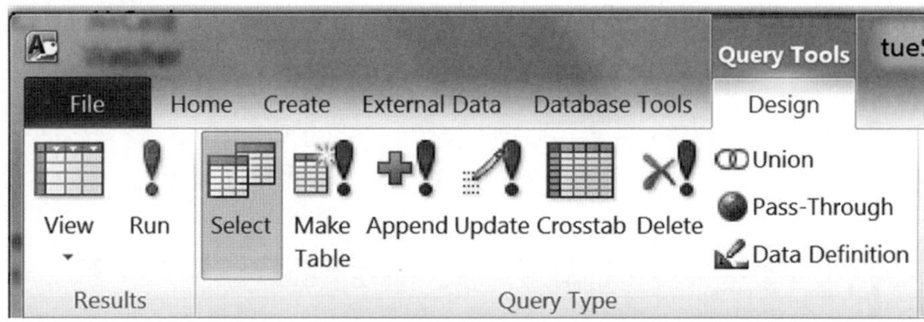

Query Tools and Action options

An **Action Query** normally consists of two parts:

1. A select query to obtain a record set based on certain criteria.
2. An action based on the records returned.

Managing data in a database

It is possible to:

- Append – add data from one table to another.
- Delete – delete records from a table.
- Update – alter information in tables at the same time.
- Make-table – create a table with the results of a query.

Caution: It is essential to have a backup of records before performing these queries. Access (and most other databases) will make changes based on the action and save immediately. There is no option to undo and the results of the action cannot be reversed.

Complex database management systems have the capacity to **rollback** before committing changes to data. A rollback returns the database to the state that it was in before the data was altered (eg updated or deleted). It is technically possible to do this in Access but it is difficult. It is better to ensure that the database is backed up before significant changes are made to the data.

Unit 12.2 Activity 4A: Managing data

At the end of each school year, what would happen to the records in the sports information system?

How to run append queries to add records

Maintenance of an information system requires archiving of records at regular intervals. Archiving records means storing records that are no longer required for current use. However, these records may be needed for historical purposes at a later date. Archived records are not modified when accessed at a later date.

The figure below shows the query design that will find records where 'YearLevel = 12' and will archive those records by adding them to a table in the current file. They can alternatively be stored in another file by selecting **Browse ...** and choosing the file.

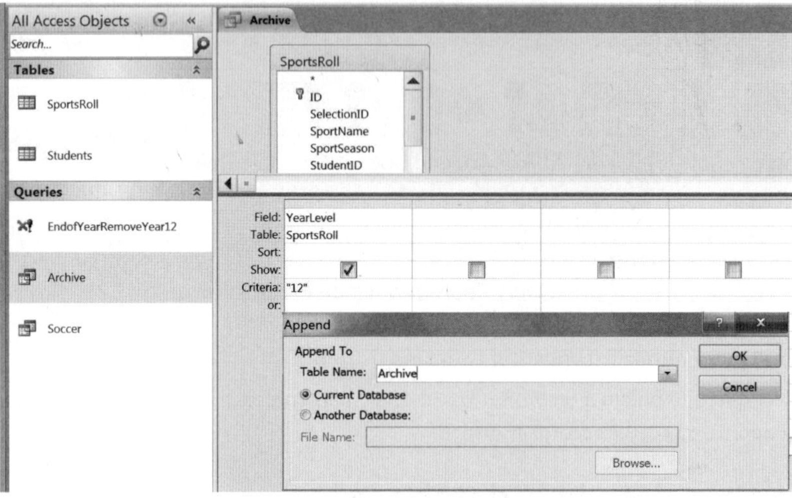

Adding fields to an archive table

How to run delete queries to remove records

Removing records is a final step in management of a database. When the records are gone they cannot be retrieved. Backing up a database before deleting records is most important.

The figure below shows a query that will delete records from the Sports Roll where the 'YearLevel = 12'. Note the symbol next to the query name in the navigation panel.

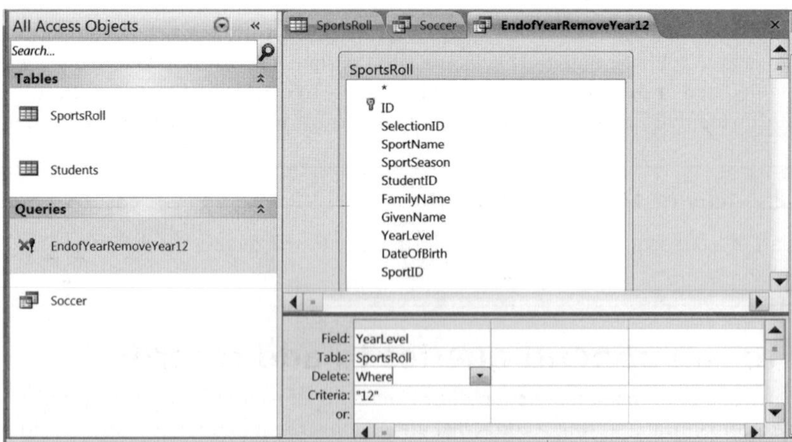

Query that will delete records

A warning dialog is displayed when the query is being run prior to the deletion; it provides the option not to run the query. The figure below displays the dialog.

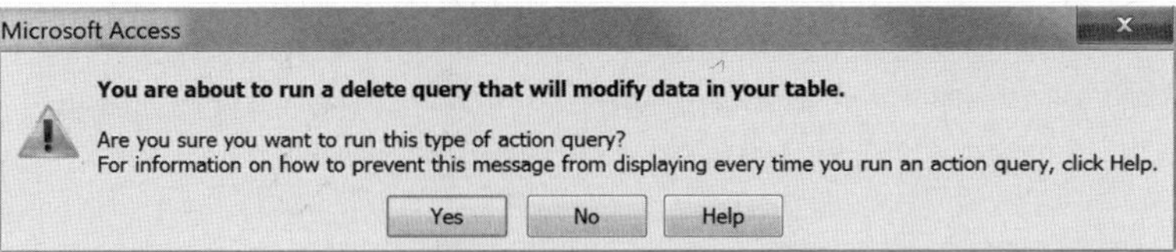

Delete query warning dialog

Make table

A query could be set to create a table with the recordset returned by a query. The figure below shows the option for the table to be included in either the current database or another database.

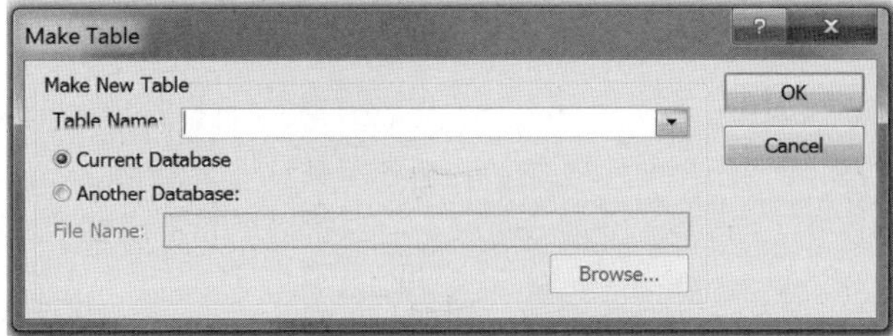

The option to 'make table', which is the result of an action query

Unit 12.2 Database 2

Topic 5: Forms

Topic 5 looks at forms in detail. It includes:

- Creating a form using Form Wizard.
- Viewing form design.
- Repositioning controls and labels.
- Controlling cursor with tab order.
- Changing control properties.
- Selecting multiple controls.
- Creating form header and footer.
- Inserting label.
- Formatting text properties.
- Applying special effects.
- Working with controls.
- Inserting command button.

Maintenance of data in table view is difficult. Tables easily give an overview of the data they contain, but they are not particularly useful for day to day administration such as:

- Creating new records, editing records or deleting records.
- Displaying information including images.
- Displaying fields that may be lengthy, such as 'notes'.
- Helping the provision of easy navigation.
- Providing a user interface for people using the information system who are not familiar with databases.

The *Form View* of a table can be created to show a single record and to display all or some of its fields. Not all fields from a table need to be shown on a form.

Information systems typically use forms for the entry of key information into a system. For example, a form would be used to add a new student to a school's records or to create an invoice for a customer.

Aims of form design

The design of a form should aim to help a person enter data efficiently and effectively in the required fields. Where possible, it should take a minimum of time and keystrokes. The form should include suitable validation on the fields to ensure the data is correct.

The design features of a form that will help achieve these aims are:

- A title on the form that identifies the organisation and the purpose of the form.
- Fields displayed in a logical order that is consistent with those on a written form.
- Captions and fields formatted to assist readability of the form.
- High contrast between the foreground and background of the form. The best contrast is black text on a white background, although light colours on areas of the form may help in defining form areas.

Creating a form using Form Wizard

A **wizard** provides a pre-set series of steps to assist in the creation of a form. The wizard will enable the:

- Selection of a table or tables (if those tables have a relationship) to be used in the form.
- Selection of fields from the table (or tables) to be included on the form.
- Selection of the form layout from four options.
- Naming of the form.
- Creation of the form with the fields in a default layout, and identifying the fields by field name.

The **Form Wizard** button is located on the **Create** menu.

The figure below shows the first screen of the **Form Wizard** where the tables and fields can be selected for the form.

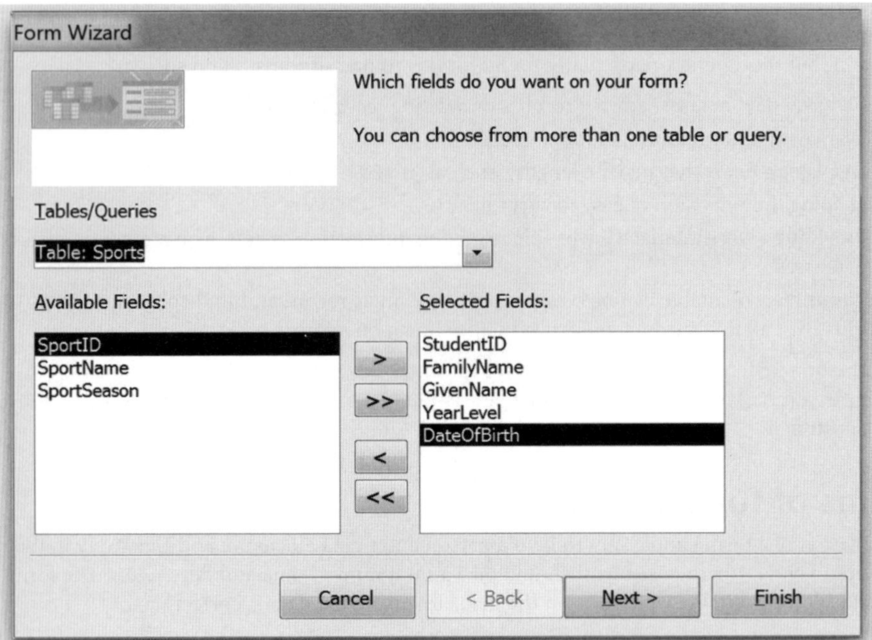

Form Wizard tables and field selection

After the tables and fields options, there are options available for the form layout.

The figure below gives a condensed view of the layout selected by the radio button.

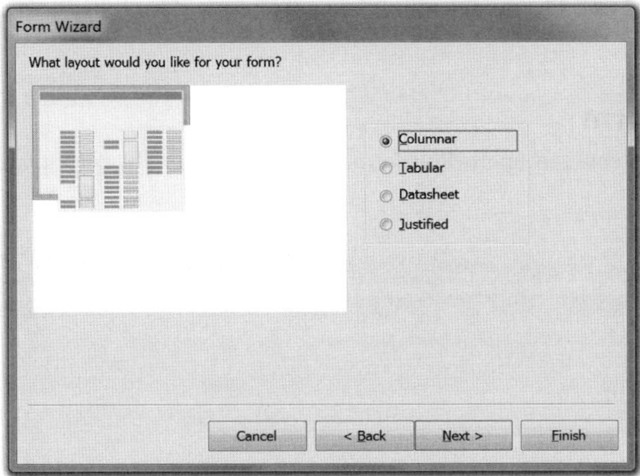

Layout options for forms selection

Tabular	*Datasheet*	*Justified*

Other form options that could be selected

The figure above shows the other layout options if the alternative radio button were selected:

The name or title of the form should indicate its purpose. The figure below shows the name given to the form and the options to open the form or modify its design.

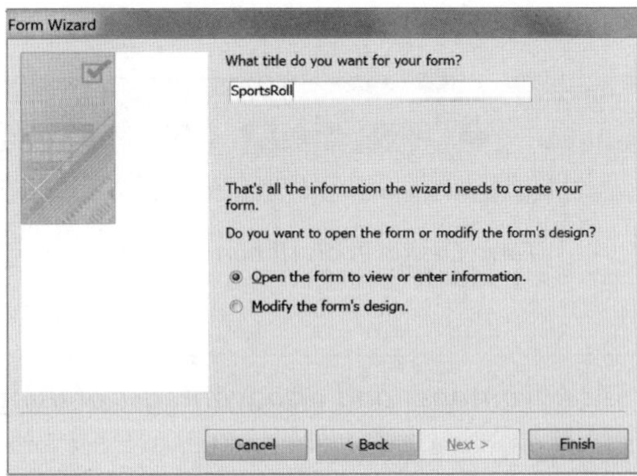

Naming the form

The form prepared by a wizard achieves selection of tables and fields but does not attempt to design the form.

Parts of a form

The figure below shows the 'Sports Roll' form with data entry on the default layout.

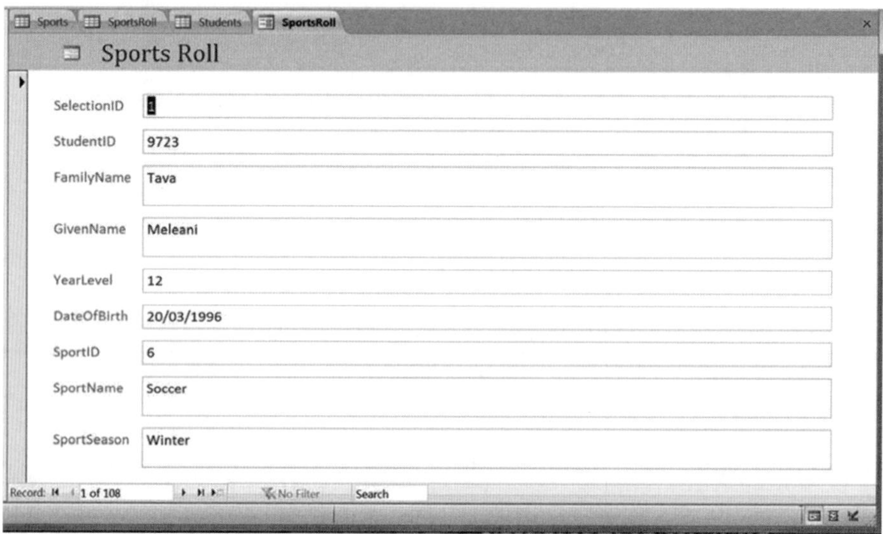

Default form with entry fields and field captions

The layout of a form, sequence and order of the fields, headings on the form, and buttons used for navigation are a matter of design. The figure below shows the **Design Tools** ribbon.

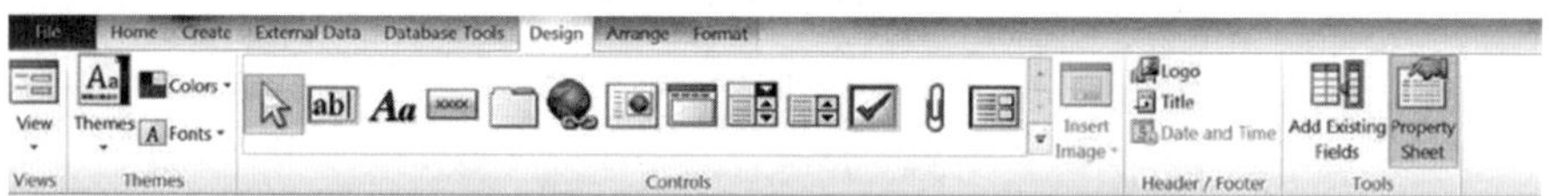

Form Design Tools ribbon options

Unit 12.2 Activity 5A: Advantages and disadvantages of using wizards

What are the advantages and disadvantages of using wizards to create forms in Access?

Split forms

A split form is an alternative method for navigation around a set of records. A split form can show a form area with a datasheet area as well. With the table selected, choose **Create > More Forms > Split Form**. The bar between the forms can be moved to determine the area each part takes up. The split form has the form and datasheet view on the same form.

The figure below shows the split form with records from the same table.

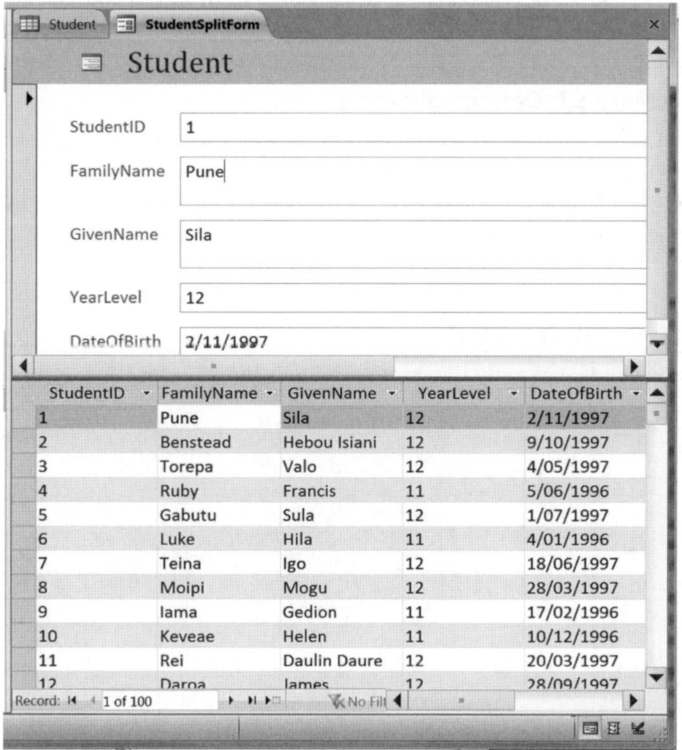

StudentID	FamilyName	GivenName	YearLevel	DateOfBirth
1	Pune	Sila	12	2/11/1997
2	Benstead	Hebou Isiani	12	9/10/1997
3	Torepa	Valo	12	4/05/1997
4	Ruby	Francis	11	5/06/1996
5	Gabutu	Sula	12	1/07/1997
6	Luke	Hila	11	4/01/1996
7	Teina	Igo	12	18/06/1997
8	Moipi	Mogu	12	28/03/1997
9	Iama	Gedion	11	17/02/1996
10	Keveae	Helen	11	10/12/1996
11	Rei	Daulin Daure	12	20/03/1997
12	Daroa	James	12	28/09/1997

A form in split view

Changing field name display

By default, the field name is displayed on a form. Usually the field name caption needs to be modified to make the form easier to understand. In particular, the 'ID' fields need an appropriate name. For example, the StudentID field could become 'Student Number'.

The table below shows an example of how field names may be given a 'caption' different to the field name.

Field Name	Field Caption
StudentID	Student No. or Student Number
GivenName	Given Name
FamilyName	Family Name
FullName	Full Name

Field names modified for display on a form with a caption

Unit 12.2 Activity 5B: Designing a form

The Port Moresby Computer Company sells computers and accessories. Orders are delivered by various contractors after orders are received by the store.

Using pen and paper, design a form that shows the delivery details for an order that would be printed and then included with the delivery.

Viewing form design

The form created by the wizard for the sport selection is shown below in design mode.

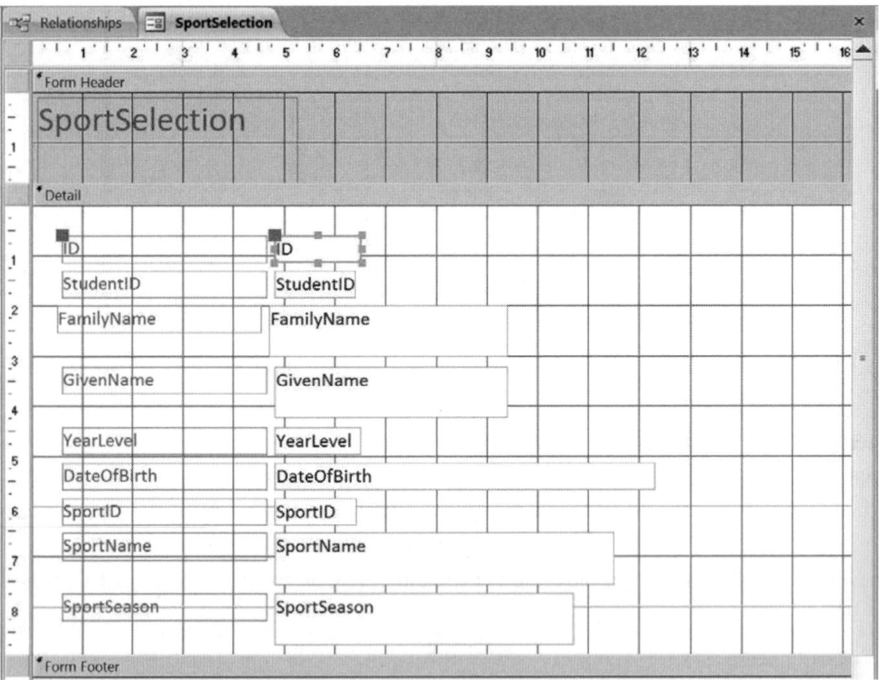

Default layout of a form using the Form Wizard

Note the form has the parts:

- Form Header.
- Detail.
- Form Footer.

The font, font style and font formatting for all fields and field captions in the 'Detail' area are the same; these are the default settings.

Unit 12.2 Activity 5C: Viewing form design

What advice could you offer to a form designer so that a form is easy to use and understand for the person entering the data? In your answer discuss the relevance of:

- Screen dimensions of the form.
- Background and foreground colour.
- Size of headings relative to labels.
- Position of form controls.
- Font type, font size and font formatting of field captions

Repositioning controls and labels

A **control** is an object that is on a form or report. The type and number of controls will vary according to whether a form or a report is being designed. They also vary from design to layout view.

The following refers to a form in **Design View**.

Examples of controls are labels, buttons and text boxes. The figure below of the Design ribbon shows controls that can be added to a form.

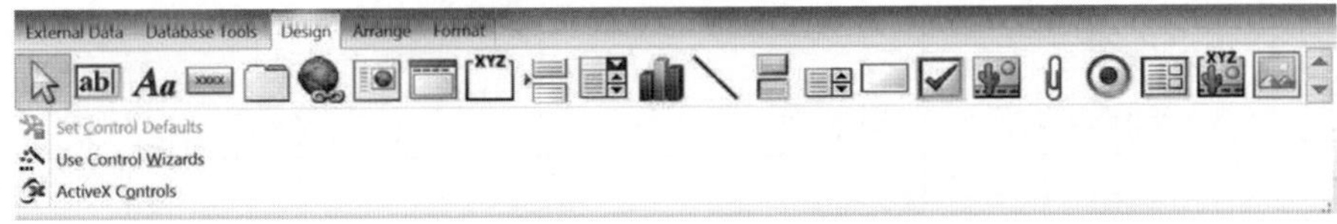

Controls on the Design ribbon

As a control is added to a form, it is unbound. That is, it needs to be associated with a field.

Unit 12.2 Activity 5D: Identifying control icons in the Design ribbon

1. In the table below are control icons from the Design ribbon. Open Microsoft Access and identify what the control icons represent. The names of the controls are:
   1. Attachment
   2. Bound Object Frame
   3. Button
   4. Chart
   5. Check Box
   6. Combo Box
   7. Hyperlink
   8. Image
   9. Insert Page Break
   10. Label
   11. Line
   12. List Box
   13. Navigation Control
   14. Option Button
   15. Option Group
   16. Rectangle
   17. Select
   18. Subform/Subreport
   19. Tab control
   20. Text Box
   21. Toggle Button
   22. Unbound Object Frame
   23. Web Browser Control

Icon from toolbar	Name of control	Purpose, how would you use it?
A		
B ab|		
C Aa		

Icon from toolbar	Name of control	Purpose, how would you use it?
D		
E		
F 		
G 		
H 		
I 		
J 		
K 		
L 		
M 		
N 		
O 		
P 		
Q 		
R 		
S 		
T 		

Icon from toolbar	Name of control	Purpose, how would you use it?
U		
V		
W		

Identifying the controls on the Design ribbon

Moving controls and labels

Controls and labels on forms can be altered from their initial default position. When selected, 'handles' appear, and with these the controls and labels can be:

- Resized.
- Moved to a new position.
- Aligned (vertically and horizontally).
- Grouped together.

Moving a control and label separately

The figure below shows a label with its field in **Design View**. Usually the label and the field are moved as one item. To move either the label or the field separately, select the top left rectangle of either the label or the field and then move it. Once moved, it will maintain the relative position to the other item if moved in the default manner.

Moving a label independently of the field to which it belongs

Controlling cursor with tab order

To assist in keyboard data entry on a form, the **tab** key moves the cursor to the next field. The default order of sequence for the tab key can be altered. Fields that are automatically entered, and thus not required on a particular form, can be placed last in the order, where they effectively will not be used.

The default tab order sequence before modification

For example, the order in the form above could be changed because:

- The ID is created automatically and does not require input.
- The StudentID and SportID enable a lookup to other fields.

The tab order would therefore become 'StudentID' followed by 'SportID'.

Changing control properties

Control properties can be altered by displaying the **Property Sheet** with the **Data** tab. The figure below shows the **Data > Control Source** for a text box field. In this case it is the 'YearLevel' field of the associated table.

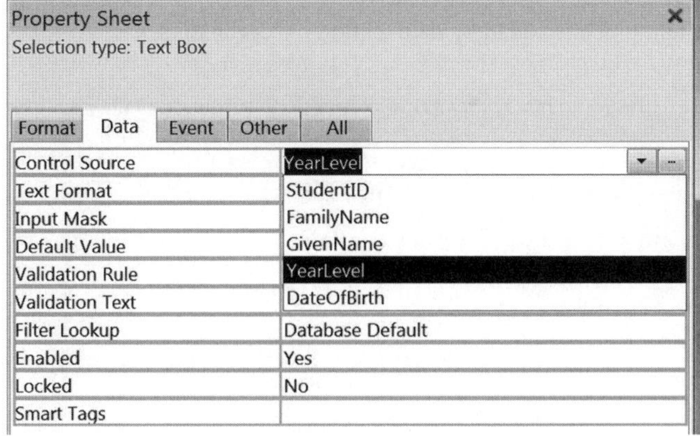

Control Source for a field on a form

Navigation

Moving around an information system should be intuitive and designed to enable a user to do it without thinking about it.

Navigation around the information system can be created by:

- Using navigation forms that have tabs with labels for selection.
- Using a form with buttons and hyperlinks to the key objects in the system.

A blank form with buttons that act as a menu can be used as a user interface to the information system.

Buttons and hyperlinks

The figure below shows a hyperlink being attached to a button on a form to link to the 'Students' table. Pressing the button will take the user to the 'Students' table.

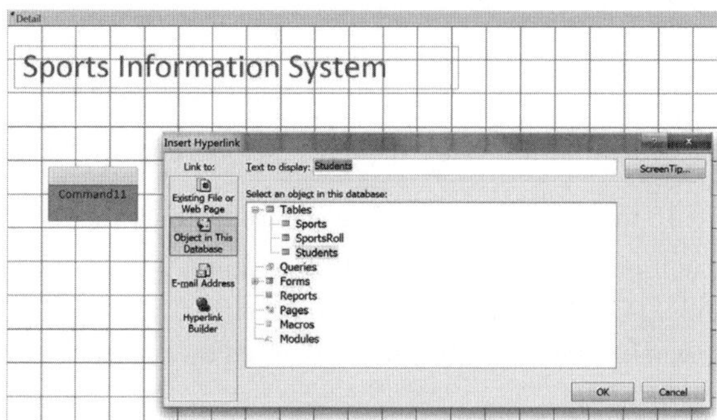

Creation of a hyperlink navigation button

A **Main Menu** screen that has buttons linking to the main components of the information system is a simple and easy navigation system to use.

The **Main Menu** below has buttons linking to the Student List, Selection Form and Sports Roll. The current date and time are added by date and time placeholders.

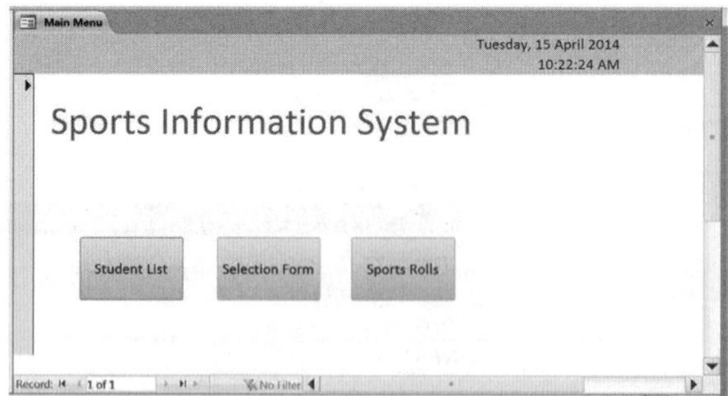

Simple main menu screen with buttons and attached hyperlinks

By using buttons, a user can navigate and operate the information system without needing to resort to the use of menus driven by text.

Many information systems use menu screens with buttons for navigation. Often the normal Access menus will be hidden or modified, and the information system will not appear to be an Access database.

Later in the chapter a **command button** will be added to the form to quit the system.

Selecting multiple controls

In **Design View** it is possible to select a control and place multiple instances of the control on the form. A right click on the control will allow the selection '**Drop Multiple Controls**'. Moving the cursor to the body of the form keeps the tool active as controls are added. The figure shows the activation of **Drop Multiple Controls**.

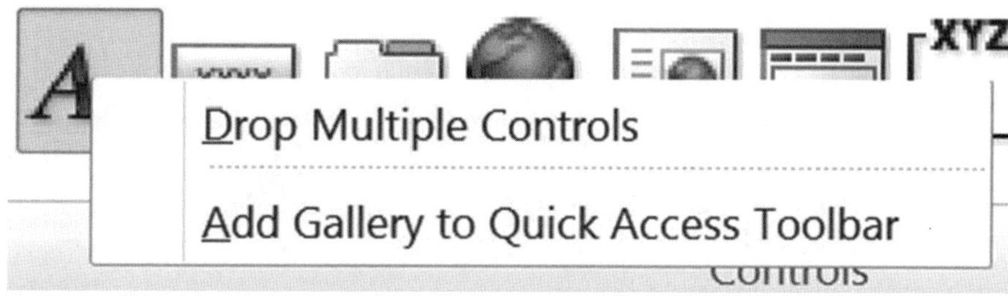

Right-click to activate Drop Multiple Controls

To return the control to its default state, click on the control on the ribbon.

As a multiple number of controls are added at the same time, depending on the control, they may need to be associated with a field.

Creating a form header and footer

Forms can have a number of parts as shown by the following figure. A header appears at the top of the form and a footer at the bottom of the form.

The **Header** and **Footer** parts can be 'toggled' on or off by selecting the part on the form in **Design** view, and then right-clicking and selecting the item from the menu. The figure below shows the formatting options for parts of a form.

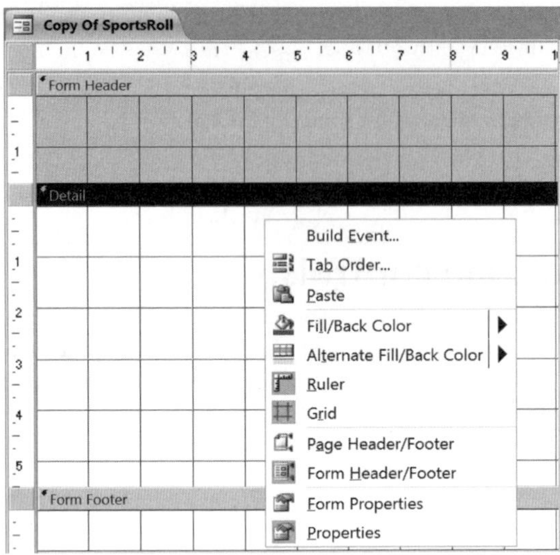

Design View with parts of a form

The header usually contains information that will remain the same for all forms, such as:

- The name of the organisation.
- A name to identify the form.
- The current date.

The footer may contain information such as:

- The current time.
- When the record was created and modified.
- The page number of the form.

Inserting a label

The figure below shows a new label added to a form. The alert symbol at the left of the label, when clicked, provides a message that indicates that the label is a text item only and not related to a control.

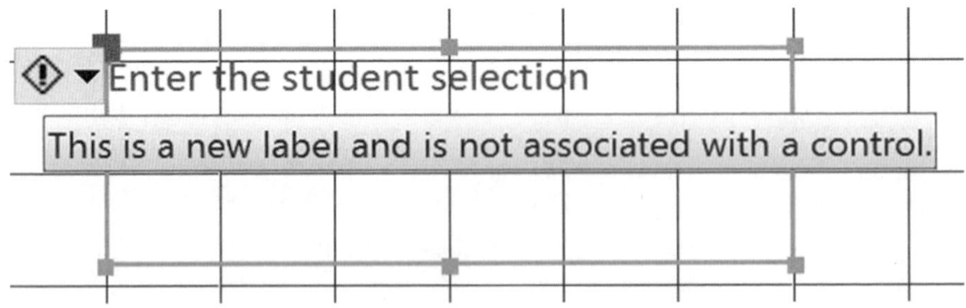

A new label is added to a form with an alert message

The above label is to provide **Help** for data entry. It does not need to be associated with a field, but it should be placed on the screen near to where the data entry will occur.

Formatting text properties

In **Design View**, the controls on a form can be formatted, in particular the text labels and fields.

The figure below shows the **Form Design** tools with formatting being applied to the lblGivenName. Note the appearance of the label below the **File** menu in the top left of the ribbon.

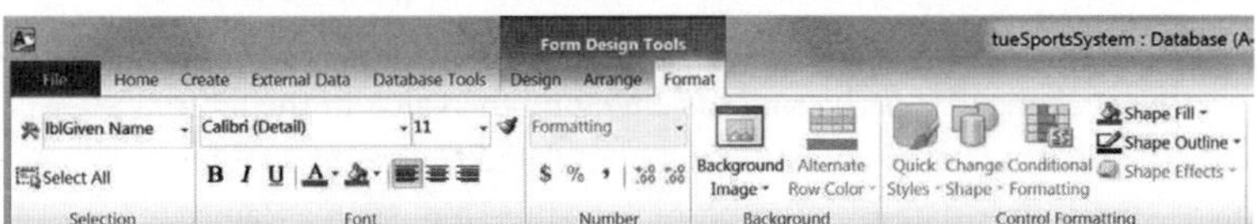

Form Design tools

The figure below shows the caption for the lblGivenName is 'Given Name' and the formatting will be applied to this text label.

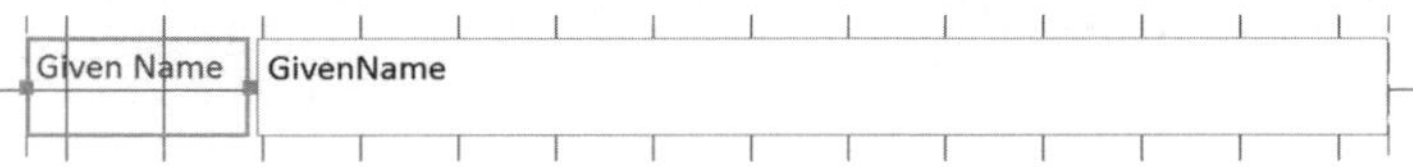

Label to which the formatting will be applied

Formatting affects how the controls will appear on the form, regarding:

- Text font (the ribbon will show the default font as the selection).
- Text font size.
- Text font style (such as bold, italic or underline).
- Text font colour.
- Text font **alignment**.
- Text background.

Care should be taken to apply appropriate formatting. For example, black text on a white background provides the highest contrast and is easiest to read. Variations can be made to improve the design of forms, but they must be assessed for readability.

Applying special effects

Images can be added to forms. Logos, insignias and pictures are common additions. For example:

- A company or school will have its logo on forms to identify the organisation.
- A stock form for a product may have a picture of the product.
- A school's student record form may have an image of the student.

A logo can be added to a form by:

- Selecting the **Logo** command from the **Controls** section of the ribbon.
- Choosing the graphic image that is used for the logo from the dialog box.

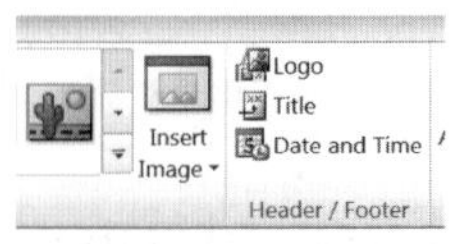

Use the Logo command to put an image on a form

Controls

The most common **control** in Microsoft Access is a text box. Controls can be:

- Bound – the values are from a field in a table, for example 'Family Name', in a text box. When a value is changed it is the same as changing the value in the table.
- Unbound – a line or rectangle on a form is not related to data in a table.
- Calculated – the source data is the result of an expression, such as 'amount = price * quantity', where price and quantity are fields that are multiplied together.

In **Design View**, by right-clicking on a field, the control can be changed to another option.

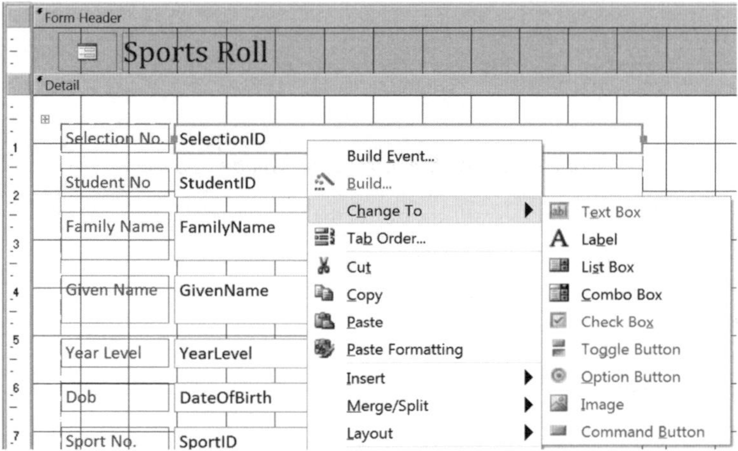

Changing the control for a field

Adding a text box field control

In **Design Mode**, by using form design tools, existing fields can be added to a form from the field list of the current record source. They can also be added from related tables. The figure below shows the **Add Existing Fields** and selections available.

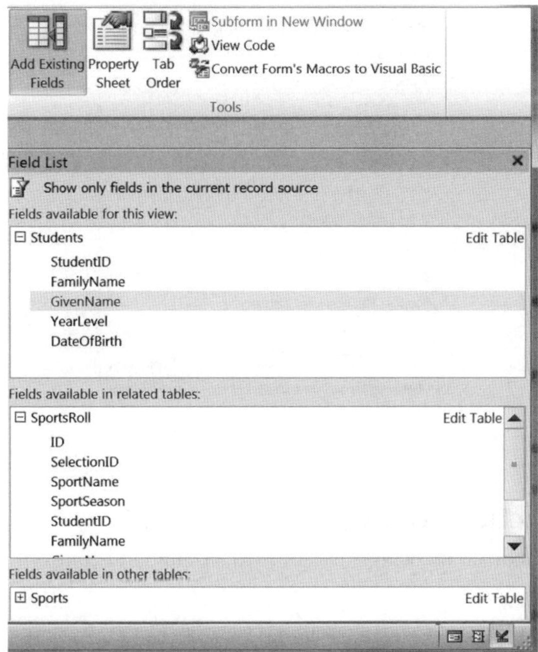

Adding existing fields to a form

Adding an unbound text box control

On a form it is usual to display information such as page numbers, the current date and time controls.

An unbound text box is not related to a field in a table or a query. For example, to include page numbers, date and time controls, particularly in headers and footers, would be to include an unbound text box.

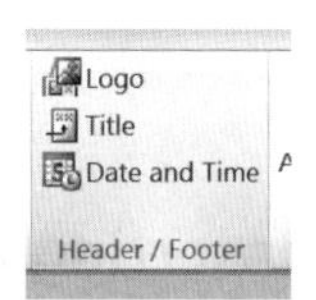

Header and footer options on the Design Tools tab

The figure at right shows the **Header/Footer** section of the **Design Tools** ribbon.

The following figure shows how Microsoft Access provides options for the date and time that will appear after the date and time is selected.

The following figure also shows how the date appears in **Design** view. The date is automatically placed and the value of the date is retrieved from the computer system clock at the time the form is displayed.

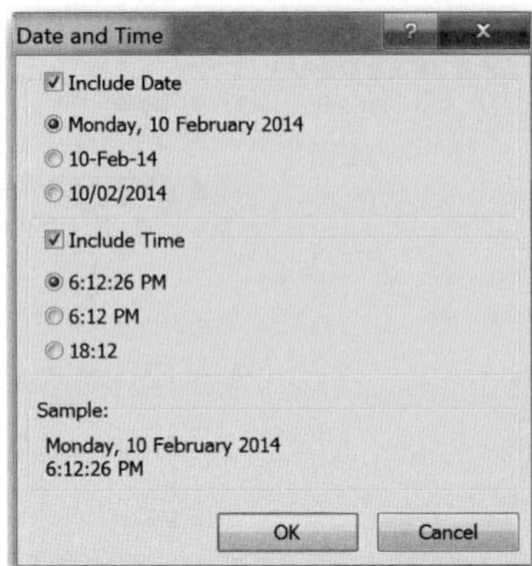

Date and time options

Inserting a function in a control

A date could also be included by using a text box (as an unbound control).

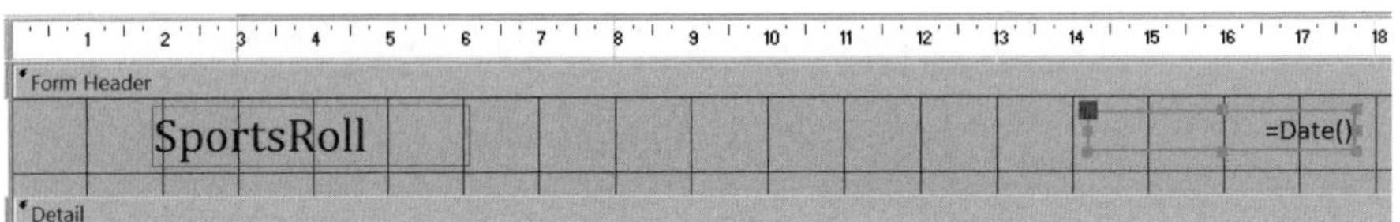

A date field is inserted in a form.

Inserting a calculated control

A calculated control is unbound, although it references fields on a form. The data from the calculation does not form part of the table.

The figure below shows a part of a form. The field 'Age at January' is a calculated control. The text box is unbound. It returns the result of a calculation using the date of birth as part of the calculation.

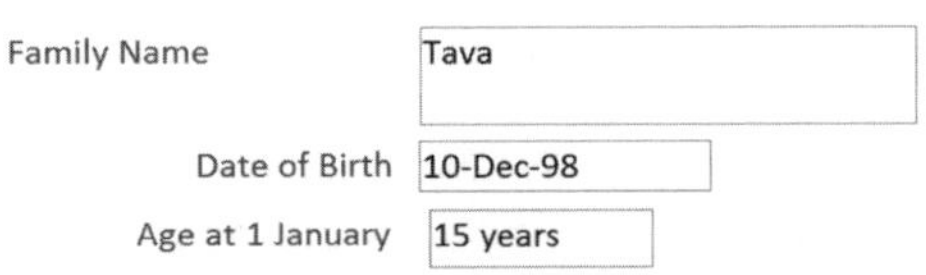

Part of a form: 'Age at 1 January' is a calculation

For example, with sports teams, competition is often based on the age of the participants. Age limits may be determined as at 1 January of a particular year.

Note: There are many formulae available to use in calculations and they do not always have to be built from scratch.

The following **function** is from Microsoft. It goes part way to providing a solution by calculating a person's age in years using their birthday, as entered in a field 'Birthdate'.

```
=DateDiff("yyyy", [Birthdate], Now())+ Int(
Format(now(), "mmdd") < Format( [Birthdate],
"mmdd") )
```

Calculating an age

The calculation uses the built-in functions: DateDiff, Now, Int and Format. It requires the year (yyyy) to be four digits, the month and day (mmdd) in US format.

Editing

The first step is to make sure the field names match (DateOfBirth for Birthdate) and the correct format for months and days is used (ddmm for mmdd).

Pre-existing formulae may not exactly match the problem being solved and may require editing.

Example: Editing the calculation: =DateDiff("yyyy",[DateOfBirth],Now())+Int (Format(Now(),"ddmm")<Format([DateOfBirth], "ddmm"))-1&" years"

The calculation is amended to subtract 1 (to give the age as at 1 January) and the text 'years' is added to enhance its appearance in the field.

Tip: The calculation can be built using **Expression Builder** or created in a text editor and pasted into the field in **Design View**.

The figure below shows part of the form in **Design View** with the details from the Property Sheet showing the control source for the text box, the formula above.

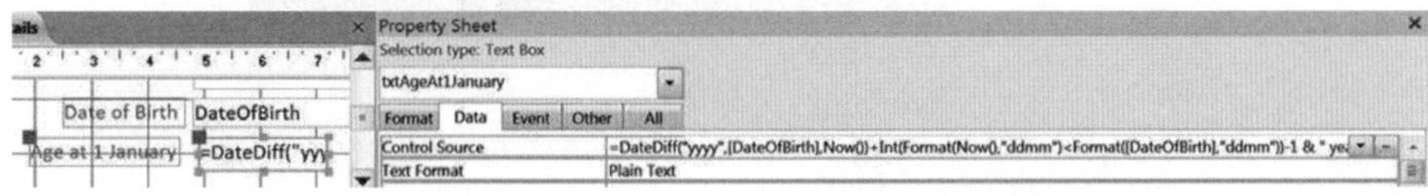

Formula that is the calculation for the calculated control

Testing

Test DateOfBirth data	Age at 1 January	Expected result

A table such as this can be used for testing the calculations

It is essential that a calculation be tested independently to ensure the calculation is correct. When calculating an age, you could use some examples from your family and friends as the test data. Alternatively, test data can be created and the results compared.

Inserting option group control

An option box is useful for displaying a set of values; the options are all visible with a button that is clicked to activate the selection.

Example

The combo box and list box allow a list of predetermined values to form the basis of a selection for the data to be entered by the user. In some cases the lists can be long; for example, a list of the states of the United States would contain fifty items. The advantage is that the list is complete and the spelling is correct.

Inserting combo box control

A **combo box control** allows a selection from a list of data options. The combo box must be clicked to open the list. A combo box does allow the editing of values, therefore a value that is not in the list can be added upon entering.

Combo box control showing field selections when clicked

Inserting a list box control

A **list box control** allows a selection from a list of data options. Unlike a combo box, it does not need to be clicked to open or allow editing of the list.

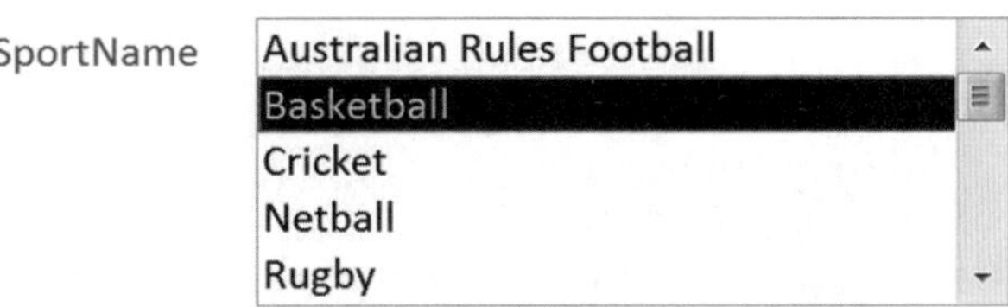

A list box control does not require 'clicking' to show the list

Date picker

For Date/Time data fields the **Date Picker** can appear when the field is clicked. This makes it easier to enter the date, as the display shows the year, month, day of the week and date number.

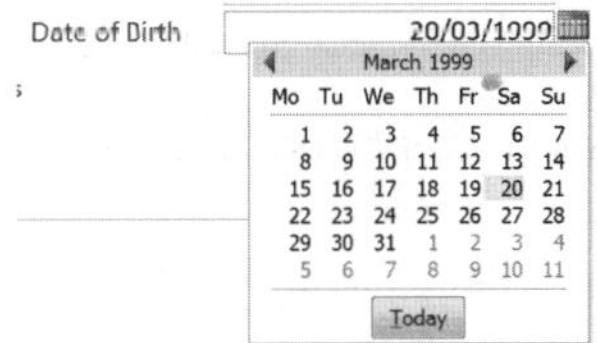

Date picker control

Inserting command buttons

Buttons on screen can be created to allow a user to perform important functions to administer an information system.

In the **Layout View** with the **Design** ribbon selected, invoke **Use Control Wizards** by clicking in the scroll box on the right.

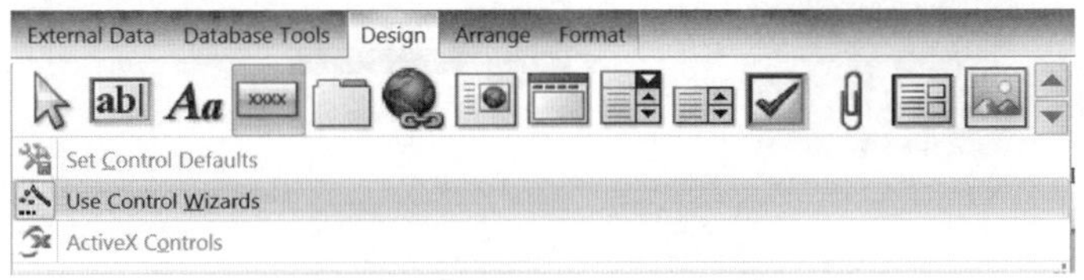

Control Wizards buttons from the Design ribbon

Then select the **Button** tool and drag it to the form. This creates a button to which an action can be attached.

This method is useful for attaching a single action to a button. From the categories, a basic range of actions can be attached. These can be edited to add further steps.

For example, the figure below shows the **Record Operations** category. This can be used to attach actions related to individual records of a table, such as **Add New Record**, among others.

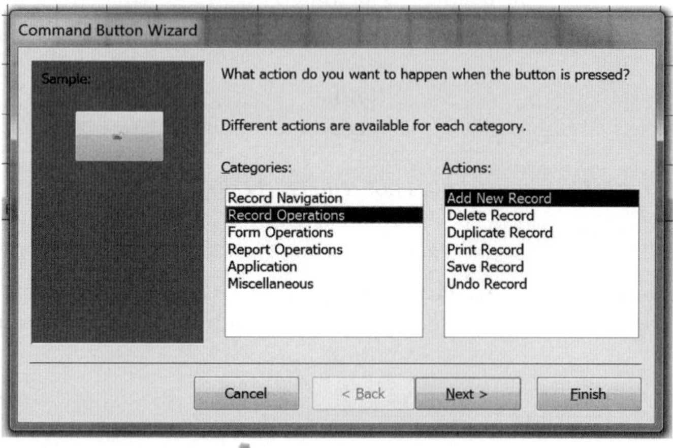

Record Operations that can be attached to a command button

The figure below shows how text and also a picture can be added to the button.

The text placement for a button can be set in **Properties**. The button has been named '**New**', for '**New Record**'.

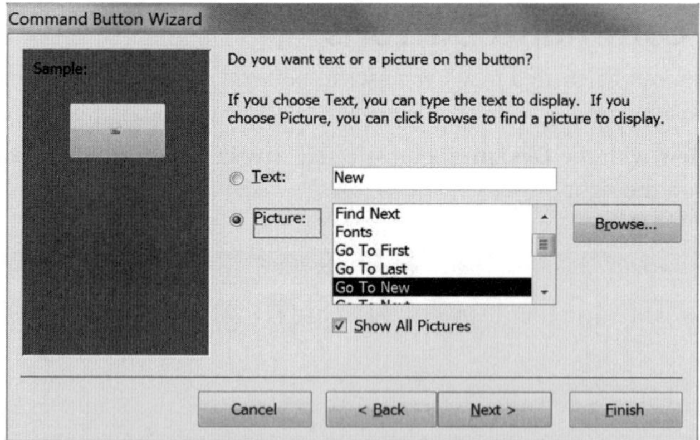

Adding a text caption and a picture to a button

Give the button a name for future reference. There are default images in Access for selection. Using **Browse** allows a different image to be selected.

The final step of the wizard is to name the button. This name is for reference in the macro and can be a different name to the caption.

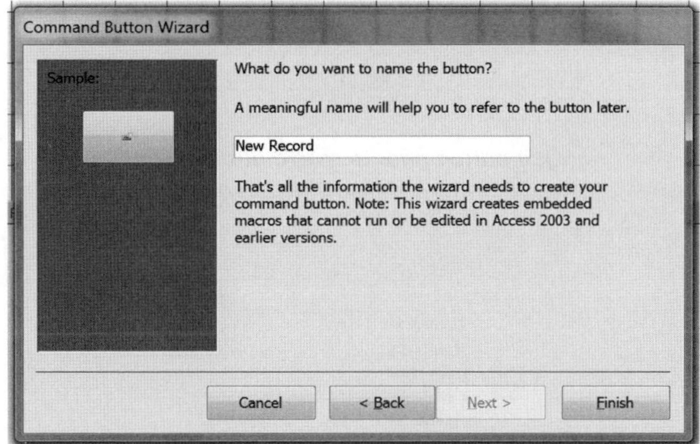

Naming the button for reference in the macro

The figure below shows the command buttons for the Sports Information System. The command button creates functions for the data form to:

- Create a new record.
- Navigate to the first, previous, next or last record.
- Delete a record.

Note the **Control Tip** displayed as the cursor hovers over the button. The tip has been added to the button properties.

Command buttons with captions and New button with the New Record tool tip

Add Quit button

A macro is capable of incorporating a series of steps, just as if they had been selected from menus and the ribbon.

The **Quit** button is used to save the files, close the files and quit Access.

Create > Macro allows a variety of settings to be selected for the macro that can be run by clicking the button.

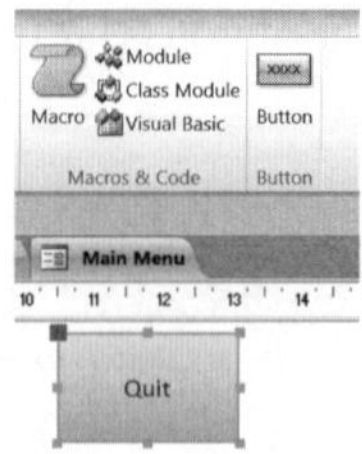

Quit button prior to macro attachment

The figure below shows a sample of these settings.

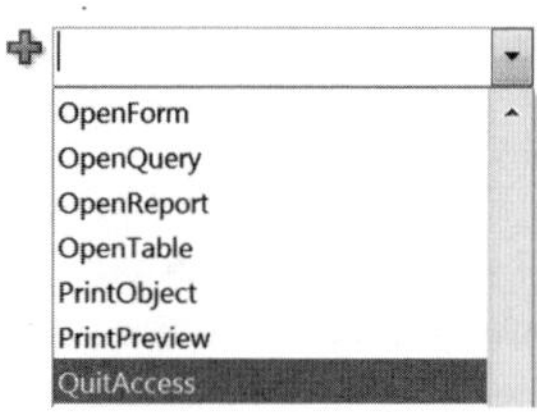

Adding the Quit Access step to the macro

The **Quit Access** selection also includes the **Save All** option when it is selected.

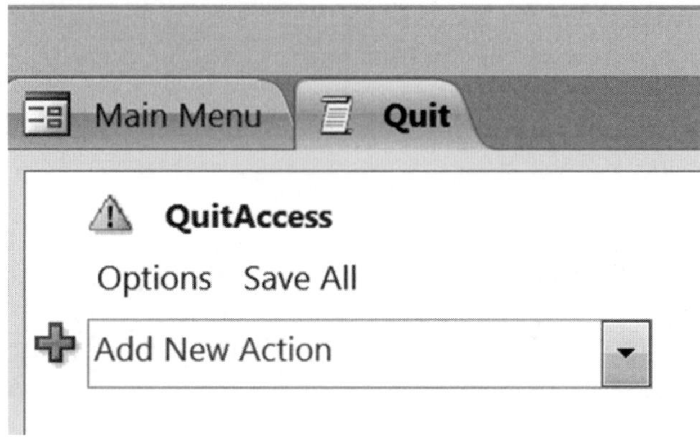

Editing the steps of the macro

The macro needs to be given a name, which will appear in the **Navigation** pane upon creation.

Macro with its name as it appears in the navigation pane

The **Quit** macro could be attached to the **Main Menu** screen by drawing a button on the screen.

Sports Information System

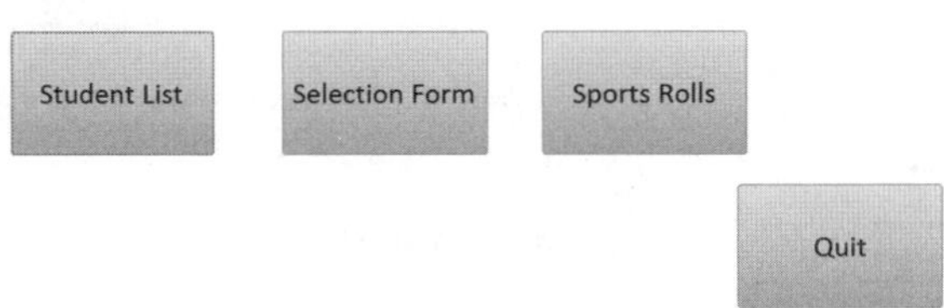

Main Menu screen with Quit button attached

Expression Builder

Creating a calculated field activates the **Expression Builder**. **Expression Builder** can be used with database elements such as fields, forms, reports, queries and tables.

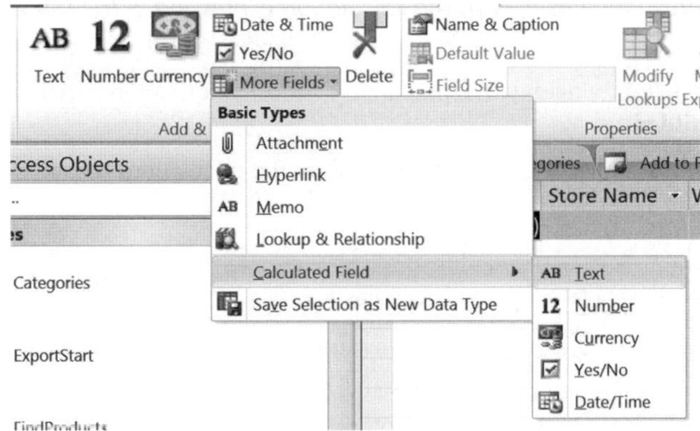

Selecting a calculated field

Expression Builder enables a value to be calculated using appropriate syntax, comprising elements, categories and values.

Example of an expression

String expression

It is possible to add items of text to each other, sometimes called 'concatenation' of text. The figure below shows the expression element 'Operators' for the category 'String'. The value '&', the ampersand character, can be used with a string.

In this case the field 'GivenName', then a single space character, then 'FamilyName' are joined as a single item of data in another field. The '&' character enables the items to be joined.

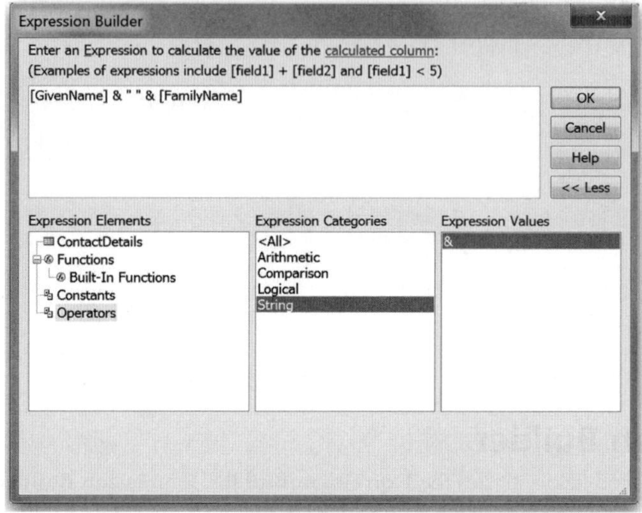

Expression Builder, with the calculation expression in the top window

Text field items (that is, a field with alphanumeric information) are referred to as a 'string' in **Expression Builder**.

Shown below in the 'Full Name' field is the result of the calculation.

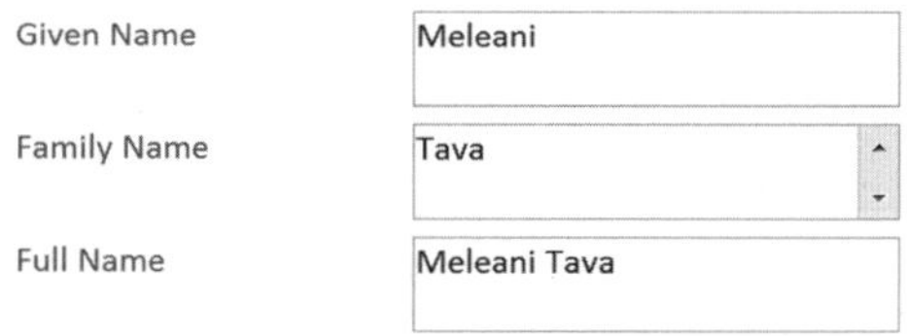

Result of the calculation in the 'Full Name' field

Expression categories

The expressions (or functions) are similar in construction to those in Excel. Expressions are grouped into categories and functions can be selected from the values.

For example, there are a variety of functions that can be applied to text. The **Trim** function could be used to clean up text. It would remove spaces at the start (leading) and at the end (trailing) of the text.

The figure below shows that the **Trim** function could be used as part of an expression. The expression removes any excess space characters during the 'concatenation' of the text. At the bottom of the window is an explanation of the function.

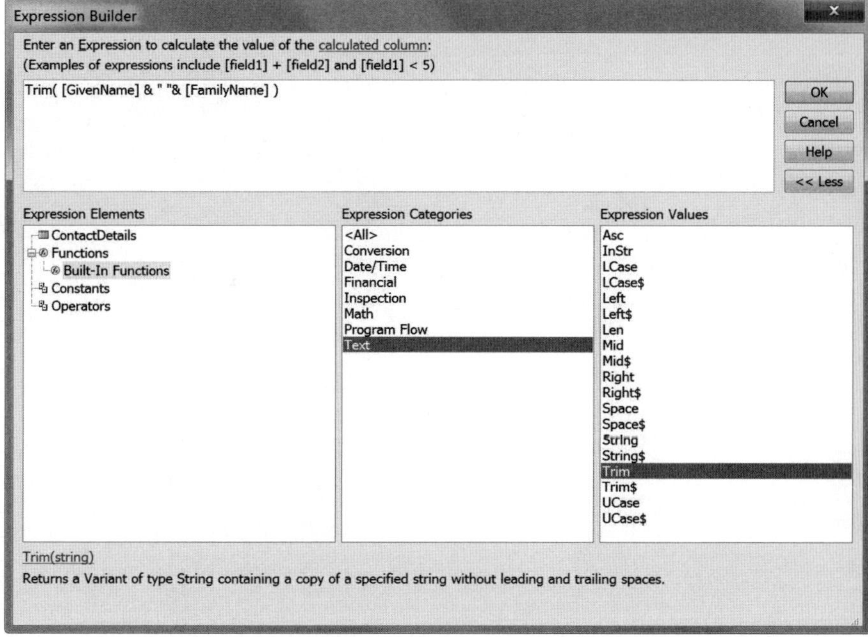

Use of the Trim function

Unit 12.2 Database 2

Topic 6: Integrating main form and subforms

Topic 6 focuses on integrating main form and subforms:

- Creating subform, creating main form and integrating subform into main form.
- Selecting the control from design tools.

A **subform** is a technique where data from different tables or queries is displayed in a single form. It is like a split form but has data from related tables.

Before developing a subform you need to have a clear idea of how it will relate to the form. The tables need to have suitable relationships to allow you to manage the subform.

Creating subform, creating main form and integrating subform into main form

The **Subform Wizard** is one method of creating a subform. The figure at right shows the steps outlined by Microsoft Online.

Selecting the control from design tools

A subform can be created in **Design View** by dragging the **Subform** control onto a form. It will appear similar to the figure below and is 'unbound' to the form. It is a 'child' item of its 'master' table.

TOP OF PAGE

Add one or more subforms to an existing form by using the SubForm Wizard

Use this procedure to add one or more subforms to an existing form. For each subform, you can choose to have Access create a new form or use an existing form as the subform.

1. Right-click the existing form in the Navigation Pane, and then click **Design View**.

1. On the **Design** tab, in the **Controls** group, ensure that **Use Control Wizards** is selected.
2. On the **Design** tab, in the **Controls** group, click the **Subform/Subreport** button.
3. Click on the form where you want to place the subform.
4. Follow the directions in the wizard.

When you click **Finish**, Access adds a subform control to your form. If you chose to have Access create a new form for the subform instead of using an existing form, Access creates the new form object and adds it to the Navigation Pane.

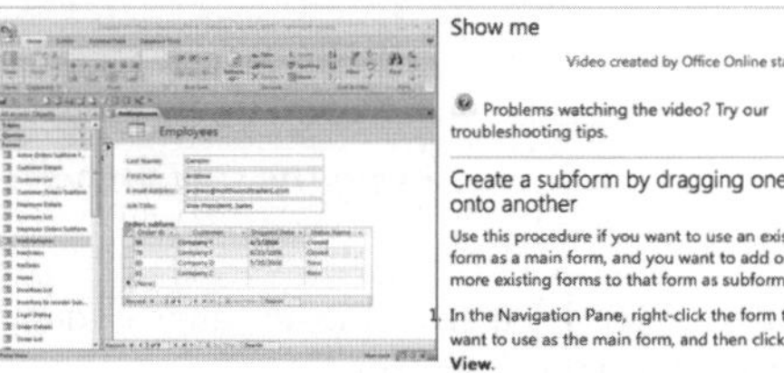

Show me

Video created by Office Online staff writers

Problems watching the video? Try our troubleshooting tips.

Create a subform by dragging one form onto another

Use this procedure if you want to use an existing form as a main form, and you want to add one or more existing forms to that form as subforms.

1. In the Navigation Pane, right-click the form that you want to use as the main form, and then click **Layout View**.
2. Drag the form that you want to use as the subform from the Navigation Pane onto the main form.

Access adds a subform control to the main form and binds the control to the form that you dragged from the Navigation Pane. Access also tries to link the subform to the main form, based on the relationships that have been defined in your database.

3. Repeat this step to add any additional subforms to the main form.
4. To verify that the linking was successful, on the **Home** tab, in the **Views** group, click **View**, click **Form View**, and then use the main form's record selector to advance through several records. If the subform filters itself correctly for each employee, then the procedure is complete.

If the previous test does not work, Access was unable to determine how to link the subform to the main form, and the Link Child Fields and Link Master Fields properties of the subform control are blank. You must set these properties manually by doing the following:

1. Right-click the main form in the Navigation Pane, and then click **Design View**.
2. Click the subform control one time to select it.
3. If the **Property Sheet** task pane is not displayed, press F4 to display it.
4. Click the **Data** tab.
5. Click next to the **Link Child Fields** property box.
    1. The **Subform Field Linker** dialog box appears.
6. In the **Master Fields** and **Child Fields** drop-down lists, select the fields that you want to link the forms with, and then click **OK**. If you are not sure which fields to use, click **Suggest** to have Access try to determine the linking fields.
    1. TIP If you do not see the field that you want to use to link the forms, you might need to edit the record source of the master form or child form to help make sure that the linking field is in it. For example, if the form is based on a query, you should make sure that the linking field is present in the query results.
7. Save the main form, switch to Form view, and then verify that the form works as expected.

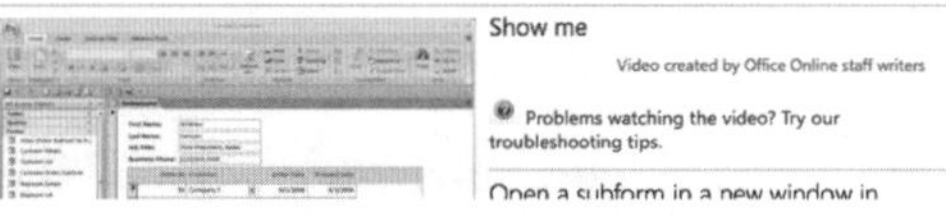

Show me

Video created by Office Online staff writers

Problems watching the video? Try our troubleshooting tips.

Open a subform in a new window in

Microsoft Online steps for creating a subform

Unbound subform control placed on form in Design View

With the property sheet open, the necessary links can be made. It requires the selection of the relationship with the '**Link Master Fields**' and '**Link Child Fields**'. This is shown in the example below.

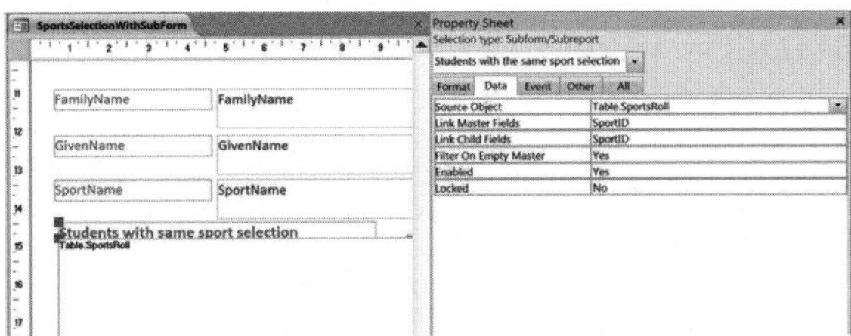

Linking the subform with its master using fields

The subform has been given the heading 'Students with the same sport selection' and the link to the 'SportsRoll' table is shown.

The figure below shows part of the form with the subform and data. When a student has selected a sport, the subform shows all students who have made the same selection.

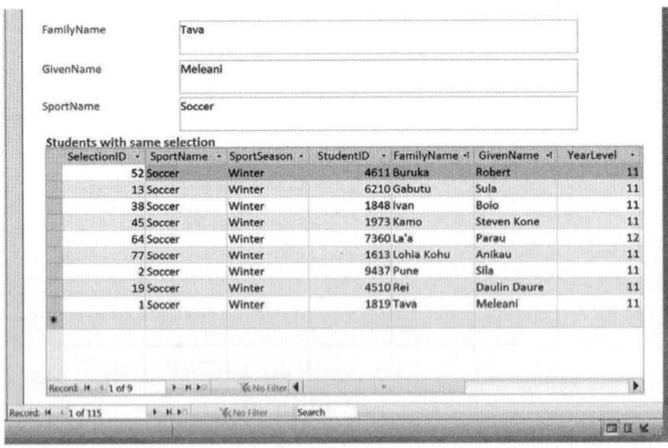

SelectionID	SportName	SportSeason	StudentID	FamilyName	GivenName	YearLevel
52	Soccer	Winter	4611	Buruka	Robert	11
13	Soccer	Winter	6210	Gabutu	Sula	11
38	Soccer	Winter	1848	Ivan	Boio	11
45	Soccer	Winter	1973	Kamo	Steven Kone	11
64	Soccer	Winter	7360	La'a	Parau	12
77	Soccer	Winter	1613	Lohia Kohu	Anikau	11
2	Soccer	Winter	9437	Pune	Sila	11
19	Soccer	Winter	4510	Rei	Daulin Daure	11
1	Soccer	Winter	1819	Tava	Meleani	11

Form and subform with sport selection

Unit 12.2 Database 2

Topic 7: Working with report sections

Topic 7 looks more closely at working with report sections. It focuses on:

- Creating a report using a wizard.
- Reorganising labels and controls in sections.
- Inserting a calculated control.
- Changing the format for a control.

Creating reports

An information system should be capable of creating professional-looking reports for analysis and decision making. Reports summarise data so that organisations can make judgments about performance and trends.

Most organisations would create a report on a regular basis. For example, a supermarket may create a sales report daily. They may also create regular stock level reports that enable timely re-ordering of stock.

The same report but with a weekly, monthly, quarterly, six-monthly or yearly time period will provide information allowing management decisions to be made based on accurate information.

The data in reports is typically sorted in a manner that makes it easy to read and understand:

- Alphabetical order (A–Z or Z–A).
- Numerical order (0–9 or 9–0).
- Date order (ascending or descending, a range of dates).

A report from the sports information system could show the students who have selected particular sports. In particular, the report should:

- Group the students according to sport chosen.
- Sort the sports from A to Z.
- Sort the students' family names alphabetically.
- Show a count of the number of students taking each sport.
- Show a total of all students who have selected a sport.

Alternatively, another report could filter out those students who have selected a particular sport, such as soccer, or students in Grade 12 only.

Identifying information on a report

A report should have a number of details to identify it clearly. These include:

- The name of the organisation.
- A statement of the time period it covers (eg 'Sales for month of February', 'Stock on Hand at a particular date').
- The date the report has been produced.
- The author of the report.
- The page number of the report and how many pages there are in the report (eg 'Page 1 of 4').

Formatting a report

Report formats require decisions about:

- Text font type and size of headings.
- How to arrange sections of the reports, including page breaks.
- Page numbers.

Creating a report using a wizard

The Sports Information System should be able to produce lists of students and the sports they have selected. The command **Create > Report Wizard** walks you through the steps.

The figure below shows the selection of the tables and the fields required for the report.

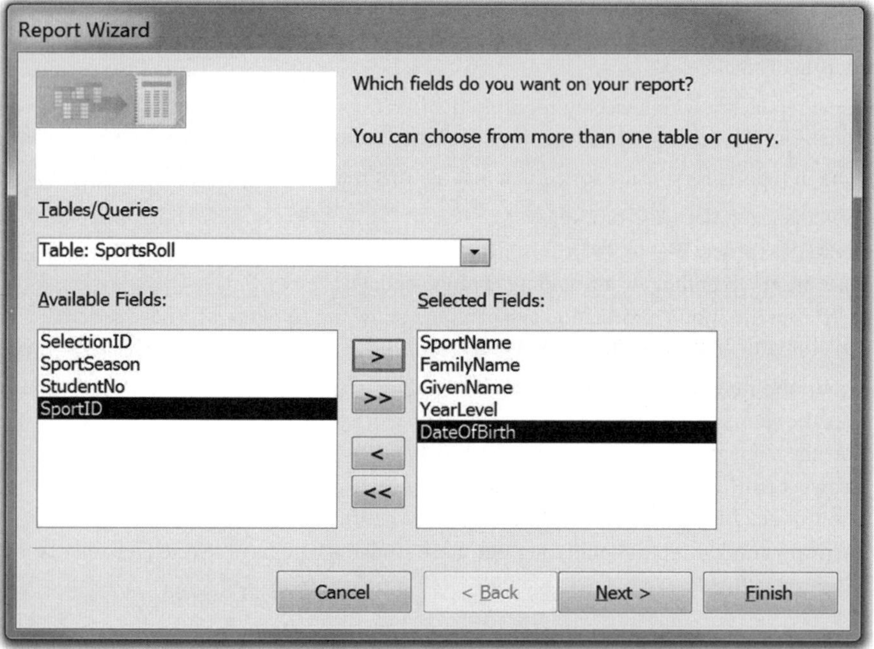

Report Wizard with tables and fields being selected

Grouping is the name of the technique used to select all the items of data with a similar characteristic, in this case all students who have selected the same sport.

The figure below shows how the report will successively display each sport, followed by the students who have selected each sport.

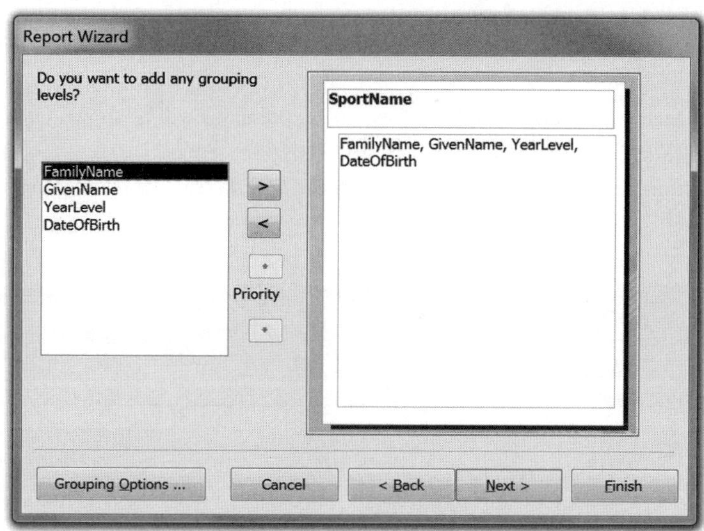

Grouping level for the report, in this case by field 'SportName'

To add structure to the body of the report, the records can be sorted.

The figure below shows options for the Sports Selection Report. Students will be listed in descending year level order (9–0), then within the group by family name, ascending (A to Z).

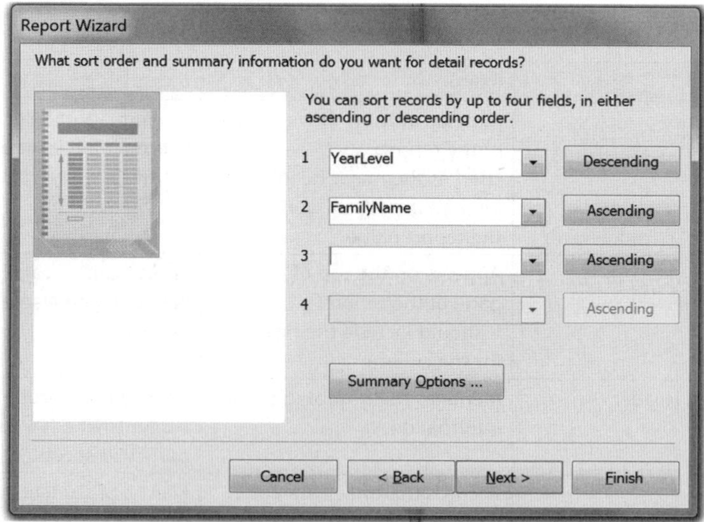

Sorting order in the report

The figure below shows how the report would look in **Design View**. Note the report sections that are indicated by the grey strips. This sets up the structure of the report with placeholders for the data to be placed.

For each part, except the **Detail**, the fields, text and expressions will be shown once according to how they have been created (eg '=Now()' will show today's date).

The **Detail** section will include the data that meets the criteria (eg data relating to students selecting Soccer).

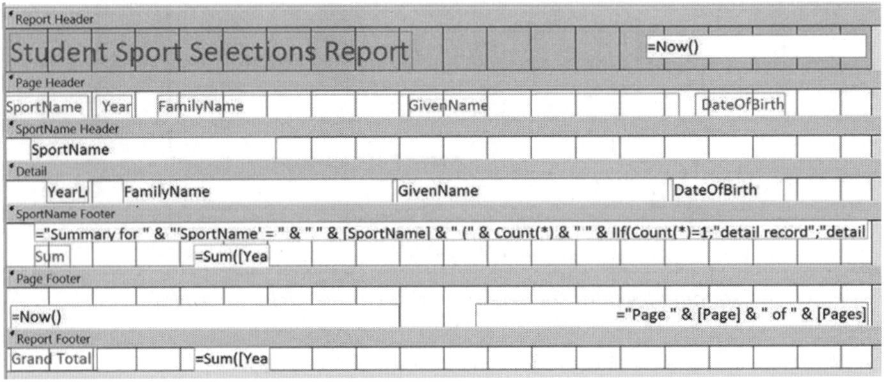

Report Header
Student Sport Selections Report =Now()
Page Header
SportName Year FamilyName GivenName DateOfBirth
SportName Header
SportName
Detail
YearL FamilyName GivenName DateOfBirth
SportName Footer
="Summary for " & "'SportName' = " & " " & [SportName] & " (" & Count(*) & " " & IIf(Count(*)=1;"detail record";"detail
Sum =Sum([Yea
Page Footer
=Now() ="Page " & [Page] & " of " & [Pages]
Report Footer
Grand Total =Sum([Yea

Report in Design View showing report sections

Report sections

The table below shows where the report sections will appear.

Report part	Purpose	Example
Report Header	Appears only on the first page of the report. Used as the major heading to identify the organisation and the report name.	Student Sport Selection Report Current date inserted with '=Now()'.
Page Header	Appears on the top of each page of the report. It should include the headings for the columns.	Sport Name, Year, Family Name, Given Name and Date of Birth.
(SportName) Header	Identifies the grouping of the information.	For example, grouping students who have selected particular sports (eg Soccer).
Detail	Records that meet the particular criteria for the report.	Names of students who are playing soccer showing the information in the fields.

(continues)

Report part	Purpose	Example
(SportName) Footer	Appears after the grouping of records, it can be used to show the count of students.	Shows that nine students have selected Soccer.
Page Footer	Can be used for the numbering of pages and include the date and time the report was made.	Current date inserted with '=Now()'.
Report Footer	This appears only on the last page. It could be used for a 'Grand total'.	Total of all students who have selected a sport.

Different sections available in a report

Shown below is an extract of the report showing the SportName Header, Detail and SportName Footer for the Soccer Grouping. There are nine students who have selected Soccer.

Soccer			
12	La'a	Parau	29/09/1996
12	Tava	Meleani	20/03/1996
11	Buruka	Robert	15/01/1997
11	Gabutu	Sula	01/07/1997
11	Ivan	Boio	22/04/1997
11	Kamo	Steven Kone	30/07/1997
11	Kohu	Andrew	19/05/1997
11	Lohia Kohu	Anikau	17/02/1997
11	Rei	Daulin Daure	20/03/1997
Summary for 'SportName' = Soccer (9 detail records)			

Header, detail and footer for Soccer grouping

Reorganising labels and controls in sections

Labels and controls can appear in different parts of a report. Text controls that have a calculation can provide different information depending on which section they are placed in.

The figure above shows a count that displays the number of records (9) that appear in that part of the report.

Inserting a calculated control

A calculated control can be added to a form and a report, but it does not need to be bound to the fields in the tables if that is desired.

An expression can be created using the data in the underlying tables and representing the result.

Changing the format for a control

Conditional formatting

A report display can be enhanced by applying **conditional formatting**. Font colour, text background and font display of the record detail can be adjusted based on certain rules.

The figure shows the 'Sports Roll' report in **Design View**. The field 'SportName' is selected and the Conditional Formatting Rules Manager has a rule 'Value ="soccer"'. The formatting applied has a background to the field and the text is bold.

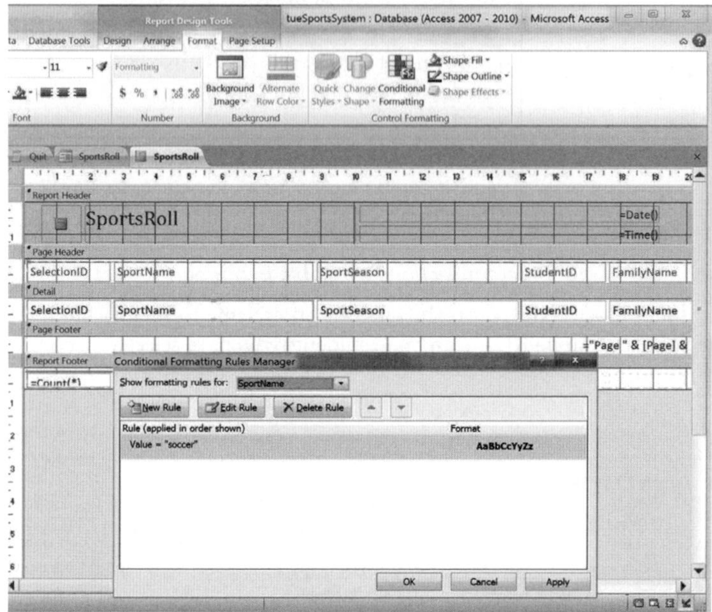

Setting the rules to apply for conditional formatting of a report

The figure below shows how the value of a field can be tested.

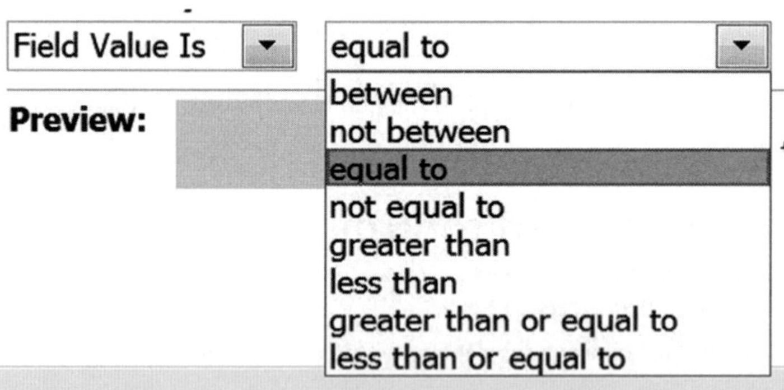

Tests that can be applied to a field for conditional formatting

It is easier to draw attention to an item of data that requires attention, for example. The figure below shows a selection of the report to illustrate the conditional formatting.

SportsRoll

SelectionID	SportName	SportSeason	FamilyName	GivenName
1	Basketball	Winter	Tava	Meleani
2	***Soccer***	Winter	Pune	Sila
3	Basketball	Winter	Benstead	Hebou Isiani
4	Volleyball	Summer	Torepa	Valo
5	Rugby	Winter	Igo	Patrick
6	Basketball	Winter	Gabutu	Sula
7	Australian Rules Football	Winter	Lohia Sisia	Joe
8	Cricket	Summer	Dikana	Arau
9	Basketball	Winter	Pune	Sila
10	Cricket	Summer	Benstead	Hebou Isiani
11	Netball	Winter	Torepa	Valo
12	Cricket	Summer	Ruby	Francis
13	***Soccer***	Winter	Gabutu	Sula

Conditional formatting applied to a report

Printing a report

By selecting **File > Print** the following options are shown.

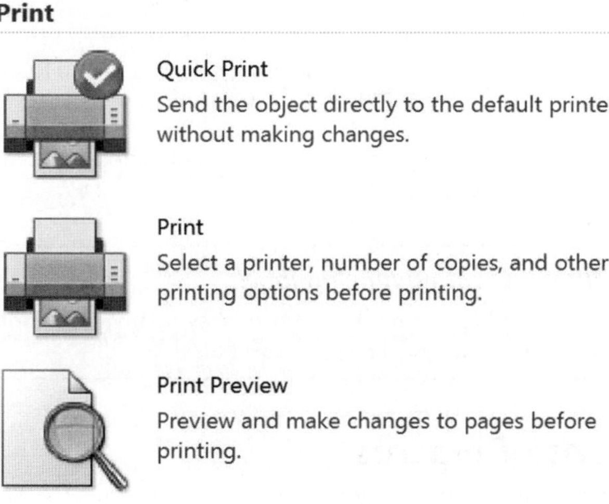

File and Print options

Print Preview is particularly useful to review the parts of the report and check that the information being conveyed is clear and accurate. In the development stage of an information system, all reports need 'dummy data' to test that a generated report will display the data as intended.

Orientation of reports, either landscape or portrait, depends on the nature of the report. The most regularly used page size for a report is A4.

The figure below shows the options with **Print Preview** selected. It shows options related to the print version as well as formats in which the data could also be exported.

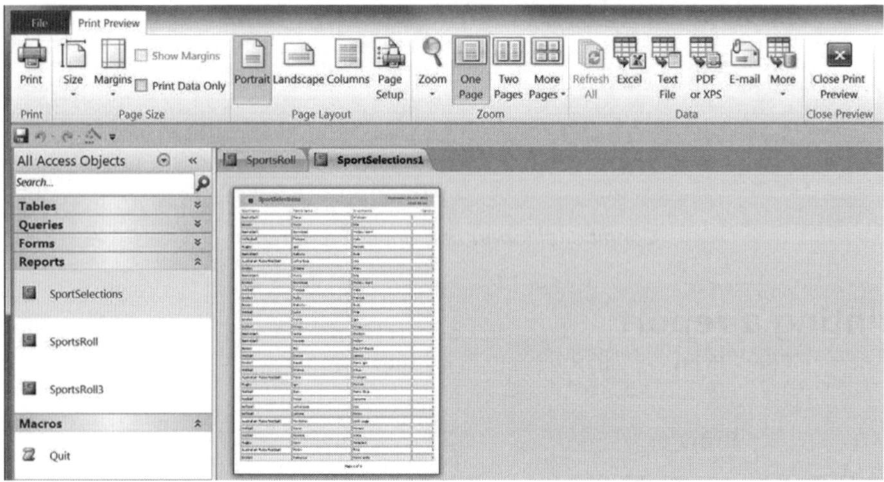

Print Preview for a report

Report generation is often included in the macros that are built into an information system so that the reports can be created easily by the user.

Unit 12.2 Activity 7A: Creating mailing labels

Mailing labels are a common report from an information system. What information should be contained on a mailing label and how should it be set out?

Management of macros

With **Macro Tools**, the editing and management of macros can occur. The **Action Catalog** can be accessed to add steps. The macro can be run with 'single step' to walk through a macro to see if the macro has:

- The required actions.
- The actions in the correct sequence.

The figure below shows the 'Quit' macro in the Macro Tools environment.

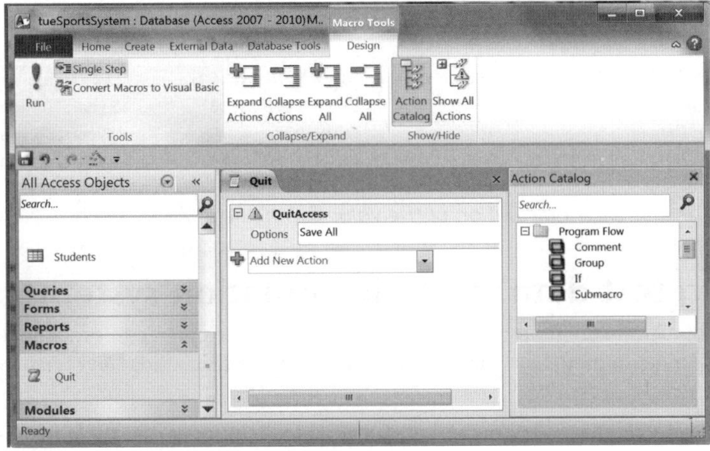

Macro tools

A feature favoured by developers is the conversion of a macro to Visual Basic for Applications.

Visual Basic and Microsoft Access

Access can be extended with Visual Basic integration to provide programming and extended features. The Visual Basic for Applications is the same integration provided for other Microsoft Office software.

Visual Basic is a programming language built on the original BASIC language. BASIC is an acronym for 'Beginners All-purpose Symbolic Instruction Code'. Visual Basic is used by many programmers to develop a range of applications.

A database solution may call on Visual Basic to provide a method of calculation for data or to enable procedures to create a stand-alone executable program from the Access database. A stand-alone executable program can be run without having to open the programming language.

For example, a sample from Microsoft (Knowledge Base Article) enables calculation of ages.

KBArticle	Title	Explanation
290190	How to create two functions to calculate age in months and in years	This sample includes two Visual Basic functions that help you calculate an age based on a date that you enter in a table. One of the functions shows the number of years expired from today's date. The other function shows the number of months expired between today's date and the number of years expired. You can cut and paste either or both functions into a module in your own database.

Microsoft Knowledge Base Article

The figure below from the sample file shows the 'Age' and 'Age with months' calculated from the Birth Date.

ID	Last Name	First Name	Birth Date	Age	Age with months
1	Freehafer	Nancy	17/04/1968	46	46 years, 0 months
2	Cencini	Andrew	2/05/1983	30	30 years, 11 months
3	Kotas	Jan	29/02/1960	54	54 years, 1 months

Calculation of the value for the field 'Age'

Creating test data for an information system

During development of an information system, test data will be entered to simulate how the system will operate. In particular, the test data should ensure that validation of data occurs during data entry.

Often test data (sometimes called dummy data) is created in a spreadsheet and then imported into the system. Existing data can be manipulated and new information created to de-identify individuals.

Some useful functions

Sum, RandBetween and Index are three functions that are useful in creating test data.

Create 30 unique numbers for ID in sequence

Do the following in an Excel worksheet:

1. Enter '1' in the Cell A1.
2. Enter '=A1+1' in Cell A2.
3. Drag Cell A2 to Cell A30 to create the values.

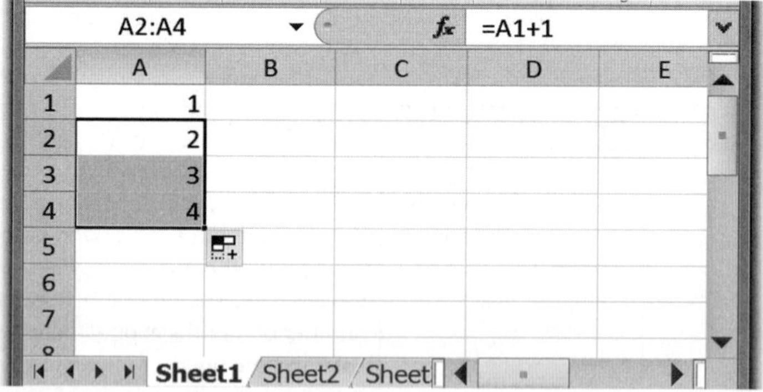

Creating a range of numbers in a worksheet

Create a range of values within a range

The RandBetween function will create values at random with a minimum and maximum value specified in the function. For example, =RANDBETWEEN(1000,9999) would create a number at random between and including 1000 and 9999.

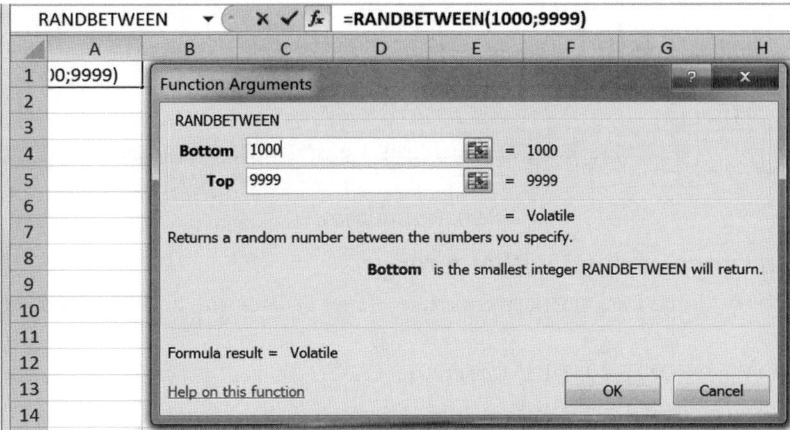

Creating random numbers

Note: the 'Formula result = Volatile'. It is subject to recalculation and as other actions on the worksheet are performed new values will be calculated.

Create a range of values, with unique numbers within a range

The RandBetween function does not prevent the possibility of duplicate values. The simplest method to ensure unique numbers would be to use the RandBetween function but create a larger number of values than required.

Select the values and in another column **Paste Special** and select **Values** only. Shown here is a column of values. The last three have been copied in this example to illustrate that duplicate values exist.

6116
7529
5290
6628
9695
5791
5842
9345
9767
9251
9345
9767
9251

Random numbers in a worksheet

Select the **Data** tab and **Remove Duplicates**. The number of duplicate values will be identified and can be removed.

Removing duplicates

Create a range of dates within a range

The RandBetween and Date functions can create a series of dates with a start and end date. For example:

=RANDBETWEEN(DATE(2015,1,1),DATE(2015,12,31))

would create a random date for dates in 2015. The result of the expression is a number (Excel stores dates as numbers). It can be formatted to appear in date form.

Create a random set of text values

The RandBetween and Index functions can achieve this by retrieving an item of data at random.

C2 =INDEX($G$2:$G$9,RANDBETWEEN(1,8))

	A	B	C	D	E	F	G	H
1	FamilyName	GivenName	SportName				SportName	
2	Tava	Meleani	Rugby				Australian Rules Football	
3	Pune	Sila	Basketball				Basketball	
4	Benstead	Hebou Isiani	Cricket				Cricket	
5	Torepa	Valo	Cricket				Netball	
6	Igo	Patrick	Netball				Rugby	
7	Gabutu	Sula	Australian Rules Football				Soccer	
8	Lohia Sisia	Joe	Softball				Softball	
9	Dikana	Arau	Australian Rules Football				Volleyball	
10								

Creating a random set of text values

In Column G is a list of sports. Cells G2 to G9 show eight different sports.

In Cell C2 the sports are indexed (placed in a list). The RandBetween function then makes a selection, at random from the list of eight.

Unit 12.2 Activity 7B: Creating a set of names

1. Put a list of five friends' given and family names into an Excel worksheet.
2. Use the RandBetween and Index functions to create a set of names.

Import data into an Access database

Access can import data from a variety of sources, including text and spreadsheet files.

After identifying the source file the data can be:

- Imported into a new table.
- Appended to an existing table.
- Linked with the creation of a linked table.

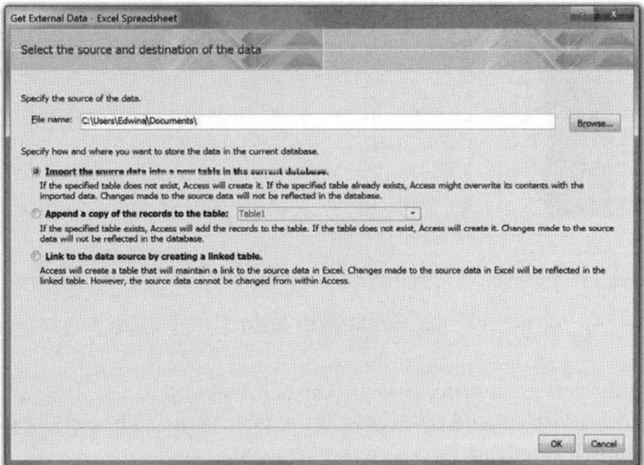

Importing data into Access

The **Import Spreadsheet Wizard** checks if the first row contains the column headings for the data. That row is then discarded during the import.

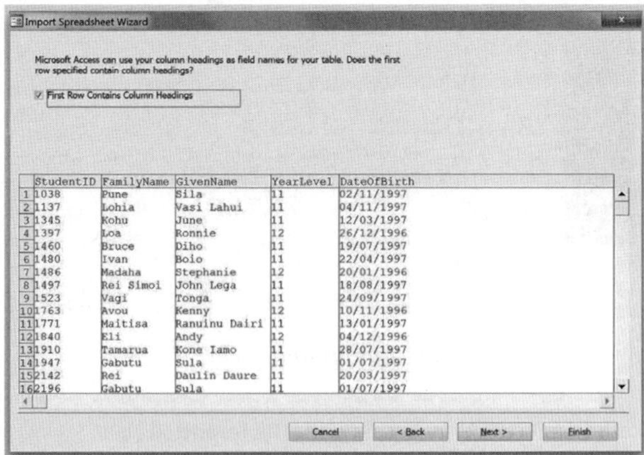

	StudentID	FamilyName	GivenName	YearLevel	DateOfBirth
1	1038	Pune	Sila	11	02/11/1997
2	1137	Lohia	Vasi Lahui	11	04/11/1997
3	1345	Kohu	June	11	12/03/1997
4	1397	Loa	Ronnie	12	26/12/1996
5	1460	Bruce	Diho	11	19/07/1997
6	1480	Ivan	Boio	11	22/04/1997
7	1486	Madaha	Stephanie	12	20/01/1996
8	1497	Rei Simoi	John Lega	11	18/08/1997
9	1523	Vagi	Tonga	11	24/09/1997
10	1763	Avou	Kenny	12	10/11/1996
11	1771	Maitisa	Ranuinu Dairi	11	13/01/1997
12	1840	Eli	Andy	12	04/12/1996
13	1910	Tamarua	Kone Iamo	11	28/07/1997
14	1947	Gabutu	Sula	11	01/07/1997
15	2142	Rei	Daulin Daure	11	20/03/1997
16	2196	Gabutu	Sula	11	01/07/1997

Importing data from a spreadsheet

Information can be specified about the field name, the data type, and if the field is to be indexed.

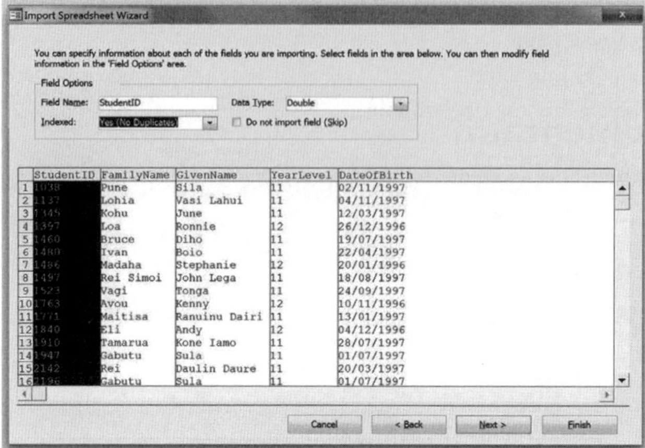

Importing data

If the data being imported has a primary key, there is the option to use those values rather than the default that is otherwise created by Access. If the table is the source of the primary key, then it is most important that duplicate values are not allowed.

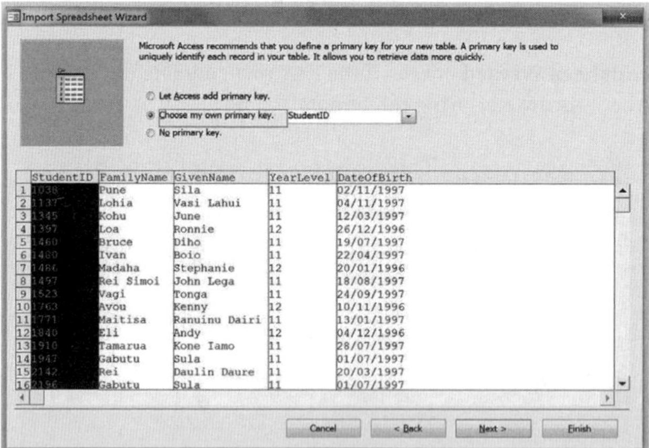

Setting a primary key

The table is in this case then created in Access with the imported data.

Export data from an Access database

A variety of formats are available for export from a database including:

- Excel.
- XML.
- Text.

User documentation

Information system user documentation is prepared to point out the key features of the system and what it is trying to achieve. Features that may be obvious to information technology professionals are not always apparent to the people who use the systems.

Working with key objects in Microsoft Access

The objects in Access can be viewed in two main ways: 'Datasheet View' and **Design View**. **Home > View** enables this.

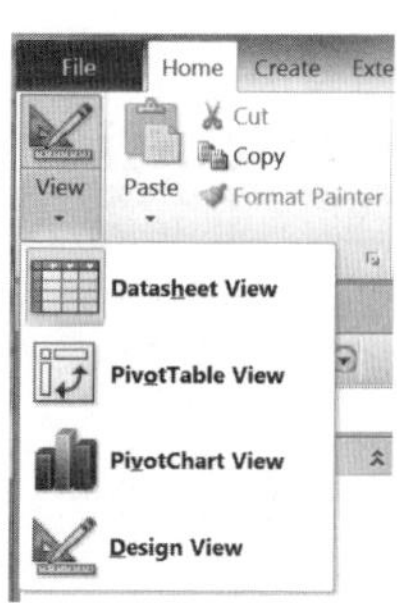

Views in Access

Both of these views have been used in the text for this Unit.

The **Datasheet View** shows the data according to the object being viewed (eg records in the table).

The **Design View** shows the elements of the object in a layout very much like a drawing program. The elements and fields, their position, placement and properties can be altered in **Design View**.

The **PivotTable View** and the **PivotChart View** enable interactive data analysis.

The figure below shows a new file with a table in Datasheet View.

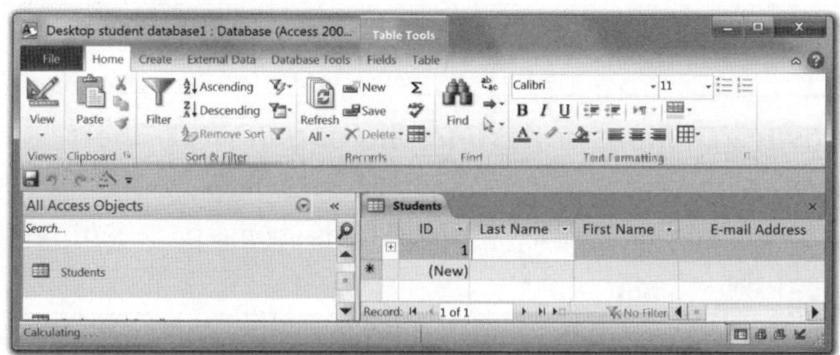

The Datasheet View shows the data

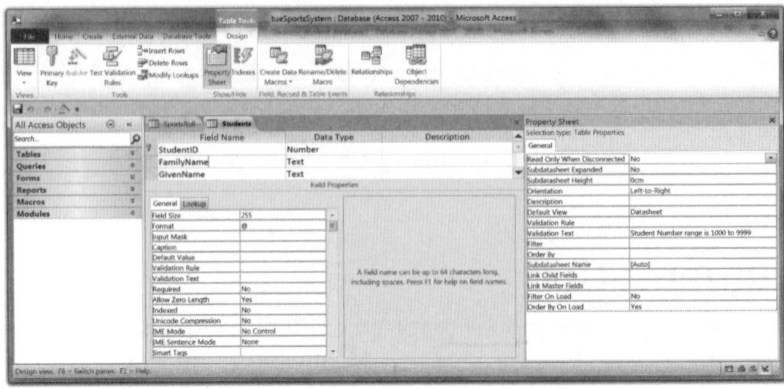

The Design View shows the properties in this view for both 'fields' and the 'Table'

Conclusion

Microsoft Access is a powerful database management package that enables people and organisations to create and manage both simple and complex information systems. One of its great strengths is its consistency in approach to other applications in the Microsoft Office product suite.

The development of complex database management packages requires significant programming expertise.

Unit 12.2 Activity 7C: Entity relationship diagram (ERD)

A supermarket sells items to customers and produces an invoice as a record of the transaction.

1. Identify the entities involved in this transaction.
2. Create an Entity relationship diagram to reflect the entities involved.

Unit 12.2 Activity 7D: Input processing and output (IPO) chart

A customer enters a supermarket and does the weekly shopping.

1. What information processing occurs when the transaction is processed?
2. Complete the table.

Input	Processing	Output

Unit 12.2 Activity 7E: Creating a table in Microsoft Access

Explain the role of each of these in a database:

- **a.** Field
- **b.** Table
- **c.** Form
- **d.** File

Unit 12.2 Activity 7F: Conventions for naming fields

What is your preferred method of naming fields?

In your answer, describe how you would create field names from a person's name and address. You could use your own details as an example.

Unit 12.2 Activity 7G: Table fields properties

This table shows field types that can be used in Microsoft Access.

For each data type, give two examples of an item of data suited to that type of field. Also give two actual items of data.

Data type	Type of data	Examples (2)
Text		
Numbers		
Calculated		
Logical		
Web addresses		

Unit 12.2 Activity 7H: Data in a supermarket

A supermarket has information to be entered into their products database. In column 1 is data that relates to an item for sale. In column 2 are fields used in the product database. What would be the best match for each of the fields and data?

Item	Fields
Corn Flakes 500g	Supplier Code
11 November 2014	Product Code
64	Price
2	Order Quantity
Breakfast Cereal	Item Description

CF14978	Date Entered
4k	Category
ASS	Aisle Location

Unit 12.2 Activity 7I: Data structure table

The Internet Movie Database at http://www.imdb.com/ has information about movies.

1. Identify 10 key data fields used to manage and arrange this information.
2. What type of field would be used?
3. Suggest a field size for each field.
4. What could be used as a primary key identifier field for a movie?
5. What types of data could be suited to having an input mask?
6. How would the input mask appear in the field?

	Data field	**Data type**	**Field size**
1			
2			
3			
4			
5			
6			
7			
8			
9			
10			

Unit 12.2 Activity 7J: Changing the display of a field name

The following an example shows field names in a table of invoices for a transaction processing system.

1. What suggestions could you make for the caption of the field appearing on the form?
2. What description could be added to help explain the purpose of the field?

Field name	Data type	Field size	Field caption	Description
Customer ID			Customer number	Unique identifier for a customer
Product ID				
Date				
Item description				
Qty				
Last name				
Family name				
Invoice ID				
Salesperson ID				

Unit 12.2 Activity 7K: Validation rules for fields

Use the field names in the invoices table for a transaction processing system.

1. What validation could be applied (if any) to the fields?
2. In the event of an item of data failing validation, what custom message could be applied?

Field name	Validation rule	Validation text
Customer ID		
Product ID		
Date		
Item description		
Qty		
Last name		
Family name		
Invoice ID		
Salesperson ID		

Unit 12.2 Activity 7L: Transaction processing system

This diagram depicts the tables for a simple transaction processing system. Customers purchase items and an invoice is created to record the transaction.

1. Explain the purpose of each of the tables in the information system.
2. Identify the key fields that you would use for each of the tables. What names would you give to the fields?

3. How would the tables be linked using those key fields?
4. What events would occur that would require changes to be made to the records in each table?

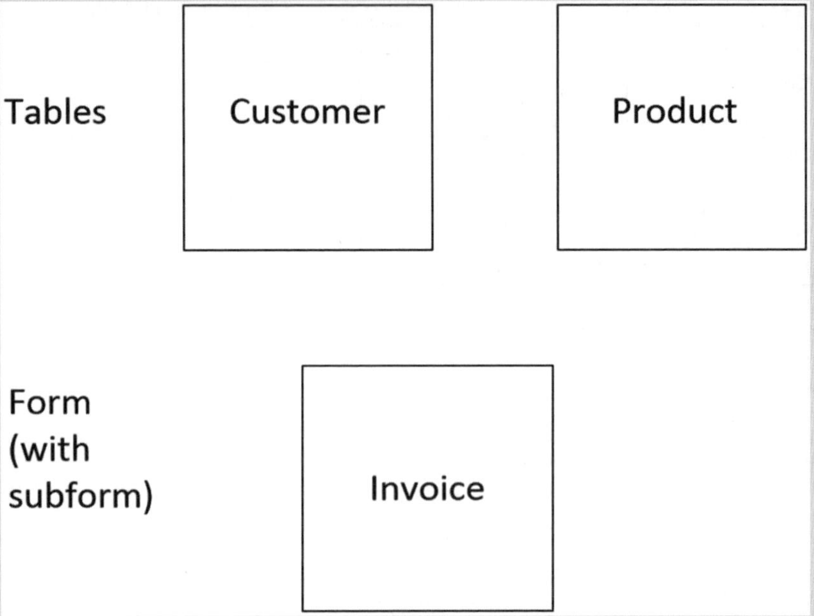

Tables	Customer	Product
Form (with subform)	Invoice	

Unit 12.2 Activity 7M: Validation techniques

Consider a school information system with regard to the data recorded about each student.

1. What types of validation (if any) would be suitable to ensure data is entered correctly in the fields in the following table?
2. What are the advantages of having a custom validation message rather than rely on the generic message produced by Access?
3. For these fields, suggest the type of field that would be best suited for input from this list:
   a. Text box
   b. Option group
   c. Calculated control
   d. Option group control
   e. Combo box control

Field name	Validation method	Validation message if validation fails
Family name	Manual, human, verification by checking source, ensure field has a name	Please enter the family name for the student
Date of birth		
Age		
Year level		
Address		
Date record created		
Date record modified		
Student ID		

Unit 12.2 Activity 7N: Sort and query

1. What is meant by: 'a sort can be "ascending" or "descending"'?
2. The direction of a sort varies according to the field type. Explain those differences for a 'text' as compared to a 'number' field.
3. What is the difference between a 'sort' and a 'query' when using a database?

Unit 12.2 Activity 7O: Layout for a data entry form

Here is an extract from an 'Excel' file that is used by the Paxton Sailing Club for recording subscriptions. The extract identifies the fields currently used to collect the information. It also shows a line of sample data. The Sailing Club is going to maintain the data in an information system using *Microsoft Access*.

Name 1	Name 2	Town	Region	Postcode	Membership	Address Line 1
Alan	Spencer	Pt Moresby	PT MORESBY	3206	Junior	Lahara Ave

Address Line 2	Subscription	Last Subscription	Phone
	95	27/1/08	3 508 5716

1. Design an entry form/screen that would be appropriate for the system. Make sure that you include appropriate headings and prompts.
2. Use appropriate names to identify the field areas on the form and annotate the diagram with instructions for font size and type.

Unit 12.2 Activity 7P: You be the consultant

The Raiders Rugby Club has a paper card index for membership records. George, the Membership Secretary, is given a computer for his birthday and begins the task of converting the card records to an information system on the computer. You suggest he should think about the way the information is entered and how the system is to be used. George feels his approach is correct as he has modelled his system on the one his cousin implemented for the now defunct Lae Bocce Club.

This information system shows field definitions. Assume all fields are 'text' only fields and comment upon the field definitions. Are they suitable? How would you define the fields? Could the data be entered into the system in an efficient and effective manner?

Unit 12.2 Activity 7Q: George's next attempt

George asks Leni about Microsoft Access. Leni tells George that an easy way to start the information system is to have the data in an Excel spreadsheet which Access can read. He does this and is provided with two layouts, one of which is shown below. What are the advantages and disadvantages of this approach?

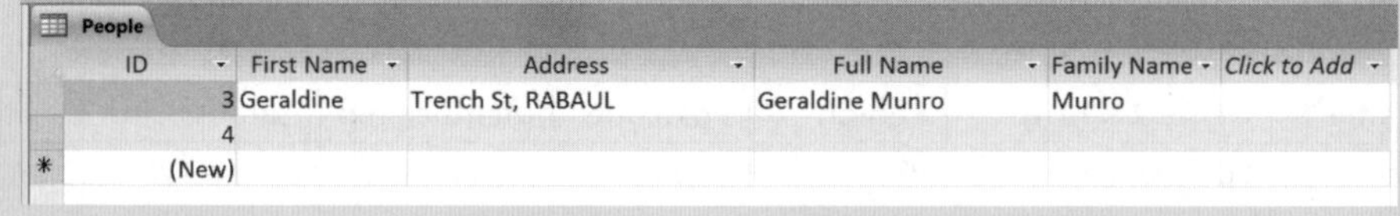

Unit 12.2 Activity 7R: Unique field (unique identifier)

George did not include a membership number on the card index. He felt it was not required as each card itself was unique. Should the information system have a membership number? Why? What would be the advantages of having a unique value for each member? In your answer, discuss the advantage when converting the existing records and when entering new members into the system.

Leni suggests a four-digit membership number. What are the advantages and disadvantages of this system? If the names are imported from Excel into Access, will Access automatically create a unique field identifier?

Unit 12.2 Activity 7S: Identifying, naming and validating the fields for the information system

George and asks you for assistance to create a 'data dictionary' for the Raiders Rugby Club. The club wishes to include member information which will be suitable for membership details, subscription details and social occasions. The club will need to know the name and address of each member, contact details, date of joining the club, length of membership, membership category and current subscription rate. The club would also like to identify office bearers. The club will print mailing labels from the system.

The four main categories of members and four subscription rates are shown in this table:

	Member type	Subscription (current) Kina
1	Junior (16 years and below)	30
2	Youth (21 years and below, above 16 years)	45
3	Adult – social	110
4	Adult – competition	165

Complete the following table for the Data Dictionary showing all the required fields. Add extra rows if required.

Field name	Field type	Validation type	Validation details	Validation tests
Given	text	Spelling	Capitalisation of first letter of given	visual check
Family				

Design an input screen with the fields you think are suitable for the information system. Show headings and titles for the screen and where the fields are to be located. Identify the font type, font size, font style, font alignment and font color of all fields to be shown on the screen.

Unit 12.2 Activity 7T: Format of a date

A date can be formatted in many ways. What is your preferred format? Could the format depend on the use in the database or a report produced by the database? See this list of different date formats.

21/02/2015

21 February 2015

21/02/15

02/21/2015

21st Feb 2015

21st February 2015

Monday 21 February 2015

Unit 12.2 Activity 7U: Designing and creating an information system

The secretary of the local tennis club has asked you to design and develop a software solution to manage the records of the tennis club. The software package should handle the information set out in this table. Identify the field name and field type for the information. In your answer, show one item of sample data that you would use as sample data for your solution.

Classification	Field type	Field name	Sample data
membership number			
family name			
given name			
title			
number and street			
suburb			
postcode			
telephone number			
type of membership (full, senior, junior, under 18 and mid-week)			
date of birth			
date of joining			
date of last payment			

Classification	Field type	Field name	Sample data
method of payment			
amount of payment			
membership status			

In the next table there are three fields. What validation would be suitable for the field? Provide two items of data which you would use to test the field and the validation you have used.

Field	Validation	Data examples
Title		
postcode		
date of birth		

Unit 12.3 Internet 2

Topic 1: Creating a new web page

Unit 12.3 introduces students to the various authoring languages required to design and publish web pages on the World Wide Web. Students are given the opportunity to design and develop web pages using web design applications or an HTML editor, and are shown the procedures involved in publishing their web pages (ICT syllabus p. 38).

In Topic 1, students are introduced to concepts and techniques relating to creating a new web page, including:

- Creating a one-page website.
- Creating a website using wizard or templates.
- Working with web folders.

What is a web page?

The **World Wide Web** is that part of the Internet where information is organised into 'pages' and is delivered to browsers. A web page is information delivered over a network to a screen.

The screen on a device such as a computer, phone or tablet is viewed using software called a browser. The 'page' is delivered over a network, the Internet or an intranet from a web server. A **browser** makes a request to a web server to deliver the page using the **hypertext transfer protocol (HTTP)**.

A web page is a text file comprising mark-up in the form of 'tags' and 'links' to files that then enables the browser to lay out the content of the page on screen.

The notion of '**hypertext**' goes back to at least the 1940s. Hypertext refers to a document that has a link (or links) to another document. The link is called a **hyperlink** – the user clicks on the hyperlink to move to the other document. A link can be recognised because it is underlined and in a different colour (usually blue.) By clicking the link, the user can go to:

- A different place on the same page;
- Another page within the same **website**; or
- Any other page on any site on the World Wide Web.

The author of the document decides what the link is and where it will go.

HTML – the mark-up behind the web page

When word processors were first developed, they used codes for all the text formatting. These codes applied text styles such as bold and italic, paragraph formatting and document control. The development of 'what you see is what you get' (WYSIWYG) word processors such as Microsoft Word meant that those codes were now hidden and the user just concentrated on the text.

In the same way, tags are inserted into text to create pages for the World Wide Web. **Hypertext mark-up language (HTML)** sets out the specifications for use of tags that are used to create these pages. The World Wide Web Consortium manages and develops standards for the web; the current version of HTML is HTML5. Websites can be created using a text editor and HTML. These documents will show all the tags. Website editors such as Adobe Dreamweaver now allow users to create websites and pages without needing to know HTML. However, the HTML code is crucial in the development of sites and web designers must be able to work with HTML.

Sir Tim Berners Lee, an Englishman, developed a hypertext proposal while at the CERN laboratory in Switzerland. Initially it was seen as a method to access information on internal networks at CERN and he termed the project the 'World Wide Web'. He is today a leading advocate for keeping web standards open and ensuring that the web continues to be developed by the community at large.

Berners Lee's work led to the specifications for HTML and, from about 1990, the development of that part of the **Internet** we now know as the World Wide Web. It dramatically changed the way information is distributed as well as the way our society functions today.

Sir Tim Berners Lee

The personal computer/desktop computer era from the early 1980s is now developing into a smartphone and tablet environment. Internet access is available from both mobile devices and desktop computers and from wired and wireless networks.

The technology and methods of producing and delivering information to a screen are developing at a significant rate. The Internet has become a communication medium and is an important way of sharing information and resources.

It is easy for a web developer to be overwhelmed by the choice and different opinions about the best approach to web design. It needs a calm approach and a realisation that, for any approach, there will be compromises – there is not necessarily 'one' best method.

Is a web page a page?

The notion of a web 'page' comes from the notion of a page in the print age. A printed page is fixed in time once it is committed to paper. It is an entity in its own right, until a later printed version supersedes it. The print industry is over 400 years old; the digital page is about twenty years old and is far from a mature industry.

A **web page** is a 'digital' document. It can be updated at any time and published immediately. The HTML that is used to create a page on the web can be viewed by a browser; it is actually a text file.

A web page, unlike a printed page, does not necessarily have a pre-determined height or width. A web page could scroll over a number of screens, depending on the amount of content. The reader of the page may view it on a variety of devices, using a variety of operating systems, browsers and browser versions, with screens of different dimensions and various resolutions.

A printed page has a fixed size, determined at the time of printing based on a relatively small number of paper sizes, A4 being the most common size in use.

Unit 12.3 Activity 1A: Comparison of pages and screens

Complete the following table.

Medium	Name	Dimensions	Resolution	Technology to view content
Printed page	A4 paper	Standard international page size, 210 × 297 mm (portrait view)		
Computer monitor				
Tablet computer				
Smartphone screen				

Creating a one-page website

A one-page website could be created using a range of software, using the **Save As** command so that the finished document is saved as a web page. This is part of normal document production and does not require any additional skills.

Most software types support a **Save to HTML** or **Export to HTML** option. The file needs to have an extension that is either .html or .htm for the browser to recognise it as a file it is able to open. The extensions .htm and .html are used interchangeably in this Unit.

For example, Microsoft Word, PowerPoint and Excel support saving a document as a web page. However, the nature of the HTML generated to create the web page can vary considerably. This method would not be used by those operating anything other than a basic one-page website.

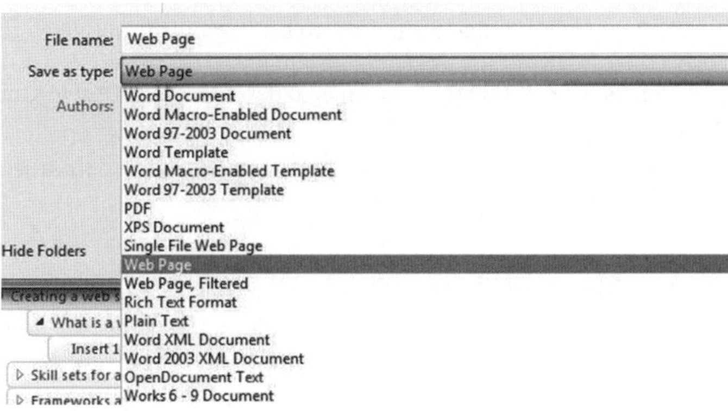

Saving a Microsoft Word document as a web page

Advantages of a creating a single web page using 'Save As' or 'Export to HTML'

The following are advantages of using the **Save As** option:

- A document can be converted to a web page quickly.
- The author does not need to know HTML to create the page.
- The author can work in a WYSIWYG view.
- Images are converted if needed to .png, .gif or .jpg formats automatically.
- Images are usually stored in a folder created during the save process.
- A single web page does not need site management and organisation with other files.

Disadvantages of creating a single web page using 'Save As' or 'Export to HTML'

- Software may use non-standard HTML when creating the page.
- It can be difficult to maintain the look and feel of a website if the page is to be included in an existing site.
- The software will maintain the layout and design as it would if the document were to be printed, rather than viewed on screen.
- The original document needs to be retained in case it needs editing.
- It can be laborious to edit the page with HTML editors to fit to existing websites and maintain the look and feel of a website.

Is knowledge of HTML required to publish a page?

It is not necessary to know HTML to make web pages. Most software (such as a word processor, spreadsheet or presentation file) can save a document as a web page with necessary HTML code.

However, an understanding of some basic HTML codes is important in understanding how a browser renders a page.

Is HTML 'WYSIWYG' ('what you see is what you get')?

HTML was originally designed to enable documents to be distributed over networks, where pages could be viewed regardless of the operating system of the computer. When the web became popular designers pushed HTML to its limits to develop ways of having more control over a page's presentation and appearance.

Some site development software has both 'code' and 'design' views that enable the user to edit the source HTML or work in a 'design' environment.

Software to create a web page

The most suitable software for creating a web page depends on the skill of the user and the task being undertaken. The cost of the software is also a consideration.

In most cases, a web page editor with site management tools is best for preparing pages for the web. A web page saved in HTML format can be opened in many different software applications. A web page is saved with the extension .htm or .html.

Some of the software types that may be used are shown in the table below:

Method to create web page(s)	Examples of software	Advantages	Disadvantages
Text editor	Notepad	Creator of the page has absolute control of the page; editing is done completely in a text only environment.	Detailed knowledge and understanding of HTML required. Professional web workers prefer editing in the text environment.
HTML editors	Many freeware editors available	HTML tags can be entered from software.	Limited or no site management tools
Commercial web editor and site management software	Adobe Dreamweaver; Microsoft Visual Studio 2013 with 'Blend'	A small to large website. Templates and wizards assist in page development. Can edit the HTML if required. Changes to pages or links can be automatically updated. Usually support 'drag and drop' for content.	The software will usually create some of its own files and folders to administer the site and track changes. Software can interfere with the code used to create the pages.

Unit 12.3 Activity 1B: Web software

1. Investigate HTML editors that are available in 'free' versions. Choose two examples that you would consider using and give reasons why you have chosen them.
2. Investigate site management software that allows development on the World Wide Web.

An HTML web page

An **HTML page** is a 'text' file with tags and content. A browser will recognise and open a file with a .htm or .html file extension.

The first opening tag, <html>, tells the browser that the document is created in HTML. The final tag, </html>, closes the opening tag and tells the browser it is the end of the page.

A simple web page written using HTML

The image on the left shows a notepad file, myPage.htm, with the HTML tags including a <p> tag containing a line of text. Below is the file itself. The file has been saved with the extension .htm, which means it can now be recognised by the browser and displayed. The right side of the image shows the page in Internet Explorer.

Unit 12.3 Activity 1C: Using HTML

Recreate the example in the figure above by doing the following:

1. Open Notepad.
2. Enter the text as shown in the example.
3. Save the file. The default is to save it as a text file.
4. Change the name of the file so that the extension is .htm.
5. Double-click on the file with the extension .htm. The file will be displayed in a browser.

About tags

A **tag** is a marker in HTML that is interpreted by the browser as a formatting command. The tag is enclosed between a 'less than' and a 'greater than' sign: <tag>.

Usually tags are made up of lower-case letters, although browsers will recognise upper-case letters.

A tag, once opened, also needs to be closed, indicated by a forward slash after the 'less than' sign (eg <tag> </tag>).

There are some exceptions, such as the 'break' tag, <br>. The <br> tag is equivalent to holding **Shift** and pressing **Return** in a word processor and moves the content to the immediate line below, whereas a paragraph tag leaves space between the lines.

A browser would render the first <p> tag below as a single line of text. The next <p> tag is a paragraph tag, followed by a second line of text, with the <br> tag placing the third line of text immediately below the second line.

A paragraph tag defines a block of text as a paragraph. It is in the form:

<p>This is the paragraph text.</p>

The paragraph tag adds space before and after the paragraph text.

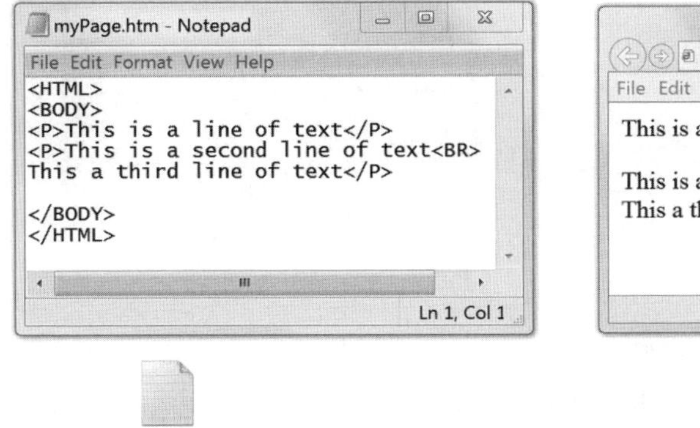

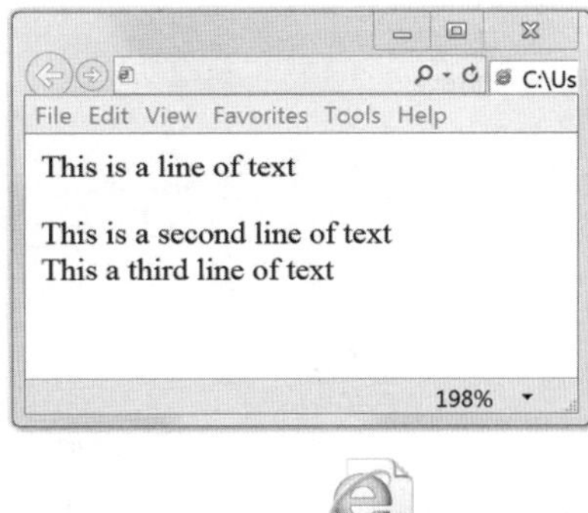

Using the paragraph and break tags

The image above shows the earlier page with the new HTML code added and then saved to the HTML file and displayed in the browser. The browser was refreshed to display the update.

Unit 12.3 Activity 1D: HTML

1. Edit the previous example to replicate the example shown above. Save the page and test it in the browser.
2. The World Wide Web consortium at http://www.w3.org/TR/html5/ documents the HTML5 specifications. Read the specification and its information.
   a. Who do the editors of the specifications represent?
   b. What do you think of the amount of detail?
   c. What can you find out about the 'p' element, that is, the <p> tag?

Examples of tags

The World Wide Web consortium sets out the specifications for tags that can be used in HTML.

Headings

HTML has six pre-defined heading styles for text in HTML. Heading sizes five and six are relatively small and difficult to read. In most documents, only two heading styles are usually needed.

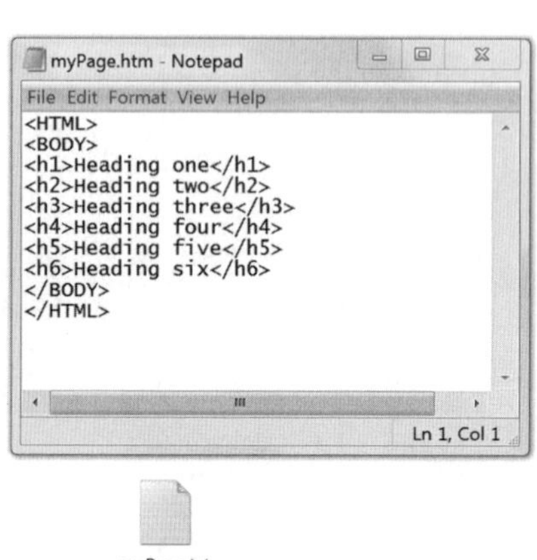

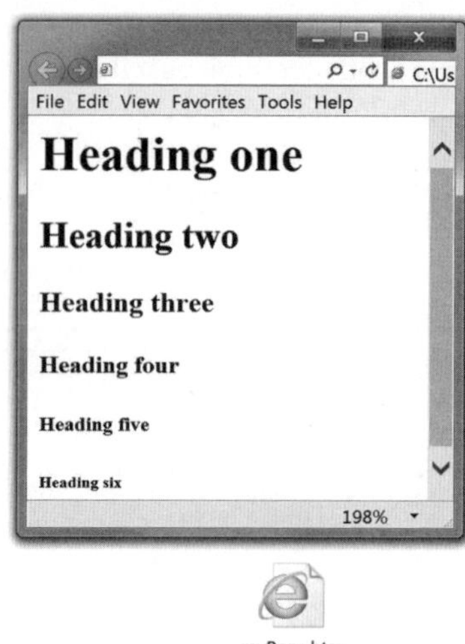

Headings and their tags in HTML

The image shows the HTML code and how the heading styles are rendered in the browser. There is no information in the HTML about font type, font size or font style. The browser is programmed to render the tags in that manner.

Unit 12.3 Activity 1E: HTML headings

Recreate the example in the figure shown above.

Page properties

The figure below shows how in Dreamweaver the **Page Properties** can set the size and colour of the heading styles for a page and override the default browser settings.

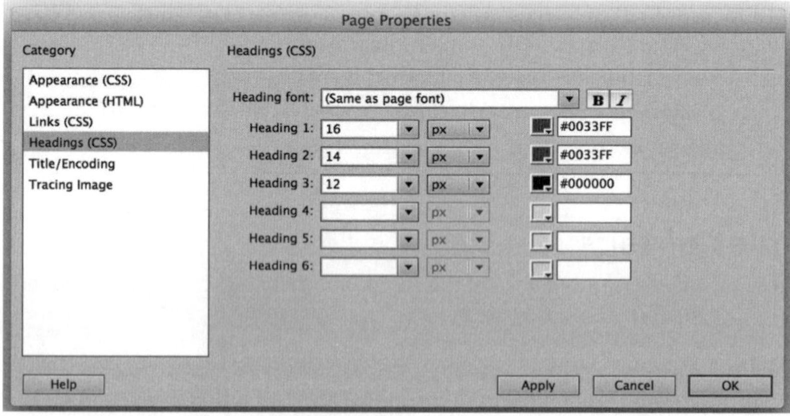

Heading specifications in Dreamweaver

Lists

Lists provide a way to organise information and reduce the number of words.

Using dot points (unordered list)

Each text item appears as a dot point in a list indented from the current text margin. A dot point list of links can be used for a large number of links under a sub-heading. The figure shows how an unordered list would appear.

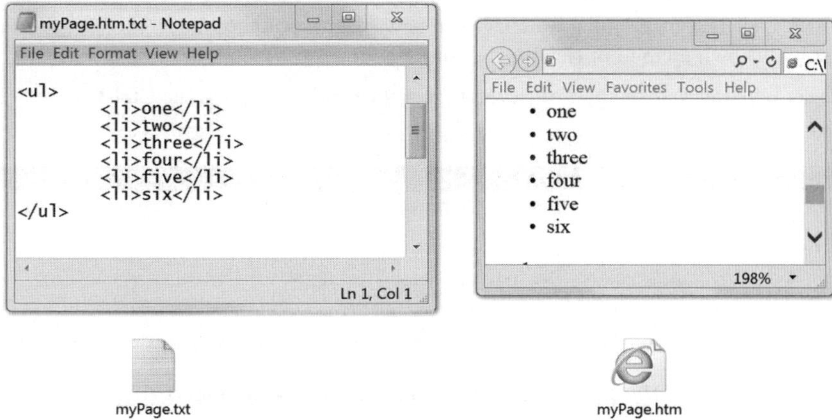

Unordered list

Using a numbered list (ordered list)

Each text item appears as an automatically numbered point in a list indented from the margin. The HTML tags are identical except for the letter 'o' in the opening and closing tag. The figure shows how an ordered list would appear.

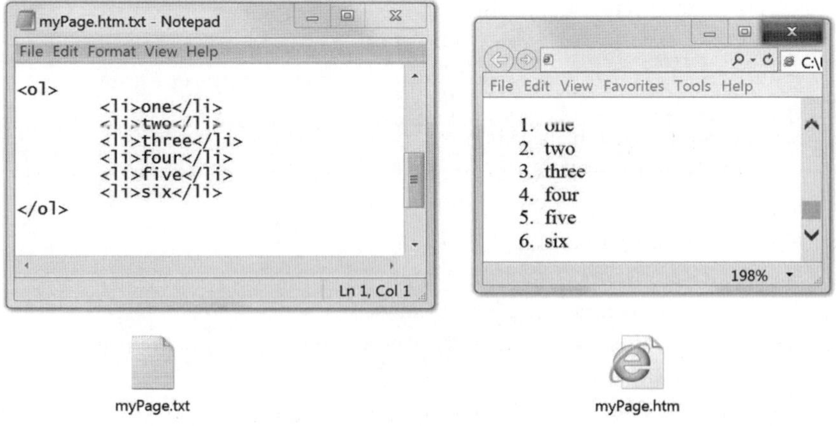

Ordered list

Unit 12.3 Activity 1F: Lists in HTML

1. Create a web page using HTML and include the 'unordered' list. Save the page and test in the browser.
2. In the same file, alter the opening and closing <ul> tags to make it an ordered list. Save the page and test in the browser.

View HTML source

The HTML code that makes up a web page can be viewed as source code by the browser. Each browser has its own method of viewing the source code.

In Internet Explorer, one method of viewing the source code is to press the **Ctrl-U** keys together.

```
http://www.pngfacts.com/ - Original Source
File  Edit  Format
<!DOCTYPE html>
<html>
<head>
<title>Papua New Guinea Facts - PNG News</title>
<meta name='description' content='Home of PNG News. Bringing all the latest Papua New Guinea News online' />
<meta name='keywords' content='PNG News, Papua New Guinea News,' />
<meta property='og:site_name' content='Papua New Guinea Facts' />
<meta property='og:title' content='PNG News' />
<meta property='og:description' content='Home of PNG News. Bringing all the latest Papua New Guinea News online' />
```

Part of the source code for the site http://www.pngfacts.com/

Unit 12.3 Activity 1G: Source code

1. Open a web page in a browser and display the source code.
2. Create a page with the HTML code below.

```
<!DOCTYPE html>
<html lang="en">
<head>
</head>
<body>
<p>
This is a line of text
</p>
</body>
</html>
```

   a. Save the file as mysamplepage.htm.
   b. Open the file in your browser to test. Does the browser recognise the file as a web page and display the text?
   c. Open the file in Microsoft Word.
   d. Save the file as mysamplewordpage.htm.
   e. Open mysamplewordpage.htm in the browser.
   f. Are there any differences in the browser display of mysamplepage.htm and mysamplewordpage.htm?
   g. In the browser, view the source of the mysamplewordpage.htm to reveal the HTML.
   h. Are there differences in the pages?

Files for page, presentation and interactivity

HTML can use other files that contribute to how the page looks and also alter the level of interactivity. Shown below are some of the file types that may be used to present the page and content.

File extension	File type	How to use
htm or html	HTML (text file)	Browser composes page according to HTML tags and text in the document.
css	Cascading Style Sheet (text file)	Gives the browser additional information about the page presentation. Used for layout (grid structure) and formatting of text (font size and colour) and how other content appears.
js	JavaScript (text file)	Adds interactivity to page with scripting, Examples of use include 'plug-in' detection (eg is Flash installed on the computer?), client-side validation (eg initial testing of the validity of an email address added to a form, such as does it contain an '@' symbol?).

File types that can be used in an HTML file

The links to these files are commonly in the <head> tag of the page.

A style is a rule about how to format a particular piece of HTML. A Cascading Style Sheet (CSS) is a set of rule styles that can be used to format HTML. The style is a similar concept to the style that is used in Microsoft Word. Using a CSS defines many of the formatting tasks and provides consistency throughout a set of web pages.

Content file formats

Some types of content are supported by all browsers. The following file types for images are used by all browsers:

File extension	File type	How to use
jpg or jpeg	Image compressed file format (Joint Photographics Expert Group)	Images, usually photographs.
gif	Restricted colours; can be animated (Graphic Interchange Format)	Images, usually flat colour, such as cartoons, logos. Can be interlaced; shows progressive loading.
png	Image file (Portable Network Graphics)	Recognised by most browsers. Can show progressive loading; allows images to have transparent background.

Image file types that can be used in an HTML file

Plug-in

A **plug-in** is a piece of software that is an add-on to a browser. The plug-in gives extra functions to the browser and it allows the browser to display different types of content. The plug-in is usually downloaded from the Internet and installed in the browser.

The following types of content require a plug-in for the browser to support them:

swf/flv	Small web format (Flash content such as movie)
mov	QuickTime (audio, movie)
ram	RealAudio (audio, movie)
pdf	Portable document format

Content types that require a plug-in

A web page that is created with content that requires a plug-in usually applies a test to see if the plug-in is installed so the content can be viewed. If it is not installed, it directs the user to a site where the plug-in can be obtained.

How does a browser work?

A **browser** has to read the HTML code and work out how to display the content. All browsers treat the main tags in a similar manner.

There are many different types of browser engines that are used by the browser. These engines include WebKit (used by Safari), Blink (Chrome), Opera and Trident (Internet Explorer). Each of these has possible variations in the manner in which it may render or display a page.

Browsers are also used to render **Epub** books and by some email clients. Epub is a file extension for an open publication e-book standard (ie for publishing electronic books).

Most browser providers, however, express support for open web standards and WWC3 standards.

The site 'How browsers work' provides a detailed examination of the processes a browser must use to render a page. The URL of the site is:

http://www.html5rocks.com/en/tutorials/internals/howbrowserswork/

What happens if there are mistakes in the HTML?

It is easy for a page to be created that contains errors in the HTML. A browser always attempts to render the page. However, if the HTML is unclear, browsers will have to make some assumptions about what was intended.

In some cases the page will render satisfactorily. However, not all browsers work the same, and a page that is satisfactory in one browser may not work in a different browser. All pages and sites should be checked using validation tools to ensure the HTML does not contain syntax errors.

A syntax error is an error in the language of the HTML. Examples are not using a closing tag, not including a compulsory tag (such as <body>), or closing a tag incorrectly.

HTML5

The specifications of HTML have developed over a number of years. There are many derivations and versions of HTML, including XHTML. At the time of writing, HTML5 was the current version.

Versions of HTML prior to HTML5 required a very detailed 'Document Type' tag to specify the language version in which the page was created. This was to assist the browser in rendering the page.

HTML5 attempted to simplify the creation of pages and it greatly simplified the document type tag. It also introduced new tags to develop and enhance web pages.

Some tags were introduced after investigation of many pages on the web and examination of the patterns used by web developers. For example, a tag such as 'nav' for navigation, and 'footer' for 'footer' elements, was reflected in common usage.

The tag <b>, used by developers for 'bolding', has been replaced in the specification by the <strong> tag. <b> is still a valid tag but its specification for use has altered.

When a tag is no longer in the specification it is said to be 'deprecated' (ie existing browsers may support the tag but the WWC3 recommends that the tag no longer be used and its specifications will no longer be developed).

The 'font' tag is an example of a tag that can appear when a document is saved from some software that was deprecated in the move to the earlier HTML 4.0.

Some new tags for HTML5

HTML5 was released in 2011. It introduced many new tags to enhance the web. These included geolocation, which allows real-time geographic location of a device. Others were web storage and web workers.

The Canvas element enables a greater variety of graphics options. The Video element supports two formats natively (ie without the use of plug-ins: 'ogg' and 'mp4'). The Audio element supports three formats natively: 'mp3', 'wav' and 'ogg'.

Video and audio are two areas on the web where there are competing technologies. Their support in the browser and the various operating systems can be crucial to owner of the technology. **Flash**, for example, was an important plug-in providing content, particularly animation and media, on web pages. Most recently it became a container for delivery of video through the '.flv' file format. However, it fell out of favour and is being replaced by a combination of HTML5, CSS3 and JavaScript, using native web technologies without a proprietary format that requires a plug-in.

The figure below shows an example of a message that is displayed if a JavaScript script on a page detects that the plug-in required to play a video is not installed.

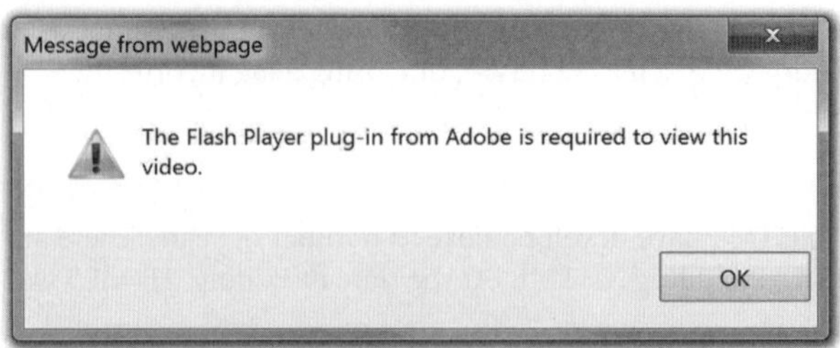

Message if the Flash plug-in is not installed

Main components of a web page

A **web page** is usually not just one single HTML file; it can also link to other files that are used by the browser to render the content.

The main components can be:

- HTML – mark-up language that the browser uses to render a page (.htm or .html).
- CSS – style specifications for layout and presentation of a page (.css).
- JavaScript – scripting language that interacts with HTML and can be 'client' side; that is, it performs within the browser on the computer where the page is rendered (.js).
- Images – image files that are displayed to enhance a page's content (.jpg, .gif, .png).
- Media – various file formats including .mp4, .flv, .wav, .ogg.

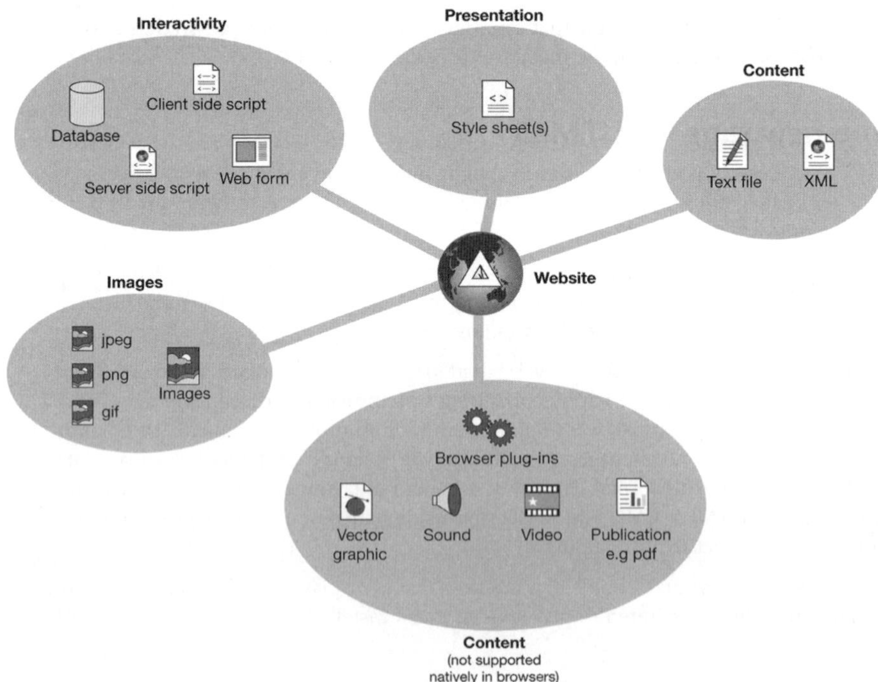

Main components of a web page

Creating a website

What is a website?

A **website** is made up of files (such as .html and image files) that are arranged in folders on a storage medium. The top folder usually contains the homepage for the site. When a browser makes a request for a page to be viewed, the page is returned to the browser together with the text, images and other content from its location within the website.

Websites are of many different types. Some examples are:

- 'Static' HTML sites with a few pages. These can be created on a personal computer and files transferred to a web server for delivery.
- Those produced in the 'cloud' using web publishing platforms, often by individuals such as bloggers.
- Large-scale commercial sites, usually utilising considerable 'server side' technology. These require back-end programming on the web server, where content is delivered dynamically on request.
- **Content Management Systems (CMS)**, where content is stored in databases. Data is delivered by a database query through search requests to a database and the information is returned dynamically to the user.

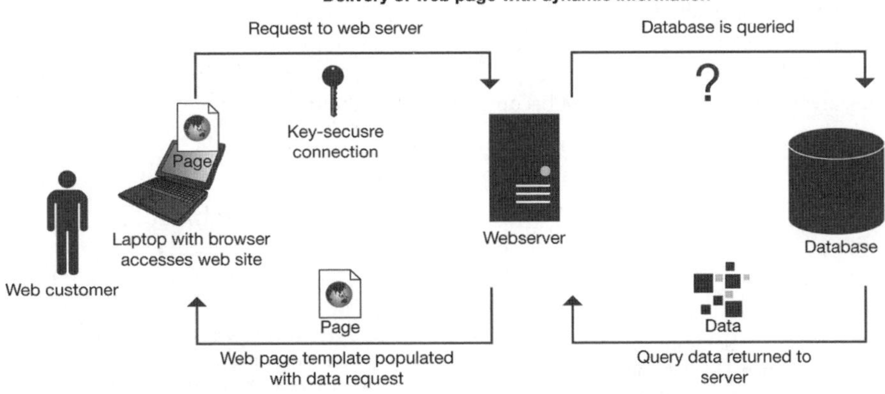

Delivering data dynamically through a website

When a page has been produced using this back end server side database technology the URL will not have the suffix '.htm' but something such as '.aspx', 'php', 'cfm'. This will indicate the environment used.

URL suffix	Name	Vendor	Comment
.aspx	Active Server Pages	Microsoft	Microsoft Access Database
.php	Hypertext Preprocessor	Open source	Usually open source databases such as SQL
.cfm	Cold Fusion	Adobe	Variety of databases

URL suffixes used for dynamic sites

Large-scale sites that would use technology such as the above require teams of specialists to enable the website to be created and, most importantly, maintained.

Skill sets for a large commercial website

The development and maintenance of a commercial website is a complex process and requires many different skills. Some of the specialist roles and skills required to produce a large site include:

- Web administrator.
- Project manager.
- Content editor and manager.
- Programmer.
- Site architect.
- Graphic designer.
- Usability expert.
- Database engineers.
- Technicians.
- Network and security managers.
- Marketing and advertising specialists.
- E-commerce specialists.

In this context, teams are established to take responsibility for such a site. The 'back-end' of the site would be created to enable levels of permissions and passwords for content creation in specific areas to be administered and become the responsibility of others.

Unit 12.5 contains more information about roles in the ICT industry.

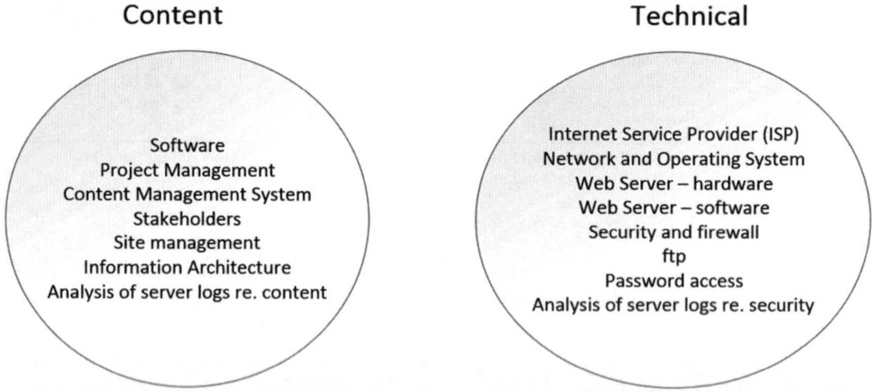

Developing a commercial website is a complex process

The figure above illustrates the difference in focus and in the areas that are dealt with at a content level compared with the technical aspects of a website.

Resources for creating websites

The Internet has many resources for web development. Careful consideration must be given to the source of the content to make sure it is useful. It takes time to develop an understanding of worthy sources of commentary, tutorials and tips.

The University of Minnesota Duluth has a Web Design References section that is a portal to a vast pool of resources with its large compendium of links through the work of its maintainer, Laura Carlson.

Creating a website using wizard or templates

A **wizard** is a tool for building a website. Many organisations and Internet Service Providers have a wizard that can allow anyone to build a website. A wizard takes the user through a number of pre-defined steps to design the site. The user has some choices to make in terms of the look and feel of the design. However, the user is restricted to the templates and themes provided by the vendor.

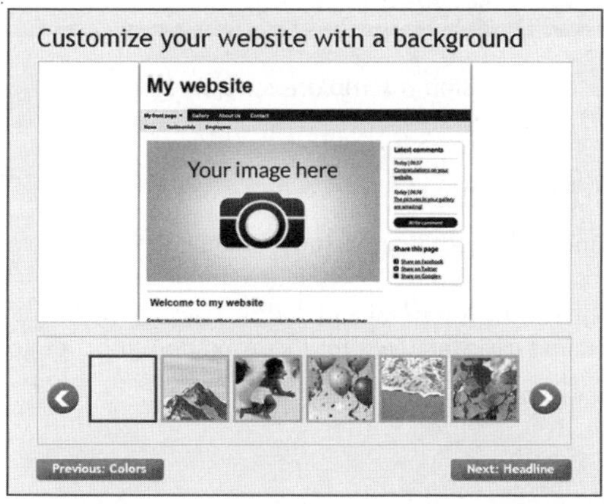

Using an online wizard to design a website

Templating is the common way for any website to be produced. A **template** is a sample document or page that has many of the details of the page already set up, including the layout, menu structure and font selection. A template provides a consistent look and feel to the pages as they are developed. The template is the starting point for each page on the site and new content is added to the template to create the page.

The underlying HTML, CSS and JavaScript used to build the page are developed and then used to create the template. Most pages use some form of a grid (similar to the desktop publishing model). Using a grid involves decisions about how CSS and HTML will create the page.

Most web publishing software provides ready-to-use templates. However, it is not always easy to modify or adjust these templates without a reasonable knowledge of HTML and CSS.

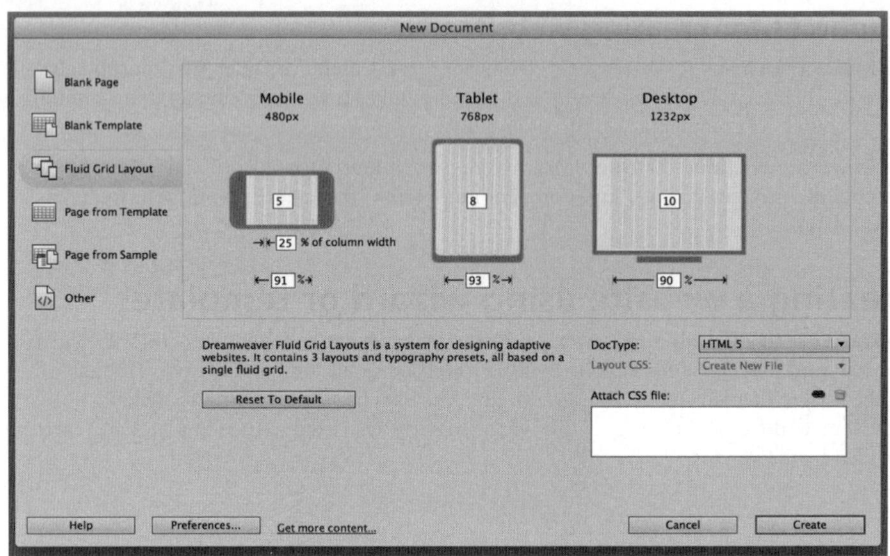

Using a template for a website

Frameworks and libraries

In the last two years frameworks and libraries have become very popular to aid the process of creating and styling websites. These often open-source frameworks and libraries are now very robust, being continually developed, tested and coded to accommodate browsers and devices. The code can be selected and easily adapted for incorporation into a project.

Some examples of frameworks are:

- Twitter Bootstrap.
- 960 Grid.
- Fluid 960 Grid.

A **web framework** is a software framework designed to simplify web development. Typically, frameworks provide libraries for accessing a database, managing sessions and cookies, and creating templates to display HTML and promote the reuse of code. Essentially, a framework is a set of tools.

Frameworks provide the basic HTML with predetermined names for elements and predetermined settings when they are used. A framework will have some underlying 'grid' structure. A framework can simplify the procedure for creating a site while providing scope for customisation.

Frameworks do provide 'drag and drop' of components to build the page by arranging those components.

Frameworks usually provide the HTML for an underlying grid by which a page can be built. The Bootstrap 'fluid' page has an underlying 12-section set up; the columns for a section will add up to 12 depending on the combination.

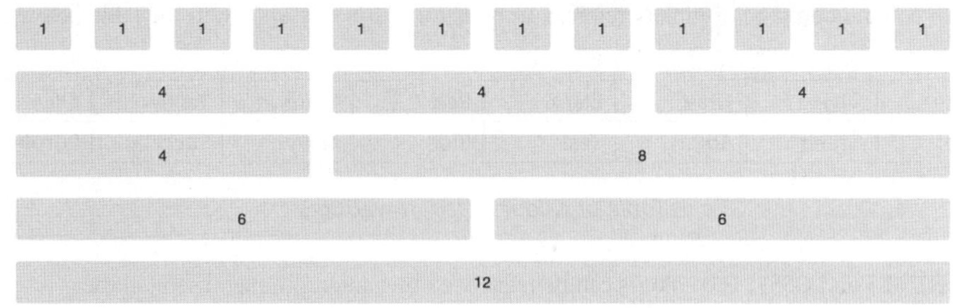

A grid for a web page in Bootstrap

However, any framework involves compromise among the alternative methods that could be used to create a site. There is also the prospect for the framework to be further developed in the light of developments in the web.

The various templates provided by frameworks can allow very quick prototyping of a page. However, some knowledge of HTML and CSS is required to make changes to the design and layout of a page.

Units of measure

Text

Different templates apply different units of measurement to various elements.

The font size of any text element in a browser can be set in a style sheet using a variety of measures. The most common are:

- Pixel.
- Em.
- Percentage.

The following may be used, but are not widely used:

- Pica.
- Inch.
- Point.
- Ex.
- Millimetre.
- Centimetre.

Color

Colours can be referred to in HTML in a variety of ways. There is continuing development in this area. When referring to colour in html note the need to use the American spelling of the word: 'color'.

Early in the development of the web Netscape determined the 216 'web-safe colors' that would look the same on all monitors used at that time and be appropriate for different operating systems.

Sixteen colours could be originally referred to by name. These are shown in the table below.

White	Silver	Gray	Black	Red	Maroon	Yellow	Olive
Lime	Green	Aqua	Teal	Blue	Navy	Fuchsia	Purple

Table of colours used in websites

With HTML5 and CSS3, 140 colours can be referenced by name. Although useful in the development of a site, it is not usual to reference a colour by name in HTML.

Colours can also be referred to by:

Form	HTML reference	Color
Hexadecimal (hex)	#FFFFFF or #FFF	white
RGB	rgb(255,255,255)	white
HSL	hsl(-,0%,100%)	white

Colours in websites

The quality of monitors and screen displays has improved dramatically since Netscape determined the 12 'safe colors' and there are now over 16 million colours at the web developer's disposal. Most current monitors can display at least 16,384 colours.

Shown in the figure below is the option for selecting the colour of the background for a page in Dreamweaver.

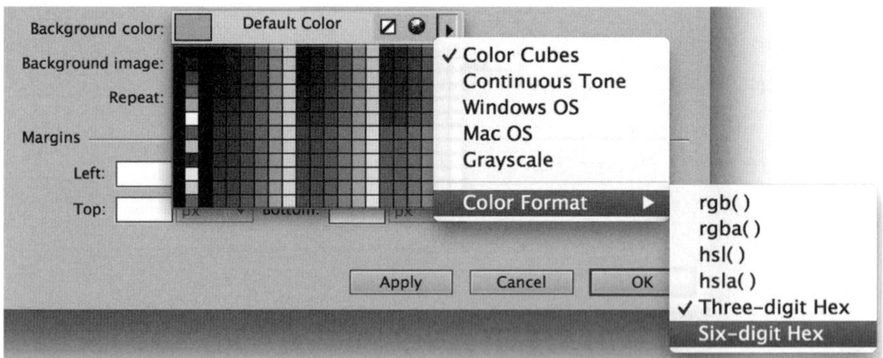

Selecting colours in Dreamweaver

Colour and design

The design element of colour and contrast on a web page is as important as the actual colour and its shade. For example, the use of the following colours may be suggestive to the user.

Color	Meaning and use
Blue	Dark blue is a strong and conservative colour. It indicates stability and is popular with financial institutions. It has a high contrast with a white background.
Red	Some reds indicate warning, danger and fire. A dark red shows strength and is a noble colour. Red for the Chinese symbolises joy and fortune and is very popular.
Green	Dark green is a calm colour, environmental and a reminder of nature. Very light greens, however, are indicative of jealousy.

Using colours on a web page

Unit 12.3 Activity 1H: Colour analysis

Fill in the table for the following colours using the above analysis as a guide.

Colour	Meaning and use
Yellow	
Black	
Grey	
Brown	

Colour wheels

Colour wheels can be used to see how different colours complement and interact with each other. A colour wheel is a visual representation of colours arranged according to their chromatic relationship. Complementary colours are placed next to each other, while contrasting colours are placed opposite each other.

Page background and foreground colour settings should be selected with care to ensure ease of readability. White space, as in the printed world, is an essential element of readability.

Responsive web design

This is an approach to creating content for the web in which fluid grids and media queries are managed by style sheets that can enable easier viewing of the content regardless of the screen display size of the monitor or device. For example, when a device accesses a web page, the design adjusts so that it is suitable for that particular device.

Unit 12.3 Activity 1I: Responsive web design

1. Go to the website http://blog.teamtreehouse.com/beginners-guide-to-responsive-web-design. Vary the size of the window that displays the site by making it narrower and then wider.
2. What happens to the page as you vary the window size?

Libraries

The term **library** when used in relation to a website can refer to:

- A collection of common items used in a particular website that is organised into a 'library' for easy access while building the website (eg graphic icons such as a 'shopping cart').
- A collection of code that has been developed by third parties but used in the website. A very popular JavaScript library is jQuery. JQuery also provides for third party add-ons to the base library.

Preliminary steps to creating a website

A number of steps must be completed before creating a website.

Page editing and site management programs

Applications such as Microsoft Visual Studio and Adobe Dreamweaver can be used to create and manage sites. This includes creating web pages, managing content, and creating and maintaining links.

The choices of menus, windows and settings can be overwhelming for the first-time user. It takes time to organise the screen and workspaces available. The interface of these software applications is complex, with a mixture of menus, windows and different icons.

Dreamweaver has a number of tools displayed as windows that include:

- An editor window that creates pages, and allows a code view, a design view and a split view that shows both the code and design views. The code view shows the HTML for the page. The design view shows the page as it will appear in the browser.
- A properties window that shows the attributes of content items when placed on a page or when selected on a page.
- A site files window that shows the relationship of files in the site.
- A snippets window that is used for storing items of HTML, CSS, JavaScript and other code that is used on a regular basis to fine tune the working of the site.
- An asset window that manages the content items, including: URLs, colours, images, scripts and templates for the site.
- A library window that stores items that will be used on more than one page, such as navigation items and nested navigation menus.

The administrator of a site can set it up with a page template that has both **editable** and **non-editable** regions. An editable region allows content to be added and managed. This does not usually include navigation links. A non-editable region contains site navigation links and other HTML that is not directly related to the content on the page. The non-editable regions can be applied to one or many pages; the editable region is specific to just one page. Typically the non-editable region is part of the site template. Usually the navigation items remain the same for the site or a group of pages.

If changes are made to the navigation or the names of page links, then those changes are written through to all pages based on the template by altering the non-editable region.

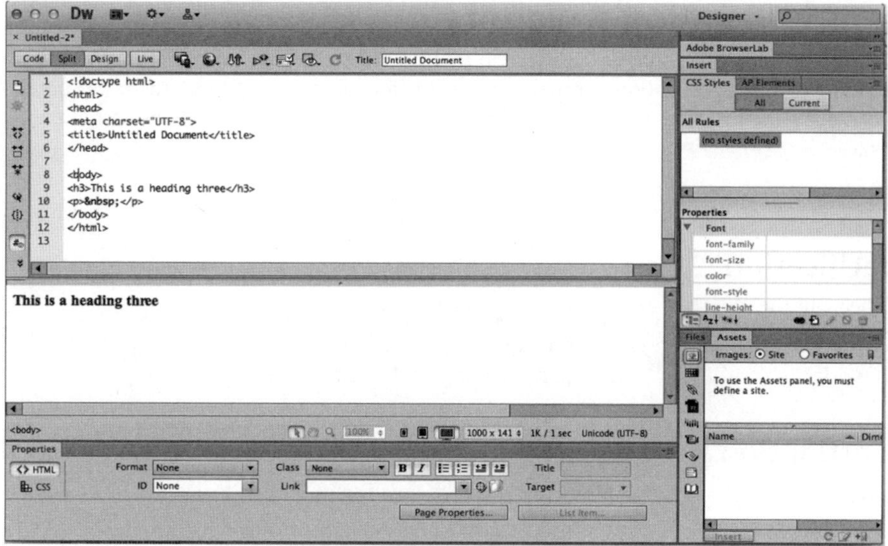

A Dreamweaver window

What can a site management tool do?

Site management software tools can show a site arranged as a collection of folders and files; that is, show a site map. A site map can only be seen after pages and folders have been created.

A site map should be prepared before embarking on creating the site with web software. This enables the site to develop in an organised and logical manner.

Site architecture

Sketching site architecture with pen and paper is a good way to start a site. This brings together the goals of the site, the content, and how that content is to be linked together and displayed.

A template for the relationship between the various items of content is established. It will also show how the files and folders that contain the content will to be managed.

If site management is to be carried out by more than one person, then consistency in approach and clear guidelines are needed to manage the site effectively.

Site management tools provide for:

- Viewing and organising a series of pages with appropriate links to other pages.
- Checking that URLs are correct and valid.
- Adjusting URLs so that if pages are moved within a site, the URLs are updated to reflect the change.
- Validation of the syntax used to code the HTML.

Steps in creating a website

A website comprises files that are arranged in folders. The homepage for the site is stored within one of the folders. When a browser makes a request for a page to be viewed, the page content is returned to the browser. The images and content come from various locations within the website.

Creating a website requires the following steps:

Specification

This sets out the nature of the project to be undertaken.

To create a website for an organisation requires many decisions to be made prior to undertaking the task. It is a very similar process to designing an information system as discussed in Unit 12.1.

Investigation

- What are the goals of the website? What is the organisation trying to achieve by creating a website?
- What are the expected results from designing this website? What will be delivered? It might be increased revenue, better communication or providing up-to-date information more quickly.
- Who is the audience of the site and what are their goals?
- Is there a website design brief to follow?
- What will be the scope of the project?
- What resources and budget are available pre-site and post-site?
- What is the timeline for the site and how will it be evaluated?
- What technology is available for use? Is that technology suitable for the task?

Drafts or prototype

A variety of tools can be used in site development. Some are related to design, others to site construction.

Where a site is being created by a team of people they assist in clarification and communication in the group. This stage should involve a schema and site architecture that reflects the goals of the organisation.

A prototype can help key users evaluate the site design.

Tools for developing a site design

The tools that can be used include:

- **Site map**.
- Content list.
- Wire frame.
- File table.
- Timeline.

- Annotated layout diagrams.
- Style guide.

Examples of each of the following tools are shown below. The examples relate to a proposed school site (with the generic name of My School) that has a homepage and five other pages. It has the scope to expand the site over time.

Tool	Description	Possible tool or software to use	Software professionals may use
Site map	A diagram like a concept map showing pages in the site and their relationship to each other. It is a hierarchal diagram. The main content of the page and name of the page on the map could be used for the <title> tag in the browser.	Pen and paper, Inspiration	Inspiration, Visio
Content list	The content that is essential to the website needs to be listed to ensure it is adapted from existing content or created to suit the site.	Excel, table in Word	Excel, database software
Wire frame	A simple line drawing showing the design elements of key pages of the site. It is a quick, simple representation of the key page layout design. Most pages have a title, header, navigation areas, content and footer. The templates could be developed using these as a basis.	Pen and paper	Photoshop, Visio
File table	From the site map (above), files, file names and content are listed in a table. It should help to organise the files, folders and directories. Folders within a website will group together similar items of content. They will be located in their folders in a similar structure to the hierarchy. Conventions for naming of files and folders should be determined. The homepage file name convention is 'index.htm' or 'index.html'.	Excel, table in Word	Excel, database software

(*continues*)

Tool	Description	Possible tool or software to use	Software professionals may use
Folder structure	Diagram of how the folders within the website will be named and arranged to manage the files	Pen and paper, screen dump of dummy files and folders	-
Timeline	Chart of tasks and responsibilities according to key dates. A Gantt chart shows a timeline of the tasks and their duration for a 'project'.	Timeliner, Excel	Microsoft Project, Visio
Annotated layout diagrams	This shows the templates for key pages in the site, annotated with details about content. The relative size of headings, menu items and body text can be shown with position of other elements such as images. Dummy text (lorem ipsum dolor) is often used to represent the body text; it tends not to distract the reader during the design process.	Pen and paper	Photoshop, drawing software
Style guide	Specifications on how content should be formatted and appear. This includes font type, font size, font color and style of headings.	Mock up in browser	Photoshop, browser.

Site map and design tools

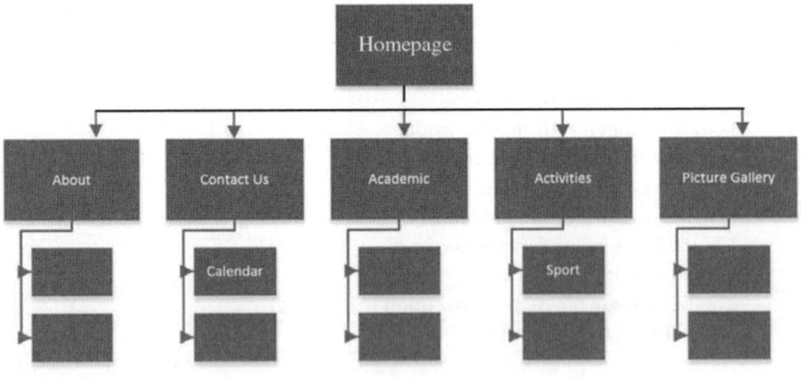

A site map

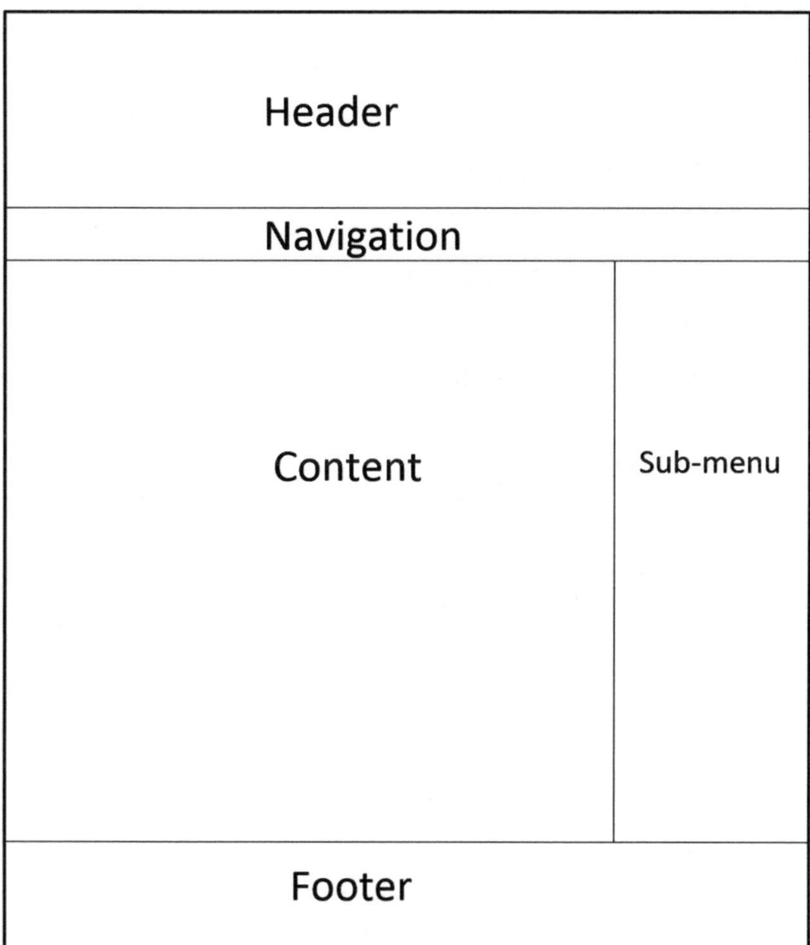

A wire frame

	A	B	C	D	E	F	G
1	File Table for School site						
2	**Page**	**HTML Title tag**	**File name**	**Key images**	**Notes**		
3	Home page	School home page	index.html	school.jpg	School photo and navigation to site		
4	About	School > About Us	about.html	principal.jpg	General information about the school		
5	Contact Us	School > Contact Us	contact.html	staff.jpg	Phone, fax and email, maps - local and school		
6	Academic	School > Academic	academic.html	grade12.jpg	List of subjects		
7	Activities	School > Activities	activities.html	rugby1.jpg	List of activities		
8	Picture gallery	School > Picture Gallery	picturegallery.html		Gallery of recent events		
9							
10							

A file table

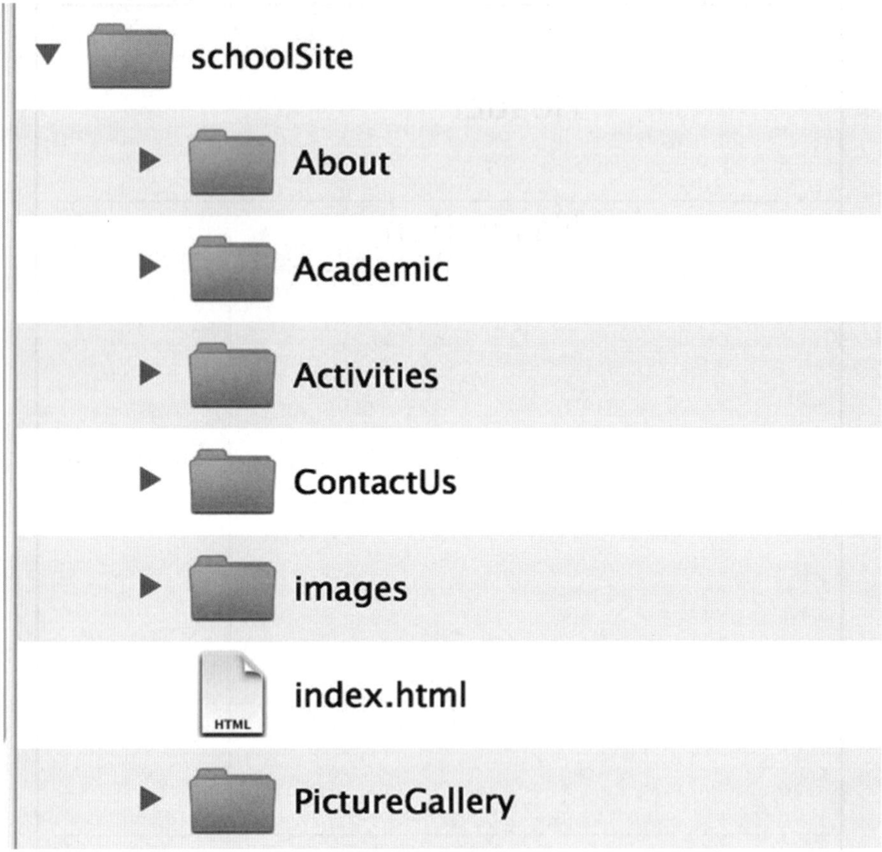

- schoolSite
  - About
  - Academic
  - Activities
  - ContactUs
  - images
  - index.html
  - PictureGallery

Folder structure of a site

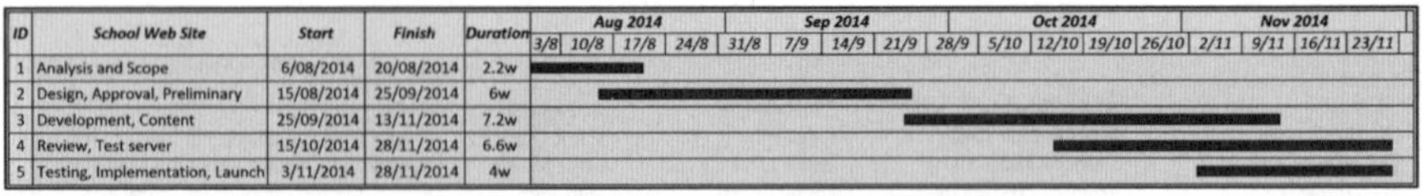

ID	School Web Site	Start	Finish	Duration	Aug 2014				Sep 2014				Oct 2014					Nov 2014			
					3/8	10/8	17/8	24/8	31/8	7/9	14/9	21/9	28/9	5/10	12/10	19/10	26/10	2/11	9/11	16/11	23/11
1	Analysis and Scope	6/08/2014	20/08/2014	2.2w																	
2	Design, Approval, Preliminary	15/08/2014	25/09/2014	6w																	
3	Development, Content	25/09/2014	13/11/2014	7.2w																	
4	Review, Test server	15/10/2014	28/11/2014	6.6w																	
5	Testing, Implementation, Launch	3/11/2014	28/11/2014	4w																	

A timeline for a site

The annotated layout in the figure shown is ready to be marked up with specifications to show how it should be created.

A style guide is used in mainly large sites where there are many people creating content. It enables a consistency in the appearance of a site.

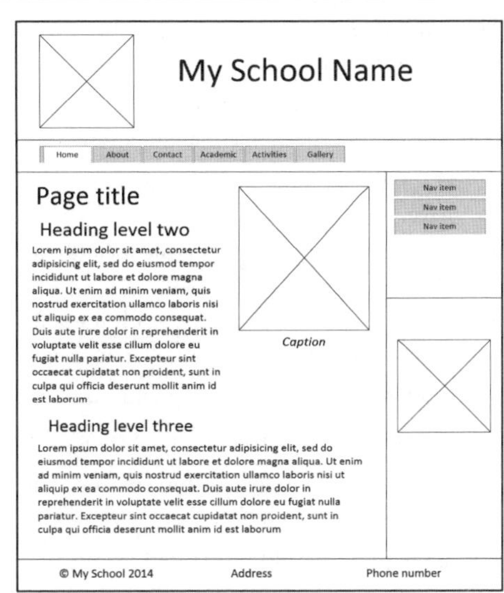

Annotated layout of a web page

Producing the site

Once the site has been planned and designed, to become a website it needs to become a series of folders and files in a directory on a computer drive. This task should be simplified by the decisions regarding the file table and organisation of content.

First, the designer must create a folder to hold the site.

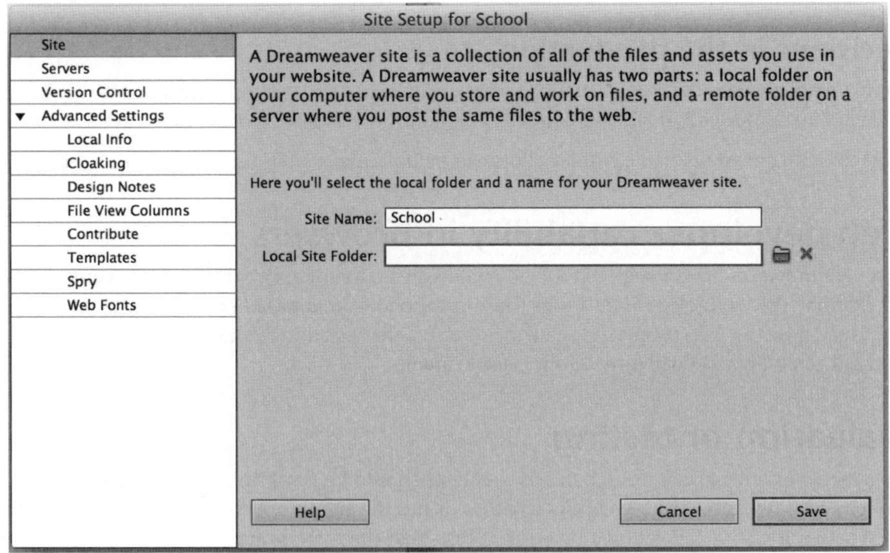

Defining a site

Then the site is created by locating the site folder using site management software. This could be done using Dreamweaver.

At this stage a check should ensure how the site management tool references the links to the homepage and other pages. There are two main types of referencing:

- Absolute. All links map the file location of the page according to its location on the hard drive.
- Relative. All links map the file location according to their relationship to the other pages or files in that site.

Relative is the preferred manner of linking for most sites. If the site is moved to another computer, directory or web server, then the links within the site will still work.

Most web server hosts will map and point to index.htm as being the homepage for a site.

Now create the homepage, in most sites called index.htm or index.html.

Next, create other folders within the site. The folder structure and its nesting of folders should reflect the site hierarchy.

A **master page** should be created for use as a template. (Note that it is possible to create a template with links to pages even though those pages have not yet been created.) Dreamweaver enables regions on a page to be nominated as 'editable' or 'non-editable'.

When a file is first saved as a template in a Dreamweaver site, it automatically creates a **templates** folder and saves the template with a .dwt extension – this is a Dreamweaver extension.

Decisions in the production

There are times when the design that has been created, particularly a pen and paper design, is not able to be produced in HTML. Often some compromise has to be obtained.

There are different ways that a similar effect can be obtained. Often there is no one right way.

Web developer capability in browsers

Most web browsers have a suite of tools to enable dissection of a web page into its components and examine the technology that brings those components to a page. These range from being able to see how the CSS properties of elements affect the visual presentation of the pages to a 'waterfall' showing the 'load' time of the page elements.

Evaluation or testing

Once the website has been created, a series of tests should be performed to minimise the errors that may be in the site. Testing checks whether or not the site has been constructed effectively and whether it can be viewed in a browser. It tests that the hyperlinks, including navigation, are correct and that content, including images, is displayed as expected.

The checks of syntax and links can be performed by software and a report is produced showing the errors.

Check of HTML syntax

This is to check that the HTML used to mark up the page accords with the rules of HTML. For example, that:

- A tag that has been opened has been closed and not left open.
- A tag when opened has been closed with the correct tag.
- A tag used is a valid tag (eg <P1> would be an error); there is no <P1> tag in HTML.
- The HTML mark-up used in the page accords with the document type the page denotes as being applicable.

For example, if the page is identified with the following:

<!DOCTYPE html>

<html lang="en">

<head>

then the page is HTML5, and tags such as <header> and <footer> are valid. In earlier versions of HTML they do not exist.

The W3C has an online validator at http://validator.w3.org/. Dreamweaver refers pages to this W3C validator.

The figure below shows the error generated as a result of attempting to use a <P1> tag. The error message itself is highly technical and does not need to be understood. Most developers would, however, understand that there is, in fact, no <P1> tag.

Line 29, Column 4: **Element p1 not allowed as child of element body in this context. (Suppressing further errors from this subtree.)**

```
<p1>this is a line of text</p1>
```

Content model for element body:
Flow content.

Syntax error

Check of hyperlinks

Hyperlinks that need to be checked include links to:

- URLs.
- Images, sound and video content.
- Files, such as CSS and JavaScript.

Most software has a built-in link checker that will search the URLs in the page and create a list of errors.

There is a variety of reasons why a link will be flagged as invalid. These include:

- The object of the link does not exist, or if it did, it now no longer exists.
- The object of the link does exist, but it is in a different location to that of the link.
- The actual link name does not correspond to the link in the page, often through a spelling or typing error.

It is also possible that a link will be flagged as valid, but there is an error. When a link is created, a user navigates to a large folder of files and, through inadvertence, the wrong file from the list is selected.

Browser preview

Pages should be routinely examined in the browser to see if they appear correctly. More than one browser and more than one operating system should be used. This is more important with templates and pages that are used as the templates for other pages.

- Check that the pages can be shown in a browser through preview.
- Establish that the pages are easy to use and that information can be found.
- Check that the pages and content on the pages meets accessibility tests.

Proliferation of screens and devices

In the United States it has been estimated that there are at least 250 different screen sizes for devices capable of viewing web pages.

A page may display differently depending on:

- The size of the screen on which it is being displayed.
- The resolution of the screen.
- The browser or the browser version used to render the screen.
- The operating system and its version on the device.

It is now regarded as impossible to produce a page that will appear exactly the same on all screens and devices. The general aim is to minimise the variations that may occur and to accept that some variations will occur.

Whilst testing, however, it is useful to display and test:

- The page on the same computer using a different browser.
- The page on a different device.
- The page on a different operating system with a different browser to the development browser.
- The page in different versions of Microsoft Internet Explorer.

Evaluation

After a site is launched, the evaluation process can commence. First, a check must be made to ensure that the site meets its objectives and that it is a suitable medium for communication. This will require a variety of techniques and a number of people to accomplish successfully.

Accessibility

A website design should take into account that a range of people will be viewing it. This can affect their interaction with the site, and, for an organisation, affect the amount of business generated by the site.

Some of these factors are:

- Age – younger people may be better at interacting with the web than older or senior citizens.
- Language skills and types of languages – alternative language versions could be provided where the website is to be used by people of different nationalities.
- Computer and Internet literacy – developers of websites have a different level of computer literacy compared to many users.

- Quality of eyesight – some people may require larger fonts for viewing.
- Culture – people of different culture can react to content in a different manner. For example, the colour red has a different social meaning in context in different societies.
- Gender – a site that has a mostly female clientele may have colours and language that appeals to that audience.

Some governments have mandatory guidelines regarding accessibility. See http://webguide.gov .au/accessibility-usability/accessibility/, for example.

Usability

A study of web usability and how people use websites has developed as an area of research and interest. A wide variety of techniques are used to determine if a website is functional and how people can interact with it to carry out their tasks.

These techniques include:

- Eye tracking – following the path of a user's eyes as he or she views a web page.
- Observing users interacting with a website.
- Asking users to carry out a particular task on a website and seeing how long it takes to complete the task.
- Examining how much time a web page takes to download.

Jacob Neilson has been writing about usability in his 'Alertbox' column since 1995. He has compiled many top-10 lists of mistakes in web design. His column at http://www.nngroup.com/articles/top-10-mistakes-web-design/ has links to other columns of a similar nature.

Some issues for consideration when designing a website

Opening and/or closing a website

Even a relatively small website can contain many files and folders. **Folders** need to be managed, arranged and organised so that administration and maintenance of the files is efficient and effective.

Think carefully about the organisation of the folders.

Display or hide the folder list

Working with a web folder involves working with folders, finding the appropriate folder and navigating around the site. Make sure the navigation paths are clearly understood.

Small site

Images can be placed in one folder or located in a folder next to their associated HTML file. Images used across the site should have a folder in the top directory.

Large site

Images that are used by a number of pages (such as navigation buttons) can be located in a directory near the top of the site for convenience. Images that might only be used once can be located near the HTML file they relate to. Many content folders will have a folder inside called 'images'.

The figure below shows how Dreamweaver will display the file and folder list for the School site.

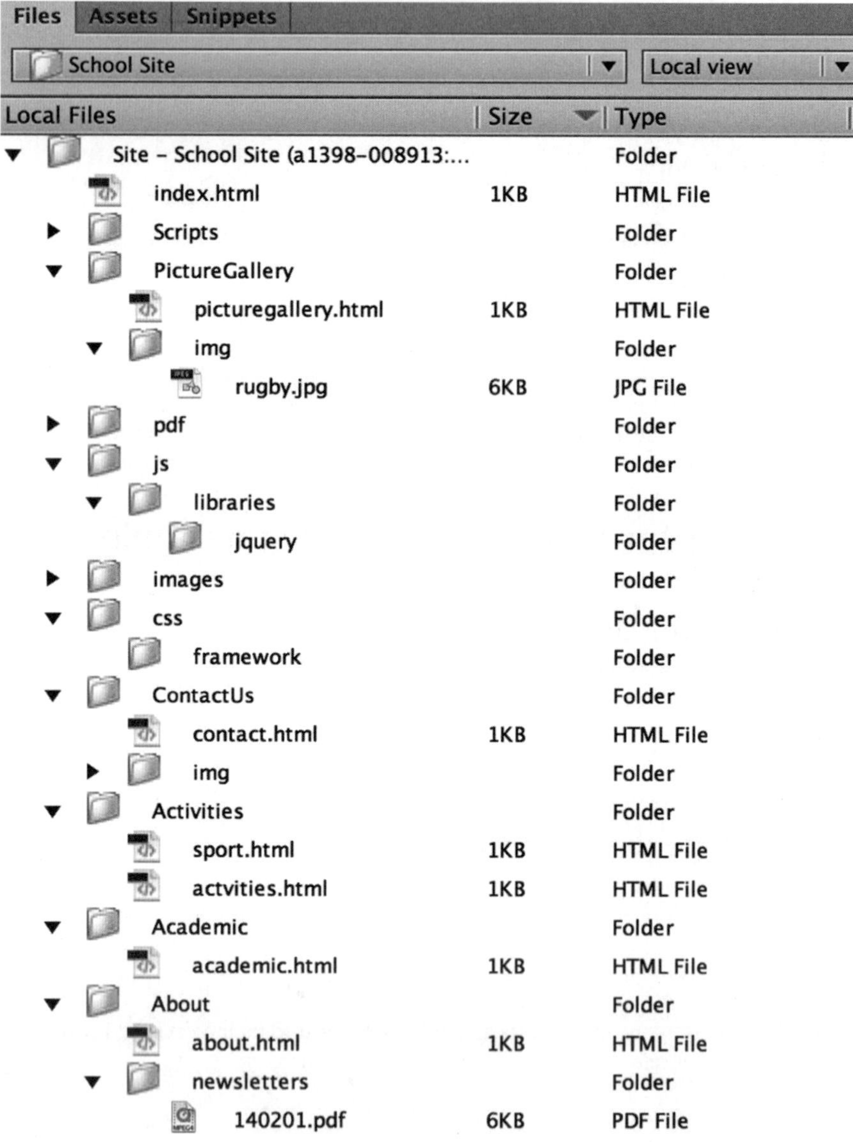

A website's folders

The figure above is the site referred to earlier in the chapter. The site folders and files are being developed as the site is built. It is becoming more complex as folders and files are created.

The main structure of folders reflects the key areas of the site, with some other folders being added to manage the files. If all the files were in one folder it may be difficult to distinguish the area of the site the files belong to.

Site management software, including Dreamweaver, can import existing sites and display the files and folders for easy access to edit.

Creating a folder

Folder naming conventions

Having a standardised approach to file and folder naming has benefits for the organisation and management of a website. This is because:

- Folders and files need to be located, relocated and updated.
- Folder and file names are significant for search engine results.
- Folder and file names are part of web addresses.

A name that provides a clue to the contents helps on a site where many people are involved in its maintenance.

Some useful conventions to consider are:

- Use lower case characters (some web servers are case sensitive).
- Use only characters [a–z], [0–9], hyphen and underscore.
- Do not use spaces (web servers use different ways to encode the space character).

Folder names should resemble the area of the website the pages inside the folder relate to.

Renaming a folder

It is best to map a site and name the folders before creating them to avoid having to rename the folders and files. However, most software tracks the names of files and folders so that if names are changed or folders are moved then references to the files or folders are also changed.

Dreamweaver has a 'hidden' file in each folder where changes are recorded.

Often when creating a new content area, an existing folder is used as the basis for the new content. The existing folder is copied and then moved and renamed.

Moving a file to a folder

A new file can be moved to a folder by saving using **Save As** and then navigating to the folder. The file is then ready to be linked as content.

Files can also be moved by selecting the file, dragging it to another folder and dropping it there.

Note that if the file is in an existing folder and is hyperlinked to provide content, then moving the file would break the hyperlink. However, some the site management tools (such as Dreamweaver) track the file and can remake the link based on its new location.

Deleting a folder

To delete a folder:

- Select the folder using a right-click on the mouse.
- Choose **Delete** from the drop-down list that appears.

A lot of care should be taken when deleting a folder on a site, particularly if the folder has a large number of files. The files may still be used as content.

An interim method is to leave the folder where it is but change its name – for example, prefix the folder name with letter 'x'. This means the hyperlinks are no longer valid but the files could be restored if a hyperlink check of the site reveals broken links.

A folder on a website does not usually represent a large amount of storage; however, deleting a folder is useful for tidying up and housekeeping.

Designing text for a screen

It is difficult to read large amounts of text on a screen. Most people scan a web page before deciding whether they will read the entire page. Usability studies indicate that people scan a screen before reading it. They may then read the content in detail, but not always.

The resolution and quality of screen displays is improving dramatically but it is not as good as high quality, printed text.

Writing text for a screen

The creator of a web page does not know on what device and at what screen size or resolution a page will be viewed. It is prudent to prepare text to be able to accommodate the variations as well as possible.

Screen displays

When writing text to be displayed on screen, use the following guidelines:

- Use short sentences.
- Have a single idea for each sentence.
- Use short paragraphs rather than large blocks of text.
- Use bold for headings – do not use for extended text.
- Use text in italics only occasionally.
- Do not use underlining – this is reserved for hyperlinks.

The use of blank white space around headings, text and graphics helps to make a page easy to read. In most cases, text will word wrap in the browser window.

Formatting text

Text is styled for most websites with Cascading Style Sheets (CSS); see below.

Text colour

The background page colour impacts on text readability. The greater the contrast between the colour of the text and the colour of the background, the greater the readability.

A white background with black text is easiest to read. Black text on a white background is easier to read than white text on a black background. Background colours and text colours should be tested to see if they provide the appropriate design effect as well as ensure readability.

Headings

HTML has six pre-defined heading styles for text. Heading sizes five and six are relatively small and difficult to read. In most documents, only two, usually at most three, heading styles are needed.

Cascading Style Sheets

Cascading Style Sheets (CSS) are often used to manage the presentation and layout of a web page. Styles enable a similar site-wide 'look and feel' for a site.

Consistency of presentation is important for a website. It focuses a reader on content rather than how the page looks. CSS are used in many sites on the web today.

Browsers have 'default' styles applied to elements in line with W3C specifications. With the heading styles <H1> to <H6>, for example, <H1> has a larger font-size than a <H2> tag, as does <H2> to <H3> and so on to <H6>. There is little difference in how various browsers render these tags.

However, with other specifications, such as margins and paddings, there can be great variation in how browsers render elements.

Why is CSS used?

Cascading Style Sheets are used for the following reasons:

- Site-wide changes to the look and feel of a site can be made globally by simply changing the settings in a single file.
- The CSS file(s) can be referred to by every page on the site through the head tag.
- They allow HTML tags to be specifically targeted for formatting.
- They allow the creation of user-defined styles.
- They enable more precise settings for elements and tags in a page rather than the basic specifications of HTML.
- It makes a site easier to maintain, particularly a large site.
- They are still under active development and improvement as well as the new features being incorporated into browsers.
- Media queries allow alternative style sheets to be used depending upon the specifications of the device that is being used to view the content. For example, the printed version of a page can be different to the screen version, as can the mobile phone version.

Applying CSS to style HTML tags

CSS is able to style the standard HTML tags. The following image shows how a browser (Chrome) by default (user agent style sheet) renders an H1 heading.

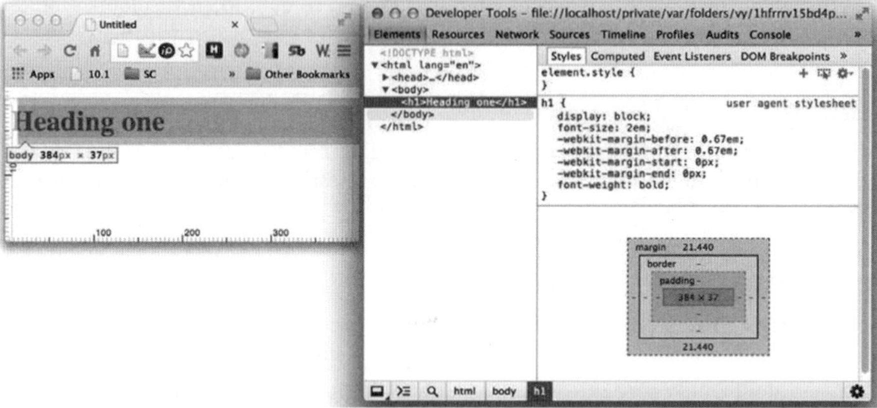

<H1> tag in Chrome

The following image shows where the H1 heading has been styled using CSS, in this case to add a border, increase the font size and increase the padding around the heading.

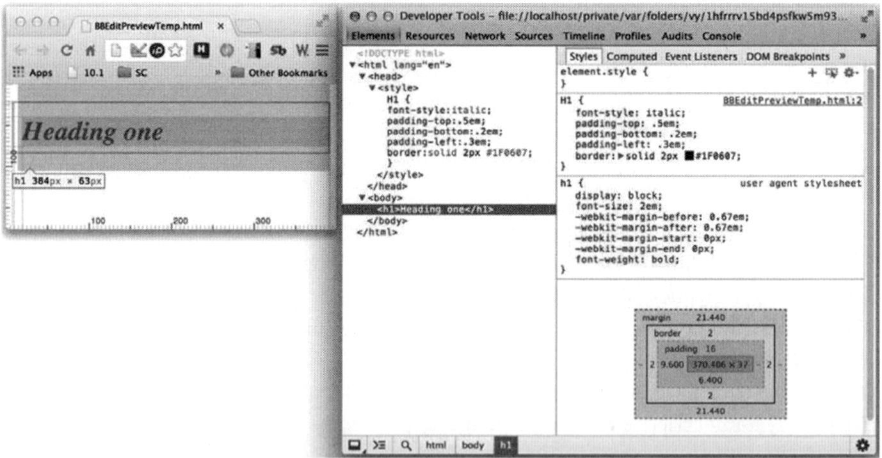

<H1> tag displayed that has been defined using CSS

The colour of the H1 text and the background colour of the H1 are some of the many other settings that could be applied with CSS to the H1.

Division tag

The division or 'div' tag is used to specify a section in an HTML page. It is an essential element in the layout of pages as 'divs' lay out the grid. A div is like a container: it could, for example, be used for an image and its caption and some accompanying text. It enables a consistent look and feel for images across a site.

IDs and classes

IDs and classes are 'hooks' that can be used to associate style and presentation with HTML and in particular 'div' tags.

The ID and class essentially allow web developers to add onto HTML and CSS with user-defined specifications.

IDs

An ID attribute is used to point to a style in a style sheet and can be used to manipulate an HTML element. Note that:

- An ID can only be used once on any page (a specification of the WW3C).
- An element can only have one ID.
- It is mainly used to identify structural elements on the page, such as a major content region.

Class

The class attribute is mostly used to point to a class in a style sheet. Note that:

- It can be used on multiple elements and any number of times on a page.
- An element can have multiple classes.

The use of classes is illustrated later in the chapter when applied to formatting images.

How is CSS applied?

There are three main ways that CSS can be applied to an element:

1. Using a separate CSS file. This is referred to by the page prior to loading – it references the link in the HEAD tag to a separate CSS file.
2. Defining the style in the Head tag – this is read by the browser before it renders the page and applies to all instances of that tag on that page.
3. Applying the style 'Inline' – that is, the style is added to a specific tag in the body of the document. It is read as part of the tag and only applies to that specific tag in that part of the page.

The following figure shows how the style has been set using the above three methods.

1. The separate CSS file, called 'styles.css', with the link in the 'Head' tag.
2. The style definition in the Head tag for the H1 tag.
3. The style definition in the body where the H1 tag is used.

```html
<!DOCTYPE html>
<html lang="en">
<head>
<!-- This is a comment line and will be ignored by the browser-->

<!-- Link to css file, style.css in the folder css in the same directory -->
<link href="css/style.css" rel="stylesheet" type="text/css" media="all">

<!-- Style declaration in head tag, will apply to all H1 tags on this page -->
<style>
H1 {
font-size:300%;
}
</style>
</head>

<body>


<!--
Inline style declaration, will only apply to this H1 tag
 -->


<h1 style="font-size:300%;">Heading one</h1>

<h1>Heading one</h1>

</body>
</html>
```

style.css

```css
/*This is a comment - note different syntax to a html file */

/* A css file is a text file with file extension of .css */

H1 {
font-size:300%;
}
```

Setting up the style

Tips for making a page easier to read

Here are some tips to make a page easier to read:

- Create and use headings from key points in the text.
- Items of equal weight should have the same heading style to show they are of equal importance.
- Use lower case for headings.
- Do not include full stops at the end of headings.

Unit 12.3 Activity 1J: Using CSS

1. Create the example shown in the figure above and display in the browser.
2. Change the size in the style.css file to 400%. What happens?
3. Change the size in the style declaration in the head tag to 400%. What happens?
4. Experiment with the sizes by choosing some font sizes of your own.
5. What conclusions can you draw regarding the precedence of the declarations on the size of the font being displayed?
6. The following are other style declarations that could be applied to the H1 tag. To begin with change the style declaration in the Head tag only.
   - font-style:italic;
   - font-weight:800;
   - font-family: 'Times New Roman', Georgia,Serif;
   - color:blue;

Unit 12.3 Internet 2

Topic 2: Working with images and multimedia effects

Topic 2 focuses on the techniques used to work with images and multimedia effects. It covers:

- Inserting images.
- Customising images.
- Inserting background sound and video clips.

Using images

Images have an important role to play in communication and are very important in websites. Here are some suggestions about the use of images on websites:

- Images should be relevant to the content and be meaningful.
- The better the original image quality, the better the final image.
- Always keep the original image, even after the final editing is complete.
- Use clip art sparingly.

Image composition

Image processing software should be used to carry out the final editing. Once the editing is complete, the image can be placed on the web page.

Typical editing tasks are:

- Resizing – changing the height and/or the width of an image.
- Cropping – removing part of the image.
- Colour correction – adjusting the lightness and brightness of the image.
- Adding filters and special effects, such as creating a vignette.
- Converting an image file format to a web file format
- Saving the image with compression to reduce the file size.

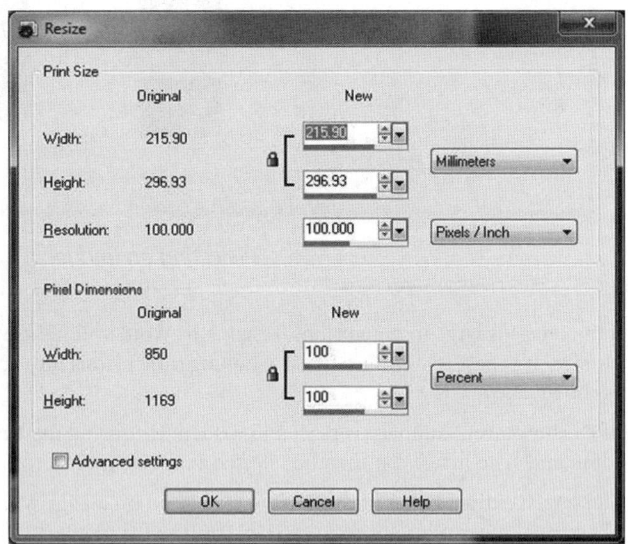

Resizing an image

Inserting an image or an AutoShape

In Microsoft Word, images are placed using the **Insert** tab. The **Illustrations** section of the **Insert** tab includes Picture, Clip Art, Shapes, and SmartArt, among others.

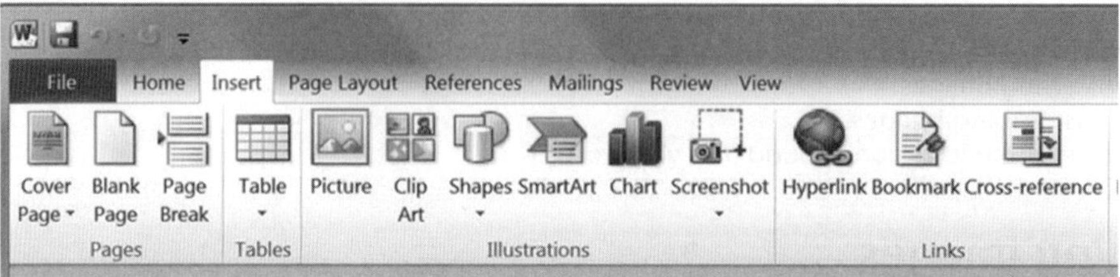

The Insert tab in Microsoft Word

Choose the **Picture** command to select an image.

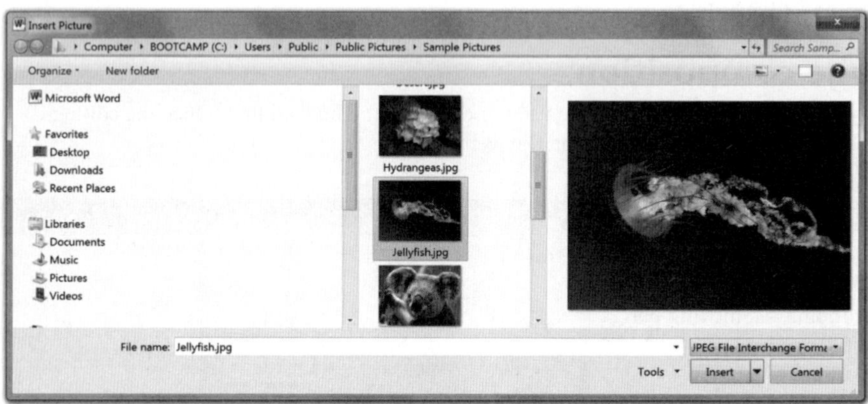

Selecting an image

If the image is large in dimensions, resizing in Word will reduce the screen size but not alter the file size. It is best to optimise file size (taking dimensions into account) prior to selecting the file, as shown above.

In Dreamweaver, an image is placed in a document using the **Insert** menu and the **Image** command. The image can then be selected in a dialog box.

The screen extract below shows the image placed on a page with the **Properties** for the image. The image dimensions are 602 × 451 pixels, the file size is 38 kB, and the alt text is 'jellyfish'.

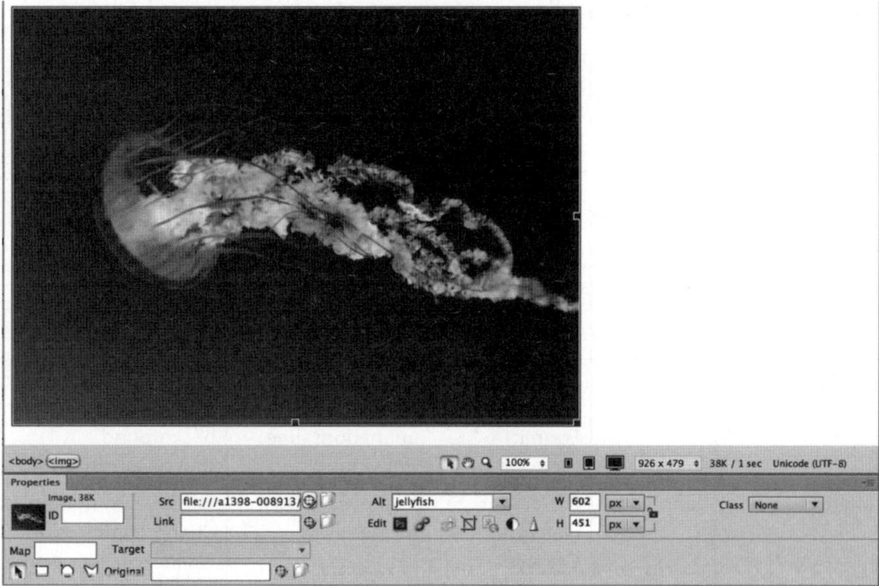

An image in a Dreamweaver file

Adding fill colour to an AutoShape

To add a fill colour to a shape:

- Choose the shape from the **Insert** menu and put it in position.
- Select the shape and choose the **Shape Fill** color from the **Format** section of the **Table Tools** tab.

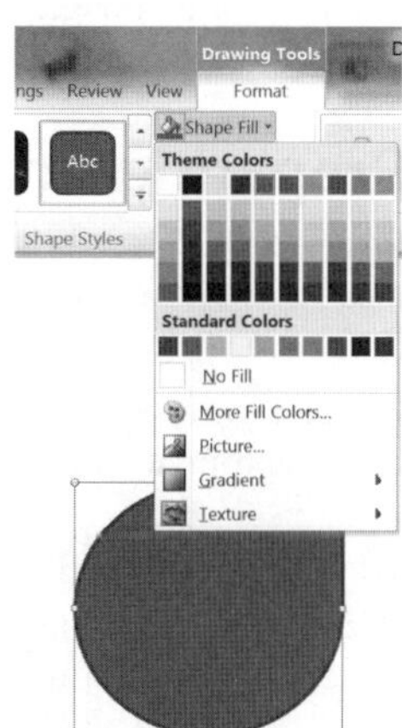

Choosing a fill colour for a shape

Images and graphics file types

Images for use in web pages are of three main types:

- gif (Graphic Interchange Format).
- jpg (Joint Photographics Experts Group).
- png (Progressive Network Graphics).

Table of image file formats

Use	File extension	Full name	Specialisation	Key features
Internet/digital cameras	.jpg	Joint Photographics Experts Group	Continuous tone images such as photographs from digital cameras or the Internet	Can display millions of colours. Has varying levels of compression that can affect quality. During compression unwanted information is discarded.
Internet	.gif	Graphic Interchange Format	Flat colour images, such as cartoons, animations, line drawings	Maximum 256 colours. Can have a transparent background. Can be animated.
Internet	.png	Portable Network Graphic	Improved gif format	Information not discarded during compression. Greater file size. Some .png can have transparent backgrounds.

Image file formats

There are other images types that are generally not used on the Web: these include Tagged Interchange Format (TIF), Bit Mapped Images (BMP) and Vector Graphic Images (FHLL).

Preparing images for the web

Images should be edited and sized using image editing software before being placed in a web page. One of the reasons for resizing an image is to reduce its file size. If an image is resized by the web editing software, it retains the original image file size.

It is best to compare images in a variety of formats with a variety of settings to determine the most appropriate image file type and size.

Feature	Definition	Comment	Use on screen
Size	Image size as measured in kilobytes or megabytes	Image size depends the camera or scanner.	Smaller file sizes are suitable for monitors and the Internet. Image download time is important. Smaller file sizes are significant in web production.
Dimensions	The height and width of an image is measured in pixels	Dimensions affect the amount of area on the screen that the image will need.	The larger the dimensions, the more time it will take an image to download.

Feature	Definition	Comment	Use on screen
Resolution	The quality of the image, measured by ppi (pixels per inch) or dpi (dots per inch)	Screen is measured in ppi.	72 ppi is used on a monitor.
File format	File formats for a monitor		Use one of jpg, gif or png format,
File name	File names should be meaningful.	Give the file a name related to its content.	
File location	Folder in which the image is located	Often located in a folder called *Images*.	Image is accessed from its location for display.

Preparing images for the web

Cropping an image

Cropping an image is removing unwanted parts of it. The image is examined to see which parts are most useful.

An image to be cropped

The figure above shows an image of Buckingham Palace, taken with a digital device. The original image is 2592 × 1936 pixels at 72 dpi and has a file size of 1.5 MB in .jpg file format. The resolution is relatively low but satisfactory.

The image is cropped (the lighter area to be discarded) to 1876 × 932 pixels and file size of 999 KB. Both the dimensions and the file size are too large for a page.

Cropped image

Resizing

Resizing alters the size of the image by setting the height or width in pixels or by reducing an image to a percentage size of the original image.

The figure shows a dialog box that allows resizing by altering the height or width of the image.

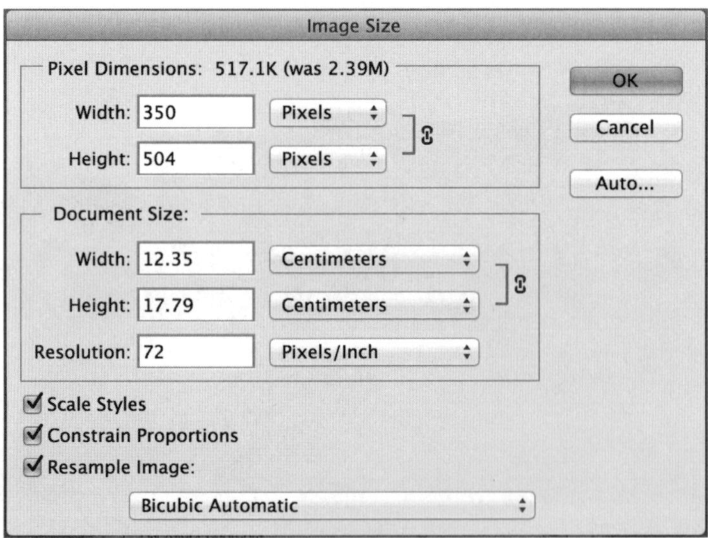

Image compression – jpg (changing the file size and quality)

JPEG is a long-established image file format and is a widely used with digital cameras. It is a 'lossy' compression scheme, meaning that as the image is compressed data is discarded, the file size of the image is reduced and the quality of the image is downgraded. It is best to keep copies of original JPEG files as once information is discarded it cannot be retrieved.

The trade-off between file size and quality depends on each particular image. The image should be previewed in the browser to see if the quality is acceptable.

Image degradation is often easily noticed with images with people's faces.

The figure below shows the 'Save for Web' dialog box in Photoshop. The options for JPEG are:

Quality	Image size	Download at 56.6 Kbps
100	101.1 K	19 seconds
60	34 K	7 seconds
25	17.1 K	4 seconds

Image compression and download times

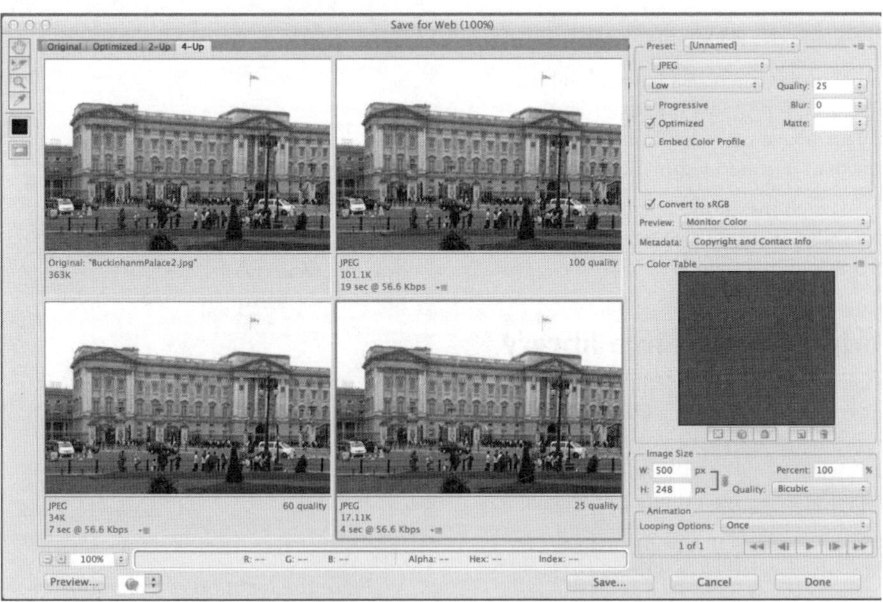

Different image qualities when compressing an image

Unit 12.3 Activity 2A

1. What is the nature of the information in the table?
2. What would be the best choice for the image to be included in the website?

Placement of images

Graphics can be aligned to the left or right of a page. Some tips for the placement of graphics are:

- Larger graphics should be placed on a page below the first screen; the first screen can be read while the remainder of the page is downloading.
- Images should be placed so that they line up on a grid (eg right aligned).
- The largest image should be the most important.
- Avoid having a lot of images the same size across a page.

Location of images and associated page content files

For a site with many images it is better for site management to distribute the files to image folders in different locations. These should be close to the content to which they relate. They have relevance to those files and it prevents long listings of images in a single folder.

Site-wide images could be in a folder in a top directory, with other images kept inside the folder where the HTML file resides.

A single image, such as a navigation button, can be used repeatedly on a page and in a site. This image is loaded from the cache rather than repeatedly downloaded.

Some web editors store images in a separate folder called 'images' that can make it easier to create and maintain links.

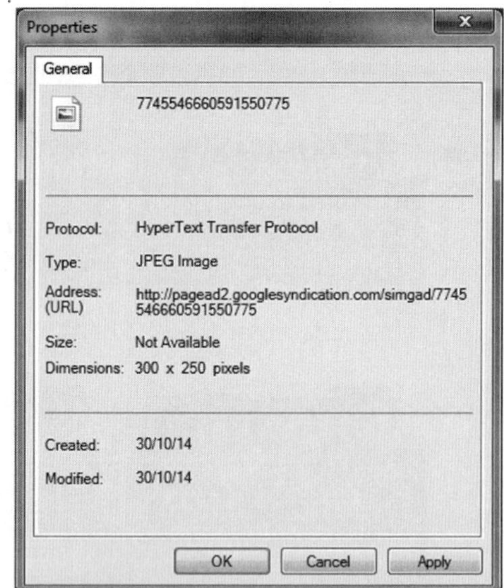

Note the location of the image in Melbourne's The Age *website*

Storing content in a library

Site content items can be stored by site management software in a library. This includes images, hyperlinks, flash animations and movies. Items can be dragged and dropped onto a page from the library.

Information stored in this manner is commonly referred to as 'libraries', 'snippings' or 'clippings'.

Repeating images

To add an effect to a page on its background, a single image can be 'tiled' so that the image is rendered and then repeated. The image can be repeated on just the *x*-axis, just the *y*-axis, or on both.

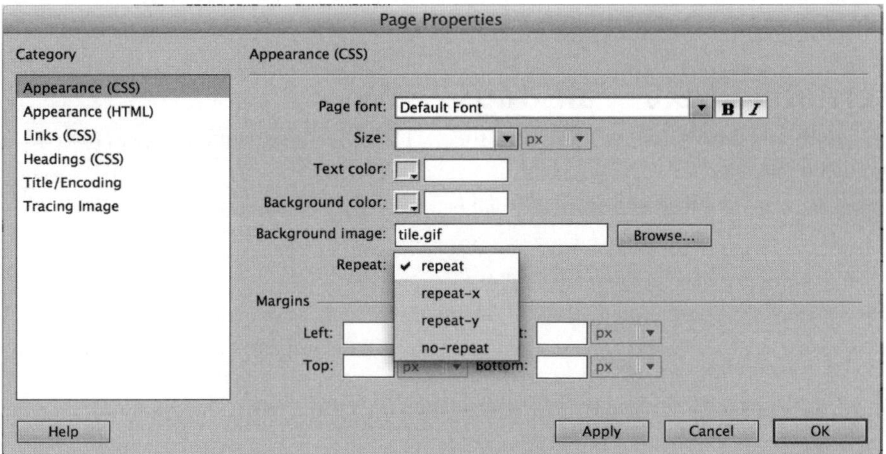

Setting up a repeating graphic

Very simple, light, washed-out images can add a stylish background that aids contrast.

Inserting WordArt

WordArt can be used to quickly add an unusual effect on a page. The WordArt is saved as a .png image when the Word document is saved as a web page. It can then be added as an image to a page.

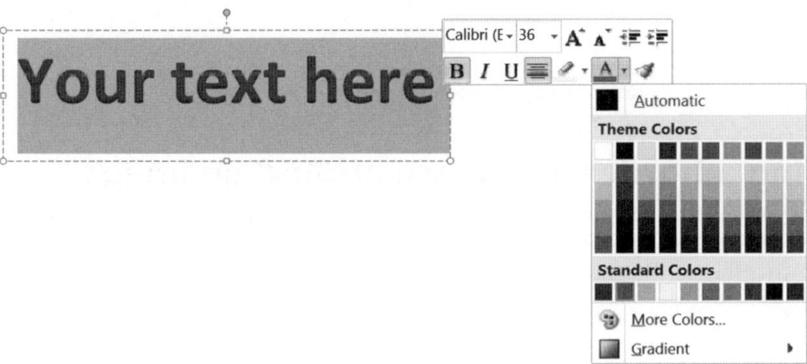

A WordArt image

Inserting a clip art image

Clip art should be used sparingly on a website. There are some standard icons, such as an envelope to indicate 'email', and a house to indicate 'Home' (as in homepage), where the meaning is clear and unambiguous.

Microsoft Office has a range of clip art images both within the package and online. There is a large amount of clip art available on the Internet.

Alternative text – 'alt' tags

Image tags should include 'alt' text as part of their HTML tag. This should be two or three words to describe the image.

In normal viewing of the page the 'alt' text will be ignored. The alt text, however, will be:

- Seen if the image is not downloaded and displayed correctly.
- Seen if a browser does not display graphics.
- Seen if a user has set the preferences to disable the viewing of graphics.
- Read using 'speech recognition' for those who are visually impaired and are using a screen reader.

The following shows the 'alt' text display when the image has not been displayed.

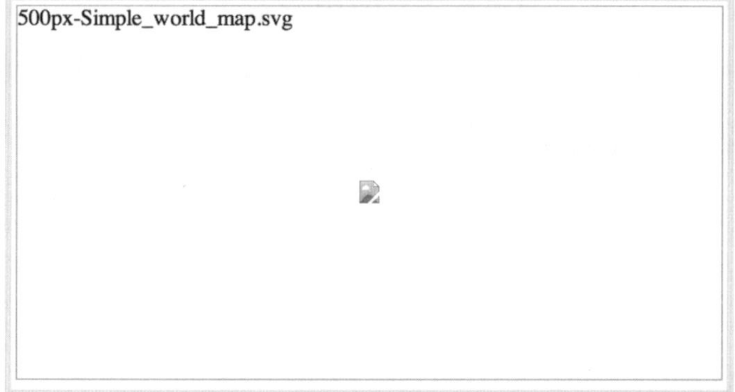

Text displayed when an image is not displayed

Adding a border and space around an image

A border and space around an image offsets the image from the text and makes the text easier to read. It also highlights the image. This could be accomplished with CSS using a 'class' and a div tag. Shown is the HTML mark-up for an example.

```
¬
<style>¬
¬
.imageRight·{¬
float:right;¬
border:5px·solid·#EEEEEE;¬
padding:3px;¬
margin-left:20px;¬
margin-bottom:20px;¬
}¬
¬
</style>¬
</head>¬
<body>¬
¬
<div·class="imageRight">¬
<img·src="img/500px-Simple_world_map.svg.png"·
width="500"·height="269"·
alt="500px-Simple_world_map.svg">¬
</div>¬
¬
<h3>Image·floated·and·border</h3>¬
¬
<p>¬
Lorem·ipsum·dolor·sit·amet,·consectetur·adipiscing·elit.·
```

Inserting space and line around an image

The key parts of the mark-up as shown by the figure are:

- A 'style' tag in the 'head' element of a page that creates a class called 'imageRight'. (Note the period in front of the name to indicate that it is a class.)
- A 'div' tag in the body of the page that is assigned the class 'imageRight'. The key part of the mark-up is that the 'div' is floated, meaning it will move to the right of the browser viewport.
- The link to the image. (It is in a folder in the same folder as the page. The actual source of the file is: http://commons.wikimedia.org/wiki/File:Simple_world_map.svg)
- An 'alt' tag, in this case added automatically with its text as the image, was inserted into the page.
- An H3 heading.
- The first line of the text to accompany the image, in this case dummy text, 'Lorem ipsum dolor'. (There are websites that can automatically generate this dummy text.)

The figure below shows how the page appears in the browser.

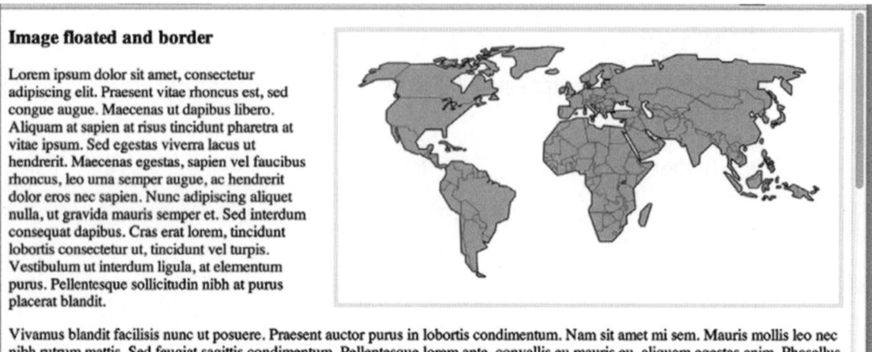

An image with a floating border

Shown below is part of the web developer window in Chrome. It shows how the image is rendered with the mark-up.

There is 3 pixels of 'padding' around the image, then the border, 5 pixels wide, of a grey shade. On the left and bottom borders there is a 20-pixel margin to the text, while there is none on the top or right.

Shown below is the relevant information from the page the image was obtained from regarding use of the image. It identifies the creator of the map and the use granted by the creator.

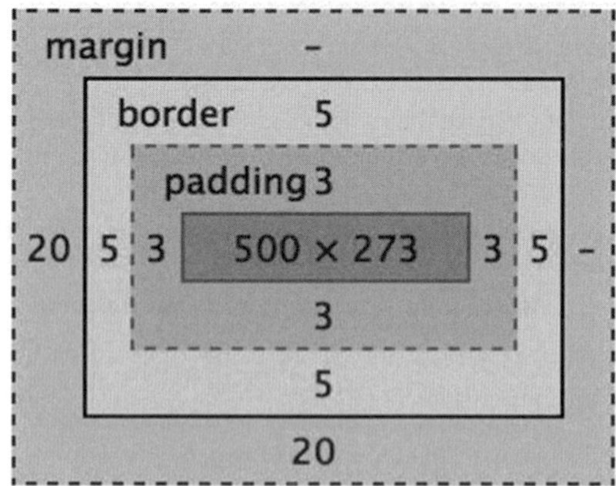

Dimensions of an image

Information about an image

Unit 12.3 Activity 2B: Images

1. Consider the image referred to in the figure above.
   a. What rights does the creator grant to others (if any) regarding the use of the image?
   b. Is there any copyright associated with the image?
   c. If you required a map of the world would you regard this as being suitable? Give reasons for your answer. There is a link on the URL cited above to the creator that can assist you with your answer.
2. Using the information in the HTML mark-up for the image floated right, how would you alter the mark-up so that the image could appear on the left-hand side of the page?

Creating a thumbnail image

A **thumbnail** is a copy of an image that has been reduced in size. A thumbnail image is very common on e-commerce sites to give a quick look at an image of a product. Clicking or hovering over the image may then show a larger image of the product. There is no set dimension size for a thumbnail; it depends on the purpose for which it is being used.

There are a variety of techniques used by web developers to display the larger image. If a large number of images were to be created, then this process would be automated. Photoshop, for example, has an image processor that would resize images to suit in a batch.

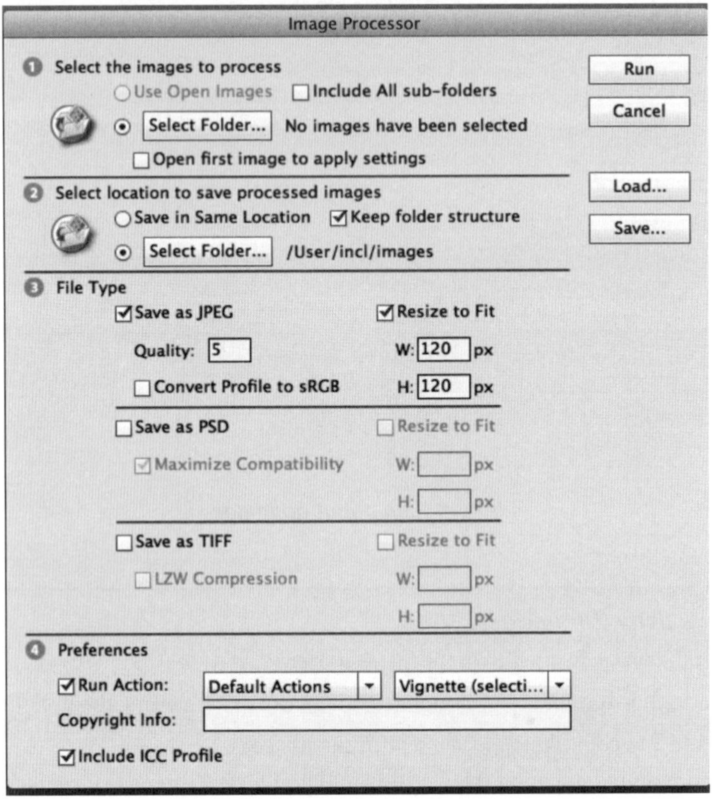

Image Processor

1 Select the images to process
Use Open Images | Include All sub-folders
Select Folder... No images have been selected
Open first image to apply settings

2 Select location to save processed images
Save in Same Location | Keep folder structure
Select Folder... /User/incl/images

3 File Type
Save as JPEG | Resize to Fit
Quality: 5 | W: 120 px
Convert Profile to sRGB | H: 120 px
Save as PSD | Resize to Fit
Maximize Compatibility | W: px
H: px
Save as TIFF | Resize to Fit
LZW Compression | W: px
H: px

4 Preferences
Run Action: Default Actions | Vignette (selecti...
Copyright Info:
Include ICC Profile

Run
Cancel
Load...
Save...

Image processing in Photoshop

Unit 12.3 Activity 2C: Thumbnails on e-commerce websites

1. Investigate three e-commerce websites that use thumbnails. Include Amazon.com as one of the sites. What are the sizes (in dimensions) and kilobytes of the images?
2. How does the site for eBay (www.ebay.com) show product thumbnails and larger images?

Media on a web page

Video and audio can be embedded in a web page in a variety of ways. The approach to using media content depends on:

- The size of the media file – video files can have very large file sizes.
- The quality of the media – video varies considerably in quality.
- The version of HTML – HTML5 has tried to simplify the process of including media.
- The file format of the media.
- Browser support for the media and whether or not a plug-in is required.

Video

For many years there have been a variety of containers for **video**, such as Flash and QuickTime. However, these are proprietary formats that require plug-ins for the browser to display the video. YouTube video uses the Flash .flv format. Flash files cannot be played on some tablet computers, notably the iPad.

There is strong support within the web community for the use of HTML5 and the 'open' standard file formats.

There are many patents and licensing rights that impact on the use of formats for video. Most video is 'lossy', meaning that as the video is compressed information is discarded. Even with the video element, there are differences in the browser support. Not all video formats are supported natively in the browser.

HTML5 approach to video

Including video in an HTML5 site requires a variety of formats to be created. This gives the browsers options of playing the first video format in the list that the browser supports.

The figure shows the table of support for video formats in the main browsers.

Browser	MP4	WebM	Ogg
Internet Explorer 9	Yes	No	No
Firefox 4.0	No	Yes	Yes
Google Chrome 6	Yes	Yes	Yes
Apple Safari 5	Yes	No	No
Opera 10.6	No	Yes	Yes

Video support in different browsers

An open source video converter is Miro Video Converter. It can be used to convert between formats and it is also useful for particular devices.

Dreamweaver CS6 at this stage does not yet have direct support for the video element, so the code needs to be entered as html.

```
<video autoplay="autoplay" controls="controls" preload="auto">
<source src="MyFirstMovie.mp4" type="video/mp4">
<source src="MyFirstMovie.ogv" type="video/ogg">
<source src="MyFirstMovie.webm" type="video/webm">
</video>
```

Code to place a video source in a site using Dreamweaver

Above is an extract of the HTML used for display of the video. The first line ensures the video is loaded as the page loads; it will show the browser native video controls and will automatically play the video when ready. The figure shows a video being displayed in the Chrome browser.

Video with controls in Chrome

The video element supports a number of attributes including:

- Height (in pixels).
- Width (in pixels).
- Poster (URL – link to an image that will show until the video begins to play). If no poster is provided the area will be blank until the first frame is available and it will be displayed.

The video controls are customisable and both CSS and JavaScript can be used to ensure that they are uniform across the browsers.

Test the HTML and video

As the support across browsers and devices may differ, the video needs to be tested on a variety of devices and also browsers.

Audio

With HTML5 the <audio> tag was introduced, although browser support for audio files varies.

Browser	MP4	Wav	Ogg
Internet Explorer 9	Yes	No	No
Firefox 4.0	No	Yes	Yes
Google Chrome 6	Yes	Yes	Yes
Apple Safari 5	Yes	Yes	No
Opera 10.6	No	Yes	Yes

Support for audio formats

Similar to video, the use of a number of file formats will enable the browser to play the first of the formats it supports. Below is the HTML for this site.

```
--------------------
<audio controls autoplay loop>
<source src="myFirstSong.mp3">
<source src="myFirstSong.ogg">
<source src="myFirstSong.wav">
</audio>
-------------------------------
```

Attributes for the audio tag include:

- Autoplay – audio will begin playing as soon as it is able.
- Loop – when completed the audio will restart.
- Controls – the default browser controls will display.

The first figure below shows the controls in Chrome and the second figure shows the controls in Safari.

Audio controls in Chrome

Audio controls in Safari

Inserting background sound on a web page

The HTML from above with the first line altered as shown will insert the sound in the background:

```
---------------------
<audio autoplay loop>
-------------
```

This removes the control so that the sound appears to be in the background.

Removing a background sound from a web page

Deleting the lines of code above removes the sound from the web page.

Displaying a message if the video cannot play

If video is included on a web page and it requires a browser plug-in to view, then JavaScript is generally included to:

- Interrogate the browser to see if the plug-in is installed.
- Direct the user to a location on the web where the plug-in can be obtained and installed; or
- Display a message that the video cannot be displayed because the format cannot be supported.

The Chrome browser has built-in support for the Flash Player so that the .flv format can be played.

Removing a video from a web page

Select the video player window and then press delete. The video file will not now be linked to the page.

Unit 12.3 Internet 2

Topic 3: Creating hyperlinks

Topic 3 explains how text and image hyperlinks can be inserted into a web page. It also explores the issue of usability on the web.

Inserting text and image hyperlinks

It is best if the text for a hyperlink is directly related to the content rather than using a generic statement. For example, '2014 Annual Report' is better than 'Click here to download the 2014 Annual Report'.

Blue and underlined text on a web page is the browser default for a hyperlink. The cursor changes its shape to a hand as it moves over the link. When the hyperlink is clicked, it points the browser to an address embedded in HTML. The hyperlink colour changes to red when the link is activated. This shows which links have been followed.

However, the default behaviour of 'underline' for links can be modified by CSS styles, such as making the text a blue colour and 'strong' text.

Where does a hyperlink point?

A hyperlink can point to:

- Another part of the same page (called an anchor).
- A different page on the same site.
- A page on a different computer on the same network.
- A page anywhere on a website.

The destination of a hyperlink is not always apparent from the text. However, the address of the link can be seen in the status bar at the bottom of the browser window

Visited hyperlink

The text colour of a hyperlink changes after it has been clicked. The default colour of a hypertext link is blue before it has been clicked and purple after it has been clicked. These browser default settings allow a user to distinguish the links as visited or not yet visited.

A hyperlink also can be located in a button or image on a page.

Clickable image maps

As an image or graphic on a web page can be a hyperlink, so can a specific part of that image or graphic. It is very common to include these on maps.

A clickable image map is a graphic that has hotspots embedded in it. A hotspot is an area inside an image that has a URL embedded in HTML. The URL will be activated when the image is clicked. Navigation graphics such as maps are common examples of clickable image maps.

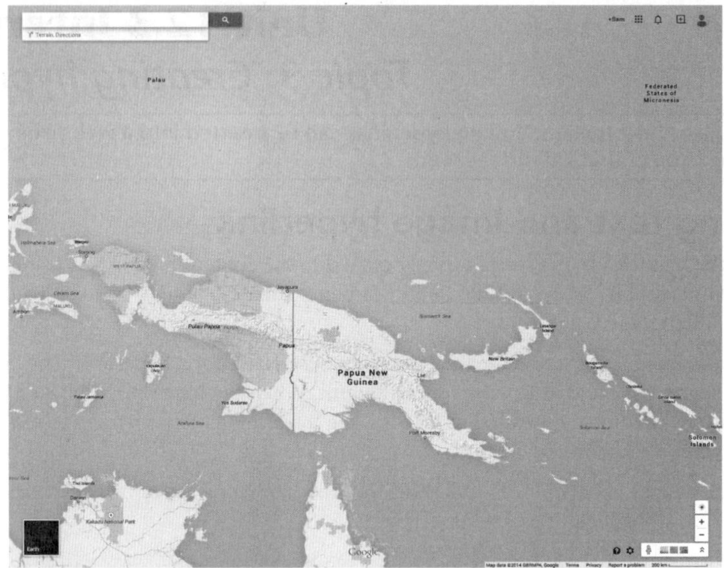

Google Maps is an example of a clickable map

Alt tags for images

The **'alt' tag** provides a description of an image to be included in the HTML code of the page. It will be displayed if:

- The image is not displayed (if the link to the image is incorrect, for example).
- The page is slow to download, and will therefore appear before the image has loaded.

Inserting a text or image link to a page on a different website

A link to a different website is the absolute URL, the one that would be displayed in the browser window. An image can be linked in the same way.

Inserting an email link

An email link, when clicked, activates the default email client on the host computer. The email address is embedded in the link and displays in the email client. The HTML can be edited to include a 'subject' line that will be automatically included.

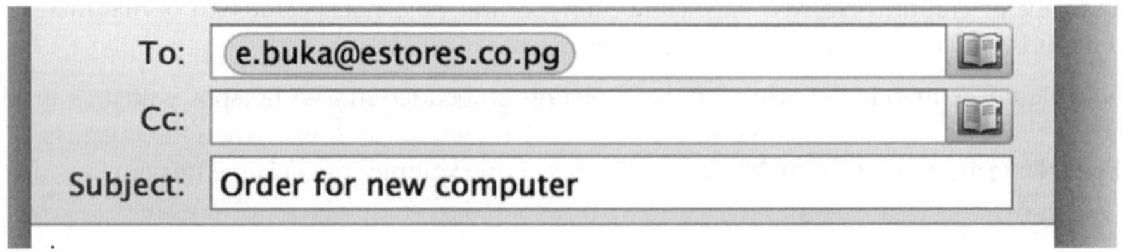

Email message load from a link in a website

Like hyperlinks, the text for the link should be brief to indicate that it is an email. Sometimes a visual clue such as an envelope icon will be used to show an email link.

Changing link colours

The purpose of changing link colours is to give feedback to the reader: first, that the text is a hyperlink, and then to indicate if it has been visited.

It is not essential that a hyperlink be underlined, provided the reader is able to identify that the text is a hyperlink.

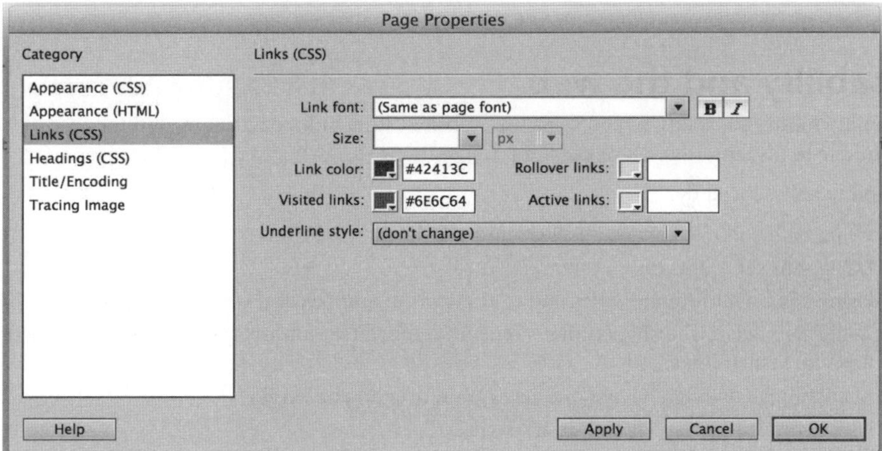

Link properties

The figure shows the Dreamweaver **Page Properties** with settings for **Links**. This sets the link display for the current page.

Hyperlinks can be styled using CSS. There are essentially four states for a hyperlink. Using CSS styling, the default could be changed to a different colour as well as other styling on the link itself.

The examples for the colours below are only for the purpose of illustration.

Link state	Default colour	CSS style, hexadecimal colour	Link colour
unvisited	blue	a:link {color:#C0C0C0}	silver
visited	purple	a:visited {color:#00FF00}	lime
mouseover	-	a:hover {color:#000080}	navy
active (ie selected link)	-	a:active {color:#00FFFF}	aqua

Link colours

The above CSS for the mouseover could be modified to more easily show it is a hyperlink by showing the underline as the cursor is over the text by:

```
a:hover {color:#000080; text-decoration:underline;}
```

What information should identify a web page?

Identifying information on a web page should include the following:

- A page title, to be included in the title bar of the browser window. This should be unique for each page.
- The name of the author or the person authorising the page.
- The date the page was created or last modified.

Usability and the web

Usability means the ability of people to use websites. It includes navigation, and the ease of use of the site to find information or carry out transactions.

Usability is enhanced by:

- Using high contrast between background and foreground colours.
- Using sans serif fonts rather than serif fonts.
- Using consistent heading styles and restricting the number of text styles per page.
- Using web defaults for hyperlinks – blue underlined text for links and purple underlined links for visited links.
- Maintaining consistent layout and navigation over an entire site.
- Using simple page layout and design template.

Some sites include 'breadcrumb navigation' in addition to the normal navigation. A breadcrumb is usually a horizontal single line (often near the header or navigation bar of a page) showing the path to the home page.

The website for the Law and Justice Department of Papua New Guinea uses breadcrumbs. Shown is an example from the site:

www.lawandjustice.gov.pg/www/html/565-goroka-university-keen-to-partner-sector.asp

Home » Sector Activities » **Goroka University keen to partner sector**

Using breadcrumbs

Usability testing

Testing can be done by:

- Observing people as they experience a website. This can include timing them to find out how long it takes to carry out a specific task.
- Conducting surveys, questionnaires and interviews about a website.
- Studying the web server log analysis that shows user interaction with the website and the links followed.

Unit 12.3 Internet 2

Topic 4: Working with special effects

Topic 4 focuses on the use of special effects on a website. It covers:

- Inserting and editing an animation.
- Reversing the scroll direction of the animation.
- Setting the speed and movement of the animation.
- Changing animation size.
- Changing animation background colour.
- Inserting a hit counter.

The use of special effects requires special care. Usability studies show that users tend to turn off and ignore content (apart from video) that is moving and changing on a page, particularly if people feel the animation is an advertisement or 'click through' link.

There is a range of components that can be added to a website.

Inserting and editing an animation

For many years a Flash file was used for animation and other effects on the web. However, Flash is a proprietary file format from Adobe. It requires a plug-in to use in a browser and it also requires specialist software to create the animation. Flash is not supported by all the tablet computers and smartphones.

The successor to Flash may well be open HTML, with the 'canvas' element used with CSS and JavaScript.

Creating animated gifs

A gif (graphic interchange file) image is able to be created as an animation. The image can be designed as a series of layers that are combined into one file.

Each layer is like a 'frame' of a movie. The file format is supported by all browsers and does not require a plug-in. Most graphics software is able to save a file in this format.

For example, a firm is about to open a store and requires 'Grand Opening Specials' as a banner across its web page. The brief is for the animation to be in a 700 pixel × 100 pixel area. For the purposes of this illustration only the text will be used for the animation.

The steps involved to creating an animated gif are as follows:

1. Decide the content for the gif. (The three words, font size, font type, font-style, font colour, 'case' for the text).

2. Using pencil and paper, create a storyboard for the animation. This will assist in deciding:

   a. The height and width of the frames (if this was not part of the brief).

   b. The content required.

   c. The colour of the background

   d. The placement of images in the animation.

   e. Allocation of the content to the frames (eg one word per frame).

f. The number of frames required and the order in which they will be shown. ('Grand' will be the text for the first frame.)
g. Length of the animation and delay between frames (if any).
h. Whether the animation will play just once, repeat a number of times, or be continuous.
i. The best method of using the software to create the frames.

Having a clear idea of what the final product will be before creating the animation enables easier and quicker creation.

For this simple example, the best method is to create three frames with 'Grand Opening Specials' and to delete the text for frames 1 and 2 that is not required. This would ensure that the text is correctly aligned horizontally and vertically across all three frames.

In this example there is a white background common to all frames.

Background – White

Frame 1 – Grand

Frame 2 – Grand Opening

Frame 3 – Grand Opening Specials

The figure shows the animation being created in Photoshop. The frames and the timeline are shown in the bottom left. The length of time for each slide can be set individually, and also the number of times the animation will play.

Graphic created in Photoshop

Unit 12.3 Activity 4A: Animated gifs

1. Find some examples of .gif animations that are available under a Creative Commons licence.
2. Open the image using image editing software and examine its settings and how it has been created.

Reversing the scroll direction of the animation

The order of the frames in the panel sets the direction of the animation. Changing the order of the layers will change the direction of the animation.

Setting the speed and movement of the animation

The speed and movement of individual frames in the animation can be set in the timeline. The figure below shows different times for the first three frames of an animation and setting about to be selected for frame 4.

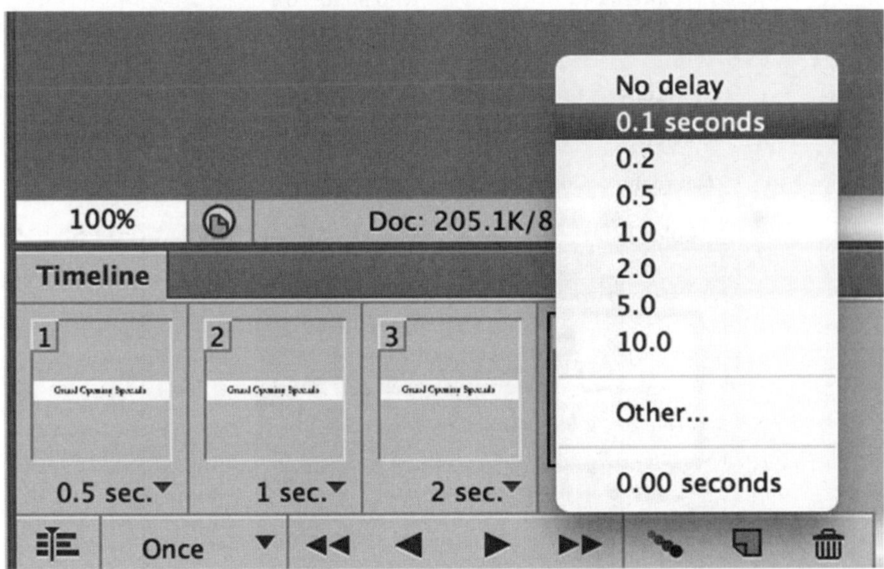

Speed and movement of an animation

Changing animation size

The actual animation size can be adjusted when saving the file as an animated gif. The figure opposite shows options for saving the file, including adjusting the size in pixels.

The size is adjusted to 600 pixels in width and the height is automatically adjusted to 86 pixels to retain the ratio between width and height.

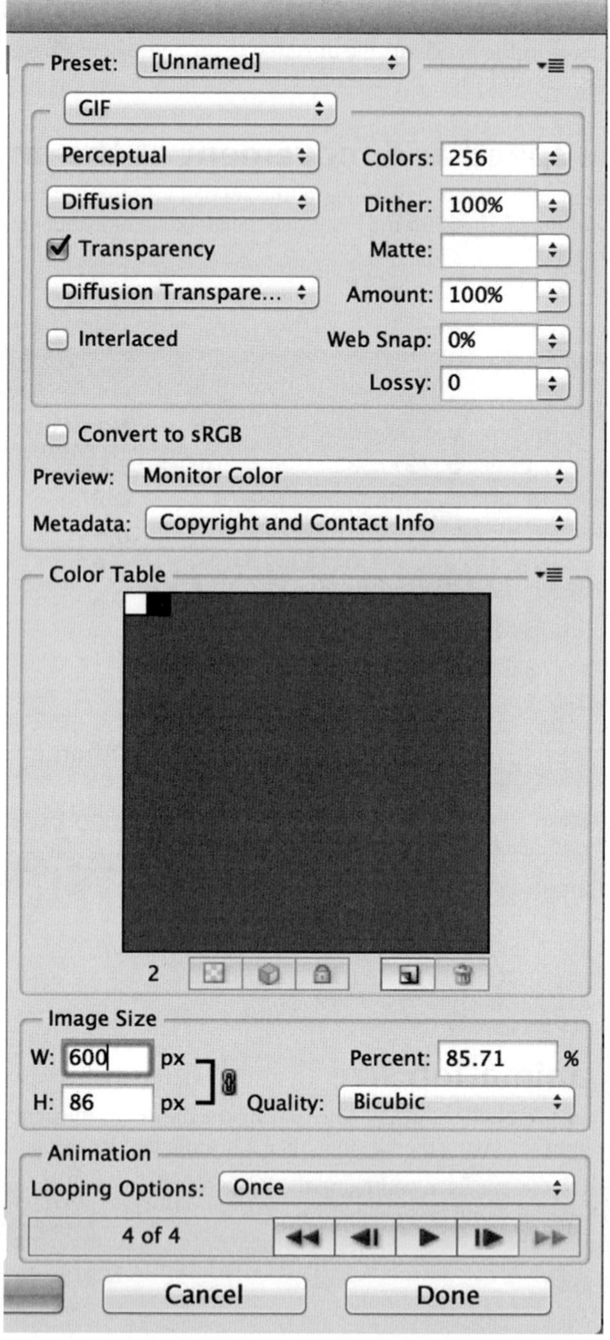

Adjusting the size of the animation

Changing animation background colour

The background colour can be set by selecting the background frame, selecting a colour and using the appropriate tool to colour the background. In this image, the Photoshop **Paint Bucket Tool** is used to colour the background.

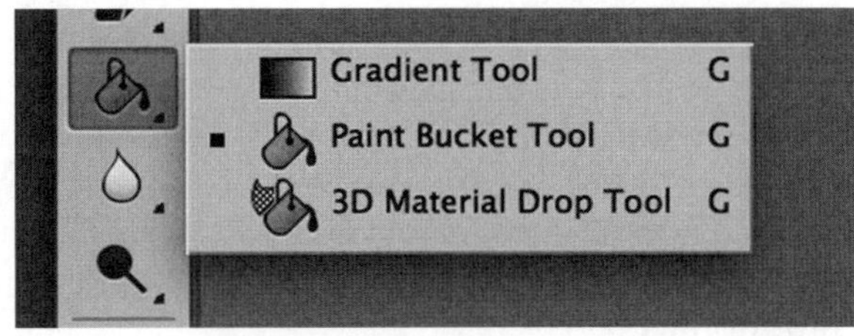

Paint Bucket Tool in Photoshop

Inserting a hit counter

Hit counters were very popular on websites in the 1990s to indicate the popularity of the site and pages.

Unfortunately, there are many sites offering 'free' hit counters, with 'free' code that merely needs to be pasted into the page. It is possible that the code is malicious and could include 'alt' tags that are intended to manipulate search engines. This means that the search engines devalue the site.

Placing a link on your site to another site is of importance to the search engines and, if it is a dubious link, the search engines regard the action as malicious.

Hit counters also tend to 'cheapen' a website and most visitors are distracted by the animation of the hit counter and doubt the usefulness to them of the counter.

To effectively analyse a website it is best to use other alternatives, usually at no cost from the industry, such as Google Analytics.

Creating animated pages with page transition

The Google development site is helpful in creating animated pages.

The figure shows the front page of a Google development site, '20 things I learned about browsers and the web'. It illustrates an approach to developing pages using animation and other effects. Examples such as this expand our understanding of what is possible and show where developments will lead.

Google development site

Resources

There are many creative initiatives at present, particularly in the area of HTML5 and CSS3. Developments mean it will be easier for individuals to be creative and to add interesting effects to web pages and sites. These developments require people with the passion, the knowledge and the technical skills to enable them to push the boundaries of what we regard as possible.

Unit 12.3 Activity 4B: Create a website

Create a prototype website for your school following the steps outlined in this Unit.
The prototype does not have to have extensive content on all pages but should be sufficient to provide the structure for the site and essential design elements so that the specific content could be placed into the appropriate areas.

The prototype should be sufficient that you could provide the materials produced and hand over to others to implement the site. They should not need to make decisions about the 'look and feel' of the site.

The site is to be limited in the range of five to ten web pages. Primarily you will be designing for the browser displaying the pages on a computer screen.

Investigation

Who is to be the audience of the website?

What key areas would be suitable for a five to ten page site?

Drafts

Prior to using a computer the following need to be created:

- Site map.
- Content list.
- Wire frame.
- File table.
- Timeline.
- Annotated layout diagrams.
- Style guide.

In the drafts you should provide advice regarding:

- Page width and length.
- Page grid and layout.
- Key navigational aids.
- Colour scheme of the site (foreground and background colours).
- School logo, size and location.
- Heading styles.

Dummy text can be used for body text in the design stage. It is useful, however, to show actual text whenever possible, as it can assist in deciding margins, the number of headings that may be required, etc.

Unit 12.3 Activity 4C: Pages from a web server

1. Find examples of three sites that serve pages from a server with each of these file extensions:
   a. .aspx
   b. .php
   c. .cfm
2. What type of web sites are they?
3. What goods or services do they provide?
4. Are they small, medium or large businesses?

Unit 12.3 Activity 4D: Analysis of a page

Look at the home page for the Air Niugini website.

1. Draw the wireframe layout for this page.
2. On the wireframe annotate the:
   a. Top navigation bar
   b. Left hand booking section
   c. Footer (navigation area).
3. Give examples of images that are hyperlinks.
4. Some screen text has been created as an image. Why is this done on some web sites?
5. What is the predominant color scheme of the page?
6. Has 'white space' been used effectively?
7. A link to the 'Site map' is shown at the bottom of the page. What is the purpose of this link?
8. Examine the page using the Chrome Browser. Choose **'Print'** and examine the page in 'Print Preview'. Comment on the display shown. How does this occur? (hint: In the 'Resources' examine the 'Stylesheets'.)

Unit 12.3 Activity 4E: Exercise images

1. Select three images that have been taken by a mobile phone.
   a. A person's face.
   b. An image taken at short range (up to 3 metres)
   c. An image taken at long range (say 100 metres)

2. Prepare the images for a web page. You will need to decide upon:
   - cropping (if required)
   - resizing (if required)
   - image dimensions (height and width)
   - compression applied and image size (kilobytes)
   - quality of the image
3. What decisions did you need to make while preparing the images?

Unit 12.3 Activity 4F: Exercise accessibility

The Australian Human Rights Commission has produced notes called 'World Wide Web Access: Disability Discrimination Act Advisory Notes'.

Section 3.3 of this section deals with web accessibility failures and is shown here.

3.3. Ten Common Web Accessibility Failures

Although there are many reasons why a web resource may be inaccessible, a number of common accessibility failures account for a significant proportion of the problems that people with a disability encounter when using the web. The following are ten such failures. Web developers should ensure that they design their websites so as to avoid them, and should take steps to rectify them if they are already present.

1. Failure to include appropriate text descriptions (such as "alt-text" labels) for images;
2. Failure to provide accessible alternatives when using a visual CAPTCHA;
3. Failure to use technologies (such as Flash and JavaScript) in ways that are accessible;
4. Failure to use HTML features appropriately to indicate content structure such as the hierarchy of headings;
5. Failure to explicitly associate form input controls with their labels;
6. Failure to ensure sufficient difference between foreground (text) colour and background colour;
7. Failure to identify data tables with Summary or Caption, and failure to mark-up data tables correctly;
8. Failure to provide a way for users to disable content such as advertisements from flashing rapidly (rapidly-flashing content may cause seizures in susceptible individuals), and failure to provide a way for users to stop a page from auto-refreshing;

9. Failure to ensure that web pages can be used from the keyboard (that is, without the mouse);
10. Failure to alert the user to changes on a web page that are triggered automatically when selecting items from a dropdown menu.

Source: https://www.humanrights.gov.au/our-work/disability-rights/standards/world-wide-web-access-disability-discrimination-act-advisory

January 14, 2014

1. Why did the Commission issue these Advisory Notes?
2. Select 3 of the 'failures' mentioned above and suggest how these could be managed and overcome when developing a website.
3. In the complete Advisory Notes (available at the web address above) there is a section dealing with 'pdf' documents. Briefly outline the key points relating to 'pdf' documents.

Unit 12.3 Activity 4G: Is a web page a page?

How does a 'web' page differ from the features of a 'printed page'? Complete this table.

	Printed page	Web page
1	Page size is pre-determined (:eg. A3, A4, A5 or newspaper tabloid or broadsheet)	
2	Page will remain the same once published	
3	Text font and font size is fixed	
4	Resolution of the page is fixed (:eg. 3200 dpi, 1600 dpi or 600 dpi)	
5	Viewing pages is immediate when the page is opened.	
6	Elements on the page remain fixed in their positions.	
7	It is easy for readers to quickly scan a page or pages to find information.	
8	Printed publications have common formats and layouts depending upon the type of publication.	
9	Readers can quickly ascertain the amount of reading by the width, height, depth and weight of a publication.	
10	Readers prefer reading a printed page	

Unit 12.3 Activity 4H: Investigate a Club

Investigate a local sporting club that operates in your area. Would the club benefit from having a web site? How would you prepare a 'prototype' website to present to the club?

Unit 12.3 Activity 4I: Create a Website

The local rugby club approaches you to help them create a web site for the club. The club is managed by a committee with office bearers including President, Secretary and Treasurer. There are three teams fielded by the club: Juniors, Seniors and Masters.

For the launch of the site they wish to have sections on the site for:

- About the Club
- Teams
- Competition
- Contact Us
- News and Events

The following is to be incorporated into the above structure:

- Newsletter
- Match Fixtures
- Competition Results
- Notices of Meetings
- Names of Raffle Winners
- Membership Application Form
- Information about each team and contract details for Team Managers
- Names and details of three local sponsors
- Map of the location of the club
    1. Create the site map for the club.
    2. Create a wireframe for the home page.
    3. Create an annotated layout for the home page.
    4. Create the folder structure for the site.
    5. Create a file table to give guidance for file naming and the type of files that may be used on the site.

In the web editor of your choice, create the homepage. What decisions would you make regarding the:

- Width of the page?
- Use of header, navigation, body and footer areas?
- Color scheme?

Unit 12.4 Multimedia
Topic 1: Introduction

In Unit 12.4 students investigate the effects of multimedia on the communicating, presentation and manipulation of information. They gain an understanding of, and experience in, developing solutions to problems using multimedia applications (ICT syllabus p. 40; Computer Studies syllabus p. 33).

Topic 1 provides a general introduction to multimedia. It covers:
- Definition of multimedia.
- Different types of media.
- Different multimedia applications.
- Terminology and jargon commonly used.
- Hardware and software requirements.
- Techniques or steps.

Definition

Multimedia is the use of computer systems to present a range of different media types integrated into a single document or applications. Media types include text, graphics, video, sound and animation.

Multimedia devices allow people to experience and use different applications that are made up of a range of media types. Devices used include computers, iPads, smartphones, DVD players and digital television sets.

Traditional forms of media offer content in a linear sequence in their presentation or delivery. Books, such as this one, provide the content in pages. The index and table of contents are used to navigate through the book to points of interest.

Multimedia allows many media types to be presented, with user interaction, choice and control. Software capable of creating multimedia combines the content, manages the files and packages the presentation.

A game played on a digital device is essentially a multimedia application. The various media combine with a display, programming and pathways based on the user interaction with the game. The existence of 'levels' and 'degrees of difficulty' mean the computer game may be a different experience for users depending on their skills, ability, and decisions made while playing the game.

The film industry is another example of large-scale multimedia. Digital creation of motion pictures enables content to be created and packaged as a single product. A film is still mostly viewed in a linear sequence but digital versions allow the user to move within the content to desired locations.

An Apple iPad Air is a device used to interact with multimedia applications

Multimedia can be used for:

- Presentations by a speaker to an audience.
- Training and educational simulations.
- Interactive games.
- Training courses, often with user control.
- Information kiosks (usually with touch screens).
- Electronic brochures.
- Databases (front-ends).

Multimedia applications and authoring software

Multimedia authoring software provides the tools to organise the content into a screen-based application. Usually the content is prepared in other applications before being imported into a multimedia format for production.

Text is usually prepared in a **word processor**, images in a graphics package and video clips in a video editing package. Multimedia authoring software enables the material to be located and assembled as required for each screen or scene.

Although multimedia software has tools for content creation, the range of tools is not as complete as that in a dedicated software package. Text in a word processor, for example, can be spell-checked as part of the validation process; the multimedia software may not have a spell-check.

The authoring software offers different ways of carrying out a desired effect. In many cases there is not a right or wrong way to create a production. The design and look and feel of a production is much up to the author. The same content may be presented in many different ways.

Multimedia industry

Many of the skills required for the production of multimedia are similar to those needed in the film and television industry. Computer skills are of great importance. Successful multimedia companies bring together people from the film and television industry, graphic designers and computer experts (programmers and interface designers).

The widespread use of computers has made it possible for many people to create multimedia productions. This was previously the province of film industry professionals, expensive studios and linear editing systems. Unfortunately, this can mean that the design of the product suffers. Design is critical to the success of a multimedia production and is easily overlooked in the rush to production. Well-designed, effective multimedia products are important in the development of a successful industry.

Terminology and jargon commonly used

Presentation

A presentation is the act of showing and explaining a topic of interest to an audience.
A presenter leads the audience and explains to the audience a range of content about the topic.
Many presenters use presentation software to enhance the explanation.

Master slide

Presentation software displays a number of slides. Each presentation has a **master slide** that has a number of design items that are included in every slide. A master slide is similar to a template as discussed earlier in this book.

Microsoft PowerPoint has a number of different themes that provide users with a master slide.

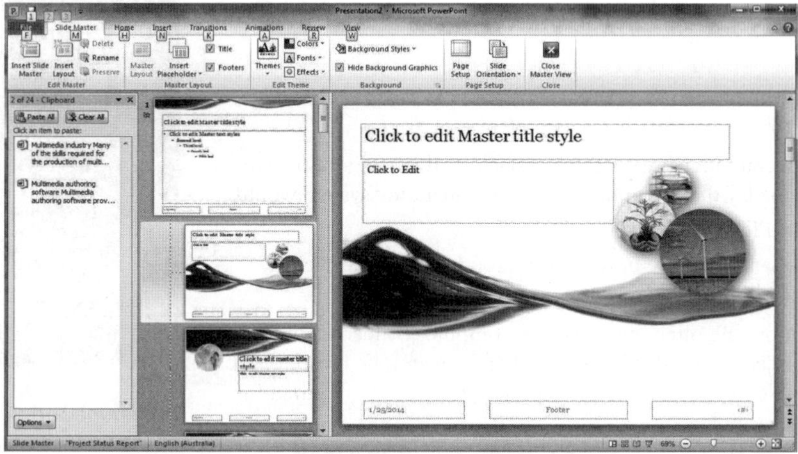

A master slide in PowerPoint

Slide

A **slide** is a single page in a presentation. A presentation is made up of a number of slides. These usually use a master slide to provide a consistent look and feel.

Transition

A transition refers to the action that takes place as the presenter moves from one slide to the next. PowerPoint provides a range of different transitions that can be used in a presentation.

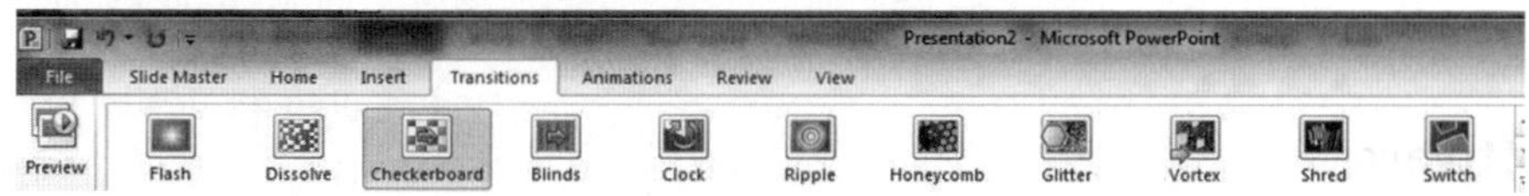

There is a range of transitions in Microsoft PowerPoint.

Animation

An **animation** is the movement of an object in a slide. That object can be text, a shape or an image. Examples of animations are discussed later in this chapter.

Hardware and software requirements

Hardware

The hardware used to develop multimedia is not necessarily the same as that used for its delivery. For high-end production involving video and intensive graphics, powerful computers with significant storage are required.

Using a variety of software concurrently requires a large amount of RAM.

An iPhone can be used to view a presentation

Delivery

A normal computer is generally satisfactory. If large monitors are used to display the presentation then the operating system would need to support the monitor setup.

Many presentations are now delivered on handheld devices including phones and tablets.

Presentations are often given using a computer connected to a digital projector and displayed on a large screen. The projector is usually able to play sounds but separate speakers are required for high-quality audio.

An example of a digital projector

Software

Presentation software

PowerPoint, Microsoft's presentation software, is synonymous with making a screen presentation. Keynote is similar to PowerPoint on the Apple platform. Google Docs also has a presentation tool that is online. It can also import PowerPoint presentations.

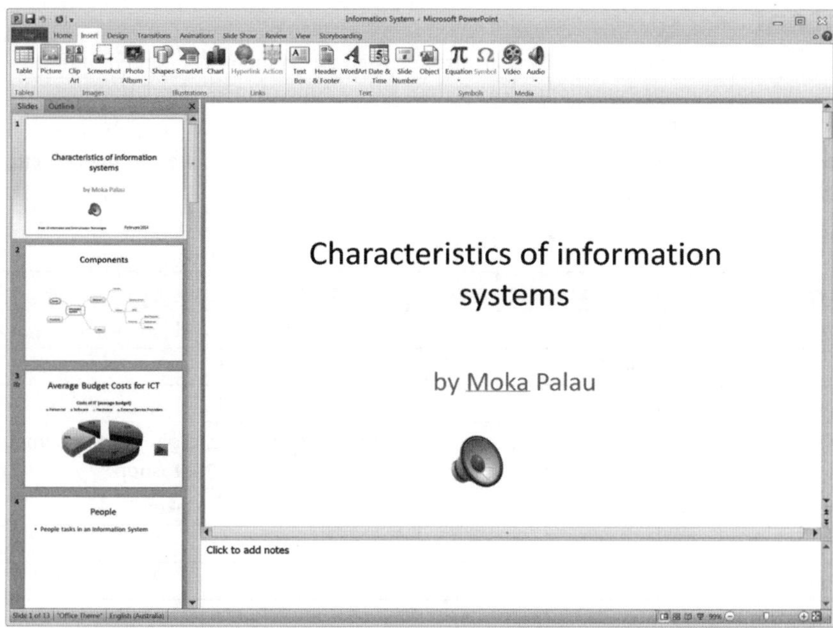

A PowerPoint screen presentation with a sound icon

PowerPoint has a number of ways to create, arrange and sort slides. The figure above shows a title slide in development with a 'default' sound icon showing on the slide.

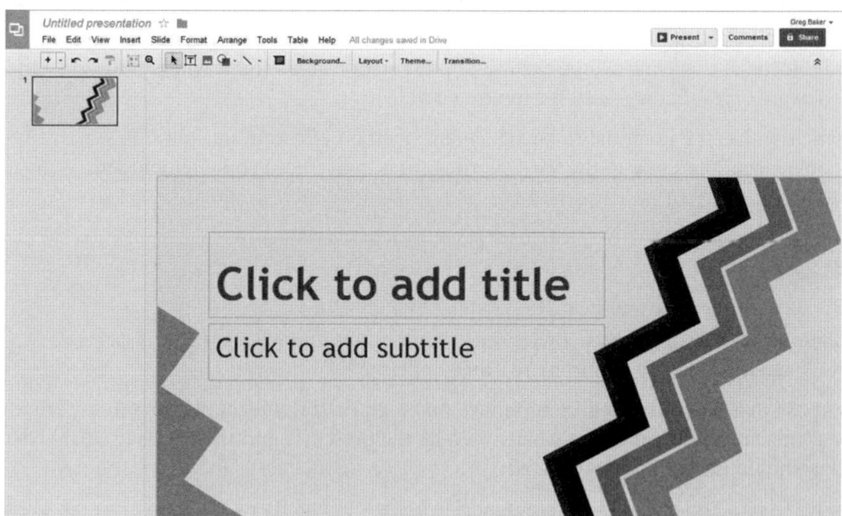

Starting a presentation in Google Docs

Content

It is best to create content in specialist software and then incorporate that content into the presentation. Although presentation software does have a suite of tools, they are not as sophisticated as those in dedicated software.

Producing content in specialist software also means the author concentrates on the content rather than the finished product.

Software to create the content can include the following:

File types	File extension	Software
Text	.txt	Notepad
Text	.doc(x)	Microsoft Word
Text outline	.rtf	Microsoft Word
Images	.png, .jpg, .gif, animated gif	Various software, digital camera, image editing such as Photoshop
Movies	.mov, .wmv	Windows Movie Maker
Audio	.mp3	Audacity
Animation	.swf	Flash

File types used in a presentation

Presentation software such as PowerPoint can enable a combination of media to deliver a presentation for an audience. The presentation displays the media and the presenter uses it to lead the audience through the key points. The presentation can include graphics, sound, video and charts to enhance the content. The presenter's screen can show notes and other information that is not seen by the audience. The presenter should know their content thoroughly and not just read the information on the screen.

The main focus of this Unit will be the use of presentation software. It will include examples of other software types that are used for multimedia.

A presentation has the potential to be an effective method of communication. Research shows that people react differently to the way information is delivered. People remember:

- 10% of what they read.
- 20% of what they hear.
- 30% of what they see.
- 70% of what they see and hear.

Presentation software offers such a wide variety of options and effects that it is easy to overwhelm an audience by including too many options.

The purpose of a presentation is communication based on the subject matter and expertise of the speaker. Care and attention to what is said by the presenter and the words used are effective tools that should not be underestimated.

It is useful to remember that the presentation is not about whether a presenter can use every effect and feature of the software, but rather that each point should have a specific purpose and aim to enhance the communication.

Different types of media

Multimedia combines the following media types:

- Text.
- Video – captured still frames and moving video.
- Graphic line artwork.
- Animation.
- Graphic images.
- Scanned photographic images.
- Digital photographic images.
- Clip art.
- Sound.
- Three-dimensional images.
- Hyperlinks to other text or images in the production.
- Text URLs that are links to websites.

Users interact with a multimedia presentation using a mouse, a touch screen or some other pointing device. A variety of screen sizes, resolutions and device types may be used to display multimedia.

Text (word processor)

Using an outline in Word, the skeleton of the presentation can be developed. Ordering and reordering of points is easier in Word than using slides in PowerPoint. It can be an advantage to have the text within just one document for spelling, grammar and consistency checks.

Images (image editing)

Using special image editing software for cropping, resizing and changing resolution allows access to a range of tools. Some of the packages also allow batch processing of a large number of files.

Movies (movie editing)

Advanced editing and frame-by-frame editing must be done in specialist software where the timeline can be altered if required. If sound is to be added, it should be added to the movie timeline.

Audio

Apart from built-in sound effects within PowerPoint, other audio may need editing and fitting to a timeline.

Animation

Sophisticated animation effects should be created using other software and imported into PowerPoint. Flash animations can be included in a presentation.

Finished multimedia

A variety of approaches can be made to developing and authoring multimedia. For example the file formats for a presentation as the finished product could be:

- Specifically programmed for that solution using a relatively high-level programming language.
- Presentation software such as PowerPoint, Google Docs or Keynote.
- Exported to a PDF (portable document format).
- Exported as a Flash file.
- Displayed in a browser using HTML5, CSS and JavaScript.

Organising content

Multimedia is predominantly a visual medium. Associations made by content develop themes and a context in which the content can be delivered. Arrangement of content involves deciding the types of content and how they relate to each other.

Associations between the types of content cannot usually be determined until the content has been collected, laid out and analysed.

Developing the topic

How the topic is developed will depend upon:

- The make-up of the audience.
- The time allocated for the presentation.
- The quality and amount of research undertaken.
- How the content can be reduced to its main points.

An information system has many components, as discussed in Unit 12.1. A concept map (also called a mind map) can be drawn to show the main parts and their relationship. It is a way of organising the information in a graphic form. This enables a topic breakdown and will give a preliminary idea of the amount of information belonging to each section.

The figure below shows the concept map in its initial stage with the basic elements of an information system.

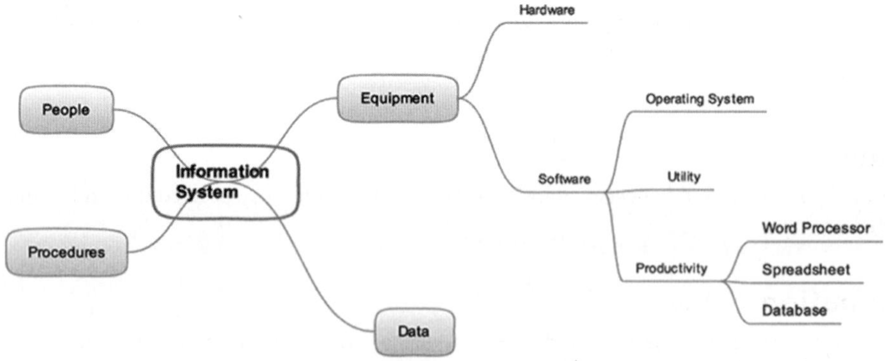

Mind map of an information system

Unit 12.4 Activity 1A: Concept map

1. What sections would you add to the diagram above to show the components of an information system?
2. Would the concept map as you have completed it give a clearer approach to the process of building a presentation?

Concept map

The **concept map** can be displayed as an outline in text showing the levels as indented text.

In outline view the order of content can be moved to reorganise it. It is possible to create an outline in other software types, such as in Word, and import it into PowerPoint.

The following image shows the appropriate 'style' heading for each part of the document using the default heading styles in Word.

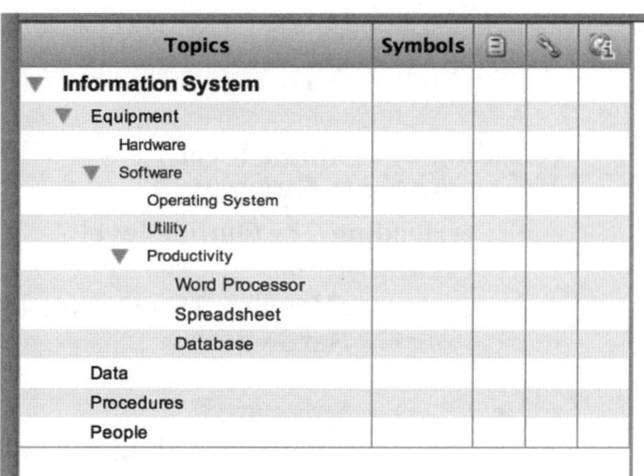

Concept map as outline text

Unit 12.4 Activity 1B: Outline text

Use an outline in Word to insert as an outline in PowerPoint. An outline created in Word then saved as an 'rtf – rich text format file' can be imported into PowerPoint and the various slides and content created by PowerPoint according to the structure in Word.

Enter the following terms into a Word document:

Information system

Equipment

Hardware

Software

Operating system

Utility

Productivity

Word Processor
Spreadsheet
Database
Data
Procedures
People

The Heading styles can be applied to each line. Place the cursor anywhere along the line and select the appropriate **Heading** selection from the ribbon.

- (Heading 1) - Outline level 1
  Information System¶
- → (Heading 2) - Outline level 2
  Equipment¶
- → → (Heading 3) - Outline level 3
  Hardware¶
- → → **Software**¶
- → → → (Heading 4) - Outline level 4
  Operating System¶
- → → → ***Utility***¶
- → → → ***Productivity***¶
- → → → → (Heading 5) - Outline level 5
  Word Processor¶
- → → → → Spreadsheet¶
- → → → → Database¶
- → **Data**¶
- → **Procedures**¶
- → **People**¶

Outline headings in Microsoft Word

To view the outline, select **View > Outline**.

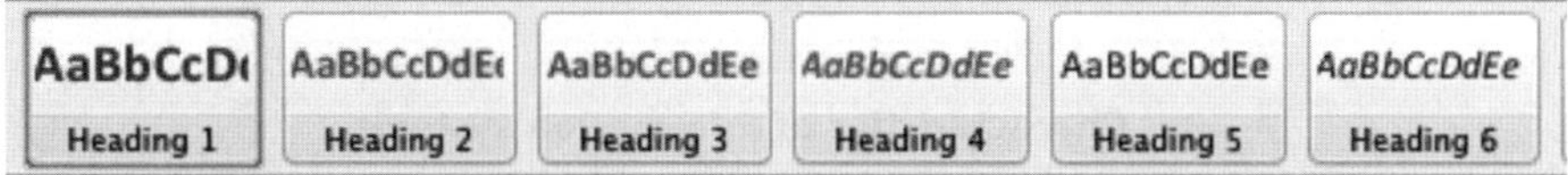

Heading styles in Microsoft Word

Note that in the outline mode, Headings 1 to 5 become Level 1 to Level 5 respectively. There are six Heading styles by default in Word. In outline view, headings can be 'promoted' and 'demoted' as well as moved to rearrange the order. The outline provides an overview of the document and is a useful tool for planning a presentation.

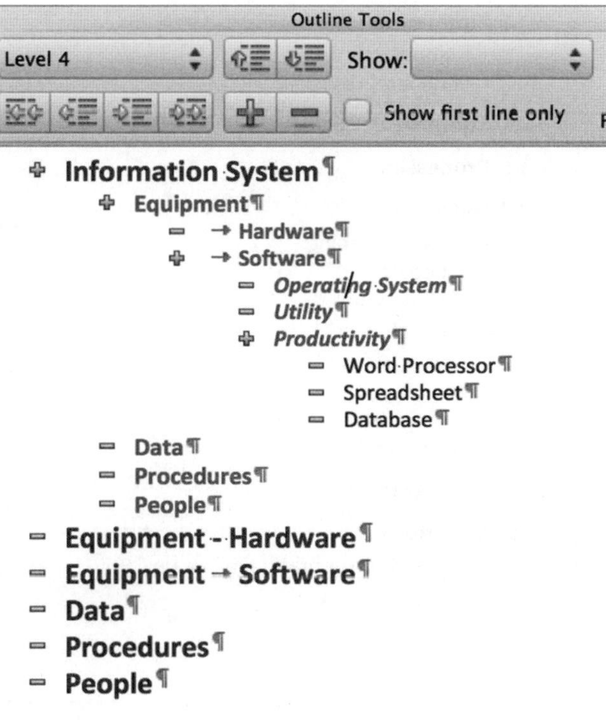

Outline view in Microsoft Word

In Word use **Save As > Rich Text Format (.rtf)**.

In PowerPoint, use **File > Home > New Slide** to insert the outline from the .rtf file. **Insert > Slides From > Outline...**

The figure below shows a presentation that was originally from an .rtf file and is now in development. Slide number 3 is being moved in Outline view to a more logical position.

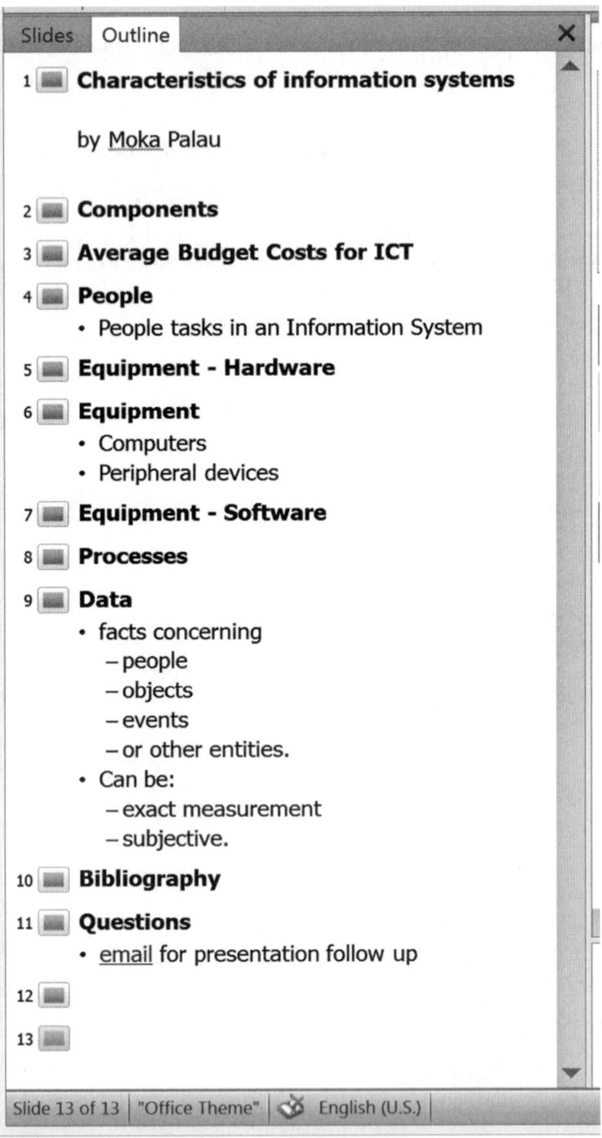

Outline view in PowerPoint

Heading 1 levels will be incorporated in the Title area of a new slide. Other heading levels below Level 1 will form the content on that slide. The number of slides added will be equal to the number of 'Heading 1' styles in the file.

A PowerPoint presentation can be exported as an .rtf file that can then be opened back in Word.

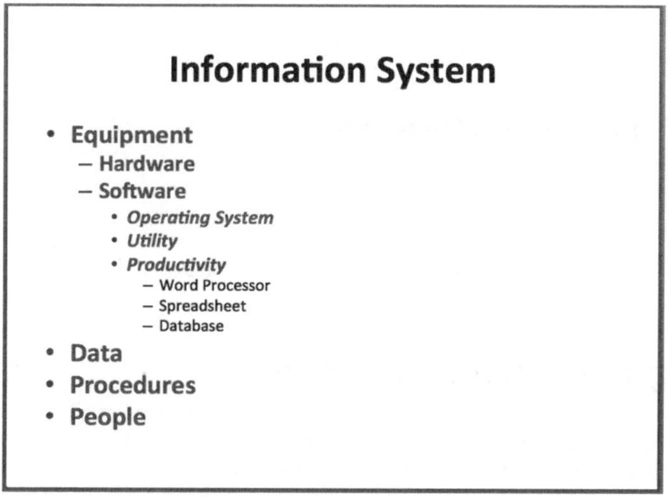

Information System

- **Equipment**
  - **Hardware**
  - **Software**
    - ***Operating System***
    - ***Utility***
    - ***Productivity***
      - Word Processor
      - Spreadsheet
      - Database
- **Data**
- **Procedures**
- **People**

PowerPoint slide produced from an outline

Unit 12.4 Activity 1C: Using an outline

1. How many slides have been added to the presentation?
2. Is the incorporation of the body content onto a slide easier using the outline?

File organisation of multimedia

A variety of file types can be used in a presentation. In some cases these will be imported and become part of the final product. In other cases there may be a stand-alone file that is referenced and accessed when required. A movie file or a large image are examples of this process.

Text, images and clip art are contained as part of the presentation in a single file. Other content contained in large files, such as audio and video, may be 'referenced' by the presentation and exist as a separate file.

It is good practice to have a folder structure of a presentation to organise the files and make it easier when making backups and for transfer to another device when completed, if required.

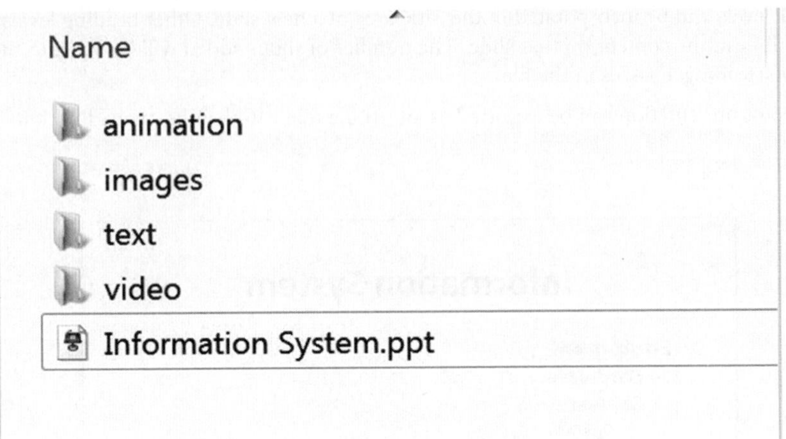

Folder structure for a PowerPoint presentation

Planning to produce multimedia

Preliminary planning for multimedia or a presentation does not necessarily need a computer. Pen and paper can allow a synthesis of content. The creator can decide on the parameters of the presentation and develop the production plan. This means that the content creation can be developed to suit the needs of the presentation.

When using a computer to construct the presentation, it is easy to be distracted by the software and to lose focus on the content and purpose of the presentation.

Techniques or steps

Storyboarding a presentation

Storyboarding is a technique used for multimedia design. The storyboard is a plan that sketches scenes in the multimedia presentation.

A mock-up on paper of important screens helps define how each screen will look and how that screen relates to others. It is a visual method of representing ideas, actions and images and can include the multimedia effects that will be used in the product.

For a storyboard to be effective with a presentation there should be a:

- Balance of information between slides.
- Balance between text and images.
- Consistent information structure.
- Consistent navigation technique.
- Consistent layout and colour.
- Slide numbering scheme that is appropriate – for example, number slides 5, 10, 15, 20 to allow inclusion of extra slides if required.

Screen design

Arrangement of content on a screen requires skill, particularly design skill. Design is a major factor contributing to the success of a multimedia product.

The screen should not dominate or distract the audience but its characteristics (eg basic colours) will affect how the audience may react. Blue is a cool calming colour, whereas red demands our attention.

People's response to colour can be affected by:

- Nationality.
- Age.
- Gender.
- Perceptions of fashion.

For example, in Western culture, red is a hot colour that can symbolise fire, danger and excitement. In Chinese culture, red represents celebration and happiness.

Elements of screen design

A screen design has to blend the various media types into a single presentation so that each content type has an integral place in the presentation. The design must take into account:

- Predominant content type.
- Types of content.
- Amount of text per screen.
- Font type and font size.

Reading large quantities of text on a screen can be difficult.

Headings will need editing, as will key terms and the words used on screen. Each item displayed on screen must earn its place.

Auto content wizards and templates

A **template** is a pre-designed slide design that can be adapted to suit the style and type of presentation. Templates include:

- Colour schemes.
- Font type and size for titles, headings and body text.
- Transition effects from one slide to the next.
- Speaker's notes.
- Outlines.
- Handouts.

Templates provide a consistent design for a set of slides. Consistent design helps make the slides easy to read and understand.

The advantages of using wizards and existing templates include:

- They are quick and require that only content is added.
- The basic design elements already exist.
- They can be easily modified to create a presentation, rather than beginning with a blank screen.

Disadvantages include:

- They can look like pre-prepared screens.
- The screens often look busy and have 'loud' colour schemes.
- The audience may have seen the screen with another presentation.
- The audience may feel the presenter has done the presentation in a hurry and suspect this might also apply to the content.

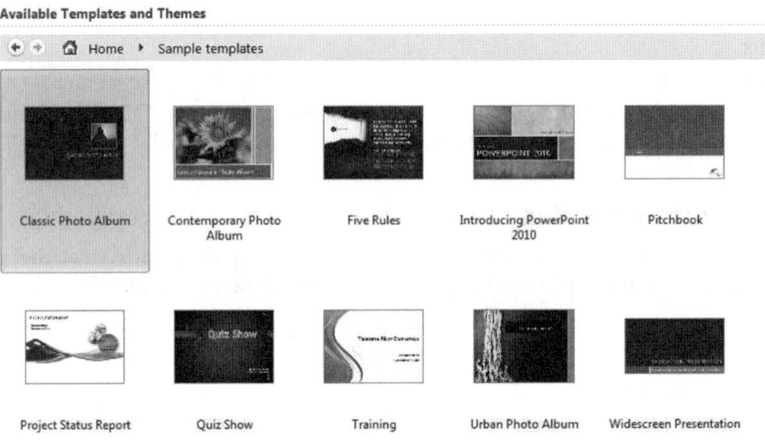

Some of the templates available in Microsoft PowerPoint

Creating a presentation

The main views for a presentation are:

- Normal – design and content prepared on slide.
- Slide sorter – slide order can be changed.
- Slide show – the slide and presentation as it will be seen by the audience.

Master views for a presentation are:

- Slide master – shared by all slides based on the master slide.
- Handout master – how printout handouts of the presentation will be placed on paper (eg 4, 8 or another number of slides per sheet).
- Notes master – the layout for notes that are referred to by the presenter but not seen by the audience. The notes are a prompt and checklist for the presenter.

PowerPoint views

The master slide can be seen and edited at **File > View > Slide Master**.

Format of a presentation

A presentation can be separated into a number of sections.

Opening screen

This should contain the presentation title, presenter name, name of event or purpose of the presentation. It could include the date of the presentation.

The background of the slide is usually common to all other slides in the presentation.

An example of an opening slide

Content slides

Generally the content slides will be of the same design throughout the presentation. Mixing colours and backgrounds for content slides will distract and unsettle the audience.

Content slides will contain a slide title in larger font at the top of the slide.

Content points are formatted the same for each slide, with graphics and other material placed in a similar position on each slide.

The slide number and the total number of slides could be shown in a smaller lighter font in the footer.

What We'll Cover Today

- A review of our current research
- 2013 sales results
- Proposed new products
- Costs on return and investment projections
- 2014 forecast sales
- Strategy and schedule
- Sales and marketing needs
- Questions and answers

A first content slide

The slide sorter view allows drag and drop rearrangement of slides. It allows:

- Arrangement of slides in logical sequence.
- Slides to be added and then placed in correct position.

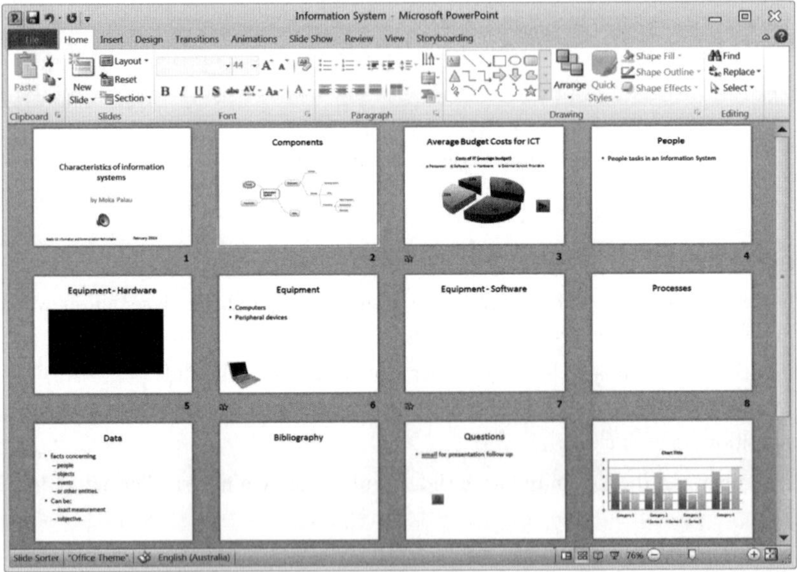

Slide sorter in Microsoft PowerPoint

Acknowledgment slide

An acknowledgment slide thanks those who have contributed to the presentation.

Bibliography

This includes references to content that has been used as source material. Hyperlinks could be added to the reference for easy access where available.

Any questions slide

Most presenters will allow for questions and discussion at the conclusion of a presentation. A slide with just a title is a prompt for the audience about which stage the presentation is at.

In some cases it is appropriate for the questioner to identify themselves, and if relevant the name of the organisation they represent. This prerequisite should therefore be included on this slide to inform the audience.

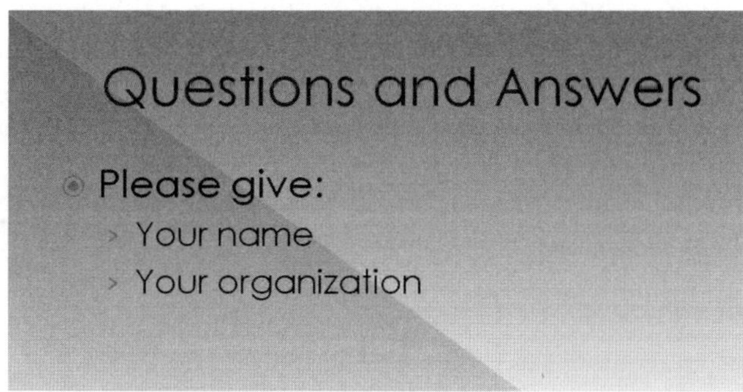

Questions and answers slide

Content

Content is the most important component of a multimedia presentation. The author of the presentation must have something to say or have information to give that is of interest to others. Multimedia is the medium of communication. It is used to present the different content types in a meaningful and interesting way.

Selecting suitable content takes careful preparation and planning so that the different types complement each other. If the content is not interesting or useful to the user, the user will lose interest. The content is enhanced with creative presentation, graphics and design. Existing content such as text, graphics, sound and video, may need modifying for inclusion in a presentation.

Although multimedia and presentation software has a large range of content and editing tools, if there is specialist software available (eg graphics, video and audio) then content specifically suited to that software should be created and edited with that software.

Text

Space on a presentation slide is at a premium. The number of words per slide should be kept to a minimum to avoid information overload.

Avoid cutting and pasting slabs of text into a presentation. At best, illustrative quotes from authoritative sources can be used, but make an intelligent selection from the quote if it is lengthy and provide reference.

- Text may need to be edited and divided into sections for screen display.
- Usually text needs to be short and succinct to be effective.
- Existing text may need to be cut, although an important document such as a speech may need to be reproduced in its entirety.
- Dot points and indented dot points are a way of getting a point across using the smallest number of words.
- Text can be imported from an outline directly into a slide presentation.

Writing for screen

Slide titles and headings should use the minimum number of words to convey the meaning. This may mean cutting the original text. For example, the slide on data uses the definition of data:

> Data 'is facts concerning people, objects, events or other entities. There are many sources of data and many types of data. Some data is an exact measurement; other data might involve subjective judgment'.

This definition is a 'chunk' of information. For a slide it could be reworked to appear as shown in the figure below.

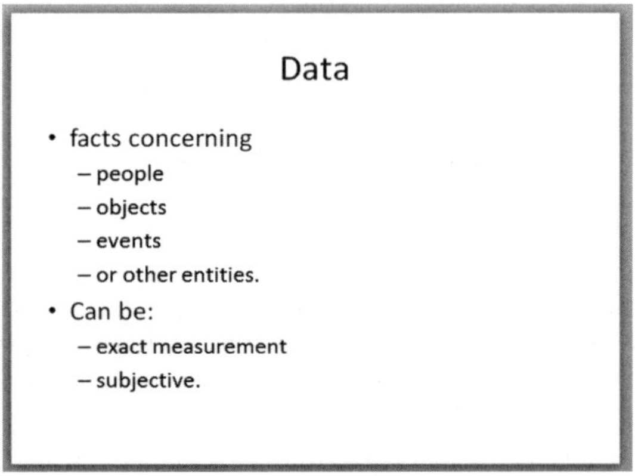

Data

- facts concerning
  - people
  - objects
  - events
  - or other entities.
- Can be:
  - exact measurement
  - subjective.

Text on a slide

Unit 12.4 Activity 1D: Writing for screen

1. What is the reduction in the words the editing has achieved?

2. Can you provide a one- or two-word example for each type of data that could be added to each dot point?

Text display

There are significant differences between screen display and the resolution for printing. The screen resolution of most computer screens is 72 dots per inch. Formatting and appearance of text on a screen affects the communication of a message in a presentation.

Characteristic	Paper	Screen
Size	With high quality printing, 8, 9, 11 point size can be used.	12 point is perhaps the smallest for suitable display. For large font size, most fonts work.
Font type	Serif fonts are usually the best, such as Times.	Need to experiment and compare. Good text fonts may not be suitable.
Font style	Italics and bold are commonly used for effect. Serif fonts work with smaller sizes. Thickness of font is an issue, as is eye fatigue.	Bold is generally satisfactory. Italic is very difficult to read. Satisfactory on large font size only. A dot can be of different size, colour and degree of lightness, indentation of dot points.
Line length	Long lines of text are difficult to read. Short lines are good for small type, as used in newspapers. Can be done to small margins.	Long lines of text are difficult to read. For maximum effect use shorter lines with plenty of white space.
Font colour	Most commonly black text on white background. Easiest to read, high contrast between foreground and background.	Softening effect of edges; some, like yellow, are hard to read.
Amount of text per page or screen	Fixed once printed.	Screens can be 'zoomed' in some cases. Screen has lower resolution than pages, so text can be harder to read.
Resolution	Print has higher resolution than screen.	A pixel is square; its size cannot change and a single pixel can only be one colour. Typically equivalent to 72 dpi. An image suitable for screen viewing will not print at high quality.
Resolution for printing	600 dpi for laser printing. 1600–3000 dpi for commercial printing.	Lower resolution images are smaller file size and allow quicker access time.
Screen and paper size	A4 is the most common printer paper size. Books and magazines can be a range of sizes.	Screen size can be set by designer for multimedia producers. Screen display window can be set by user for web browsers.

Text resolution for print and screen

Graphic artwork

Graphic images are usually imported into PowerPoint slides. PowerPoint does have some capability for creating images, similar to that in other applications within Microsoft Office.

Generally, images should be modified in a graphics application. However, they can be modified in size and also cropped to suit the presentation.

The types of images that can be added include:

- Line artwork.
- Animations.
- Scanned photographic images.
- Digital camera photographic images.
- Clip art.
- Three-dimensional images.

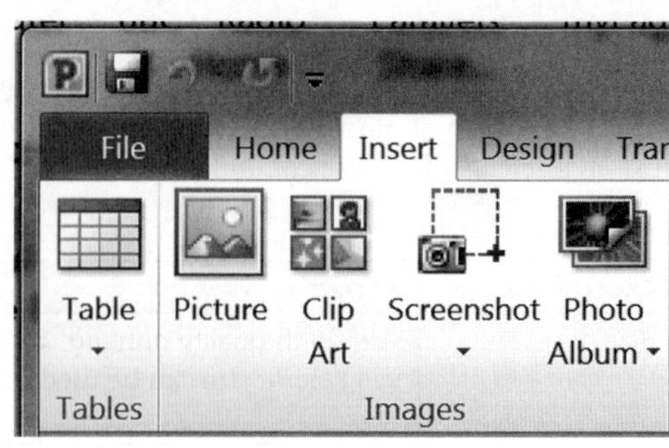

The Insert tab in Microsoft PowerPoint allows the insertion of images

Charts

PowerPoint has the capability to create simple charts and tables for the display of data. PowerPoint can link to data in an Excel spreadsheet and update edits from the spreadsheet live to the presentation.

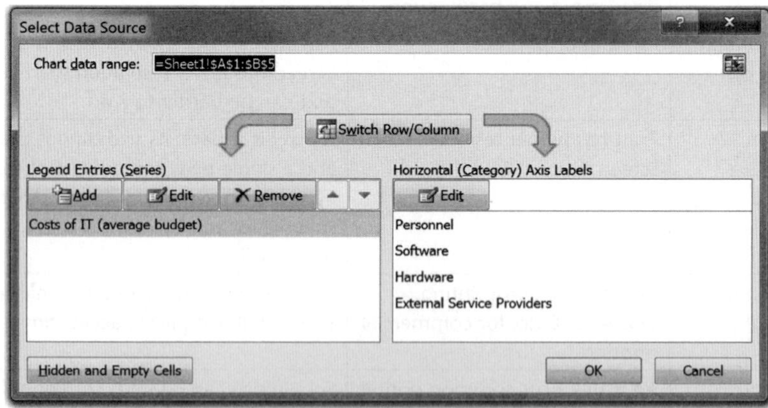

Excel data source for a chart in PowerPoint

The data is separate from the presentation. Formatting of the chart and the chart type can be selected from within PowerPoint. This is suitable for a simple chart on a single slide.

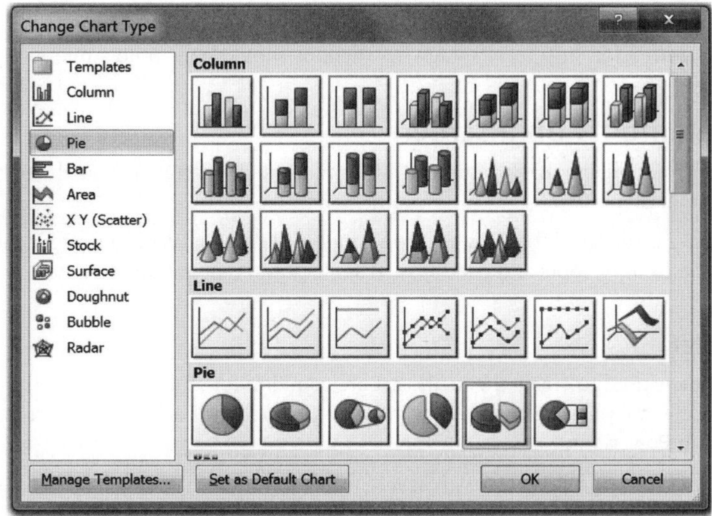

Different chart types that can be used in PowerPoint

Screen size

The user usually sets the screen presentation size. The appropriate size depends on content and its arrangement. Usually a number of prototype screens need to be designed to see what is effective.

The production may need to suit a range of screen sizes. The traditional ratio size was 4:3, with 16:9 now more common and 16:10 also available.

There is an increasing variety of monitors and projection devices so it is best to discover if there are any special requirements for correct display.

Some examples of screen sizes are shown in the table below.

Screen	Tablet (eg iPad)	Laptop	Plasma/LED TV	Projector
Ratio	4:3	16:9	16:9	16:9 Older models 4:3
Pixel dimensions (examples)	1024 × 768	1280 × 768 1920 × 1200	1280 × 768 1920 × 1200	1024 × 768 1280 × 768 1920 × 1200

Screen resolutions

Consistency of screen design

Consistency of design in a presentation helps the audience follow the presentation. The audience expects similar content to appear in similar positions on the screen. The layout should be consistent throughout the presentation.

Each screen should contain the same design elements. Buttons, icons and menus should be consistent. The need for on-screen written instructions should be kept to a minimum.

Design elements on a screen

The two main components of the setup of a slide are the slide master and the theme that is being applied to that master.

The slide master is the 'grid' that sets the layout for the slide with placeholders for the content. Themes are the colours, fonts and effects (such as shadows) that are pre-designed.

Slide master

A **master slide** is used to create the items that are common for all slides. A screen can comprise two layers: a screen layer superimposed over a background. The background layer is called a 'master slide' in PowerPoint.

The background contains elements such as text title box and body text field areas as well as navigation buttons common to a number of screens.

Elements of the master slide

The text font and size are set in the master slide and should be consistent. A new slide added to the presentation adopts the characteristics of the master slide. The figure below shows a master slide and the text levels with indent and text formatting.

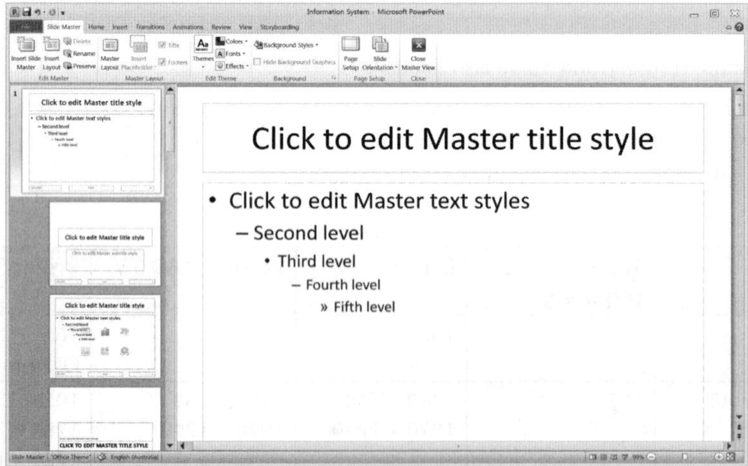

Slide master in PowerPoint

Themes

A theme can be quickly applied to a presentation. The theme colours are selected to complement each other rather than clash. There is a 'basic' theme that has no colours, but is applied to the slides as default.

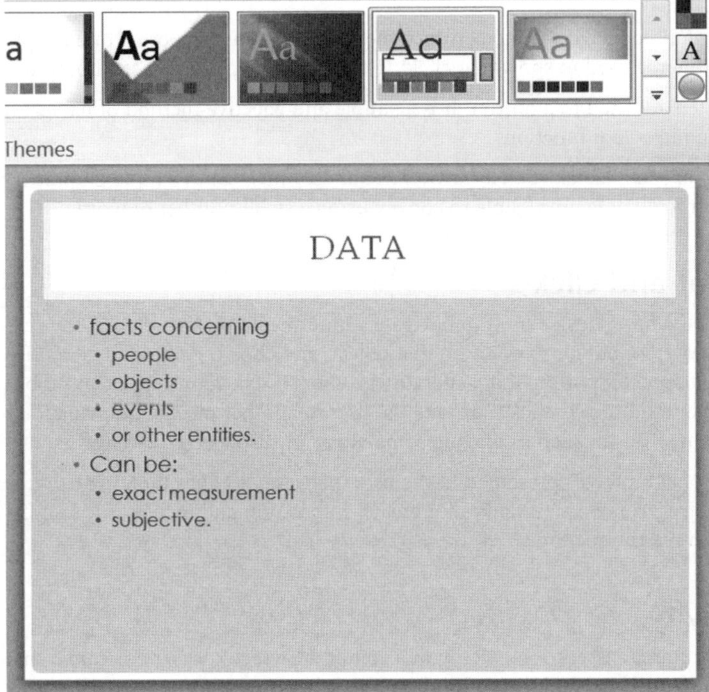

Applying a theme to a presentation

The look and feel of a presentation can be altered radically by selecting a different theme. Although easy to apply, the question still remains: 'Is this the appropriate look and feel for the presentation?'

Within a theme it is also possible to select a variant of that theme.

Buttons and hypertext links

Buttons are used to create hypertext links that move the user from one part of the presentation to another part. Buttons are objects which, when clicked, perform an action. Those actions include:

- Carrying out a hypertext link.
- Showing an image.

- Playing a sound or a digital video.
- Displaying a message or dialogue box.

By default PowerPoint includes simple navigation buttons and a screen annotation pen.

Navigation buttons in PowerPoint

Icons

An **icon** is a graphic image used to convey a meaning about its purpose. For example, a graphic image of a printer is used to show that clicking on the printer icon will send output to the printer.

An icon is often attached to a button. It is a simple and effective method of navigation or of expressing an important function.

The meaning of some icons, such as arrows, is almost universal. A simple graphic icon can convey a meaning that is impossible to convey using a small number of words.

See, point and click

The mouse is the basic device used to navigate a multimedia presentation. The user will see something, move the cursor to point on that object, and click the object. The mouse click is like pressing a 'hot spot' or 'button' that generates a response. The mouse click could be a selection from a menu or a button. A click may take the user to another piece of information, or it may cause an action to occur, such as playing some music or displaying an image.

As the range of alternatives presented to the user increases, so does the interactivity of the presentation. Easier navigation makes for greater interaction and increases the accessibility of the information in the production.

Interactivity

Multimedia requires a user to interact with a computer screen. A user can make choices about the information to access and the paths chosen to access that information. There are differing degrees of interactivity.

In a passive interaction, a series of screens is viewed in a linear sequence. An interactive activity allows the user to make choices which lead to the different scenarios.

Although there is limited research regarding the nature of interaction, it is different from other forms of communication. Some differences include:

- Short attention span – people are frustrated if response times are slow when using multimedia.
- Spatial disorientation – people can feel lost using multimedia, not knowing where they are within a presentation. Most presentations are linear in sequence; some presentations will number the screen being displayed and also show the total number of screens (slides).

Using backgrounds

Elements of a presentation, such as titles and page numbering, must be common to a number of pages. The location of screen elements such as navigation buttons, text fields and areas for graphics can be set in the background.

A background refers to those elements that appear on each page or screen of the production. The colour composition of the background is important – it must be interesting, with colours that do not clash with elements that appear in the foreground. As a new page is opened, the elements for that page are superimposed over the background.

There can be a number of backgrounds in a presentation. This allows variety in presentation, depending upon the content and the overall design. Too much variety, however, can cause the user to become disoriented.

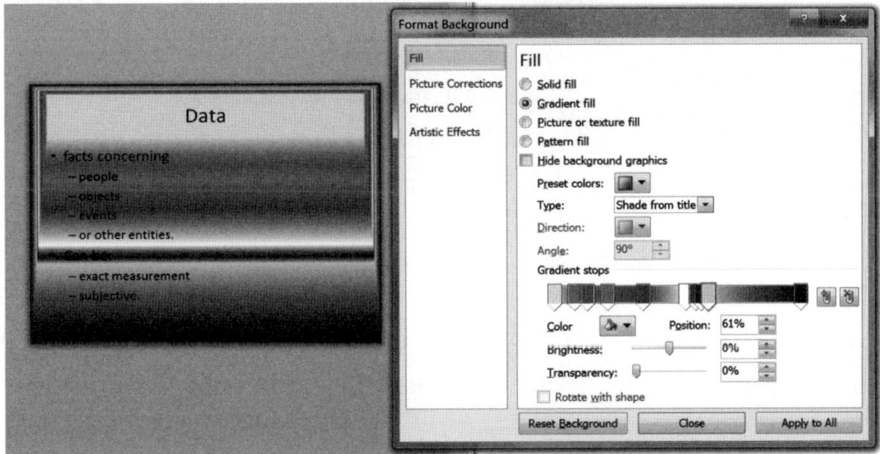

Adjusting the background of a slide

Unit 12.4 Activity 1E: Slide settings

Do you think the presenter should accept the settings as shown for the slide above? Give reasons for your answer.

Navigational design

Decisions about how a user will move around a multimedia presentation must be made in the planning stage. This determines the degree and type of user interaction to be developed. It will also determine how these links can be made to work in the production. Paths that the user decides to take must be carefully planned.

A map showing each screen and its relationship to other screens should be drawn on paper.

Navigation methods

Common examples of navigation in multimedia are:

- Menus.
- Hypertext.

- Buttons, with icons to direct the user to a particular link.
- Transparent buttons that act as hot spots on the screen.

In some cases an **index** of key terms or topics can be a useful navigation device.

PowerPoint will place a set of 'default buttons' for navigation for a presentation.

Navigation can be done using a menu as shown in the figure below.

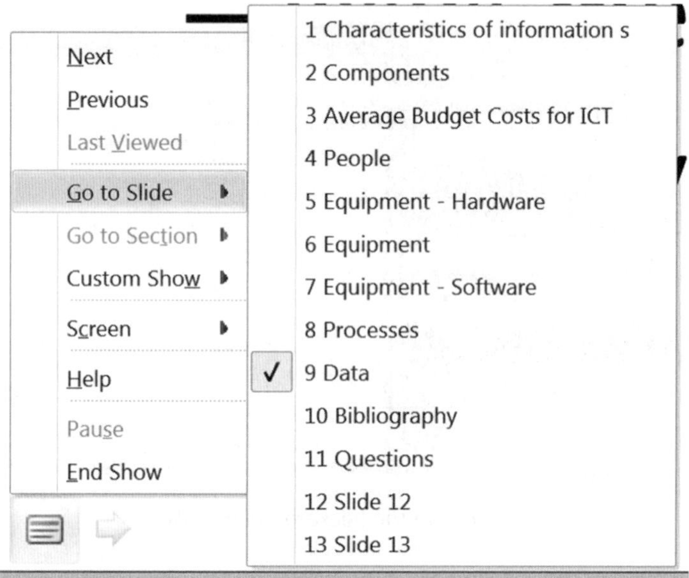

A navigation menu

Video

Carefully selected **video** can be very powerful in a presentation. It can also provide a rest for the presenter for a short period of time and stimulate the audience. Usually 'less is more': video that complements and enhances a presentation can be measured in seconds. If it is lengthy, audience attention may wane. It can become a distraction from the main message of the presentation.

Frames can be taken from the video and used as a placeholder in a presentation.

Sources of video

Video for multimedia can be:

- Recorded by a camera.
- Recorded from a television signal to a storage device.
- Obtained as 'clips' from a network or storage device.

Copyright may be an issue when including a video in a presentation.

Storyboarding a video

The motion picture industry uses **storyboarding** extensively for location shooting so that the resources required for the shoot can be planned and managed. For less complicated situations storyboarding will assist in framing the shot and determining suitable lighting.

A storyboard is a critical tool for movie shooting to record video specifically for multimedia. A video storyboard is usually a series of rough drawings representing a shot-by-shot breakdown of the planned video. The storyboard allows:

- Key scenes to be planned in relation to each other.
- The action and events related to a key scene to be planned.

The storyboard can be then used to plan more specific questions and tasks such as:

- Suitable locations to be found and checked; the time and position suitable at a single location may vary according to the time of day.
- What the scene should look like.
- Whether or not props are to be used.
- Scripting spoken words.
- Rehearsing spoken words, unless spontaneity is required.

Usually movies need to be edited and this should be done in specialist software before exporting to a format for the presentation. The original video should be retained for backup and in case it needs to be reconsidered if another edit is needed.

Video capture

There is a wide variety of formats for video. Different companies develop proprietary file types and video compression 'codecs'. Codecs enable compression or decompression of video and can be either software or hardware devices.

Examples of video file formats include .asf, .avi, .divx, .mov, .mp2, .mp2v, .mp4, .mpeg, .wm and .wmv.

While video is playing and being displayed on a computer screen, the part to be used is recorded and digitised. It is best to record three to four seconds extra at the start and end of the section to make it easier to cue and edit the footage. The section is then named as a file and compressed by the software as it is saved.

Importing files

Files can be imported for use in a movie. The figure below shows some of the video, sound and image file types that can be imported into Windows Movie Maker, from **Help** in Windows Movie Maker. Windows Movie Maker can be downloaded from the Microsoft website.

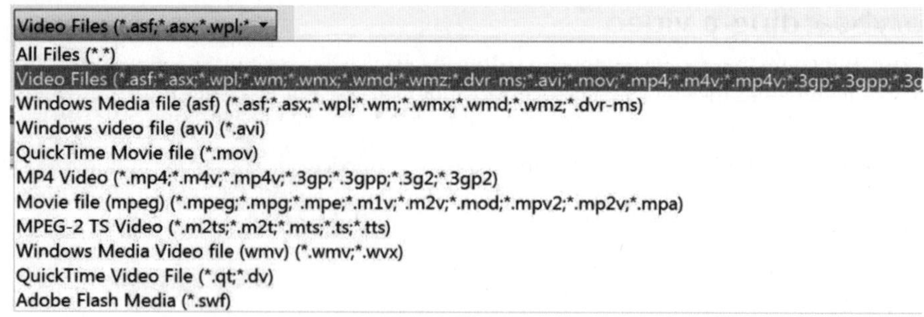

Importing video files

A movie project

A movie document is called a project. The project organises and manages files to be assembled for the movie.

Name	Size	Type
scene1.avi	1,864 KB	Video Clip
still1.jpg	33 KB	JPEG Image
sound1.wav	4,185 KB	WAVE Audio File
scene1_0001.jpg	29 KB	JPEG Image
myfirstmovie.MSWMM	53 KB	Windows Movie Maker Project
myfirstmovie.wmv	1,178 KB	Windows Media Audio/Video file

Files that can be used in a project

Providing meaningful file names for clips can make them easier to track during editing.

The figure above shows the files in a movie, the project file (with the .MSWMM extension) and a movie created from the project.

How a project works

A project file saves the arrangement of movie clips, transitions and effects applied to the clips, title and credit screens, and other edits that have been made. The project only uses references to original clips, not a copy of the actual file. If the clips are moved or renamed during the project they need to be linked back to the project.

If the original clip is deleted it can no longer be used in Movie Maker.

Organising a collection

Files that are grouped together for use in Windows Movie Maker are called collections. A collection could be made for each scene or discrete section of the movie.

Editing a movie

A movie can be edited like any other document. For example, the cut, copy and paste commands apply to movies.

Features of movie editing software

The two main tools to organise and assemble a movie are the timeline and the storyboard. The viewer at the bottom of the screen toggles between the timeline and the storyboard.

Storyboard

The storyboard shows the clips that form part of the movie. The figure below shows the storyboard at the bottom of the screen with a title, two video transitions and video.

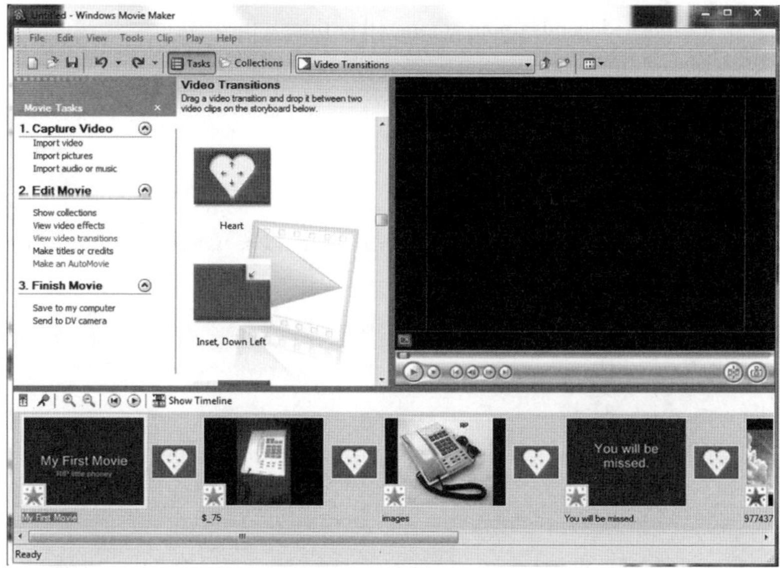

A storyboard in Movie Maker

Timeline

The timeline shows the files in the project in relation to each other and time, displayed as hours: minutes: seconds: hundredths of a second.

The timeline identifies content as:

- Video, with transition effects and video audio.
- Audio/music, including voice over or narration added in Movie Maker.
- Title screen, credit screens and text overlay.
- Effects applied to the video clips.

The figure below shows the timeline view. Note the solid line crossing the timeline elements, sometimes called a playback indicator or playhead.

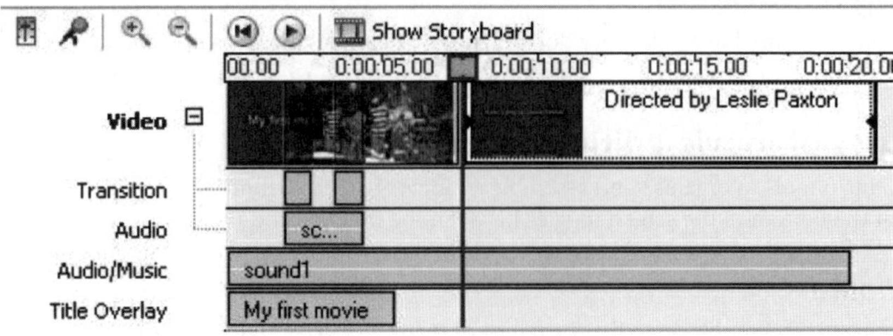

A timeline in Movie Maker

The file size of the movie depends upon, among other things, the:

- Frames per second.
- Window size of the movie.
- Compression schemes used to produce the video.

Playing a movie in PowerPoint

A movie can be part of a PowerPoint presentation and should be used to illustrate a point in the presentation.

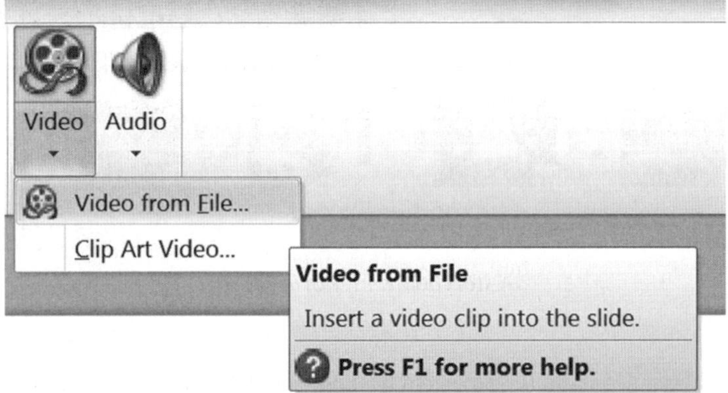

Inserting a video into a PowerPoint slide

PowerPoint displays the movie with a set of standard controls. There is a variety of settings to adjust the screen window for the movie. It needs to appear in the presentation in a manner that is consistent with other slides.

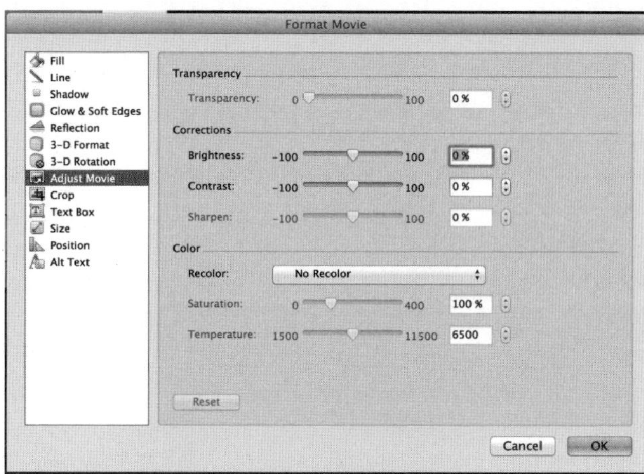

Video settings in PowerPoint

Elements of good multimedia design

Good multimedia design will:

- Make it easy to find information quickly.
- Create a presentation that the user finds interesting.
- Maintain the user's interest.

Common faults in multimedia

The following list represents some common faults in multimedia design and presentation:

- No feedback given to the user when an action is performed and it appears nothing is happening.
- Screens cluttered with too much information.
- Screens have too many different icons.
- Repetition of various effects, such as sound, animation or video, on particular screens that becomes boring.
- Using icons whose meanings are not obvious.
- A mouse click bringing up an unexpected responses.
- Not knowing how to get to a previously visited screen.

Unit 12.4 Multimedia

Topic 2: Creating interactive presentations

Topic 2 looks at the skills and techniques required to create interactive presentations.
It covers:

- Creating hyperlinks in a presentation.
- Creating action buttons.
- Adding music and sound.
- Adding movies and animated GIFs.

A variety of settings can be used to navigate and create interaction in a presentation. Some of these events occur when:

- A new screen is opened, for example an audio file may play.
- The mouse is clicked causing a movie to play.
- The mouse is clicked on text (hyperlink) that opens a browser and a website.
- The mouse is clicked on a button and the presentation moves to a new slide.
- The mouse (cursor) enters or leaves a particular object.

Creating hyperlinks in a presentation

A **hyperlink** can be attached to text, objects or any item on the screen in a presentation. The hyperlink can point to:

- An anchor within the presentation.
- An anchor in another presentation.
- A web page.
- An email client.

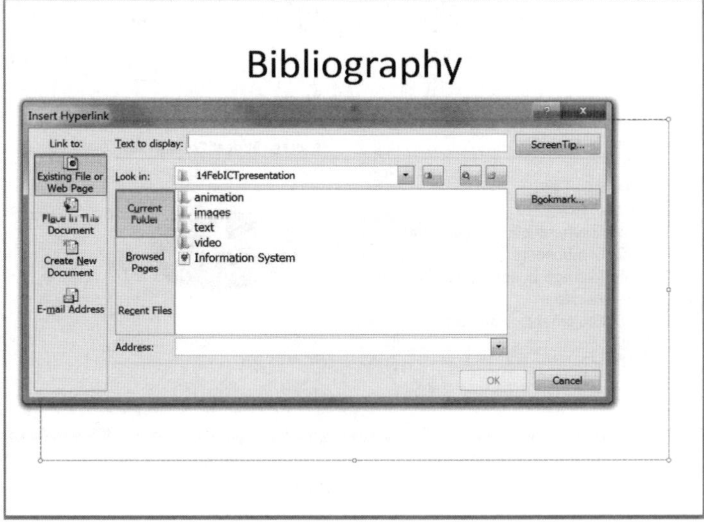

Inserting a hyperlink

Creating hyperlink action buttons

The figure on the right shows a graphic object, in this case an oval shape, that is about to be placed over the image to create a button to hold the hyperlink.

If a number of buttons were to be created, one button could be copied and then the link could be edited to go to the correct location.

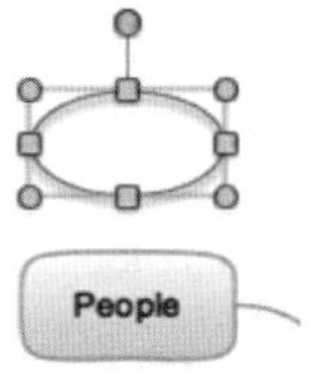

Creating a button with a hyperlink

Create a hyperlink to a location in the current presentation

A hyperlink to another location in a presentation can be created using the **Links** section of the **Insert** tab in PowerPoint.

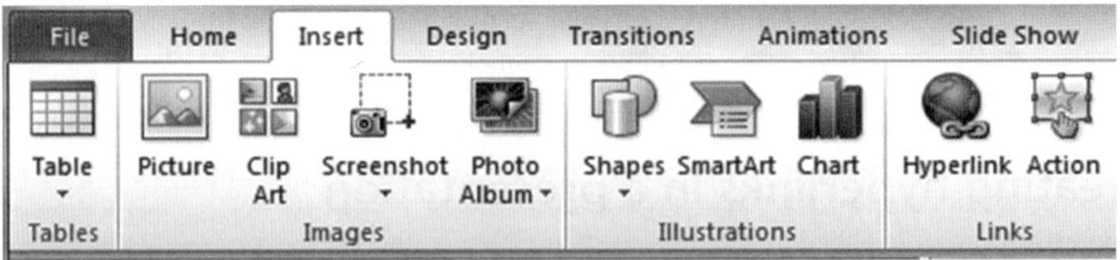

Inserting a hyperlink

The action of the hyperlink is defined within PowerPoint.

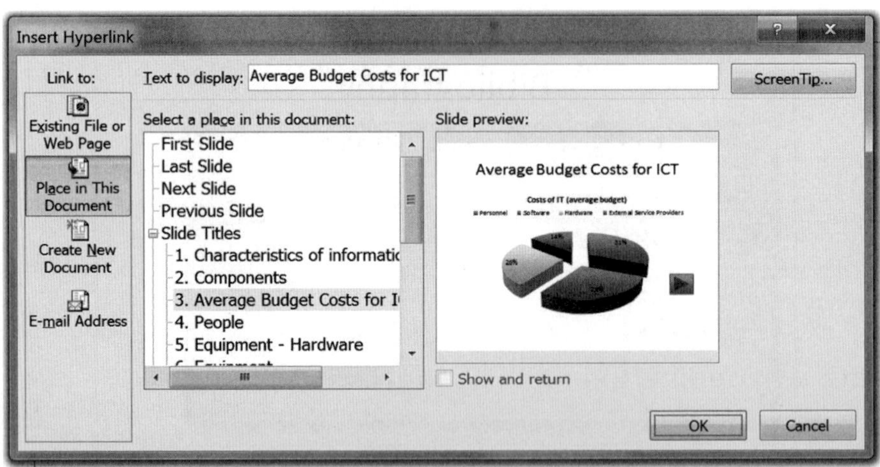

Creating the hyperlink

Create a hyperlink to a specific slide in another presentation

To create a hyperlink to a slide in another presentation, first create a button or select text for the hyperlink. With the item selected, **Insert > Hyperlink > A Bookmark**, select the file and then nominate the slide.

By right-clicking on the button or link the dialog box allows a hyperlink to select the presentation and a particular slide as the button destination.

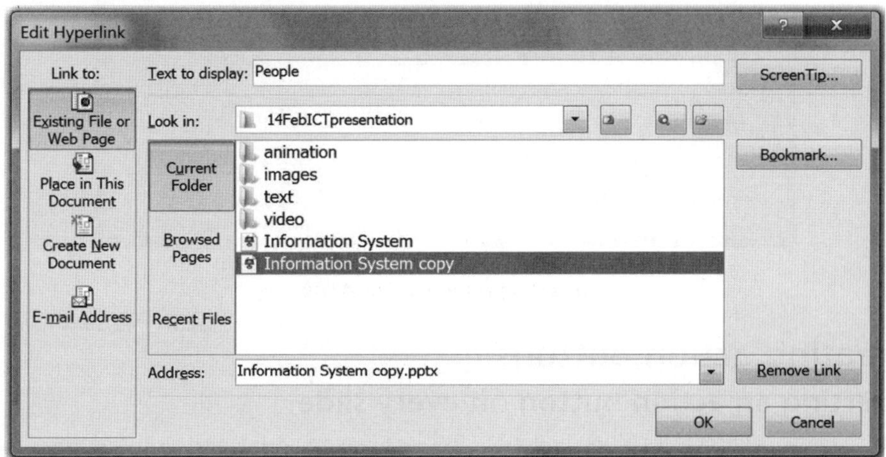

Creating a link to a slide in a different presentation

Note the actual location of the file as shown in the link (ie the URL for the file). This is an absolute reference to the file and for the link to work the files need to be on the computer where the link was created.

The linked slide will need a link back to the originating slide.

Create a hyperlink to a file or web page

This is done using the same method except that a file or a web page is selected as the destination.

Create a hyperlink to an email address

This could be a useful effect where a presentation is distributed by a presenter for later review, comment or study. By embedding an email link in the presentation, it can focus the response to the actual point of the content.

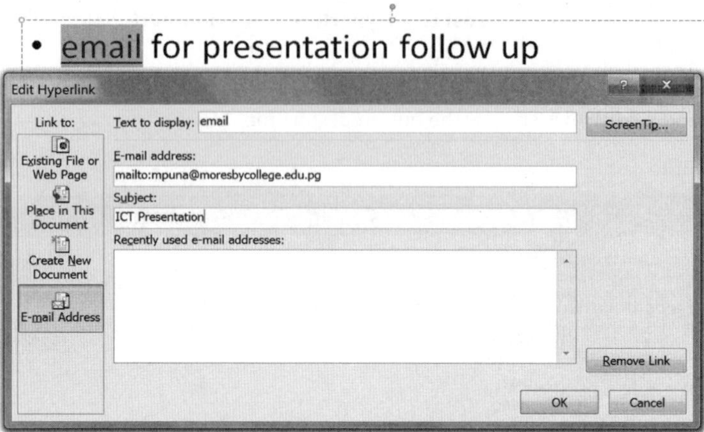

Inserting an email hyperlink

Creating action buttons

Inserting an action button on every slide

Using a master slide enables action buttons to be placed on every slide that each perform a consistent action. For example, a **Next** button could go on each slide.

A variety of options exists for placing a button on a slide. A button is placed on the screen by selecting **Slide Show > Action** Buttons. The cursor then changes to allow the button to be drawn on the screen.

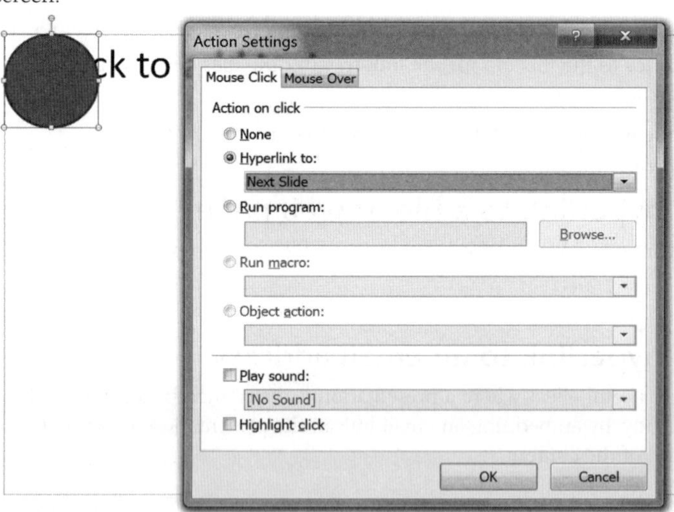

Inserting an action button

Adding music and sound

Inserting music or sound effects on a slide

Music can be added from a file to a slide. This is done using the **Audio** button on the **Media** section of the **Insert** tab in PowerPoint.

Care needs to be taken when adding sound to a slide. It is easy for the audience to be distracted by superfluous noise – in particular, sound effects from clip art audio can be distracting.

Audio when added to a slide should be directly related to its content and shorter, rather than longer, in duration.

The figure on the right shows options for adding sound to a slide using the menu items **Insert > Audio**.

Inserting audio into a slide

The options:

- Audio from a File would be suited to music.
- Clip Art Audio would be a short sound affect.
- Record Audio would be a snippet of speech, for example, recorded during the slide creation.

The figure below shows a recording being made. The name **Comment** is added to the slide. It has a duration of 4.3 seconds.

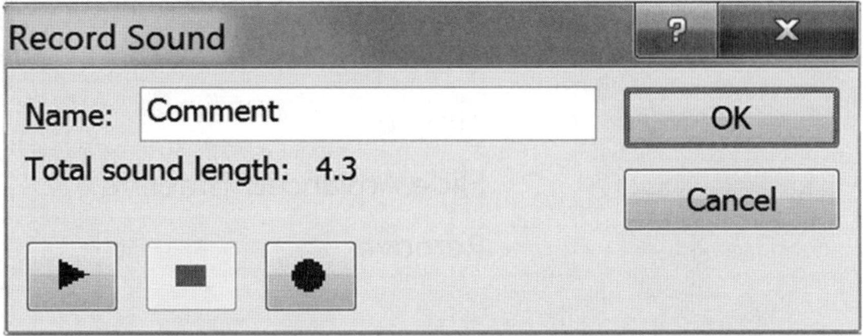

Recorded audio. It is 4.3 seconds long and has the name 'Comment'.

The figure below shows how the sound will be seen on the slide with the 'sound' icon and *playback controls*.

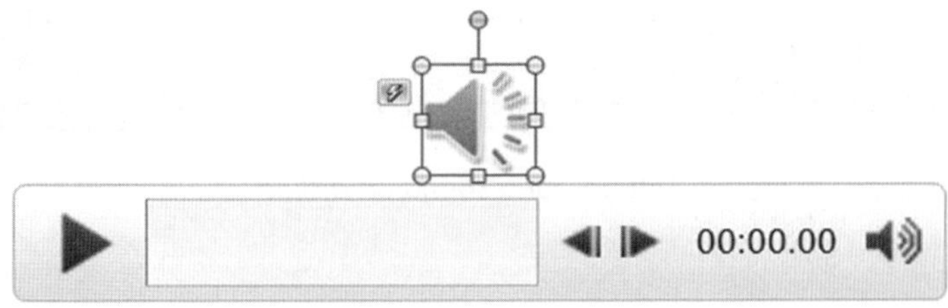

Sound inserted onto a slide with controls

The figure below shows the settings that can be applied to a sound. This pane appears when the sound is selected on the slide.

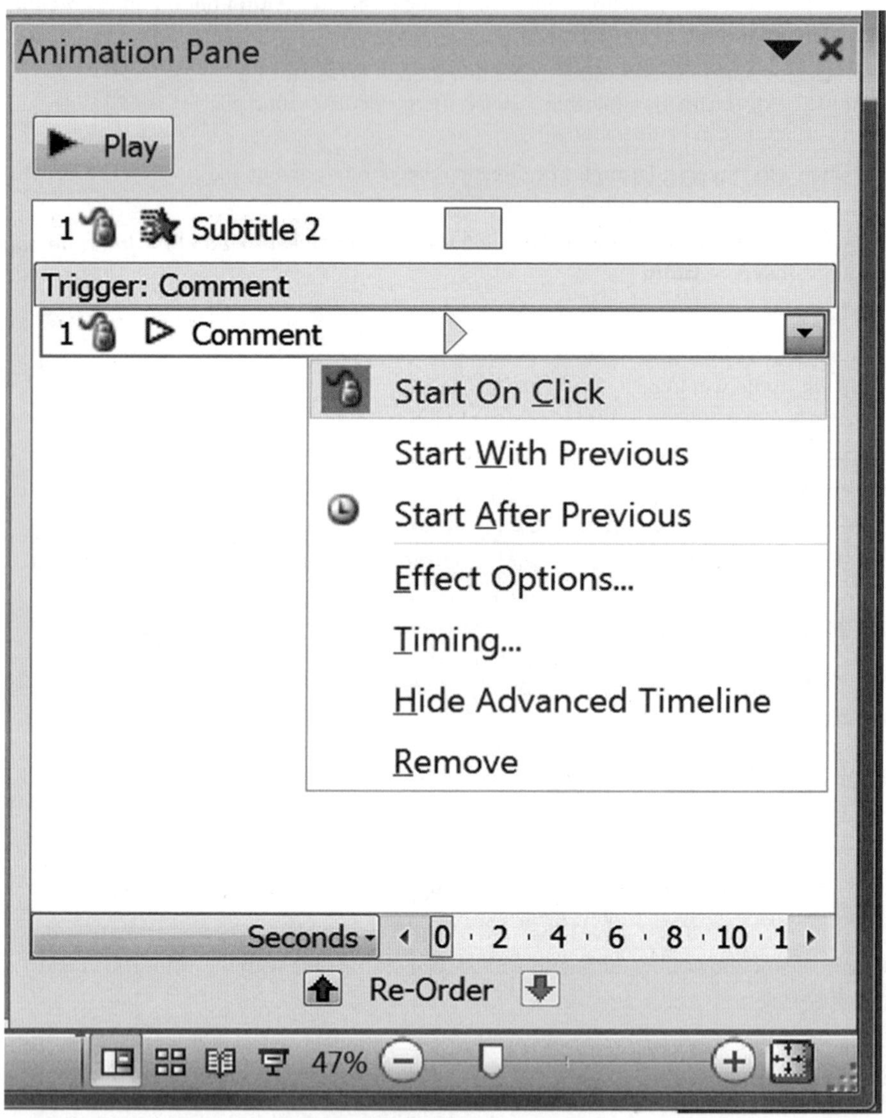

Settings for a sound on a slide

Stopping the sound during a presentation

The sound playing can be stopped by clicking on the stop button on the controls. At the end of the time of the sound, it will stop automatically (unless it is looping) when complete.

Playing a CD during a presentation

A sound file can be set to play from the start of the presentation.

Adding movies and animated GIFs

Starting a movie on a mouse click

With a video selected on the slide, the **File > Video** tools provide a variety of options that can be selected to arrange the playback on the slide. A video could be selected to play automatically or on a mouse click.

The figure below shows the options for playback of a video.

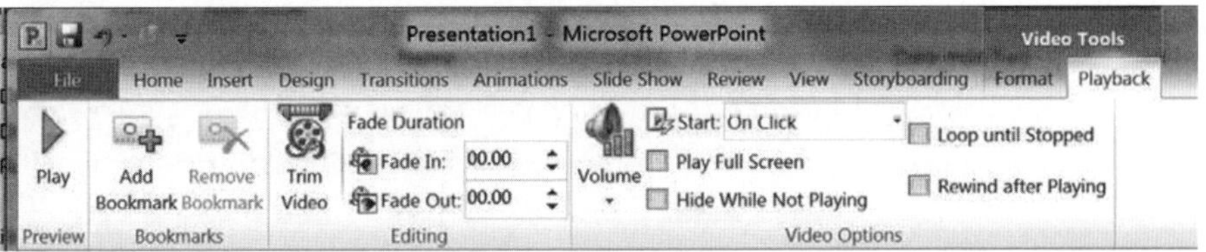

Video playback options

Unit 12.4 Multimedia

Topic 3: Delivering and controlling a presentation

Topic 3 looks at the skills and techniques required to deliver and control a multimedia presentation. It covers:

- Applying animated effects and transitions.
- Delivering your presentation.
- Setting timing and creating self-running presentations.
- Creating custom shows within a presentation.
- Packaging a presentation.

Applying animation effects and transitions

Animation effects and transitions should be applied with care. They can be very obtrusive and detract from the presentation.

Their usefulness depends on the subject matter of the presentation and the demographic of the audience. Older audiences may find animation distracting. Younger audiences may be less inclined to find them distracting.

Applying an animation scheme

An animation scheme can be applied to a slide by selecting the required animation on the **Animations** tab in PowerPoint.

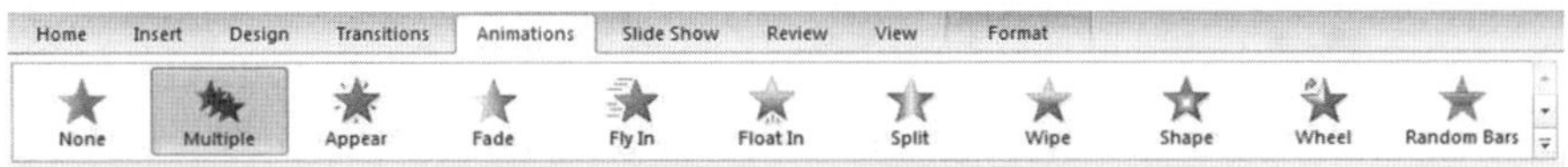

Applying an animation on a slide

Applying custom animations to text and objects

Text and other objects can be animated on a slide by setting a 'path' for the object that will be played when the slide is displayed in presentation mode.

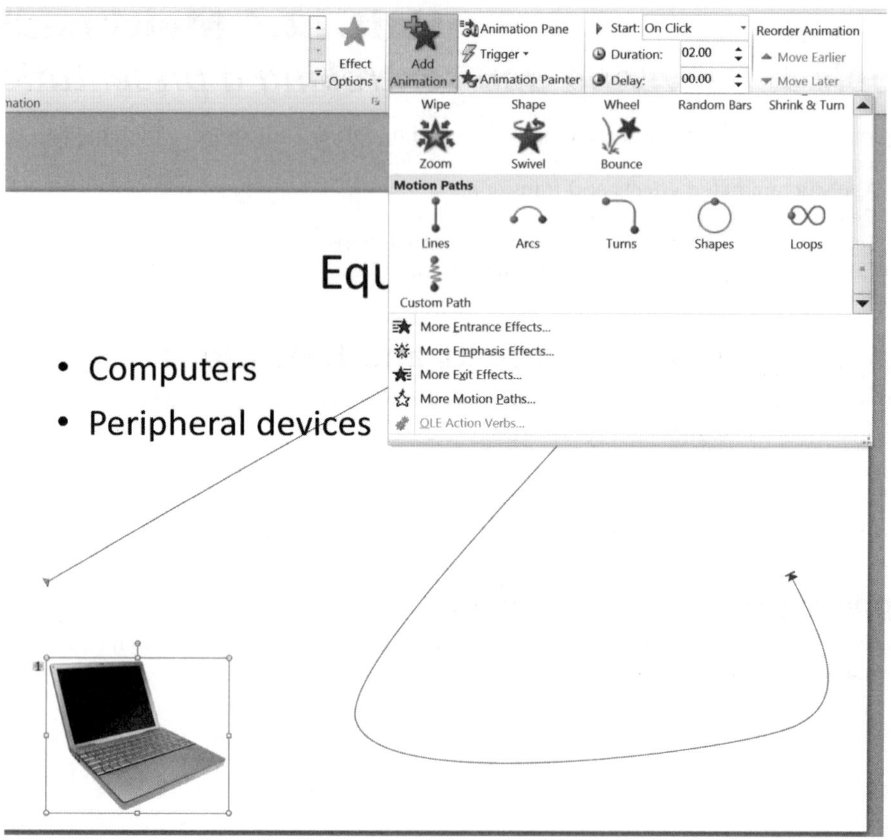

Creating a custom animation path

The animation can be tested on a single slide with **Animation > Preview > Play**.

Applying custom animations to the elements of a chart

By selecting an element in a chart a custom animation can be selected and a range of animations applied to the element.

Adding transitions to a slide

A transition effect (how the screen displays a move to another slide) can be applied to all slides or to individual slides. For example 'dissolve', 'fade' or 'flash' would change the screen appearance whereas 'push', 'split' or 'reveal' show movement from one slide to another.

Transition effects should be used with care. They can have an unsettling effect on the audience as well as distracting them from the content. Inexperienced presenters often try to use too many effects.

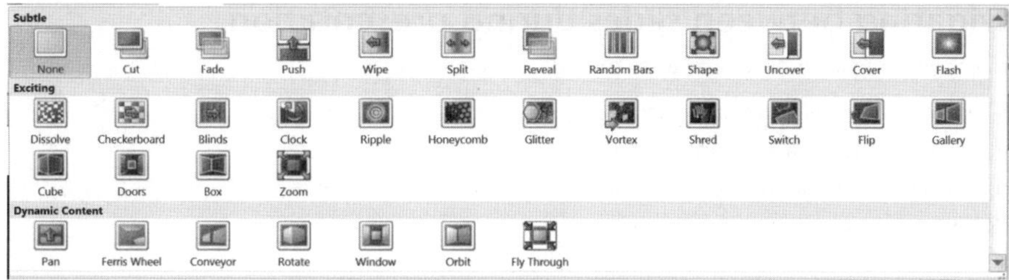

Transition choices in PowerPoint

Delivering your presentation

After the development of a presentation, it is essential to have **backup** copies that are easily accessible. These backups should themselves be tested to make sure that they are viable.

The delivery of a presentation may take place in a different area to where it was developed.

The following could impact on the effectiveness of the presentation:

- Room orientation and lighting.
- Size of the room.
- Size of the screen for the presentation.
- Position and orientation of the presenter to the audience.
- The type of computer being used to operate the presentation.

If a presentation device is used, a check must be made to see if it replicates the colours used in the presentation. High contrast between foreground and background will help minimise problems in this area.

Where possible, the environment should be tested before the presentation.

Tips for making better presentations

Here are some tips when making a presentation:

- Speak slowly and clearly; it is important not to rush through the presentation.
- Face the audience and not the screen.
- Speak to a central point in the room.
- Do not be distracted by movements in the audience
- Use the points on a slide as a guide for the audience; try not to read the slides 'word for word'.
- Watch other presenters and examine their presentations. See what works and what does not work.

An old adage in making a presentation is to tell the audience:

- What you are going to say (ie introduce the main points).
- The presentation content in detail.
- What you have just said (ie summarise the main points).

Navigating between slides during presentation

Choices for navigating between slides include:

- Onscreen buttons (shown by default by PowerPoint).
- Onscreen buttons added and customised.
- Left (previous slide) and right (next slide) keyboard cursor keys.
- Remote control replacing the mouse.

Marking up slides using a pen during presentation

PowerPoint default pen options are available during a presentation.

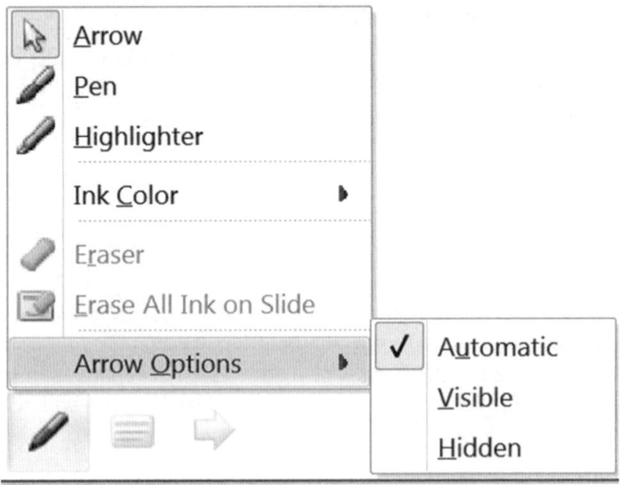

Pen options for marking up a slide

Mark-up is useful to expand on an explanation, particularly if a chart or picture is being used. It is sometimes useful to mark up during a presentation. The pen can also be used if there are questions from the audience that require further explanation.

Using highlight annotations during a presentation

The figure below shows a section of text that has been annotated as the slide show has been running. The highlight colour is yellow.

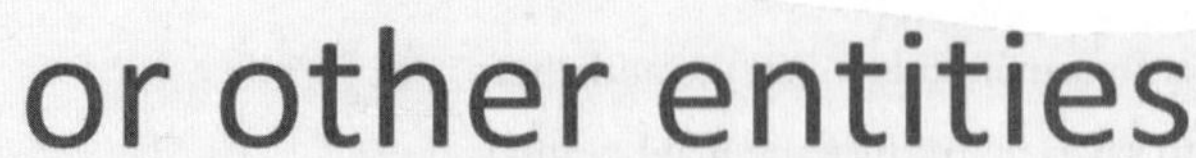

Annotation to slide

Keeping ink annotations after a presentation

The figure below shows what happens when the slide show is finished. If annotations have been made, then PowerPoint will prompt for the annotations to be saved or discarded.

Dialog box to save or discard annotations

Setting timing and creating self-running presentations

A slide show can be set up using the **Set Up** section of the **Slide Show** tab in PowerPoint.

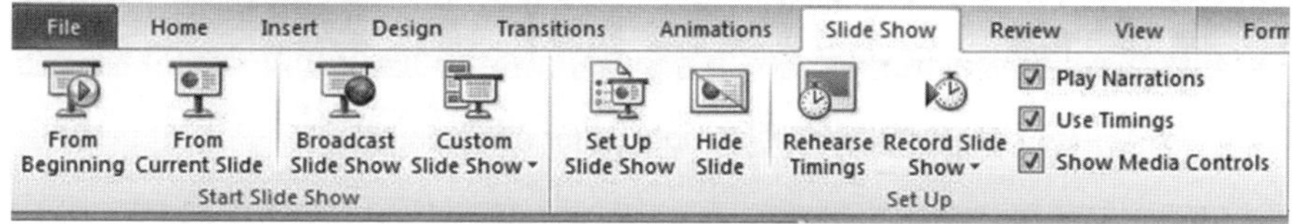

Setting up a slide show

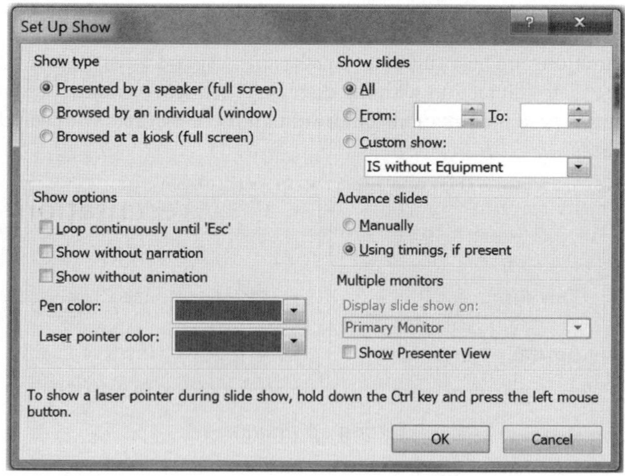

Set-up options for a slide show

Set timing for a slide show manually

Manual operation of a slide show is usually done by the presenter.

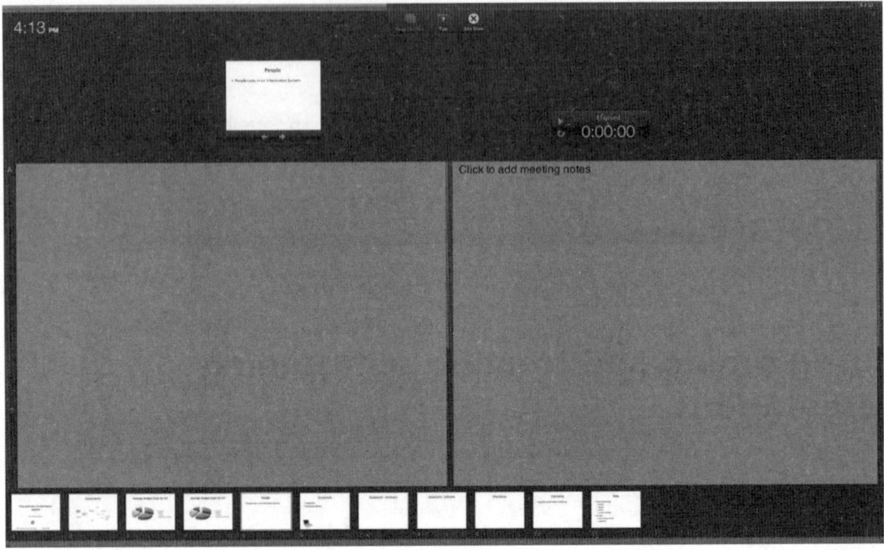

Some of the set-up options for a presentation

Create a self-running presentation

A presenter would use a self-running presentation only if he or she was very confident about both the content and the delivery and if the presentation was very short.

Self-running presentations are best suited for kiosks and displays where the audience refers to the screen and there is no interaction with the display. These self-running presentations are often in a continuous loop. These presentations often contain more pictures, video and audio than a regular presentation.

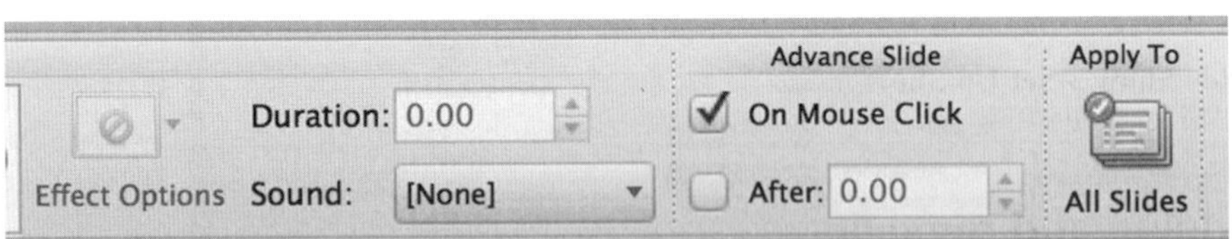

Setting up timings

Creating custom shows within a presentation

There may be occasions where a presentation needs adjustment for a specific audience, or perhaps the timing needs to be adjusted.

A custom show could also be used for a speaker to rehearse the presentation prior to its delivery. The speaker could rehearse only the key slides and any other slides where the content and slide effects were more complicated.

A custom show could also be used to eliminate slides that are in development and not quite complete or for some reason do not quite work. Those slides can be improved and used at a later date.

Creating and presenting a custom show

A separate presentation can be set up by selecting only specific slides to be shown, rather than all the slides in the presentation. This can be done using the **Custom Slide Show** command on the **Slide Show** tab of the ribbon.

The **Edit Custom Show** command enables a custom show to be created and for the slides included to be edited.

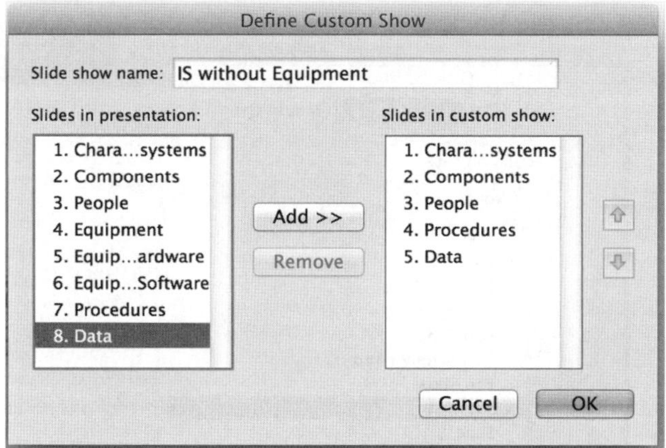

Setting up a custom show

Slide Show > Set Up Show makes the selected Custom Show with a range of settings active in Presenter mode.

Adding and removing slides in a custom show

From the Slide Show menu, **Custom Shows > Edit Custom Shows** enables the slides in a custom show to be added or removed.

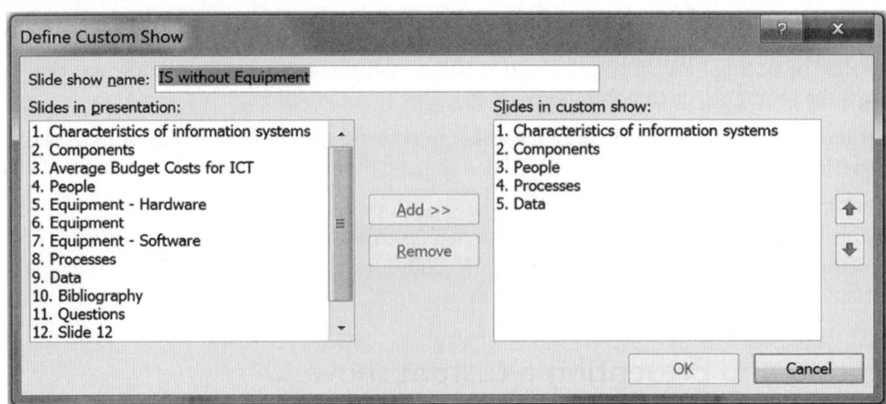

Choosing the slides for a custom show

Creating a hyperlink to a custom show

An action button added to a screen is the best way to store the hyperlink. The destination for the custom show can be selected by right-clicking on the button.

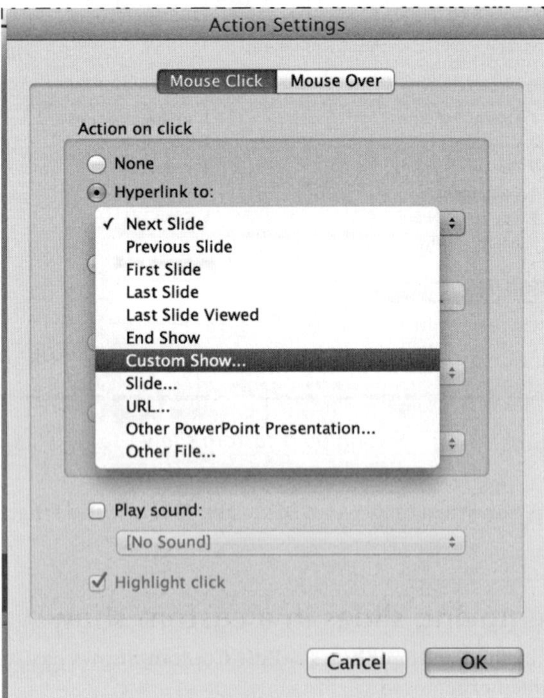

A hyperlink to a custom show

Removing a custom show

From **Slide Show > Custom Shows > Edit Custom Shows** a custom show can be removed from the presentation.

Review a presentation

PowerPoint has a number of tools to review a presentation prior to its delivery. These tools are available on the **Review** tab on the ribbon.

Review options

Packaging a presentation

A presentation can be password-protected to limit access. This is done using the **File > Info** menu items.

When a presentation is finished it can be distributed. For this purpose PowerPoint files can be saved as:

- A native PowerPoint presentation.
- A movie file.
- An image sequence, with each screen becoming a separate image file.
- A portable document format (PDF).

These, and other, options are available using the **Save As** command.

Unit 12.4 Activity 3A: Packaging a presentation

1. From a completed presentation create each of the above file types.
2. Compare the files by:
    - File size.
    - Ease of editing.
    - Software that that is now able to access the files.
3. Consider the advantages and disadvantages of each file type. Discuss whether all aspects of the presentation can be displayed or seen in the new file.

Packaging for CD

Some versions of PowerPoint enable all the files associated with a presentation to be organised and then written to **CD**, **DVD** or other **storage device** at the one time. For example, the presentation may reference audio and video files that are kept separately.

The folder structure shown earlier in the Topic will enable just one folder to be copied as it contains the folders with all the content. That folder could also be archived (compressed) as a single file for attachment to email.

A presentation can be packaged as a stand-alone presentation. To do this, choose the File menu and then select **Save As**. Now choose the file type as **PowerPoint Presentation**.

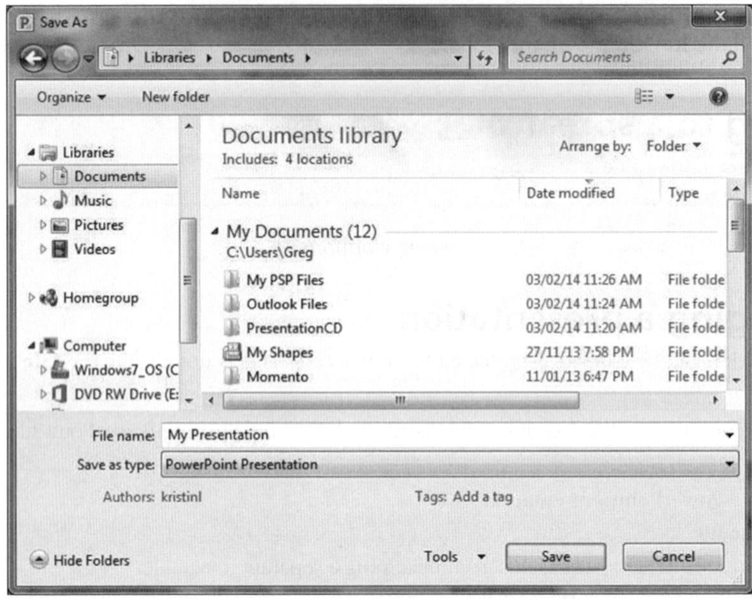

Saving a document as a PowerPoint presentation

This is now saved as a stand-alone presentation.

Viewing a packaged presentation

A packaged presentation can be viewed on another computer without the need to purchase a copy of Microsoft PowerPoint. This allows the viewer to see a fully featured presentation. PowerPoint Viewer can be downloaded from the Microsoft site (www.Microsoft.com).

Testing the presentation

A presentation should be given test runs to check:

- Slide timings.
- That sound, video and animation files are successfully linked and operate correctly in the presentation.
- That navigation buttons and special effects operate correctly.

Unit 12.4 Multimedia

Topic 4: Integrating multimedia with other applications

Topic 4 focuses on methods for integrating multimedia with other applications, such as:

- Linking to a spreadsheet.
- Embedding an object.
- Exporting multimedia files to another document.

Linking to a spreadsheet

PowerPoint can link to data in an Excel spreadsheet and update edits from the spreadsheet live to the presentation.

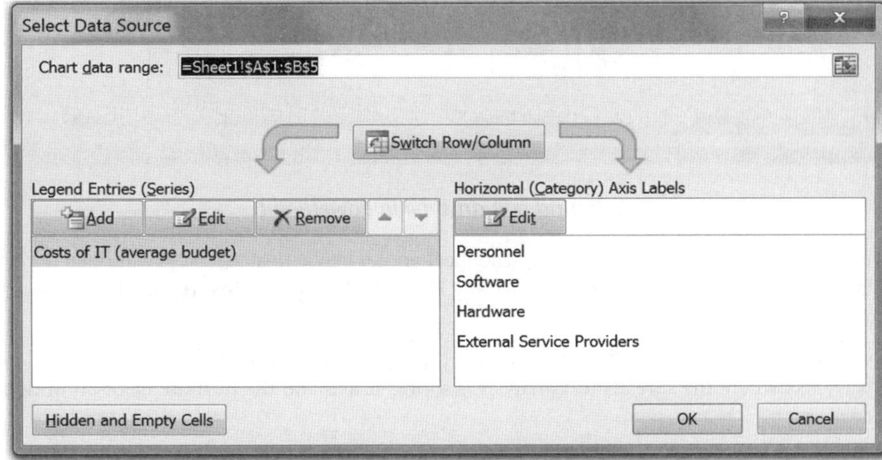

Selecting an Excel data source for a PowerPoint slide

The data is separate and the formatting and chart type can be selected from within PowerPoint.

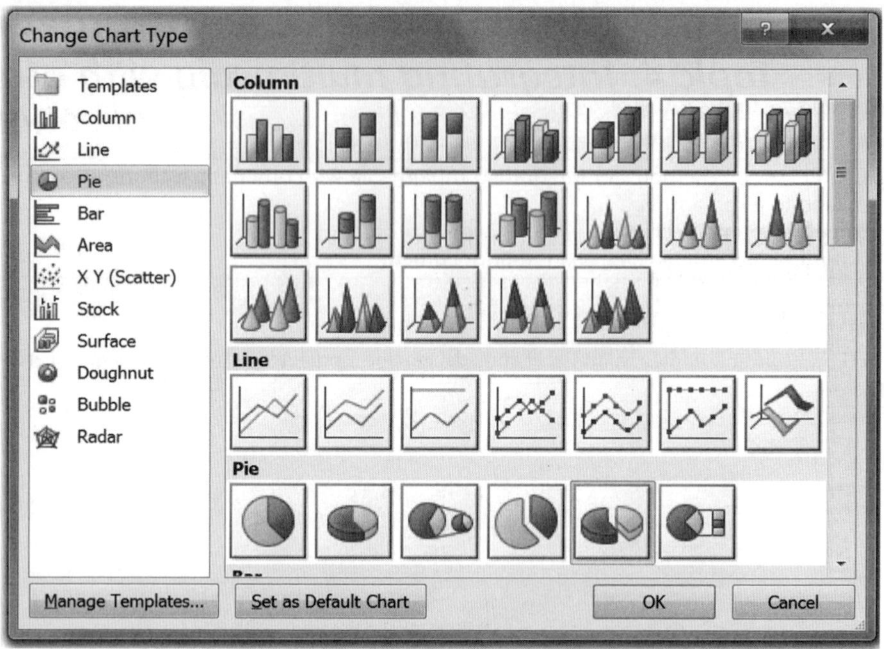

Selecting a chart type in PowerPoint

PowerPoint can hyperlink to an Excel spreadsheet and, when activated, Excel will open and display the sheet. This can be done by selecting **Hyperlink** from the **Insert** menu and selecting the required file.

If, for example, there were a number of charts on the same sheet it might be preferable to do it this way; also where the spreadsheet analysis is sophisticated and the purpose is for an in-depth explanation.

Embedding an object

An object can be embedded in a PowerPoint slide using the **Object** menu item on the **Text** section of the **Insert** tab. The object can be created from a range of applications.

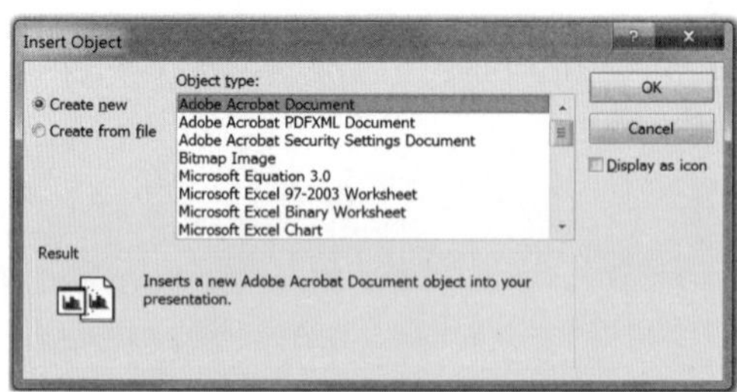

Inserting an embedded object in a PowerPoint slide

The object can then be edited from within PowerPoint by double-clicking on it.

Unit 12.4 Activity 4A: Create a multimedia presentation

Create a multimedia presentation about a career in ICT that interests you.

Exporting multimedia files to another document

A PowerPoint multimedia presentation can be saved in a variety of formats and used in a range of different ways.

This is done using the **Save & Send** command on the **File** menu.

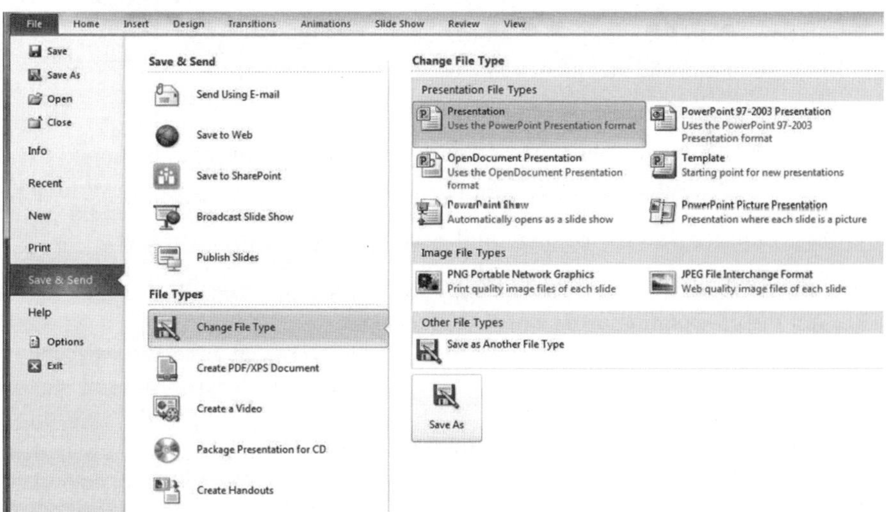

Saving a PowerPoint presentation in a different file type

These file types include:

- PDF.
- Video.
- A packaged presentation.

Note that the presentation can be directly emailed from within PowerPoint using the **Send Using E-mail** command.

Unit 12.4 Activity 4B: Presentation software task

Presentation software can accompany a talk, training seminar, lecture or sales presentation, among other things.

1. List the steps that need to be carried out to create a presentation to a group of people. Assume that you will be preparing at least six slides.

2. Choose a topic and then complete the following tasks:

- **a.** Analyse the topic and decide on the key aspects of the presentation.
- **b.** Create a list of key points to be covered in the presentation.
- **c.** Decide the order of the points in the presentation.
- **d.** Prepare text for the presentation using Microsoft Word.
- **e.** Prepare speaker's notes to accompany the presentation.
- **f.** Select a master slide template to be used.
- **g.** Create the master slide.
- **h.** Select the font type, font size and font style for slides in the presentation
- **i.** Determine the final order of the slides and rearrange the presentation.
- **j.** Select images that may be used on the slides
- **k.** Create graphics and charts for slides
- **l.** Test the presentation using a projection device
- **m.** Create navigation buttons on slides
- **n.** Test the buttons on slides.
- **o.** Test the presentation before a controlled audience.
- **p.** Walk through the presentation and determine suitable timings.
- **q.** Adjust the material on slides to suit the time for the presentation.
- **r.** Create a 'main menu' slide after the opening slide.
- **s.** Use the 'outline' view to order text and the slide order.
- **t.** Print 'reduced view' slides for the audience to follow the presentation.
- **u.** Save the presentation in a web format for posting on a web site.
- **v.** Test the presentation on the computer which will deliver the presentation.
- **w.** Create a back up copy for the presentation.

Unit 12.5 Computers and Employment
Topic 1: Career options in ICT

Unit 12.5 is designed to help prepare students for the workplace after Grade 12 (syllabus p. 42). You will learn how to format an electronic curriculum vitae (CV) and job application letters.

After completing this Unit students will be able to:
- Use a range of computer skills to prepare CVs and job application letters.
- Search for jobs on the Internet.
- Identify possible careers in ICT.

Topic 1 describes a range of career options that are available in the ICT field.

There are many different careers in Information Communication Technologies. In small organisations, one person may carry out a number of different roles. In large organisations, teams of people are employed to carry out the services required by those organisations.

ICT is an industry that changes quickly. As new developments are launched, the required skills change and the demands for those skills change. ICT is regarded by some as a global industry where geographic borders are not relevant.

In some cases, organisations outsource some of the ICT functions to other organisations. Some of these organisations may be located in countries different to that of the original organisation. For example, India has developed a significant ICT industry that provides outsourcing services around the world.

In Unit 12.1, the concept of an information system was examined. Its key elements are:

- People.
- Processes.
- Equipment.
- Data.

Careers in ICT have a skill set that encompasses those aspects of ICT. Many careers require specialists in a particular element of the system. For example, a systems analyst may conduct examination of an ICT system and report on that system, encompassing all areas. A technician works with the equipment and software that are used to operate the system. Within a small business or organisation, one person may have to deal with all aspects of the ICT to ensure it can operate on a daily basis.

Some terms

Career: an area of work that a person chooses to devote his or her expertise to for a significant period of time. The career includes the sum total of paid and unpaid work, learning and life roles that are undertaken throughout a significant period of time.

Occupation: a group of similar jobs found in different industries or organisations.

Job: a position in which one performs specified tasks for payment.

A career can be the life journey one undertakes in all forms of work – paid or unpaid – together with learning and a range of roles. For example, a person can have a career in education with an occupation as a teacher and a position as a teacher of mathematics.

A career in ICT may encompass a range of different jobs. The most senior positions in ICT are usually filled by skilled people with tertiary qualifications who have had a number of differing roles throughout their time in employment.

A number of different jobs in ICT are described below. This list is not exhaustive and the positions often change to reflect advances in technology and changes in business needs and structures.

Employment

A person may be employed by an organisation as a:

- Full-time, permanent employee.
- Part-time, permanent employee.
- Casual employee.
- Contract employee.

A full-time, permanent employee is usually employed on a continuing basis and is paid an annual salary. The employee is entitled to annual leave, sick leave and long service leave. Typically, an agreed amount of notice must be given if an employee leaves an organisation. Some full-time employees are entitled to be paid an overtime rate if they work longer hours than those agreed as a normal working week.

A part-time, permanent employee is usually employed on a continuing basis and is paid an annual salary. The difference to a full-time employee is that a part-time employee works a specified percentage of the full-time hours (eg 0.6 is usually three days per week or the equivalent thereof). The employee is entitled to annual leave, sick leave and long service leave. Typically, an agreed amount of notice must be given if an employee leaves an organisation.

A casual employee is usually employed on a time basis (ie he or she is paid by the hour or the day). The employee is usually not entitled to sick leave, annual leave or long service leave. A casual employee often has irregular hours.

Types of organisations

The type and size of an organisation has implications for the work environment and types of tasks that a career may involve.

Size	A small business has up to 50 employees. A small to medium organisation (SME) is defined in some quarters as having up to 255 employees. A large organisation can have many thousands of employees.

Nature of the organisation	Government (public): Government department or a business owned by the government (a statutory authority). Local government.	Non-government: Private company – owned by shareholders and has a limited liability. Public company – owned by shareholders and shares are traded on a Stock Exchange. Partnership – an association of two or more people in a business enterprise who share the responsibility for the business and the profits (or losses). Sole owner (sole trader) – this is a simple form of business structure in which there is no division between personal assets and the business assets. Sole traders often operate under their own names. Co-operative – this is a group of people acting together to meet the common needs of its membership. Co-operatives allow groups of people to make a contribution to a final product or service. Churches. Sporting and other clubs.
Organisation motive	Profit or not for profit	
Business type	Mining, manufacturing, production or service industry	

Small office home office business (SOHO)

A small office or home office business is one that is operated by one or two people and can be based at home or in a small rented serviced office.

This type of business is suitable for a single owner who offers goods or services to a limited number of people. The business owner can conduct the operations from a home office.

Sole trader

A sole trader is the simplest form of business structure. Almost anyone can set up such a business – some trade under their own name, while others register a business name.

A sole trader operates so that there is no division between private and business assets. This means that the liability is unlimited and debts owing to the business may need to be paid using private assets.

A sole trader can provide many personal services to people and small businesses that require IT support at home or in an office.

Contractor

A contractor is a person who provides his or her services to an organisation for an agreed fee. A contractor will:

- Be engaged to carry out a set task or work for an agreed number of hours.
- Invoice the organisation for the work carried out.
- Take responsibility for his or her insurance, sick leave and holidays.

A sole trader will often work as a contractor.

Franchise

A franchise is a type of business where a person (franchisee) pays a licence fee to operate a type of business that is already established. The franchisee opens a branch of that business and sells the products or provides the services of that business.

The franchisee pays a start cost and an annual fee, often based on the revenue of the business. The franchisee benefits from the business name, organisation, advertising and marketing.

IT services for the small office home office market

Franchises are often operated by sole traders or small businesses.

The role of information technology in organisations

Information technology enables many organisations to function effectively and efficiently. Some organisations have built their competitive advantage through their ability to create and use information technology in different ways.

IT has played a crucial role in the development of new ways of doing business and, in fact, in creating new businesses.

Amazon online store

Amazon was one of the first organisations to build a business selling books without a physical store. Although it took some years to begin to make a profit, it dramatically changed the way in which books are bought and sold around the world. Amazon has now expanded into offering a much wider range of products and services.

Travel industry

The travel industry has been changed significantly by the development of Internet applications that allow customers to book flights throughout the world. Most airlines have sites that enable users to search and book flights, while other sites enable comparisons between different airline offerings.

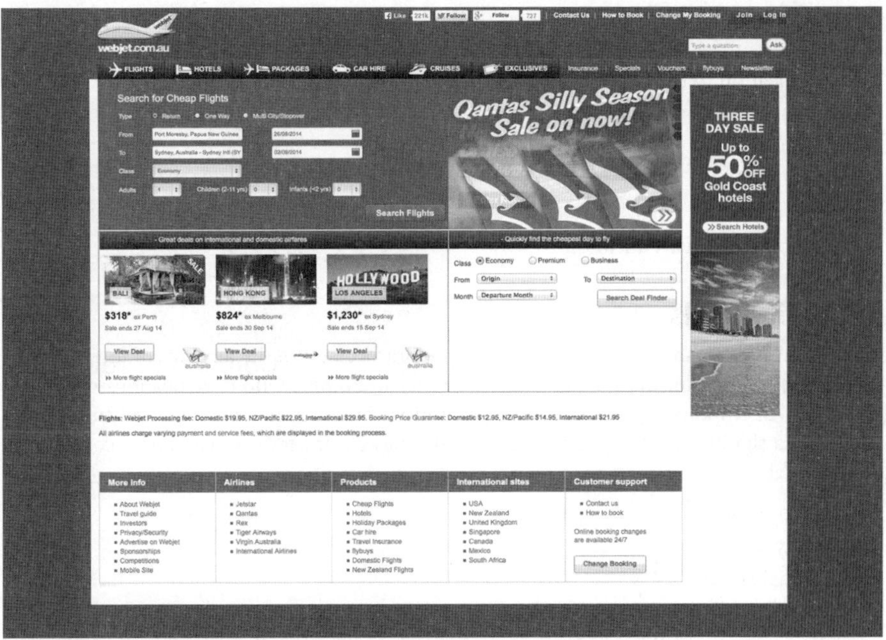

The Webjet site searches a number of other sites for the best deal

Positions created

Businesses such as Amazon and the travel industry have led to the creation of many new job types and industries: in particular, positions related to database creation and management, web design and online processing and transactions.

Many of these organisations outsource a lot of these businesses and use consultants and freelance designers. Some big organisations outsource their IT departments to businesses in different countries.

Skills

Technical skills

People in the ICT industry need satisfactory levels of ICT skills. Competency and skills in the office packages are mandatory. These include word processing, spreadsheets, presentations, project management and email.

'Soft' skills

Skills that can set a candidate apart from others are so-called 'soft skills' or 'people skills'. They are well regarded by prospective employers as they complement the talents that people have in their respective disciplines. These soft skills include:

- Leadership.
- Teaching and training.
- Communication (written and spoken) skills.
- Flexibility.
- Time management.
- Ability to work in a team.
- Proven problem solving.
- Responsibility for self-education.

Personality skills

The behaviour of a person in a workplace is important because of the amount of interaction that takes place between employees, management, clients and others who have dealings with the organisation. An employee represents the organisation for which he or she works, and human resources are a significant asset to an organisation. These characteristics can enhance the success of the organisation:

- Respect for others.
- The ability to work with others.
- Professionalism.
- Reliability.

A prospective employer is likely to gain some insight into these skills during the interview process.

Some careers in IT

There is a wide variety of careers in IT. Large organisations often employ IT specialists while small organisations may rely on IT staff who have a wide range of skills.

There are also many opportunities for sole traders, contractors and small businesses to build a career in IT.

The jobs described below are a sample of those available. Note that changes in technology, both hardware and software, ensure that a career in IT is dynamic and ever changing.

Chief information officer (CIO)

The **chief information officer** is the most senior executive in an organisation responsible for the information resources and the technology resources of that organisation.

The CIO plans and organises the ICT strategies of the organisation and ensures that the ICT infrastructure reflects the organisation's goals. A CIO typically has a bachelor degree or higher qualification and significant experience within the ICT industry.

CIO positions are often found in large organisations including government departments.

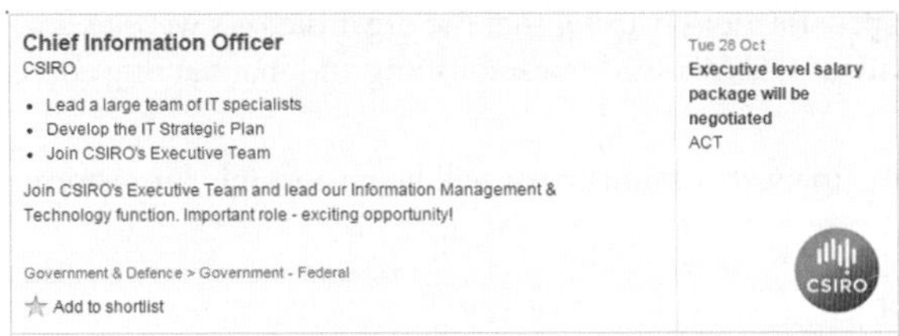

A CIO position on Seek.com.au

IT manager

An **information technology manager** is responsible for planning, implementing and maintaining the technology infrastructure for an organisation. Responsibilities also include the installation of hardware and software, the backup of systems and the purchasing of hardware and software.

Programmer

A programmer or **computer programmer** uses computer code to develop solutions to problems. A programmer typically uses a programming language such as Fortran, Cobol, Java or PHP. Most programmers can use a range of languages to develop appropriate and effective solutions.

Systems analyst

A **systems analyst** investigates the requirements of a business and makes recommendations regarding its needs in terms of hardware, software, network infrastructure, business processes and skills.

Systems administrator

A **systems administrator** carries out many of the functions of an IT manager but works at a more operational level. He or she is responsible for the provision, installation and operation of systems hardware and software.

ICT technicians will often report to the systems administrator.

Web administrator

A **web administrator** is responsible for maintaining an organisation's website. The administrator will liaise with designers, developers and the Internet Service Provider.

He or she will be responsible for ensuring that the organisation's website operates reliably and consistently. They will also be involved in establishing and maintaining content management procedures.

In the case of a failure, the web administrator will be responsible for restoring the website.

Web designer

A **web designer** is responsible for the design of a website, including a range of elements such as graphics, text, layout and the way in which the various pages interact. A web designer has a range of skills including graphic design, interface design, usability and website optimisation.

The designer is able to use a wide range of software to develop a site. The designer also needs to be able to understand the needs of the organisation for which the website is being designed and ensures that the design reflects those needs

Database administrator (DBA)

The **database administrator** is the person responsible for managing an organisation's data resources. Within an organisation, the database is usually a shared resource that belongs to the entire organisation. The DBA is responsible for the planning, design, implementation and protection of the database. The DBA ensures that the database performance is acceptable and provides training and support for users.

Security specialist

IT **security specialists** recommend and design security policies for organisations. The specialist needs to understand the ICT environment of the organisation including hardware, software and network. A knowledge and understanding of emerging trends in security threats is also important, as is an understanding of hardware and software developments.

ICT Security Advisor
Hudson

- Contract till 30 June 2016
- Minimum NV1 clearance required
- 20th December start date

Our client is seeking an experienced **ICT Security** Advisor to provide expert **security** advice for **ICT** systems

Information & Communication Technology > Security

Add to shortlist

ICT Security position on Seek.com.au

Graphic designer

A graphic designer is a professional who creates, modifies and manages images and text to provide a piece of design. Graphic designers work in the printing industry to provide documents including brochures, business cards and catalogues. They also work in the electronic media to produce interactive websites and user interfaces for organisations.

Network engineer

A **network engineer** is responsible for the design, implementation and maintenance of a computer network. An understanding of both hardware and software together with network performance is important. The network engineer needs to identify and manage appropriate network hardware and software including switches, routers and servers. Cabling standards and maintenance are also important.

Technical services manager

A technical services manager is responsible for the provision and managements of the technical services for an organisation. He or she will typically manage a team of technicians and will develop processes to ensure that the services meet the needs of the organisation.

ICT technician

An **ICT technician** configures, maintains and repairs both computer hardware and software. A technician will configure new computers that are to be used within an organisation and will ensure that the equipment operates effectively. The technician will also be responsible for resolving issues identified by users relating to both hardware and software.

ICT account manager

An **ICT account manager** is a sales professional. He or she sells a range of ICT hardware, software or services to organisations. An account manager is usually responsible for a number of established clients as well as taking responsibility for developing new clients. Sales professionals often receive a significant part of their remuneration as commission based on their level of sales.

ICT qualifications and training

Most organisations expect ICT professionals to have appropriate qualifications. The qualifications required depend upon the position. Some organisations will expect tertiary qualifications from a university or technical college. They may also look for specialised certification that is provided by major vendors. They may also take into account informal qualifications gained and experience at conferences or in user groups.

Tertiary qualifications

Most universities offer courses that allow students to complete degrees that include ICT-related subjects. For example, the University of Papua New Guinea offers computing-related subjects through the School of Natural and Physical Sciences.

The School offers the degree of Bachelor of Science (BSc) as well as postgraduate degrees that include Master of Science (MSc) and Doctor of Philosophy (PhD).

The University of Papua New Guinea is one of the leading universities in Papua New Guinea

Other universities also offer IT-related courses. The University of Goroka offers courses including Information Technology and Computer Studies.

Vendor qualifications

A number of the large vendors offer courses that lead to formal industry qualifications. Two such vendors are Microsoft and Cisco.

Microsoft certification

Microsoft is a multinational company founded in 1975 and headquartered in Redmond in Washington State in the north-west of the USA. Microsoft is the largest software development and marketing company and it dominates the personal computer market with its operating system software and application software.

Microsoft has set up a comprehensive system of training and certifications. Some organisations expect ICT staff to have successfully completed one or more of these certifications.

Microsoft argues that appropriate certification is a significant factor in gaining employment.

The types of certification include:

- MCSA – Microsoft Certified Solutions Architect.
- MCSE – Microsoft Certified Solutions Expert.
- MCITP – Microsoft Certified Information Technology Professional.

A complete list of courses is available via the Microsoft website.

These courses can be offered online, in a classroom or remotely using prepared materials provided in books and on CDs and DVDs. Microsoft Press provides much of this material.

These certifications usually include an examination.

Cisco certification

Cisco Systems Inc is an American-based multinational corporation that designs, manufactures and sells networking equipment. Cisco was founded in 1984 and its headquarters are in San Jose, California, in the heart of 'Silicon Valley'.

As networks have become a key part of most organisations' infrastructure, Cisco has become one of the most important suppliers of network equipment.

Like Microsoft, Cisco has also developed a range of training courses to provide appropriately qualified people for the ICT industry.

Cisco has created the 'Cisco Learning Network' and it provides a range of levels of qualification including:

- Associate.
- Professional.
- Expert.
- Architect.
- Specialist.

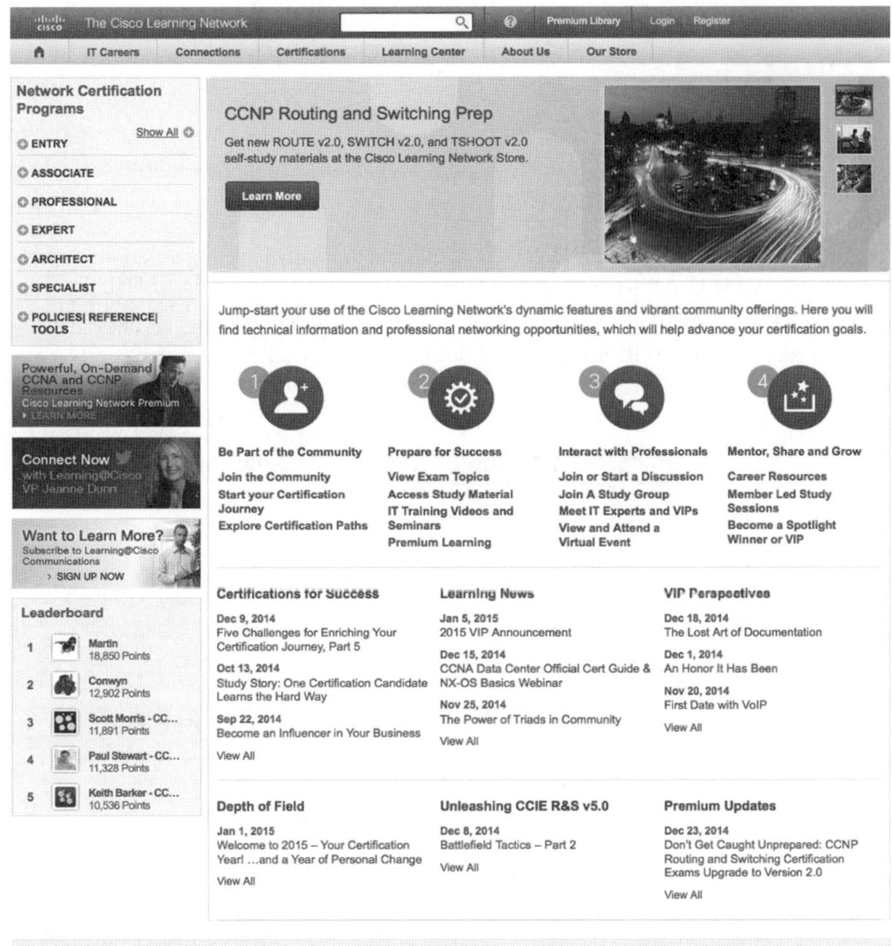

The Cisco Learning Network

Examples of such qualifications are:

- CCNP: Cisco Certified Network Professional.
- CCIE – Wireless: Cisco Certified Internetwork Expert – Wireless.

The assessment for these courses includes written examinations and, in some cases, a practical component.

ITIL

ITIL stands for the Information Technology Infrastructure Library. This is a set of processes designed in the United Kingdom to provide guidelines for best practice in IT service management, delivery and support.

The areas that ITIL addresses are:

- Service support.
- Service delivery.
- Planning to implement service management.
- ICT infrastructure management.
- Applications management.
- The business perspective.

There is a large industry focused on IT service management. Many large organisations expect service staff to receive IT service management training and that they implement ITIL processes.

A range of private organisations provide IT service management training and certification. Organisations can become ITIL–accredited, although this can be a lengthy and expensive process.

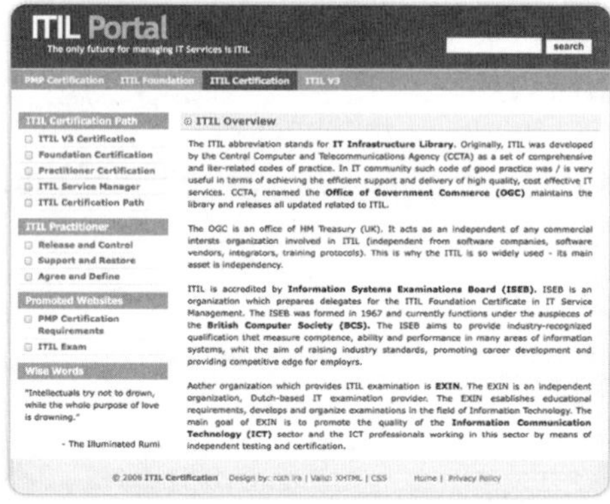

ITIL certification at www.itilcertification.org/

Informal qualifications

Many people develop their own informal qualifications through their own interest and enthusiasm. Many cities have user groups that provide support, advice and training for members. For example, in Australia the Melbourne PC User Group has more than 4000 members.

Conferences

There are many conferences and workshops that are useful in helping people involved in ICT keep their skills up to date.

Conferences run by analysts such as the Gartner Group are helpful in identifying future directions and trends.

Searching for positions

When searching for a position, a prospective employee should find out about the industry, the position and the organisation before applying for the position.

Research the industry

It is important to research the types of jobs being offered in any industry and to have an understanding of what the jobs entail. A prospective employee should also try to work out if the position actually matches the job title. Usually a job advertisement gives general information about what the job actually involves and the terms and conditions of employment.

A job hunter should work out:

- What qualifications are necessary to work in the industry.
- Where the jobs are likely to be located.
- Whether the appointments are made by the employer or by a recruitment agency.

Research the organisation

It is useful to find information about the organisation to try and determine if it is a suitable environment in which to work. Large companies, both domestic and international, publish a variety of information to promote the organisation. Their website may be a good starting point and it may include:

- Mission statement.
- Vision statement.
- Strategic plans.
- Code of conduct.
- Organisational chart.
- Corporate image.

The workplace

Workplaces are bound by a range of government laws. These laws aim to make the workplace a fairer and safer place. These are often a minimum requirement, and many employers will go beyond the basic requirements and extend their operations to promote a healthy work environment for the benefit of all.

The following are some of the areas that governments legislate with regard to the workplace:

- Equal opportunity.
- Affirmative action.
- Discrimination.
- Occupational health and safety.

ICT environment and employment policies

Within an organisation, there are procedures and policies governing the use of information technology by employees.

These may be available online and include:

- The nature of computers and communication equipment provided by the organisation.
- Guidelines regarding the use of the Internet in the workplace.
- Intranet conventions.
- Procedures for network security, passwords and file access.
- Policies about email usage and monitoring.
- Standard software employer provided
- The operating environment of the organisation.

Job description

Many organisations have job descriptions that give detail about the tasks and responsibilities to be performed by people in particular positions. The job description may also detail how people report to others in organisations to establish the chain of command.

Unit 12.5 Computers and Employment

Topic 2: Job search on the Internet and in other media

Topic 2 examines methods for searching for jobs using the Internet and other media such as newspapers. It covers:

- Using search engines to find job opportunities.
- Searching websites of businesses with career opportunities.

There are many different methods of finding jobs. These methods include:

- Specialist search engines on the Internet.
- Newspapers and classified advertisements.
- Advertisements on organisations' sites.
- The services of recruitment consultants.
- Word of mouth.

Sometimes, people are 'headhunted' for particular positions. That is, particular people are identified as being suitable for a job vacancy and those people are approached. This is often done with the help of a recruitment consultant.

Using search engines to find job opportunities

A search engine can be used to help find vacant positions. For example, entering 'IT Manager' in Google brings up a range of sites that have IT Manager positions available.

Most of these links are to recruitment consultants.

The *Post-Courier* has a classified section online that contains a Jobs section.

Classifieds in the Post-Courier

There are a number of organisations that advertise jobs on the Internet. One such organisation is Seek Ltd, which was founded in Australia in 1997. Seek enables organisations to advertise positions on the Internet and job seekers can search for available positions.

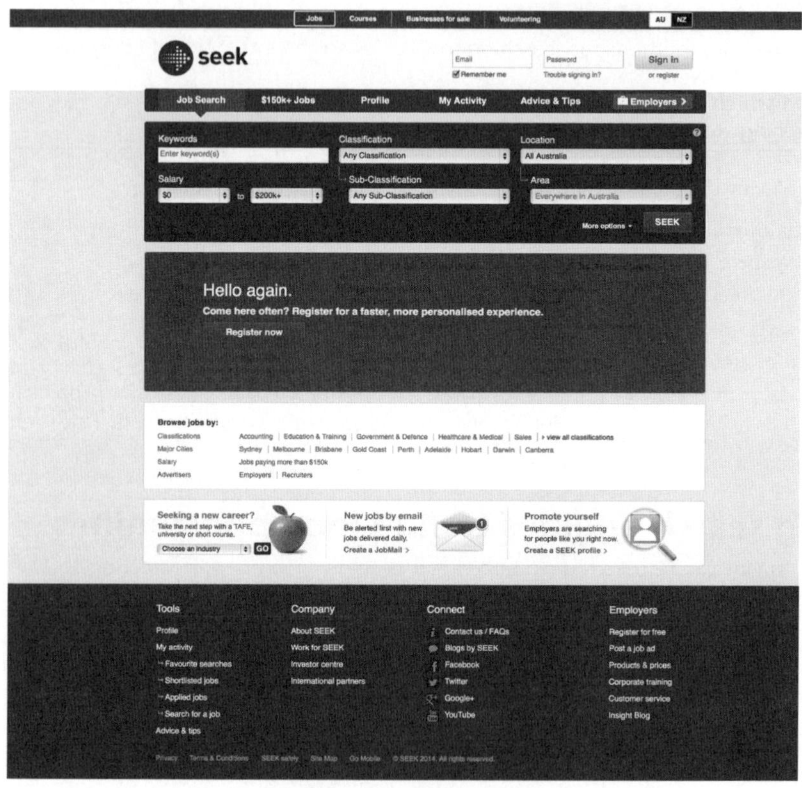

Finding a job at Seek.com.au

Although it is an Australian company, Seek also has positions available throughout the Asia–Pacific region.

Another site, Pacific Island Jobs, specialises in jobs in the region.

Some sites aggregate job advertisements from a range of organisations. For example, the site named Indeed brings together jobs from many different companies in the one website.

Latest jobs

Pacific Island Jobs

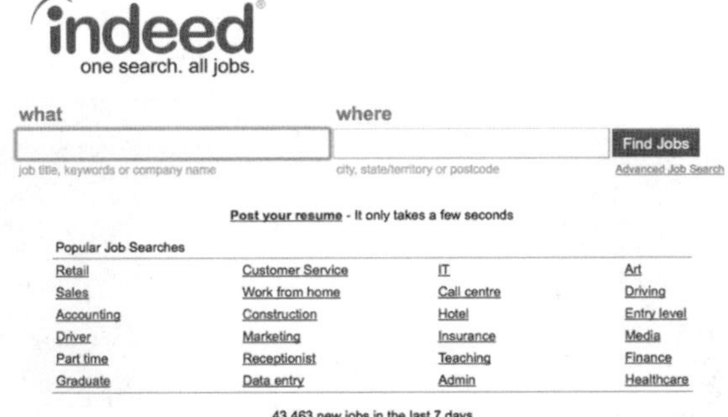

The site http://au.indeed.com/jobs shows a range of jobs in Papua New Guinea

Newspapers

Newspapers have classified advertisements for jobs. These often appear as a careers supplement with weekend newspapers. Some of the newspapers will replicate those advertisements online.

Organisations' websites

Some organisations advertise jobs on their websites. These are usually large organisations and they will have their own specialised human resources (HR) departments to deal with the employment process.

Microsoft uses this method to advertise positions throughout the world.

BHP Billiton, another multinational corporation, also places advertisements for positions on its company website. These positions are located in many different countries.

Recruitment consultants

Recruitment consultants provide services to both organisations and people. Some recruitment services specialise in ICT positions.

Organisations use recruitment consultants to find staff. The organisation places the position with the recruitment consultant who then advertises and identifies suitable candidates. The consultant will screen the applicants before presenting them to the employing organisation.

Successful recruitment consultants:

- Understand the organisation that is seeking a staff member.
- Understand the requirements of the position.
- Thoroughly vet the applicants and ensure that only appropriate candidates are presented to the organisation.

The recruitment consultant usually charges a fee that is equal to a percentage, say 15%, of the annual salary of the successful applicant. This fee is payable by the organisation that employs the applicant.

Recruitment consultants may also offer contract positions. In these cases, the applicant is hired by the consultant who then places the applicant with an organisation. The applicant is paid a fixed rate – usually hourly or daily – by the consultant. The organisation is charged a higher fixed rate by the consultant.

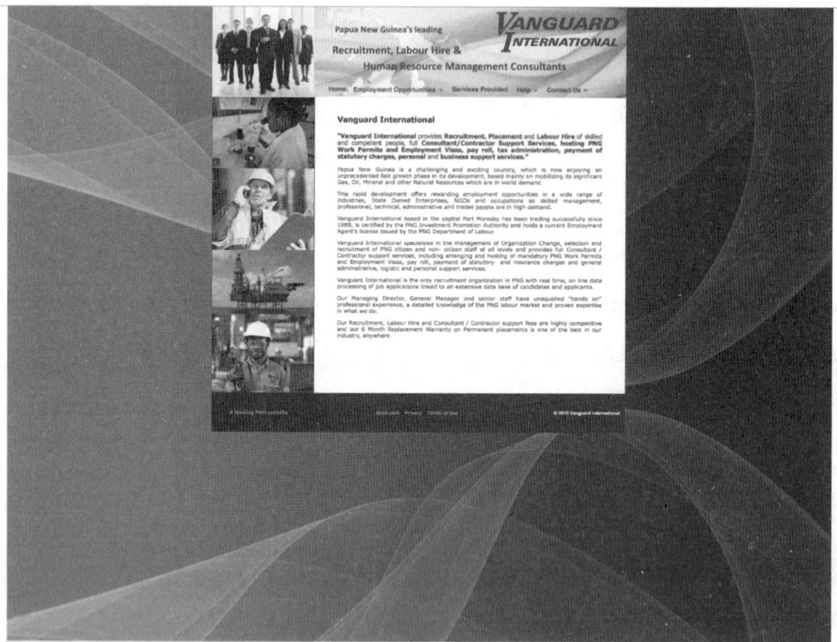

Vanguard International is an example of a recruitment consultant

Finding out about a prospective employer

Research about a business or organisation that is offering a career opportunity gives an applicant a better understanding of the organisation and provides some background for a common interview question, 'Why do you want to come and work for us?'. Prospective employees who have an understanding about the business will be more highly regarded than those who do not.

Likely avenues of finding information include:

- Company websites.
- Product/service brochures.
- Company press releases and advertising.
- Newspapers.
- Trade and industry journals and magazines.
- Conversations with current employees.

What makes up a job advertisement?

The purpose of a job advertisement is to attract a range of interested and appropriately qualified applicants. A typical job advertisement will give information about:

- The organisation.
- The job title.
- Duties and responsibilities.
- Qualifications and experience needed.

It will also describe how to make contact with the organisation.

In some cases, a guide to the remuneration will be included. In other cases, only minimal information will be included together with a link to a website.

Sample advertisement

The following advertisement is a hypothetical one, but is typical for the type of position being advertised. It sketches out the general nature of the position.

COMPUTER DEPARTMENT TECHNICIAN – MORESBY PARK

ABC Electronics, one of Papua New Guinea's largest retailers, is seeking an experienced Technician for the store in Moresby Park.

We are seeking applicants who are keen, motivated, analytical and have strong technical and managerial ability to lead the department.

The successful candidate will need to be hands-on and versatile, work well under pressure and have excellent staff communication and management skills.

Duties include technical repairs and maintenance, managing customer inquiries and returns, organising deliveries to and from repair agents and providing technical support to customers daily.

Applicants must have previous retail experience and experience with computers is essential.

We are also seeking applicants with strong communication and time management skills. Time management will also be of paramount importance. This position involves weekend work.

If you want to be part of a successful team and you are keen, motivated and have proven technical ability, please forward applications by email to recruitment@abc.co.pg or by mail to: Mark Buka, Technical Services Manager, PO Box 111, Moresby Park, Port Moresby 411.

Unit 12.5 Activity 2A: Reading a job advertisement

1. What do you think is the general nature of the position?
2. Is there any important information missing from the advertisement?
3. What specific skills would an employee need to fulfil the position? In your answer discuss the difference between the ICT skills and personality skills required.
4. What would be the advantages and disadvantages of this type of job?

Unit 12.5 Computers and Employment

Topic 3: Formatting résumés or CVs

Topic 3 provides information about formatting résumés or CVs (curriculum vitaes). Students learn about the content of a résumé or CV and how these should be formatted. Electronic CV templates such as those in Microsoft Word are also discussed.

What is a résumé or curriculum vitae (CV)?

A **résumé** or curriculum vitae is a document prepared for a prospective employer with the purpose of giving the applicant the prospect of being selected for a job interview.

It should contain:

- A statement that sets out the applicant's reasons for applying for the position.
- A summary of the applicant's schooling and subsequent education.
- Qualifications achieved by the applicant (listed in order from most recent to oldest).
- Work history of the applicant (listed in order from most recent to oldest).

The résumé is a written communication to a prospective employer and it is often the first impression the employer has of a person. If an employer has a large number of applicants the screening process begins by examining the letters and CVs.

Poorly presented documentation could greatly handicap the chances of being considered or shortlisted for the job.

Formatting résumés or CVs

There is scope in the formatting of a résumé for it to have individual styling characteristics unless the employer has an application for employment form which has specific requests for information.

The résumé should be easy to read so that the person reading it can focus on the information. The following are guidelines that enable this to occur:

- Use fonts consistently throughout the document.
- Keep the body font size and headings size consistent, such as size 12 point for body text.
- Start each new line from the left margin.
- Have an adequate margin, say 2.54 cm (for both top and bottom, left and right).
- Have adequate white space between major sections.
- Keep sentences short.
- Use bullet points where appropriate (eg when listing educational qualifications).
- Make sure the paper is good quality white and the printer is working effectively to produce good clean copy.

The reader should be drawn to the relevant information by initially scanning the document and by then taking extra time on important points.

Content of a résumé

Cover sheet

Cover sheet to résumé – contains basic information about the applicant.

Personal details

Include your name, address and contact details. Contact details should include email address and phone number.

It is not necessary to include information such as date of birth (or age), gender or marital status.

Educational qualifications

These should be listed in order from the most recent to the oldest. This list should include the level of each qualification and the organisation at which the qualification was gained.

Employment history

Positions should be listed from the most recent to the oldest and include the job title and a brief description of the duties and responsibilities.

Voluntary work history and community involvement

List any of these types of involvement.

Hobbies and interests

Listing these gives the prospective employer some insight into the applicant.

Success in previous employment

List any particularly successful project or task completed in previous employment.

Referees and references

A referee is a person who can vouch for the applicant. Most employees ask for referees. A referee can be personal (ie vouching for the personal integrity of the applicant), or professional (ie vouching for the applicant's professional qualifications and activity).

CV templates

Microsoft Office provides a range of templates that can be used for a résumé or CV. The templates give the user a structure to use and ensure that there is a consistency of style throughout.

However, the user does need to take care that the presentation reflects a look and feel with which the user is happy. It needs to distinguish the user from others who use similar templates.

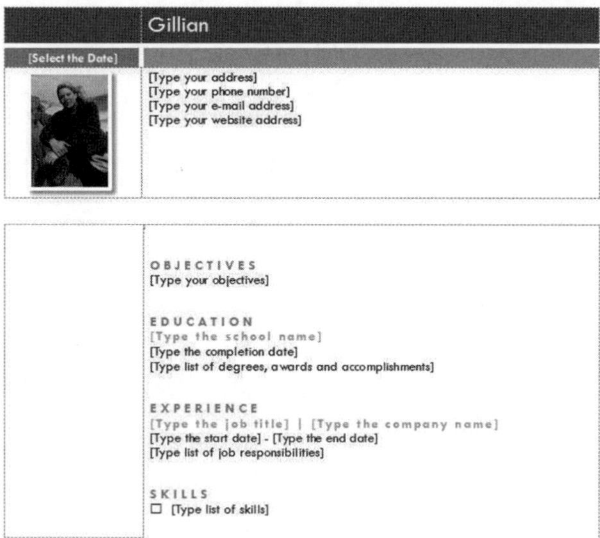

Part of a template from Microsoft Office

There are other websites that give sample CVs and templates. Many of these can be found by entering 'Sample CV format' in a search engine.

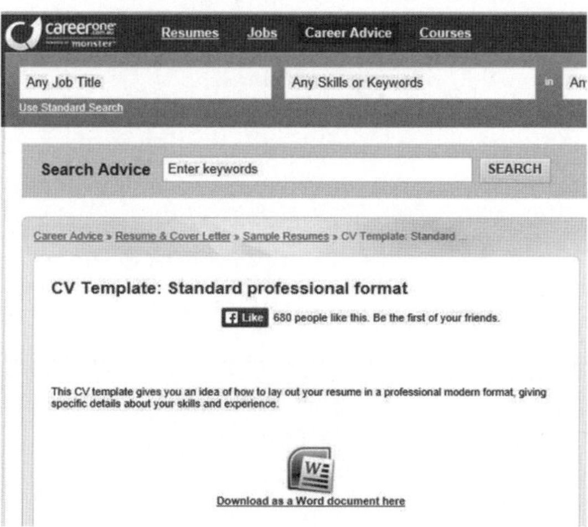

Downloading a CV template from CareerOne.com

Unit 12.5 Computers and Employment

Topic 4: Formatting job application letters

Topic 4 provides information about writing and formatting job application letters. It also discusses the use of mock interviews as a method for preparing for a real job interview.

Job application letter

A **job application letter** or cover letter is a prospective employee's introduction to a prospective employer. This is a document in its own right.

It is typically a one-page letter that is designed to show clearly that you are interested in the job. The application letter should encourage the prospective employer to read your résumé.

A cover letter for each and every application needs to be tailored for that position.

Parts of a job application letter

The parts of a job application letter are:

- Applicant's address including contact details.
- Date.
- Receiver's address.
- Name of person responsible to receive the application (if known) and their title, name of the organisation and address (postal if details provided, Internet address if job applications are to be directed to that address).
- Salutation (greeting). Make sure to use the correct salutation, such as Mr, Mrs or Ms. If you are not sure then contact the organisation to check, or use a generic term.
- Body of letter.
- The job title or position that is the subject of the letter.
- Statement about how the applicant became aware of the position.
- Statement of the intention to apply for the position.
- A brief outline of what skills the applicant would bring to the organisation.
- Statement of availability for interview.
- Complimentary close.

Sample job application letters can be found on the web. Some sites regard the cover letter as being as important as the résumé.

Michelle Puna
32 Ocean View Drive
Moresby Park
Port Moresby 411
Papua New Guinea

Mr Mark Buka
Technical Services Manager
ABC Electronics
132 Post Street,
Moresby Park
Port Moresby 411
Papua New Guinea

10 February 2014

Dear Mr Buka,

I am writing to apply for the position of 'Computer Department Technician' at your Moresby Park store as advertised in the Port Moresby Times on Saturday 28 September 2013.

I successfully completed Grade 12 last year and have been doing volunteer work for the Salvation Army since then. I am currently doing an Information Technology (ICT Systems), Year One of Three at a tertiary level.

I have done work experience at the Moresby Park supermarket in the ICT department. I find working with computers and technology interesting and exciting and would like to begin a career in this industry.

I have visited your store and I am impressed by the operation of the business and I feel that I would be able to be a part of your team and be involved in the exciting future that your business is planning.

I have enclosed a copy of my resume and would be pleased to attend an interview at your earliest convenience.

Yours sincerely,

Michelle Puna

Michelle Puna

Example of a job application letter

Mock interview

A useful preparation technique for preparing for a job interview is the 'mock interview'. Questions are asked that are typical of the questions a candidate could be asked at an interview.

Some typical questions for which a candidate should be prepared are:

- Why do you want to work for this organisation?
- Why do you wish to do this job?
- What skills and attributes could you bring to this organisation?
- Can you work well in a team environment?
- Are you punctual and reliable?
- What is your preferred career path?
- What would you like to be doing in five years' time?

- What are your hobbies and interests?
- What do you do well?
- Do you have any other questions?
- Are you available for another interview?

Conclusion

There are many opportunities for careers in the ICT industry. It is an industry that undergoes rapid change and that needs dynamic people.

People can choose to work for themselves or in large organisations.

There is a great range of educational opportunities but continual learning is a critical factor in a successful career.

IT has transformed many industries in the last twenty years and will continue to do so well into the future.

Unit 12.5 Activity 4A: Employment

1. Complete this table relating to the advantages and disadvantages of each type of employment.

	Type of Employment	Advantages	Disadvantages
1	Full-time, permanent		
2	Part-time, permanent		
3	Casual		
4	Contract		

2. Find an example of an advertisement for each type of employment. (They do not necessarily have to be ICT related). Do any of the jobs have qualifying periods?
3. Casual or short term employment is often found for ICT positions. What are the advantages and disadvantages of such employment?

Unit 12.5 Activity 4B: Skills

When looking for employees, organisations often look for and evaluate:

- Technical skills
- Soft skills
- People skills.

1. If a prospective employer asked you about any of these skills, how would you answer and provide examples to illustrate your capability?
2. The ability to work in a team is highly regarded by many employers. If the prospective job was being part of a team, how would you respond to the following scenarios?

a. 'How would you feel about working as a member of a team, would it appeal to you?'
b. 'You will be the youngest member of the team, how would you feel about that?'
c. 'An existing member of the team will be your mentor for the first three months to help you settle in. What are your thoughts about that'

Unit 12.5 Activity 4C: Search engines and employment

1. How are jobs classified and organised on job search engines?
2. How are you able to use the search engine effectively to filter the type of employment you may be seeking?

Unit 12.5 Activity 4D: Careers in IT

1. If you were to have a career in ICT, what would be your 'ideal' career?
2. How significant are computer skills in any career in this day and age?

Unit 12.5 Activity 4E: Investigation

Interview a person who uses ICT in their employment on a daily basis. Find out about their career – some of the questions below may help as a guide.

1. What is the general nature of the use of ICT?
2. Is ICT important to your job?
3. What ICT skills in particular (hardware and software) are critical?
4. How long have you been using ICT?
5. How has it changed from when you first started using ICT?
6. What ICT skills do you particularly like using and those you are less inclined to like?
7. What training do you undertake to keep up to date with ICT skills?
8. What changes in technology are likely to impact on your job?

What other questions would you ask?

Unit 12.5 Activity 4F: ICT qualifications and training

1. What courses and training in ICT are available near to where you live?
2. What courses in particular would appeal to you? Find an example of a specific course.
   a. What is the 'title' of the course?
   b. Are there any prerequisites for study?
   c. How many subjects comprise the course? Are any compulsory?

d. How long can the course take (full-time, part-time)?

e. What forms of assessment are used in the course?

f. What is the qualification that you would obtain?

g. Can you find an advertisement/job that mentions the qualification or similar?

Unit 12.5 Activity 4G: Résumé

1. Create a cover letter and a résumé for yourself as if you were applying for the ABC ICT Department Technician. You could use an existing template for the CV and modify its layout and formatting.
2. Compose the text for an email that could be sent in an application for the position.

Unit 12.5 Activity 4H: Résumé as a website

Create a résumé as a website. Use the text from the résumé created earlier as an exercise in this chapter. It could be divided into the following sections:

Résumé section	Information	Details
Personal details	Your name and address and phone number	Not required to include date of birth or marital status.
Educational qualifications	Tertiary, secondary and primary education	List details in order from latest to earliest, with more detail for most recent or highest qualifications.
Professional details	Membership of professional organisations and positions held	
Career history	Employer names and title held, time as employee	List more information and details for the most recent positions and employers
Personal interests	Hobbies, interests and positions in community and sporting organisations. Positions in voluntary organisations	Employers are interested in the things you do that are not work related. It can show skills that are looked upon favourably.
The position	Information specifically relevant to the position being applied for.	The job advertisement may specify details about the job that should be addressed in the résumé
Referees	Names and contact details of people willing to verify your credentials for the position.	It is usual to include three referees.

This site map could be used for the résumé:

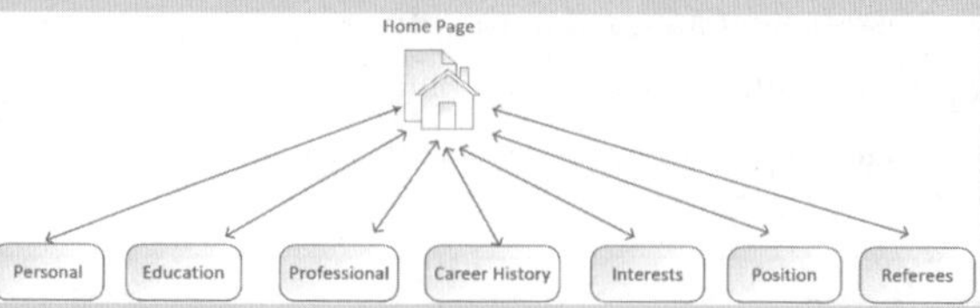

The top-down structure shows how the pages (at the first level, such as 'Personal' and 'Education') may be at the same relative position to the home page. For consistency, they should have the same design and navigational aids.

Each page needs a filename and a title that will appear in the browser window.

Page	Filename	Browser title	Names of images and other content
Homepage	index.htm	Résumé: 'Your Name'	
Personal			
Education			
Professional			
Career History			
Interests			
Position			
Referees			

1. Draw a wireframe that will show how the main pages of the site will be designed.
2. Create an annotated layout to show the key elements of the page and styling applied to key parts of the page.
3. Create the site.

Unit 12.1 Information and Communication Systems

Topic 1: Information systems

Unit 12.1 Activity 1A: Identifying information systems (page 2)

1. With the information systems, apart from your personal details, was any information used to identify you such as a number or combination of letters and numbers?

a. Electronic Funds Transfer Point of Sale (EFTPOS) allows the purchase of goods and services without the need for physical cash. It requires three parties to the transaction – the customer, the merchant and a financial institution such as a bank. Each interaction transfers funds from the customer to the merchant via the financial institution to allow the transaction to be successful.

There are generally two types of transactions:

i. Cash – the funds are transferred from customer via financial institution to the merchant at the time of sale.

ii. Credit – the obligation to pay funds transferred by the customer at a future date to the financial institution, the merchant then receives the funds from the financial institution. The merchant is usually charged a percentage fee by the financial institution; sometimes this is passed onto the customer as a charge at the time of the transaction. The customer pays the financial institution at a later date.

b. EFTPOS transactions are usually conducted over wide area networks. Security is provided by a range of methods, including authentication by the merchant of the card being used, encryption of data that is sent across the network and verification of the success of the transaction.

Unit 12.1 Activity 1B: Stakeholders in a club (page 5)

1. Refer to the list above in the text. Have you identified any stakeholders that are not listed above? Have you identified the significant stakeholders?

a. Stakeholders for a new clubroom would be those involved in providing the funds, including levels of government if there is any support from the local council or government. The other key stakeholder is the Club's committee.

b. An accurate estimate of the funds required, the timeline for the project and information about the persons who are responsible for managing the project and facilitating communication between all parties involved.

Unit 12.1 Activity 1C: Stakeholders in a company (page 7)

1. Companies are required by law to release an annual report to shareholders. This will include a balance sheet and a profit and loss statement. In some cases, half yearly reports are also provided. Dividends are usually paid every six months.

2. An annual report is provided at an organisation's annual general meeting. These reports are also provided to shareholders, either online or in print.

3. The annual general meetings of an organisation is required to make the management and Board accountable to its shareholders. The meetings make resolutions about the composition of the Board. The senior management and Board members attend and receive questions from the shareholders.

Unit 12.1 Activity 1D: Firewalls (page 18)

1. The Windows firewall control panel gives detailed information about the security of the computer. This information varies, depending upon the version of Windows being used.
2. A range of settings can be adjusted, including connection security rule and firewall rules.

Topic 3: Communication systems

Unit 12.1 Activity 3A: A library system (page 49)

1. Prior to computing information systems, a person's borrowings would be recorded on a card file. A system would need to authenticate the borrower, the title and the borrowing period.
2. The library usually provides the borrower with a paper record of the borrowing. This usually includes the borrower's name, the items and the due dates.
3. Usually, many libraries allow an extension (renewal) of the original loan, providing that the item has not been reserved by another user.
4. A letter, telephone call, email or text message are some of the options used to communicate with the borrower. Some libraries have a system of fines for overdue items.
5. Your observation will note the type of system, the input and output. Most likely, both the borrower's library card and the items use bar codes.

Unit 12.1 Activity 3B: An airline system (page 49)

1. Date, flight origin, flight destination, number of passengers (adults, children and infants), cabin class, option of price (date flexible), price or schedule, promotional code, if any.
2. **a.** Price (dates flexible) shows the fare for the flights as an amount on the calendar date, with a comparison for other days.
   b. Price. Shows the price with the flight schedules for those dates.
   c. Schedule. Shows the flights, connections and plane type.
3. **a.** Schedule.
   b. Prices (dates flexible).
   c. Price and Schedule.
4. An additional destination is added to the trip details.
5. The schedule is downloadable from the home page in a 'pdf' format.
6. At the conclusion of the booking process an e-ticket is created. With airline reservation systems the e-tickets are often emailed to the passenger. Then can be later accessed using the booking reference number provided by the airline.

Unit 12.1 Activity 3C: An airline check-in system (pages 49–50)

1. Mercator.
2. The complexity of airline systems requires a significant degree of expertise to develop a system. External providers of systems can produce them at lower costs than what an individual airline is able to do. Specialist providers have a greater pool of skilled people, including analysts and programmers. These have the advantage of being able to integrate bookings across many airlines. A key disadvantage is the reliance on an external provider for a critical part of the business.
3. There are many providers of airline reservations systems (ARS), including: Amadeus, Mercator and Navitaire.

4. a. Airline inventory: aircraft, plane schedules, passenger classes (such as business, economy) and seats for various classes.
   b. Availability. Airlines operate schedules with various flight frequencies, such as number of flights per day or number of flights per week. The timetables are changed over time.
   c. The Passenger Name Record is how the airline records all details about the passenger.
   d. Fares are constructed and can vary considerably, such as time of day, popularity of the route and according to particular seasonal factors. Airports and governments also levy charges and taxes, the type involved a component of the ticket price.
   e. Most airlines now use electronic ticketing. The ticket can be printed by the passenger. A bar code on the ticket is used for electronic verification. For international flights, passports and its photo image are also used for verification.

Unit 12.1 Activity 3D: Banking (page 50)

1. a. Answer from research.
2. a. If the customer is an existing customer, then personal and account details are recorded. These include the name, address and other contact details.
   b. Banks will require primary evidence of identity. For example, government documents to prove identity such as a passport, a birth certificate and proof of residency.
   c. A login requiring a username and password so that access to a secure server can be given. Advice regarding the suitability of a username and also password is usually provided with instructions about security of this information. For example, the password may need to be a minimum of digits with characters other than A to Z and a mix of other characters.
   d. Security questions usually have personal information answers that are person specific. For example, name of first school, name of first pet, mother's maiden name. Often there are at least three questions requiring an answer. If they are needed in an authentication process, a question may be selected at random from the set.
3. Precautions include: using secure user names and passwords, not revealing the user name or password to other people, not storing the username and password securely. Clients should not respond to emails purporting to be from a bank that directs the user to an internet page to log on. Invariably these sites are false and harvest the user name and password.

Unit 12.1 Activity 3E: A computer network (page 51)

Answer from research activity.

Unit 12.1 Activity 3F: An invoice receipt (page 51)

1. The transaction is the invoice and receipt for the purchase of fuel from a service station.
2. The name and address of the service station, the date and time of the transaction, the quantity, fuel unit price and total are shown. A card (rather than cash) has been used to finance the transaction.
3. Although a card number is recorded there is no indication of the type of card (savings or credit), or the financial institution that is handling the transaction.
4. Own answer.

Unit 12.1 Activity 3G: A supermarket or small business (pages 51–52)

Answer from research.

Unit 12.1 Activity 3H: A school (page 52)

Answer from research.

Unit 12.1 Activity 3I: Transaction processing (page 53)

1. Customer
   - **a.** Access 24/7. Electronic transactions only. Efficient for transactional banking. Requires network internet access, suitable device.
   - **b.** Telephone is existing network, many people have access. Restricted keypad on phone. Cumbersome compared with internet banking.
   - **c.** Most banking operations can be conducted. Cash withdrawals. Restricted hours of operation. Access depends on where the ATM is located.
   - **d.** Access through retail outlets, usually supermarkets, cash available.
   - **e.** Physical location of bank branches, limited hours. Other advice and bank services are available. Bank branches limited in number, especially remote areas.

   Bank
   - **a.** Fewer face-to-face staff for operation. Lower costs than maintaining a physical branch network. Technology for online banking must have high security. Difficult to develop relationships with customers.
   - **b.** Use existing telephone technology. Technology supplanted by internet banking.
   - **c.** Efficient where customer base requires cash. No need for branches. Security of ATMS.
   - **d.** Use of other business premises, reduced costs. Some payment to other businesses for providing service.
   - **e.** Provides face-to-face interaction with customers, develops relationships. Cost of maintaining bank branches is expensive. Security.
2. ATM. Cash deposits and withdrawals, account balances. Transfer of funds between accounts.

Unit 12.1 Activity 3J: Ipconfig.exe and ping (page 53)

1. Compare with figure on page 35. Network information displayed will differ.
2. Compare with figure on page 36.

Unit 12.1 Activity 3K: Using the internet (page 53)

Answer from research.

Unit 12.1 Activity 3L: Data mining (page 54)

1. Google is making links and developing relationships between items of data. It enables a greater sophistication in data handling and knowledge development. With the volume of data increasing exponentially so are more sophisticated ways of managing and interpreting the data.
2. For individuals using Google as a search engine the searches will reveal much deeper and relevant links.

Unit 12.1 Activity 3M: Networks (page 54)

Wired network

- **a.** Cable requires fit out to physical locations, siting of a cable is important for access.
- **b.** Authentication to a network is from a physical location.

c. Cable provides best network speed.
d. Range and reach of a network best determined at time of installation.

Wired and wireless network

a. Often deployed to maintain existing cable network but extends the range. Cabling can be costly to retrofit to old buildings. Weather and vermin are risk factors.
b. Security enhanced by wired network.
c. Advantage of speed in wired network area.
d. Physical layout of site may enable easier setup of network with some wireless components.

Wireless network

a. Wireless access points require less cabling. Cheaper than cable.
b. Wireless is accessible within certain ranges, authentication to network is essential.
c. Wireless not as fast as cable.
d. Coverage depends on location and number of wireless access points.

Unit 12.1 Activity 3N: Software (pages 54–55)

1.
   1. Word Processor
   2. Spreadsheet
   3. Spreadsheet or specialist software
   4. Browser
   5. Browser
   6. Email
   7. Image editing/Drawing
   8. Image editing
   9. CAD/Drawing
   10. Calendar
   11. Media player usually with operating system or specialist software
   12. CD organiser or iTunes
   13. Utility software, often with operating system
   14. Media player usually with operating system or specialist software
   15. Defacto is Adobe Reader
   16. Most software can save as a web page, specialist web authoring
   17. Media utility
   18. Presentation software
   19. System utility, specialist software
   20. Possible word processor or page layout
2. Answer from research.

Unit 12.1 Activity 3O: Evaluation and review (page 56)

1. Governance refers to decision rights – who has the rights to make decisions about structure, resources and personnel; and who is responsible to whom and for what.
2. Organisations use IT for management and administration and also to enable informed decision-making. Analysis both internal and external can help meet short-term, medium and long-term goals.
3. Costs going beyond the budget is a very common IT disaster in new projects. Often, projects 'over promise and under deliver'. Project management principles are applied to IT projects. A significant issue is often the users' inability to clearly identify its requirements and to prioritise those requirements.

Unit 12.1 Activity 3P: Privacy principles (page 56)

1. The site collects information about visitors to the website, in particular email addresses. It is used by the company to inform the visitors about information the company believes will be useful for them. Information will be kept confidential to the best of the company's ability.
2. The company will provide information if it is required by law to do so.
3. When a user visits a web site, that website may enable a cookie. A cookie is a small text file that resides on the visitor's computer and can store a variety of information. A browser has a setting that can override the capability to store cookies, but for some websites this may limit the user's interaction with the site.

Unit 12.1 Activity 3Q: Firewall (page 56)

The firewall would be located between the internet and the internal network; that is, the hub. It is placed there to ensure there is no access to the internal network.

Unit 12.1 Activity 3R: Servers on a network (page 57)

Web server – this is a computer that allows content to be delivered through the internet. The computer must be connected to the internet, and specialised software is installed to allow it to carry out the delivery of content.
Print server – this connects computers on a network to one or more printers that allows users to print documents.
Mail server – this is a computer with software that manages electronic mail. It sends, receives and controls email for an organisation's users.
File server – this gives access to separately stored files, part of a multi-user system.

Unit 12.1 Activity 3S: Peripheral devices on a network (page 57)

1. Printer – Prints from digital to hard paper copy.
   Copier – Reproduces a hard copy document.
   Scanner – Converts a hard copy to digital document.
   Multifunction device – Often combines the functions of printer, copier, scanner and fax.
   Fax (facsimile) – Transmits digital or hard copy of a document using the telephone network.
   Digital camera – Captures a digital image.
2. All of the devices can be connected to a computer or server and hence to a network.
3. These devices need 'drivers'; that is, utility software provided by the manufacturer so the devices are recognised by the operating system of a computer.

Additional functionality is often provided in applications that enable features beyond those provided by operating systems and drivers. For example, most digital cameras have software to edit, enhance images and organise collections.

Unit 12.1 Activity 3T: Communication systems (page 57)

A letter – A letter is physically delivered to the postal address. It requires an established mail network. It is not cost effective. Mail can be lost, and incorrectly addressed mail cannot be delivered.
An email – This has become the predominant method of written communication. It is cheaper than physical mail and can be very quick. However, email can go astray if the address is incorrect or a server is not working. The sender of an email does not necessarily know if

it has been received and read. Time is used in organisations to compose email – words in an email can convey different meaning to spoken a communication. Spam email can be a significant problem.

A telephone call – A telephone call provides immediate, verbal communication. However, there are many missed calls. It is an established technology and the Public Switched Telephone Network (PSTN) is well established in advanced economies. The use of mobile telephones reduces the need for a wire network, but it can be very expensive.

Unit 12.1 Activity 3U: Creating a good working environment (pages 57–58)

1. The backup is a procedure that should be documented so that more than one person in the organisation can perform it. Currently, Florence is solely responsible for the backup. Florence may be absent from work (illness, holidays and leave). In the current situation the procedure would fail.

2. Once per week is inadequate unless the volume of business and the number of users is very small. The backup should be performed automatically at least daily.

3. 100 Mb is inadequate space for an effective backup.

4. The office safe must be fireproof. Backups should also be stored offsite.

5. Backup should be at regular intervals as part of normal procedure.

6. The backup should be not used for normal access. Adline now has two versions of the file, which one is correct?

7. He should undergo a professional educational training course to improve his skills. Although magazines and manuals have useful information, they are not a substitute for comprehensive training and understanding.

8. Duplicate entries in the system will cause problems. It is likely that the same information will not be entered exactly the same and it will be difficult to establish that they are duplicates.

9. The file should be saved at regular intervals and always before printing. The cause of the computer freezing should be investigated with a view to resolving the issue.

10. If modifications are made to a person's computer, particularly software that is a new version, users need to be notified. Many software vendors issue new releases incrementally and automatically on a regular basis. The changes are not always immediately apparent.

11. The monitor is used only to display the output. If the computer is not shut down in the appropriate way data could be corrupted.

12. This could result in different versions of the same document being available. Samuel should adopt a consistent approach if copying the data onto the office computer. USB keys are prone to unreliability and loss of data. They can also be a source of virus transmission.

13. Florence should use a template so that the letters can be formatted consistently. Each new letter should be a separate document.

14. The printed memo is time consuming and inefficient. It is easier to store and search memo's in a digital format.

15. The software licence needs to be examined to see if Tabitha is licensed to install the software on more than one computer as well as at home.

16. There are risks with software downloaded from the internet. Viruses and worms may be introduced into work computers. The work computers need to be in a controlled environment to maintain them in optimum working condition.

Unit 12.2 Database 2

Topic 2: Exploring advanced table features

Unit 12.2 Activity 2A: Unique identifiers (page 72)

1. Family name would fail as a unique identifier because more than one person can have the same family name.
2. A student would usually be identified by a unique personal identification number.

Unit 12.2 Activity 2B: Data formats (page 74)

1. General date – 02/01/2015 10:40:04 AM
   Long date – Friday, 2 January, 2015
   Medium date – 02-Jan-15
   Short date – 2-01-2015
   Long time – 10:40:04 AM
   Medium time – 10:40 AM
   Short time – 10:40
2. Microsoft Access uses the General Date and Long Time formats as the default.

Unit 12.2 Activity 2C: Different date formats (page 75)

1. The date could be expressed in (general, long, medium and short), as well as a custom format that could be created using the components (d,m,y). The following are a few examples of format options:
   d/m/yy (2/1/15)
   dd/mm/yy (02/01/15)
   ddd/mmm/yyyy (Fri 02/Jan/2015).
2. Formats that identify the month by name rather than number greatly reduce the risk of incorrect data entry and differences in date conventions for different countries. If a 12-hour time clock is used then AM or PM is required to identify morning or afternoon and evening.

Unit 12.2 Activity 2D: 12-hour and 24-hour clocks (page 75)

1. **a.** 16:40 (4:40 PM)
   b. The time difference between Port Moresby and Singapore is two hours. Port Moresby is two hours ahead.
   c. 14:40 (2:40 PM)
2. The 12-hour clock is a particular feature of analogue clock faces. Twelve-hour clocks are often referred to in spoken time as compared with written time. The 24-hour clock is very common in many countries, with notable exceptions. Radio and television stations typically use 12-hour clocks. Transportation systems typically use a 24-hour clock.
3. The 24-hour clock is unambiguous, hence its use in airlines. For example, the time 12:00 with a 12-hour clock is vastly different, depending on it being AM or PM.

Unit 12.2 Activity 2E: Input mask (page 78)

1. If the date is referencing an event in history, for example, it is valid. If it is meant to reference an event in recent times, then it is in error; that is, the year 1111 is almost certainly an error.
2. Museums and historical databases might use this date.
3. An input mask enables the date to be entered, but upon entry to be displayed in a different format. Data entry is restricted to the placeholders in the mask.

Unit 12.2 Activity 2F: Variation in spelling (page 79)

No answer required.

Unit 12.2 Activity 2G: Creating a sports information system (page 89)

No answer required.

Topic 3: Using relationships

Unit 12.2 Activity 3A: SelectionID (page 95)

1. Benstead, Hebau Isiani
2. Cricket

Unit 12.2 Activity 3B: Solving many-to-many relationship problems (page 95)

1. Four tables
2. Significant fields for the tables:
Teachers – Unique identifier, Family name, Given name, Title, Subjects 1, Subjects 2 …
Students – Unique identifier, Year level, Family name, Given name, Title, Subjects 1, Subjects 2 …
Academic subjects – Unique identifier, Formal name, Year level …
Classes – Unique identifier …
3. Most fields would be text, apart from the Unique identifier and Year level.
4. The IDs could be numeric or alpha numeric.
Teacher – TeacherID
Student – StudentID
Subjects – SubjectID
Classes – ClassID

Topic 4: Creating advanced queries

Unit 12.2 Activity 4A: Managing data (page 103)

After archiving the Year 12 records, increment other year level by one. Sport selections would need to be updated where necessary.

Topic 5: Forms

Unit 12.2 Activity 5A: Advantages and disadvantages of using wizards (page 110)

Advantages – They are good for inexperienced users, as steps will demonstrate features being applied to the database. It can be very quick to design a page or a report.
Disadvantages – Not all the features available in the software will be used. It can be difficult to modify the solution to meet the exact needs of the user.

Unit 12.2 Activity 5B: Designing a form (page 112)

The form should consist of a data entry order form together with a separate delivery note form for printing. The data entry form for repeat customers would access data already in the information system regarding name, address and delivery details. A delivery note usually lists the items being delivered but is not a complete invoice.

Unit 12.2 Activity 5C: Viewing form design (page 113)

Screen dimensions – The form should fit on one screen and avoid scrolling (up or down, left or right). The actual screen dimensions of devices vary considerably so testing on the devices in use is required.
Colour – Readability enhanced by strong contrast between foreground and background. Black text on white background is the most effective. Avoid using reverse colours; for example, white on black.
Size of headings relative to labels – Ensure that the size reflects the importance of each section. Headings should be 2 points larger than labels.
Controls – These should be in a fixed position with items of the same size.
Fonts – Important headings can be in a larger font size to draw attention. The same font should be used for headings throughout, variation of bold in some cases. Field captions should be a guide and unobtrusive.

Unit 12.2 Activity 5D: Identifying control icons in the Design ribbon (pages 114–16)

No answer to be provided.

Topic 7: Working with report sections

Unit 12.2 Activity 7A: Creating mailing labels (page 144)

The mailing label could be attached to a letter or parcel. It should contain the appropriate information with name and address of receiver.
There are a variety of names for the receiver. They could be simply a given and family name, include a title, or the name of a company or organisation.
Addresses vary considerably in their structure, as well as local, domestic and international. Each item of information is normally contained on a separate line.
Most software produces the mailing label using a 'merge' from a database.
A simple mailing label comprises the elements:

Given Name & Family Name
Address Line 1
Address Line 2
Location/Town/Suburb
State & Postal Code
Country

Unit 12.2 Activity 7B: Creating a set of names (page 148)

Use functions on page 148.

Unit 12.2 Activity 7C: Entity relationship diagram (ERD) (page 152)

1. Entities would include Supermarket, Customer and Item.
   The supermarket has many customers.
   The supermarket has many items.
   The customer has many items.
2. Own diagram.

Unit 12.2 Activity 7D: Input processing and output (IPO) chart (page 152)

Input:

The information system can automatically include data relevant to the transaction. The name, address and contact details of the supermarket are the same for all customers and therefore part of the document template.

Placeholders can be used to show the date and time, retrieved from the computer. Other information such as the name of the person serving the customer would be retrieved from the information system.

Each item has:

- An item code
- Description
- Price of item.

The quantity of each item is also input.

Processing:

For each line item, the quantity is multiplied by the price to give a total.

The line item prices are added for a total on the invoice.

In some cases, a discount may be employed.

A receipt is produced to provide a record for the customer of the transaction.

The Supermarket's database of stock items is updated as is the funds received.

Output:

An invoice/receipt is printed and provided to the customer as a record of the transaction. (Refer to Unit 12.1, Activity 3G. for a list of the categories of information provided on an invoice). Internally the supermarket's records would be updated for sales and stock figures. If stock reorder levels are triggered then a report could indicate the need to re-order.

Unit 12.2 Activity 7E: Creating a table in Microsoft Access (page 153)

a. Field – A field is a particular piece of data that describes part of an entity in a database.

b. Table – A table contains the data about each record in a database.

c. Form – A form is a view of a record. All or selected fields are located on screen, by a default view or by organisation to a design.

d. File – A file is a collection of data that has a name and is stored.

Unit 12.2 Activity 7F: Conventions for naming fields (page 153)

Two common conventions are Hungarian notation (camel case) and also using underscore between words. Spaces should not form part of a database field name. Whatever convention is applied, it should be consistent within a database. Some other conventions make use of prefixes to field names to assist in identification of field type.

Unit 12.2 Activity 7G: Table fields properties (page 153)

Data type	Type of data	Examples (2)
Text	Person's name eg First Name	Meleani Andrew
Numbers	Value 0–9 eg Price	7.00 5.32
Calculated	Usually numeric calculations eg Line item	30.30 12.00

Data type	Type of data	Examples (2)
Logical	True or false eg Membership Paid	Yes No
Web addresses	Web URL's	www.parliament.gov.pg http://www.pm.gov.pg

Unit 12.2 Activity 7H: Data in a supermarket (pages 153–54)

Corn Flakes 550g	Item Description
11 November 2014	Date Entered
64	Order Quantity
2	Aisle Location
ASS	Supplier Code
Breakfast Cereal	Category
CF14978	Product Code
4k	Price

Unit 12.2 Activity 7I: Data structure table (page 154)

	Data field	Data type	Field size
1	Movie code	Number	7 digits, unique
2	Movie title	Text	200 characters
3	Movie length	Time	3
4	Classification	Text	2
5	Movie type	Text	20
6	Director	Text	40
7	Writers	Text	100
8	Actors	Text	200
9	Release year	Date	4
10	Rating	Number	1 decimal place

c. Add 'characters' to the numbers in the third column, 'field size', eg. The third row with number 3, to read '3 characters', etc.

d. Movie code, it is seven digits and a unique number.

e. Fields suitable for an input mask would be: 'Release Year', 'Rating'.

f.

Field	Input Mask - Placeholder
Release Year	9999
Rating	9

Unit 12.2 Activity 7J: Changing the display of a field name (pages 154–55)

Field name	Data type	Field size	Field caption	Description
Customer ID	Number	8	Customer number	Unique identifier for a customer
Product ID	Number	8	Product number	Unique identifier for a product
Date	Date	Date/time	Date	Date of invoice
Item description	Text	24	Item	Item
Qty	Number	3	Quantity	Quantity purchased
Last name	Text	20	Last name	Last name of purchaser
Family name	Text	20	Family name	Family name of purchaser
Invoice ID	Text	8	Invoice number	Unique identifier of invoice
Salesperson ID	Number	4	Sales person	Unique identifier of sales person

Unit 12.2 Activity 7K: Validation rules for fields (page 155)

1. Customer ID and Product ID should have validation that they meet the rules established. For example, they might include a check digit to ensure accuracy or they might display the customer name or product name for verification. The Qty field should have a range check. Salesperson ID should also display the Sale person name for verification.
2. An appropriate message could be: 'Customer ID is not valid – please check the number.'

Unit 12.2 Activity 7L: Transaction processing system (pages 155–56)

1. Tables
   Customer table stores customer data.
   Product table stores product data.
   Invoice stores the result of a sale.
2. Key fields
   Customer ID for customer table.
   Product ID for product table.
   Invoice number for invoice table.
3. Linking tables
   Each customer would have many products.
   Each product would have many customers.
   Each invoice would have one customer.
   Each invoice would have many products.
4. Changing records
   A customer record would change if contact details change or if there is a name change.
   A change in price of a product would require a change to the record in the products table.
   A new invoice record would be generated for each sale.

Unit 12.2 Activity 7M: Validation techniques (pages 156–57)

Date of birth – range check so that it is reasonable.
Age – this should be calculated and would not need validation.
Year level – check of valid year levels.

Field name	Validation method	Validation message if validation fails
Date of birth	Range check	Indicate the range acceptable, for example: 'The date of birth must be in the range 1 Jan 1998 to 31 Dec 2010.
Age	Calculation Use Date of Birth to calculate age.	Automatic, no validation message required.
Year level	Range check (1–12) for example	'Year level must be from 1 to 12'
Address	Manual, human, check source, existence check	'Please enter a address details'
Date record created	Automatic entry in field, no validation required.	Automatic, no validation message required.
Student ID	Automatic entry	Automatic, no validation message required.

Unit 12.2 Activity 7N: Sort and query (page 157)

1. Sort
Ascending sort goes from smallest to largest.
Descending sort goes from largest to smallest.

2. A text sort sorts the values alphabetically. A number sort does so using the number values.

3. A sort orders the values. A query finds a record according to a specific criterion.

Unit 12.2 Activity 7O: Layout for a data entry form (page 157)

Does not require an answer.

Unit 12.2 Activity 7P: You be the consultant (page 158)

Does not require an answer.

Unit 12.2 Activity 7Q: George's next attempt (page 158)

Advantages – easy to create a flat file.
Disadvantages – does not cater for relationships. All forms will need to be re-developed in Access.

Unit 12.2 Activity 7R: Unique field (unique identifier) (pages 158–59)

A unique identifier is critical for the information system.
An information system does need an method of distinguishing each entity. The method should entail an identifier that is unique and not related to the entity. It is common to use a number. It could however be alpha-numeric; for example, with a number that has an alphabetic prefix. An invoice could have 'INV54789', the 'INV' being an abbreviation for invoice (not unique) and '54789' its number.
By ensuring that a unique identifier is used for each entity there is certainty that the record can only relate to a single entity. For adding new records it is usual for the membership numbers to be generated automatically with, for example, a 'serial number' increment.
A four-digit numbering system would be adequate for a smallish club. It would be prudent to use a five-digit number if there were prospects over time for their need. Access by default will create a unique number for each record as it is added.

Unit 12.2 Activity 7S: Identifying, naming and validating the fields for the information system (page 159)

Field name	Field type	Validation type	Validation details	Validation tests
Given	text	Spelling	Capitalisation of the first letter given	Check primary source visual check
Family	text	Spelling	'as above'	'as above'
Address Line 1	text	Spelling	'as above'	'as above'
Address Line 2	text	Spelling	'as above'	'as above'
Town/City	text	Spelling	'as above'	'as above'
Province	text	Spelling	'as above'	'as above'
Phone	text	Input mask	Force user to enter data in prescribed manner	Enter test data with country code (675) and remaining digits
email	text	Test characters in email, for example '@'	An email needs an '@' character to be valid	Enter an email but remove the @ character
Membership Number	number	Auto enter serial	Automatic, check starting value and increment value	Check serial is entered when new record created
Joining Date	date	Range check	Create acceptable date range for field	Enter date data before, within and beyond the acceptable range
Date of Birth	date	Range check	Create acceptable date range for field	'as above'
Membership Type	text	Value list	Selected from list of options	Check the value is not empty
Subscription Rate	number	Lookup to table with subscription amounts	Amount entered upon entry of membership type	Check the value is not empty
Length of Membership	calculation	Date today less joining date	Formula requires test data to check	Test data during development

General tests applied may be to check that the value for a field is not 'empty'. Test data for range checks should involve data – below the range, within the range and above the range.

Unit 12.2 Activity 7T: Format of a date (page 160)

21/02/2015	Normal default date format, suitable if date is not critical to the report, but is there to reference the date. Could appear in the header or footer for reference.
21 February 2015	In the body of the report if the report is the basis for correspondence to a third party. Having the month name as a word rather than a number makes it easier to identify the month.
21/02/15	Very brief format, date is not primary to the document; for example, could be used to indicate date printed.
02/21/2015	Would be used where the mm/dd/yyyy date format is used.
21st Feb 2015	Abbreviated format, limited usage these days, 'st' is not common.
21st February 2015	Practice would be to use the second example in preference to this.
Monday 21 February 2015	Useful if the date is important and critical, the day name is shown. Where a document or report is part of chain of communication, particularly with legal correspondence, the day of the week may have a greater significance. For example, a letter reply may need to be made by a specified day and date.

Unit 12.2 Activity 7U: Designing and creating an information system (pages 160–61)

Classification	Field type	Field name	Sample data
membership number	Number	MemberID	8067
family name	Text	FamilyName	Lohia
given name	Text	GivenName	Kenny
title	Text	Title	Mr
number and street	Text	AddressLine1	32 Mack Street
suburb	Text	AddressLine2	Rabaul
postcode	Number	Postcode	611
telephone number	Text	Phone	3 723 8925
type of membership (full, senior, junior, under 18 and mid-week)	Text	MemberCategory	Junior
date of birth	Date	DOB	14/02/2008
date of joining	Date	DOJ	01/12/2006

Classification	Field type	Field name	Sample data
date of last payment	Date	PaymentLast	15/03/2015
method of payment	Text	PaymentMethod	Cash
amount of payment	Number	PaymentAmount	30
membership status	Text	MemberStatus	Active

Unit 12.3 Internet 2

Topic 1: Creating a new web page

Unit 12.3 Activity 1A: Comparison of pages and screens (page 165)

Medium	Name	Dimensions	Resolution	Technology to view content
Printed page	A4 paper	Standard international page size, 210 x 297 mm (portrait view)	Laser printers 600 dpi, commercial printers 3000 dpi Black and white, colour	None, although some people require glasses and or assisted reading
Computer monitor	Monitor, screen	Range of height, width and depth of monitors can vary considerably	Some monitors can have a range of resolution settings	Computer, operating system and software for the monitor
Tablet computer	Tablet	Range of dimensions depending on manufacturer of device	Resolution can vary, advances in screen technology have enabled higher resolution screens	Tablet is a device with a built in screen. Battery power and operating system. Range of operating systems. Network access
Smartphone screen	Smartphone	Range of dimensions. Smaller screen size than tablet computers.	'as above'	'as above'. Network access

Unit 12.3 Activity 1B: Web software (page 167)

1. Some factors to consider: Expiry (if any) of version, syntax colouring, edit and preview modes, whether editor is in active development, operating system and operating system version required.
2. Site management software is often a feature of html editors; in particular, commercial versions of software. Site management software requires the folder containing site files to be designated so that it can manage the files used for the site and links to those files.

Unit 12.3 Activity 1C: Using HTML (page 168)

Practical exercise – refer to page 168.

Unit 12.3 Activity 1D: HTML (page 169)

Practical exercise – refer to page 169.

Unit 12.3 Activity 1E: HTML headings (page 170)

Practical exercise – refer to page 170.

Unit 12.3 Activity 1F: Lists in HTML (page 172)

Practical exercise – refer to page 171.

Unit 12.3 Activity 1G: Source code (page 172)

1. The source code should appear as per the figure above.

2. **a.** Practical exercise.

b. With the file extension .htm or .html the browser will recognise and open the file.

c. Microsoft work can open .htm files.

d., e. Practical exercise.

f. The browser display of both is the same.

g. Practical exercise.

h. There is a substantial difference in the html of the two files. Microsoft Word has added 'proprietary' code. This is to preserve the layout as per the printed page from Microsoft Word.

Unit 12.3 Activity 1H: Colour analysis (page 183)

Colour	Meaning and use
Yellow	Usually a warning or highlight, to draw attention to something. Not as severe as red. It can also connote cheerfulness, as in sunshine.
Black	A very strong colour, could be sombre as well as convey style.
Grey	A restful colour, draws attention but without strong impressions.
Brown	The earthy colour has a feeling of warmth and security.

Unit 12.3 Activity 1I: Responsive web design (page 183)

1. & 2. The window for this page display represents the 'viewport' of the browser. Media queries act as they would if the page were seen on a device. The dimensions of the page and the content vary in width and length to fit.

Unit 12.3 Activity 1J: Using CSS (page 202)

1. Practical exercise.

2. First, the H1 tag stays at 300%, the second H1 tag will appear as 400%.

3. Same as above.

4. Practical exercise.

5. An inline style would override a style specified in the head tag if there is an inconsistency (or alternative declaration). For example an inline style declaring the colour of a <H1> tag as 'red' would override the declaration in the head tag it that colour was specified as 'green'. Similarly, a declaration in a head tag would override the declaration (if different) in the external css file.

6. Practical exercise.

Topic 2: Working with images and multimedia effects

Unit 12.3 Activity 2A (page 210)

1. The quality of an image is inversely proportional to image size and download time. Often a compromise has to be attained with image quality to allow realistic download time because of file size.
2. The best choice can be made by:
   - looking at the image at various compression settings to see how the quality is affected, particularly taking notice of people's faces if there are any
   - the importance of the image in the site, for significant images a higher quality may be justified with resultant higher file size and longer download time.

Unit 12.3 Activity 2B: Images (page 215)

1. **a.** A creative commons licence is granted for the image. It means that others can use the image without infringing copyright. There can be terms and conditions applied to the use of the image.
   b. The image depicted may not be now available. Find an example similar and examine the copyright.
   c. The image above at the time of writing did not include Australia in the image; hence, it would be unsuitable.
   d. For the image to be floated to the left, the line 'float:right;' would be changed to 'float:left;'.

Unit 12.3 Activity 2C: Thumbnails on e-commerce websites (page 216)

1. The images of thumbnails vary from site to site and the nature of the items being depicted.
2. eBay tends to show images of the product to the left and other information to the right (and below) the image.

Topic 4: Working with special effects

Unit 12.3 Activity 4A: Animated gifs (page 226)

1. & 2. Practical exercise.

Unit 12.3 Activity 4B: Create a website (page 230)

Practical exercise.

Unit 12.3 Activity 4C: Pages from a web server (page 231)

1. **a.** .aspx, Activer Server Pages – Microsoft.
   b. .php, hypertext pre-processor – Open Source.
   c. .cfm, Cold Fusion – Adobe.
2. The are used as a means by websites for the linking data in a database to web pages so that dynamic requests for information to a website, therefore server, can be populated with data to meet the request. See page 177 diagram.
3. Many web pages use this technology to display specific information to meet a web request. For example, the pages of products that meet a certain category, jobs that meet a criteria request such as within a particular area.
   Sites that require a user name and password log-in provide information specific to the user.

4. Large business will use the technology because of:
   - the number, range and type of goods or services being marketed
   - the number of customers the business services.

   Medium businesses will use the technology if they have the technical skills and can manage it effectively.

   Small businesses may use the technology, but often with assistance from a third party.

Unit 12.3 Activity 4D: Analysis of a page (page 231)

1. & 2. Practical exercise.

3. In an image that is a hyperlink the cursor will change shape to a 'hand'.

4. Having text as an image ensures it will display the same in a variety of browsers on a range of devices. Mostly today the same can be achieved with CSS. It is easier to alter and there is no image download time.

5. Airline colours are featured.

6. White space is not predominant on the viewport area where the content is displayed. It is used as the background to the page.

7. The site map provides an index to the important parts of the site as determined by the administrators of the site. They may use website statistics to see areas of high activity on the site.

8. Note the difference in the print version compared with the screen version. A 'print' style sheet is used for printed output.

Unit 12.3 Activity 4E: Exercise images (page 232)

1.–3. The type of images taken will dictate how the steps in the exercise will be displayed. The dimensions of the image and how the image appears in the browser will be the focus of the steps.

Unit 12.3 Activity 4F: Exercise accessibility (page 232–33)

1. The advisory notes are to assist website owners and developers in particular. Factors that affect the ability of people to understand the content and to be able to use a web site are identified on page 194–195. The best practice guidelines help businesses to ensure that no users are disenfranchised from a site. For example with an e-commerce site the more accessible the site is would be reflected in the sales generated from the site.
2. For this question see if you can support your answer with a practical example.
3. Practical exercise.

Unit 12.3 Activity 4G: Is a web page a page? (page 233)

1. There is no predetermined width or height of a web page.
2. A web page is fixed only at a point in time. It can be changed at any time.
3. A font and font size can be selected by the developer and set in the CSS. The font size can be increased or decreased by browsers according to user preferences.
4. Resolution is that of the device or screen viewing the page.
5. A page can be downloaded progressively (from top to bottom); depending on the speed of connection and content on the page, an image-rich page would not be downloaded immediately.
6. Animation, audio and video are common elements on a web page and the web is media rich compared with early days of the web. These elements can move and be animated using javascript, browser plug-ins and css among other technologies.

7. Copy writing for the web should ensure that the page is easily scanned. Most people scan a page before reading.
8. A web page is a digital document; it can have any range of dimensions according to need. Many web grid framework grids however provide html for the more common dimensions suitable for the plethora of screens that may eventually be displaying the page.
9. It is easy for the visitor to a website to be 'spatially disorientated'; that is, to not be able to understand the depth and breadth of a site.
10. The higher resolution of the printed page makes it easier to read.

Unit 12.3 Activity 4H: Investigate a club (page 234)

Practical exercise.

Unit 12.3 Activity 4I: Create a website (page 234)

Practical exercise.

Unit 12.4 Multimedia

Topic 1: Introduction

Unit 12.4 Activity 1A: Concept map (page 243)

1. A more detailed map would elaborate on each section. For example, people – detail the roles of people in an information system; equipment – detail types of hardware used for an information system.
2. The concept map enables an overall view of the presentation. Grouping of content and sequence of material can more easily be developed from the visual representation.

Unit 12.4 Activity 1B: Outline text (pages 243–44)

Practical exercise.

Unit 12.4 Activity 1C: Using an outline (page 247)

1. Six slides.
2. The outline levels are easily converted to content as per the outline levels maintaining structure and consistency.

Unit 12.4 Activity 1D: Writing for screen (page 254)

1. The reduction in words conveys the salient points of the information. It is easily scanned by the eye.
2. Examples of dot points:
   - people
   - objects
   - events
   - or other entities
   - exact measurement (eg temperature = 27 degrees C)
   - subjective.

Unit 12.4 Activity 1E: Slide settings (page 261)

The slide text is difficult to read given the gradient effect and its colour. A slight gradient on a slide can be effective design tool; in this case, the eye is drawn to the gradient effect rather than the text.

Topic 3: Delivering and controlling a presentation

Unit 12.4 Activity 3A: Packaging a presentation (page 285)

3. Native PowerPoint Native file format, can be viewed and edited in PowerPoint File size can be large depending on media content included.
   Movie file can be played using a variety of software. Presentation cannot be edited as text.
   Image sequence Useful to select separate slides Slides become images, not editable as text
   pdf A common file format Can be difficult to edit text.
   The file formats other than native PowerPoint are very useful for distributing a presentation for single use viewing, particularly if the setup of the computer used to display the presentation is unknown.

Topic 4: Integrating multimedia with other applications

Unit 12.4 Activity 4A: Create a multimedia presentation (page 289)

Practical exercise.

Unit 12.4 Activity 4B: Presentation software task (page 290)

Practical exercise.

Unit 12.5 Computers and employment

Topic 2: Job search on the Internet and in other media

Unit 12.5 Activity 2A: Reading a job advertisement (page 310)

1. Computer technician position in a retail store. Typically, customers would like advice prior to purchasing equipment regarding suitability, compatibility with operating systems and best value for needs. If stock were not available in store then it would need to be purchased. If customers have issues with products the technician could be the first port of call to problem solve the issue. A diagnosis might solve the issue; if not, repairs may be required. If the equipment is faulty it may need to be returned to the manufacturer. Useful advice and service to the customer would ensure customers are likely to return.
2. There is no mention of whether the job is full time or part time, the likely levels of remuneration or other employee benefits.
3. This position would require a good level of personal skills commensurate with the consumer interaction required. These people skills are different from the technical skills and expertise required by computer technician.
4. Advantages – Technology is changing, a retail store would be expected to have up-to-date products to meet the needs of customers. A technician would build up a knowledge of which products work well in their product area compared with others.
   Disadvantages – Difficult customers, weekend work, opportunities for advancement.

Topic 3: Formatting job application letters

Unit 12.5 Activity 4A: Employment (page 317)

1.
   1. Full time, permanent – Job security benefits may dissuade employees to move to better jobs.
   2. Part time, permanent – May suit those not wishing/able to work full time. An employee may prefer full-time work.
   3. Casual – No security of position. Easier to seek other position.
   4. No security – Flexibility to choose contract.
2. Practical exercise.
3. Advantages – As an employee becomes known to the organisation there are opportunities to demonstrate skills and value to it, and the ability to add worth to an organisation.

Disadvantages: If an employee wants full-time work he or she will always be on the lookout for other jobs, there is no allegiance to the organisation, or feeling valued or not may affect work output.

Unit 12.5 Activity 4B: Skills (pages 317–18)

1. Relate your answer to the text (pages 295–96).
   An employer would have a preference for a prospective employee who is capable in all areas. In your answer you need to examine your strengths and weaknesses. Once areas are identified, people can undertake training and seek assistance to maintain strengths and attend to those areas that need improvement.
   - **a.** 'I could learn from other members of the team as well as assist them in areas I am strong at.'
   - **b.** 'I am keen to learn from team members who have experience.'
   - **c.** 'A mentor will be of great benefit as they can be my first port of call with questions and queries I may have.'

Unit 12.5 Activity 4C: Search engines and employment (page 318)

1. Job search engines group jobs according to the common job titles in particular industries. The titles 'filter' jobs according to those meeting the criteria and hence narrow the number of search results.
2. To use the search engine one needs to have an understanding of how the job title is related to the actual job as well as the particular job being advertised.

Unit 12.5 Activity 4D: Careers in IT (page 318)

1. Answer depends on personal preference.
2. Increasingly, computer skills are important for many careers. Using a computer for email and communication are essential for many employees at work. Using networks, responsible computer use, knowledge and compliance with privacy laws and skills, using common software types such as word processor, spreadsheet and database.

Unit 12.5 Activity 4E: Investigation (page 318)

Answer from personal research.

Unit 12.5 Activity 4F: ICT qualifications and training (pages 318–19)

Answer from personal research.

Unit 12.5 Activity 4G: Résumé (page 319)

Practical exercise.

Unit 12.5 Activity 4H: Résumé as a website (pages 319–20)

Practical exercise.

Glossary/Index

alignment (121): the arrangement of text relative to its position on a page.

'alt' tag (222): provides a description of an image to be included in the HTML code of the page.

animation (237, 241, 277): the rapid sequencing of still images to create the appearance of motion.

application software (27): software that has been developed to solve a particular problem for users to perform useful work on specific tasks; for example, word processing, spreadsheets and Adobe Photoshop (see system software).

backup (16, 279): the procedure for copying computer data with which somebody is working and storing it in another alternative storage device or area for safe keeping as a security measure. A backup of very important files is crucial in any organisation.

binary (42): a numbering system that has only two different values: 0 and 1.

bit (42): the smallest unit of information storable in a computer or peripheral device, expressed as 0 or 1. Eight bits make a byte, the common measure of memory or storage capacity. Short for binary digit.

broadband (47): a transmission medium designed for high-speed data transfers over long distances. Cable modem services and DSL are examples of broadband networks.

buttons (135, 259): on screen they allow a user to perform important functions to administer an information system. Used to create hypertext links that move the user from one part of a presentation to another. When clicked they perform an action.

cascading style sheets (CSS) (199): often used to manage the presentation and layout of a web page.

cell (28): the basic unit of a spreadsheet or some other table of text, formed by intersection of a row and column. It contains a label, value or formula with attributes such as size, font and colour.

chief information officer (296): the most senior executive in an organisation responsible for information and technology resources of that organisation.

client/server system (42): a computer network in which processing is divided between a client program running on a user's machine and a network server program. One server can provide data to, or perform storage-intensive processing tasks in conjunction with, one or more clients.

clip art (212): simple drawings held in digital form on a computer. These items are often supplied in large libraries of files that can easily be incorporated into word processor or presentation graphics documents.

combo box control (126): allows a selection from a list of data options.

communication (13): the exchange of information between people by means of speaking, writing or using a common system of signs or behaviour.

communication system (39): processes that enable information to be passed between people.

compact disc (CD) (285): a digital optical disc data storage format that allows playback of audio, video, photos, text and other recorded information.

computer (11): an electronic device that accepts, processes, stores and outputs data at high speeds according to programmed instructions.

computer programmer (297): uses computer code to develop solutions to problems.

concept map (243): used to outline suggested relationships between concepts, and to organise and structure knowledge.

conditional formatting (141): the formatting of a cell that is dependent upon the value in a cell.

content management systems (CMS) (177): where content is stored in databases.

control (113, 122): an object on a form or report. The type and number of controls will vary according to whether a form or a report is being designed.

convention (68): a set of rules and guidelines used in developing a database.

copyright (18): exclusive legal right that prohibits copying of intellectual property without the permission of the copyright holder (see copyright law).

custom format (73): where a database creator sets his or her own format from a number.

data (19, 61): a collection of facts about an entity. The data can be numeric or it can be descriptive.

database (28, 61, 63): a body of information held within a computer system using the facilities of a database management system structure of a database and access to data.

database administrator (298): the person responsible for managing an organisation's data resources.

data mining (20): the extraction of hidden predictive information from large databases.

data structure table (69, 71): used in the design process before developing the system; it helps database construction and enables faster development via software.

data warehousing (19): retention of transaction data over a long period of time; provides management with historical data that can be used to support decision-making.

Design View (119, 121, 122): functions in which controls on a form can be formatted.

desktop publishing (24): application software and hardware system that involves mixing text and graphics to produce high-quality output for commercial printing, using a computer and devices such as digital camera, scanners and printers. Microsoft Publisher, QuarkXPress and PageMaker are examples of desktop-publishing software.

device driver (26): small piece of software that tells the operating system and other software how to communicate with a piece of hardware.

digital video disk (DVD) (285): a storage device that uses laser technology to read data from optical disks; sometimes called a digital versatile disk.

division or 'div' tag (201): used to specify a section in an HTML page.

editable region (184): allows content to be added and managed.

electronic mail (340): transmission of electronic massages over the Internet. Also known as email.

epub (174): a file extension for an open publication e-book standard (ie for publishing electronic books).

Expression Builder (131): enables a value to be calculated using appropriate syntax, comprising elements, categories and values.

file server (22): a computer that other computers access; a computer in a network that stores application programs and data files accessed by other computers.

firewall (17, 23): software or hardware that can help protect a computer from hackers or malicious software. A firewall helps prevent malicious software (such as worms) from gaining access to a computer through a network or over the Internet, and helps prevent a computer from sending malicious software to other computers.

folders (36, 195–8): a named area on a disk that is used to store related subfolders and files.

font (73): a set of characters with a specific design. Also known as typeface. A font describes a certain typeface, along with other qualities such as size, spacing, and pitch.

footer (119): a block of text that appears at the bottom of each page in a document.

format (70, 72): to the manner in which the contents of a cell are displayed in terms including font size, type and the number of decimal places for a number.

formula (28): instructions for calculations in a spreadsheet. It is an equation that performs calculation on the data contained within the cells in a spreadsheet worksheet.

function (22, 125): a variable quantity whose value depends upon the varying values of other quantities.

graphical user interface (27): a graphical user interface allows people to communicate with a computer by the use of symbols and a pointing device such as a mouse.

hacker (48): a computer user who gains unauthorised access to a computer system or data belonging to somebody else.

header (119): a block of text that appears at the top of each page in a document.

HTML page (167): a 'text' file with tags and content. A browser will recognise and open a file with a .htm or .html file extension.

hub (21, 24): a device used to connect computers on a network. The computers are connected to the hub with cables. The hub sends information received from one computer to all other computers on the network.

hyperlink (163, 221, 269): a connection between an element (such as a word, phrase, image) in a document to somewhere else in the same document, or to a different destination on the Web. Hyperlinks are usually in a different colour to the rest of the document or are underlined; they are activated by a mouse click.

hypertext (163): a system of storing images, text, and other computer files that allows direct links to related text, images, sound and other data

hypertext mark-up language (HTML) (30, 163): a text mark-up language used to create documents for the Web. HTML defines the structure and layout of a web document by using a variety of tags and attributes.

hypertext transfer protocol (HTTP) (23, 163): the client-server protocol that defines how messages are formatted and transmitted on the World Wide Web.

icon (260): a small picture that represents a file, folder, program or other object or function.

ICT account manager (299): sells ICT hardware, software or services to organisations.

ICT technician (299): configures, maintains and repairs computer hardware and software.

IDs and classes (201): 'hooks' that can be used to associate style and presentation with HTML and in particular 'div' tags.

index (85, 262): a data structure that speeds up the search for records that contain certain types of data.

information (2): the meaningful material derived from computer data by organising it and interpreting it in a specific way.

information system (1): a computer-based system with the defining characteristic that it provides information to users in one or more organisations. Information systems are thus distinguished from, for example, real-time control systems, message-switching systems, software engineering environments or personal computing systems

information technology manager (297): responsible for planning, implementing and maintaining the technology infrastructure for an organisation.

input mask (70, 75): string expression created by a developer; it establishes parameters concerning what users can enter in as inputs in text boxes. A type of template, or format, that entered data must conform to.

Internet (164): network that links computer networks all over the world by satellite and telephone, connecting users with service networks such as email and the World Wide Web.

Internet protocol (IP) (42): a protocol that that allows traffic to pass between networks. The most widely used is IP, the Internet protocol.

Internet service provider (ISP) (46): company that connects you through your communications line to its servers or central computer, and then to the Internet via another company's network access points.

intranet (23, 42): a private network, set up by an organisation or company, that resembles the World Wide Web but which is inaccessible to external users.

IT security specialist (298): recommends and designs security policies for organisations.

job application letter (315): a prospective employee's introduction to a prospective employer.

join (3): the way in which data from multiple tables is displayed at the same time.

library (184): in relation to websites: (1) a collection of common items used for easy access while building the website; (2) a collection of code developed by third parties used in the website.

list box control (127): allows selection from a list of data options.

local area network (LAN) (24): a network of computers, printers and other devices located within a relatively limited area (for example, a building). A LAN enables any connected device to interact with any other on the network. A LAN uses the infrastructure and standards of the Internet and the Web.

Main Menu (118, 131): screen that has buttons linking to the main components of an information system; a navigation system.

many-to-many relationships (95): where each record in a table has many entries in another table and vice versa.

master page (192): a template of a page design that includes the essential elements of a page including margins, text blocks and default formatting styles.

master slide (237, 258): in a presentation has a number of design items that are included in every slide. Similar to a template.

microprocessor (14): a silicon wafer with electronic switches etched on the surface to make an integrated circuit. A microprocessor is a type of microchip that has memory and logic circuits built in.

modem (23, 42, 46): a device that sends and receives data over telephone lines to and from computers. Modem stands for modulator/demodulator.

monitor (34): a computer screen, also referred to as visual display unit (VDU), that displays data or files that a user is working on. There are two types: cathode ray tube (CRT) and liquid crystal display (LCD).

multimedia (235, 241): the combined used of digitised information representing text, sound, and still or video images, or the media so used.

network (21): a number of computers linked together to share resources and to facilitate communication.

network hub (22): a device that allows multiple ethernet devices to be connected.

network engineer (298): responsible for the design, implementation and maintenance of a computer network.

network operating system (NOS) (25): specialised software designed to enhance operating systems by adding networking features.

node (21): a connection point on a network that allows the input or output of data; any device connected to the network.

non-editable region (184): contains site navigation links and other HTML not directly related to content on the page.

normalisation (64): a set of rules that is applied to the data to eliminate redundant data and to create the tables that will be used in the structure of the database.

one-to-many relationships (92): usually occurs when each record in a table has many linked records in a second table, but each record in the second table has only one corresponding record in the first table.

operating system (27): the computer program that manages all other programs on the computer. The operating system stores files, allows you to use software programs and coordinates the use of computer hardware.

paragraph tag (169): defines a block of text as a paragraph.

peer-to-peer network (23): where computers on a network share files and resources with each other; mostly used in homes or in small organisations.

PING utility (36): tool used by system administrators to see if a computer's network connections are working.

plug-in (174): software that is an add-on to a browser. It gives the browser extra functions and allows it to display different types of content.

program (27): a list of instructions in a programming language that tells a computer to perform a task.

protocols (35): rules and procedures developed by manufacturers and international standards organisations.

query (97, 99): a question or request for specific data contained in a database. Used to analyse data.

range check (82): checks if values meet a particular test or set of tests.

résumé or **curriculum vitae (CV) (311):** a document prepared for a prospective employer to give the applicant the prospect of being selected for a job interview.

relational database (64): a data model that views information in a database as a collection of distinctly named tables. Each table has a specified set of named columns, each column name (also called an attribute) being distinct within a particular table, but not necessarily between tables.

rollback (103): returns the database to the state it was in before the data was altered (eg updated or deleted).

router (23): an electronic device that directs communicating messages when networks are connected together.

satellite connection (48): connection services that use satellites and the air to download or send data to users at a rate seven times faster than dial-up connections.

sensor (12): a device, often a microprocessor, which measures a physical quantity. The measurement is read by an observer or another piece of equipment such as a computer. Sensors are used to measure temperature and light, amongst other things.

server (22): a powerful computer that manages shared devices, such as laser printers. It runs server software fr applications such as email and web browsing.

site map (186, 187): a diagram like a concept map showing pages in the site and their relationship to each other.

slide (237): a single page in a presentation.

spam (41): electronic junk mail; an unsolicited, often commercial, message transmitted through the Internet as a mass mailing to a large number of recipients.

spreadsheet (28): an application software or program that is used to manipulate numeric data and create workbook files. Popular spreadsheet programs are Microsoft Excel, Corel Quattro Pro and Lotus 1-2-3.

storage device (285): device that can be used to store data (for example, flash drive, CDRW).

storyboarding (248, 263): a technique used for multimedia design. It is a plan that sketches scenes in the multimedia presentation.

subform (135): a technique where data from different tables or queries is displayed in a single form. It is like a split form but has data from related tables.

switch (21, 22): a device used to connect computers on a network. The computers are connected to the switch with cables. A switch is similar to a hub, except that it sends the information received from one computer to the specific computers that are supposed to receive it.

systems analyst (7, 297): person who develops system requirements that can be used by designers and programmers in a way consistent with the goals of the organisation; must ensure that technical concerns, such as design specifications for input and output procedures, are met.

systems life cycle (7, 61): a step-by-step process for the development of an information system.

tab (116): a position in a line of text that allows that text to be aligned in a consistent manner.

tag (168): a marker in HTML interpreted by the browser as a formatting command. It is enclosed between a 'less than' and a 'greater than' sign (eg <tag>).

templates (62, 129, 249, 179, 192): a sample form or presentation that can be used as a pattern to help guide you in designing your own layout. For websites, a sample document or page that has many of the details of the page already set up, including layout, menu structure and font selection. The starting point for each page on the site. It is also a pre-designed slide design that can be adapted to suit the style and type of presentation.

text (69): consists of characters (eg A to Z, punctuation and symbol characters).

thumbnail (215): a copy of an image that has been reduced in size.

transmission control protocol/Internet protocol (TCP/IP) (42): the standard protocol for the Internet. The essential features of this protocol involve identifying, sending and receiving devices reformatting information for transmission across the Internet.

user interface (63): the way users interact with the information system. Elements include the menu bar, buttons, field layouts and descriptions, scroll bars and links.

utility driver (26): program that performs a specific task in the management of computer functions; the software enables these tasks to be carried out.

validation (79): checking that data is correct at time of entry.

video (217, 262): moving images displayed on a monitor.

videoconferencing (48): use of television video and sound technology as well as computer networks (including the Internet). Also called teleconferencing.

Visual Basic (145): a programming language; used by many programmers to develop a range of applications.

web administrator (297): responsible for maintaining an organisation's website.

web browser (23, 30, 163, 174): special Internet software that connects users to remote computers, opens and transfers files, displays text and images, and provides an uncomplicated interface to the Internet and Web documents.

web designer (298): responsible for the design of a website.

web framework (180): a software framework designed to simplify web development.

webpage (164, 176): a computer file, encoded in HyperText Markup Language (HTML) and containing text, graphics files and sound files, which is accessible through the World Wide Web. Browsers interpret HTML documents to display webpages.

website (163, 177): group of related webpages.

wireless (44): the transmission of information without a physical connection between the sender and the receiver. Uses radio frequencies, hardware, software and various technologies to transmit information.

wizard (97, 108, 179): a series of steps used to create an element of the information system. A tool for building websites.

word processing (27): the act of creating a word document on a computer using a program (for example, MS Word or ClarisWorks).

word processor (236, 241): an application package designed to work with text and produce documents.

World Wide Web (WWW) (163): the interconnected system of Internet servers that support documents in multimedia form and include sounds, photos and video as well as text.

WYSIWYG ('what you see is what you get') (27): an editor or program that allows a developer to visualise the end result while developing the interface or document.